The Politics Of Forced Migration:

A Conceptual, Operational and Legal Analysis

Nitza Nachmias
with Rami Goldstein, Editors

PublishAmerica
Baltimore

First printing

ISBN: 1-4137-3196-1
PUBLISHED BY PUBLISHAMERICA, LLLP
www.publishamerica.com
Baltimore

Printed in the United States of America

For Yoheved and Nahum Rubinstein, and Sidi and Hans Goldstein,
our refugee parents, who taught us tolerance and to believe in equality,
human rights, and human kindness.

Nitza Nachmias and Rami Goldstein

Contents

Part: II
Causes and Effects of Forced Migration: Case Studies

Part: III
A Look to the Future: Possibilities and Constraints

About the Authors

Index

The Politics Of Forced Migration:

A Conceptual, Operational and Legal Analysis

Nitza Nachmias
with Rami Goldstein, Editors

Roberta Cohen

Foreword

I f one were to start afresh and design an international system to address the world's humanitarian emergencies and the millions of uprooted people they produce, it would look markedly different from the one we have today.

To begin with, a new system would need to better reflect the changing nature of war—the fact that internal conflicts have become far more prevalent than interstate wars and that they often divide countries along racial, ethnic, linguistic, or religious lines and use displacement as a weapon, even a goal of war. Conflicts of such ferocity produce not only refugees, who flee across borders for safety, but large numbers of internally displaced persons (IDPs), who remain *within* their own countries after being driven from their homes by armed conflict, ethnic strife, and massive human rights abuse. Indeed, the number of IDPs has risen from a few million in the early 1980s to an estimated 25 million today, whereas the number of refugees has decreased to an estimated 12 million.

Yet for dealing with refugees the international system consists of a well-structured legal and institutional framework but makeshift, *ad hoc* arrangements for IDPs. Since 1951, refugees have benefited from a legally binding convention and a specific agency, the UN High Commissioner for Refugees (UNHCR), which has a staff of 5,000 and a budget of nearly $1 billion. For IDPs, the UN Secretary-General in 1992 created a voluntary position, a Representative on Internally Displaced Persons, with limited human and material resources at its disposal. No one operational agency has been given a global mandate for IDPs, which means that in each emergency, an array of international agencies and non-governmental organizations come forward on an *ad hoc* basis to help IDPs, under the coordination of the UN's Emergency Relief Coordinator. To assist the Coordinator, an IDP Unit was created in 2002, and soon it will become an Inter-Agency Division, but its staff is expected to total no more than 15 people. As for a normative framework, the Representative of the Secretary-General in 1998 presented to the UN a set of Guiding Principles on Internal Displacement, and while they have been widely accepted, they are non-binding. In sum, there is a great inconsistency and inequity in the current system in the way forced migrants are dealt with. The result is that IDPs receive far too little assistance, protection, and reintegration and development support from the international community.

A new international system would seek to close this gap in treatment by developing a new framework for dealing with state sovereignty. In keeping with more traditional notions of sovereignty, the refugee system created after the Second World War provided international protection to persons already outside their national territory who lacked the protection of their own government. It did not extend to persons uprooted and at risk within their own countries. However, in the past decade it has become evident that persons displaced inside their own countries also are often in need of international protection. In too many cases, they have been subjected to mass starvation, mass killings, and genocide while the international community stood by. This has stimulated ideas for a framework that would recast sovereignty as a form of responsibility toward one's citizens. Under the new framework, states, to claim the prerogatives of sovereignty, would be expected to carry out their internationally recognized responsibilities toward their citizens, namely to provide them with protection and life-supporting assistance. If unable to meet the life-saving needs of their citizens, they would be expressly required to request and accept outside offers of aid. If they deliberately obstructed or outright refused international access, they would be subject to calibrated actions that range from diplomatic demarches to political pressures, sanctions, or, as a last resort, military intervention.

Whereas refugee protection seldom requires exceptional measures such as the deployment of military force, IDP protection in the midst of civil wars often triggers calls for international humanitarian intervention and stimulates debates over when it is acceptable to override sovereignty. Some see a perceptible shift toward the view that people in need of humanitarian assistance have certain rights and claims on the international community and that the international community has a right, even a duty, to provide needed relief and also protect populations at risk. But the UN and the major powers have not always been ready to carry out this responsibility, especially when it requires the exercise of force to gain access and protect displaced populations. Nonetheless there does seem to have emerged an international responsibility to prevent mass starvation. When it comes to interventions to prevent mass killings, ethnic cleansing or the crime of genocide, the international community has been far slower to act, often considering the costs and risks too high. Clearly, criteria and triggers for intervention still need to be worked out as well as the political will to enforce a new framework.

In building an international system for effective protection of internally displaced persons, the refugee regime will also need reform. To begin with, a new international system would benefit from an expanded and updated concept of a refugee. The 1951 Convention definition, which is based on fear of individual persecution, no longer captures the refugee experience. Indeed, by the mid 1960s, the 1951 Convention did not apply to the majority of refugees being assisted by UNHCR. Although in practice UNHCR applies refugee status more broadly to include those who flee their countries because of armed conflict and generalized violence, not all states will admit refugees on this basis since universal treaty law extends only to refugees fleeing specific kinds of persecution. Moreover, temporary protection status and other improvised means of providing refuge to groups escaping violence do not always provide the full range of rights to which 1951 Convention refugees are entitled. It is left to a state's discretion to decide whether or not to return "civil war refugees" to conditions of danger. While many warn it could be counterproductive to reopen international consideration of the refugee definition, regional and national arrangements have been proposed as a means of addressing this protection gap.

Expanding protection for Palestinian refugees should also be part of a new framework. The status of Palestinian refugees is different from other refugees, since it is governed by a UN resolution, adopted prior to the 1951 Refugee Convention, and maintained by a special agency, the United Nations Relief and Works Agency (UNRWA). These differences, however, have not always worked to the benefit of the refugees. UNRWA's mandate, for example, unlike UNHCR's, has long focused on providing material assistance rather than to offering protection. Moreover, the solutions available to Palestinian refugees are limited when compared with other refugees. They have two options only —to return to their homes or receive financial compensation. Yet these options to date have proved politically unworkable and are at the core of the long-standing impasse impeding resolution of their plight. There have been calls, as a result, to end their special status and give them the full rights of other refugees, so that they might have a choice not only of returning but of locally integrating where they currently reside or of resettling in other countries. To this end, it has been advocated that UNHCR assume a comprehensive legal protection mandate for Palestinian refugees under the Refugee Convention. In line with this thinking, the *World Refugee Survey* has stopped counting as refugees those Palestinians who do resettle and become citizens of other countries, its policy analyst Ahmed Jabri arguing that the legal rights and status of Palestinians for too long have been held hostage to political negotiations far from fruition and should be brought within the protection confines of the international refugee regime.

Because protracted refugee situations often lead to violence in refugee camps, a new international framework will have to promote both political solutions and political and security frameworks for managing militarized refugee situations. Too often humanitarian organizations have been left to fend for themselves in addressing refugee security, one of the more notorious cases being in Goma, eastern Zaire. But UNHCR does not have the means to identify, intern, disarm and demobilize armed elements in refugee camps. The greater engagement of the UN Department of Peacekeeping Operations and the Security Council in procedures for separating armed elements from civilians in camps will be needed to protect the security of *bona fide* refugees and of maintaining the civilian and humanitarian nature of camps and the credibility of humanitarian operations.

While some would advocate blurring the distinction between refugees and IDPs in a new international system, the maintenance of separate legal regimes makes eminent sense given the central role that state sovereignty plays in the international system. However, in the operational realm distinctions are less persuasive, since IDPs and refugees are often intermingled on the ground, both in desperate need of protection and assistance. As a result, international organizations have increasingly been expanding their mandates over the years to include IDPs, most notably

UNHCR, which counts 5 million IDPs as of concern to the organization. Its role nonetheless has raised concerns that the greater involvement of the agency with IDPs will distract it from protecting refugees and even undermine its safeguarding of the right to asylum. Reinforcing these fears is that some governments have denied asylum to persons fleeing their countries on the grounds that in country protection was being provided to IDPs. However, it is also true that such governments would likely find other excuses to bar asylum seekers from entry. The system for IDPs currently being created by the UN Emergency Relief Coordinator will need UNHCR's greater involvement with IDPs since it is the agency with the most experience and expertise in protecting uprooted populations, especially in camp situations and during return and reintegration.

Another new feature of an improved international system for forced migrants would be more uniform criteria for knowing when displacement ends. To be sure, the 1951 Refugee Convention makes clear when refugees cease to hold that status. But the convention does not apply to Palestinian refugees and when it comes to persons fleeing armed conflict, governments have a great deal of discretion in deciding when it is time for people, who had been given temporary humanitarian status, to return home. In the case of IDPs, no criteria exist at all for deciding when displacement ends. This is particularly noticeable in protracted situations when governments may find it expedient to maintain people as IDPs in order to achieve political goals. The governments of Georgia and Azerbaijan, for example, would like their IDPs to return to Abkhazia and Nagorno Karabakh and therefore do not extend sufficient support to them to enable their successful reintegration in their new locations. IDPs are kept in a state of limbo unable to return in the absence of a peace settlement but equally unable to integrate into the localities where they fled. Because many of these have remained in temporary shelters for more than a decade, they have been called "the Palestinians of the South Caucasus."

An international regime to deal with forced migrants should include a whole range of actors internationally and domestically. Because the problem of forced migration is not a humanitarian or human rights one alone, political efforts to resolve the crises and inequities that have caused the displacement in the first place should be an integral part of the system. In the absence of political solutions, humanitarian assistance can only promote dependency over the long term and even prolong conflicts. Since up to half the population can be uprooted in countries devastated by civil wars, the rehabilitation of areas affected by conflict will be necessary to decrease tensions between the host community and the populations being reintegrated. An expanded role for international development and financial institutions in post-conflict reconstruction should therefore be part and parcel of a new system. At the national level, partnerships among national authorities, non-governmental groups and civil society should be encouraged in working out solutions for displacement.

The current fractured and often incoherent international response to humanitarian emergencies is the main subject of this important new volume, edited by Nitza Nachmias and Rami Goldstein. They are joined by refugee specialists, academics, legal experts and NGOs who span a variety of countries—Israel, Norway, the Palestinian Authority, the United Kingdom and the United States. Most of the chapters point out the gaps and inequities in the current international system and how these might best be addressed. While some of the authors argue for an evolutionary approach that builds upon the current system, others call for more radical restructuring to address the challenges facing forced migrants in the 21st century. Indeed, this is a volume that both appreciates the current system but also expresses impatience with the effectiveness of 50-year-old mandates and definitions as well as outmoded concepts of sovereignty.

Authors Rami Goldstein, Leon Gordenker, Alan James, Claudena Skran, Kendall Stiles and Abby Stoddard focus on the legal, definitional and conceptual aspects of the problem, while case studies are presented by Petter Bauck, Sari Hanafi, Joseph Rudolph, Arne Strand, Beth Elise Whitaker and the two editors, spanning refugee situations in Afghanistan, Rwanda and Yugoslavia, with three articles devoted to the Palestinian refugees.

Their overall analysis of the current international system for forced migrants and their critiques of its shortcomings are intended to stimulate reform in how governments and the international community respond to complex humanitarian emergencies. Indeed, all of the thorny questions associated with a new international system for forced migrants are discussed in this book, including the impact of international terrorism on the refugee regime and the role of donor governments. Most valuable is that the different authors comment on a variety of proposals and recommendations made for improving the refugee and IDP system and also introduce new paradigms for dealing with forced migration. The book should prove a valuable stimulus to the formulation of better policies and institutional arrangements in the 21st century for responding to the needs of the tens of millions of persons driven from their homes by armed conflict, human rights violations and related causes and who have no other recourse than to look to the international community for support.

Nitza Nachmias

Introduction

T his volume provides a thorough examination of the policies, principles and practices utilized by the international community in their effort to assist refugees and forced migrants. The essays focus on the causes and effects of the wanton, brutal killings within sovereign borders, and the ethnic and religious strife that compels millions of men, women, and children to flee their homes *ad infinitum,* out of fear for their lives. The desire to respond to man-made disasters is strong in every culture and on every continent. However, the book points out that effective and consequential results are hardly achieved. In a clear departure from the past, the disasters of today are more complex, more dangerous, and, sadly, more commonplace. Thus, an effective and well-coordinated response requires a multidisciplinary action based on specialized and well-orchestrated political, strategic and legal instruments.

The book identifies and evaluates the successes and failures of humanitarian operations and suggests necessary revisions in the existing response mechanisms. The central purpose of this book is to synthesize for the reader the authors' insight gained through their fieldwork and scholarly research. The first part of the book addresses concepts and theories that later, in the second part, are put to the test of reality. The comparative approach helps the reader to evaluate the various strategies and tactics used by assistance providers and to reach important conclusions. The main topics of this volume are: coercive and non-coercive humanitarian intervention, human rights, the increased role of civil society and Non-Governmental Organization (NGOs), the political and legal status of refugees and Internally Displaced Persons (IDPs), the various strategic and tactical instruments available, and the circumstances that hinder assistance operations. The essays clarify for the reader why, too often, a proper response is late to arrive, and why the vast resources invested in humanitarian assistance are not yielding the expected results.[1]

In their search for answers, the authors reveal the deep suspicions and lack of cooperation among the refugees, the host countries, and the assistant providers. The population-receiving countries view the unexpected influx of forced migrants as a formidable security risk. They often develop xenophobia and anti-refugee sentiments, resulting in a growing unwillingness to provide the refuge seekers with asylum and protection.[2] In regions that experience delicate ethnic balance, the host countries often exhibit fear of a spillover effect that could instigate domestic violence and ethnic strife.[3] Finally, the refugees are often viewed as an economic threat, a competitive labor resource, and a negative cultural and religious influence.

The essays show that both governments and international organizations share the blame for misjudging and underestimating the negative and violent consequences of forced migration. Years of suffering and unabated violence in refugee camps encouraged the refugees, in some cases, to resort to violence and terrorism as the ultimate recourse for their grievances. The evidence shows that in most cases the response was inconsistent, late to arrive, and structurally flawed. The UNHCR and the other assistant providers were understaffed, under financed, and operated in ambiguous legal and political environments. While "Human Rights" has become a user-friendly term,[4] in reality, only highly selective compulsory measures have been exercised, and the consequences charged a heavy toll in human lives.

Part: I
Forced Migration Revisited

Part I includes four theoretical essays identifying and reviewing the major factors determining the outcome of humanitarian intervention. The first step for a successful international intervention is the development of a coherent conceptual framework based on existing operational opportunities and constraints. The legal aspects of the "right of return," "resettlement," "repatriation," and "asylum" have to be clearly defined. However, as Alan James explains, these procedures could hardly be expected. Indeed, the source of the problem is lack of consensus regarding the definition of "Forced Migration," as well as the conflicting theoretical approached to "sovereignty" and "legitimate intervention." "With bullets flying, it would be an ultra strict semanticist who argued that such a response should not be brought within the concept of 'forced.' The concept is in the nature of a spectrum. At one of its ends the assertion that an individual or a group has been 'forced' to migrate will seem crystal clear; at its other such a claim may look very doubtful; and in between there could well be room for debate as to whether some migrations are properly designated as the outcome of the threat or use of force." Moreover, the important investigation of motives "is often a slippery business. However, a search should be undertaken to identify the particular grounds on which individuals or communities feel obliged to move or are made so to do."

Leon Gordenker expands the discussion beyond the contentious definitions. He traces the roots of the current assistance mechanisms to the 1920s, when forced migration was first recognized as an international problem. "By the early 1920s, most of the main elements of the contemporary refugee regime had been put into place." However, the early failures of the 1930s and 1940s proved that irreconcilable national interests have blocked the efforts to repatriate and resettle refugees. The United Nations High Commission for Refugees (UNHCR) was never granted the right to override a sovereign government rejection of refugees. Sovereignty has been in the past, and continues to be in the present, the most important factor in the resettlement and repatriation of forced migration.

Another question raised by Professor Gordenker concerns the rules guiding the individual treatment for refugees (asylum seekers mainly) vs. the treatment of groups of refugees. The Refugee Convention (1951) applies mainly to the few who ask for resettlement in democratic, wealthy states." Moreover, the Refugee Convention did not foresee the myriad of regional conflicts and the millions of internally displaced persons.[5] Consequently, three needed revisions took place: a) a shift in the rules and regulation toward a group, rather than an individual approach to forced migration, b) the creation of a separate category for "internally displaced persons" (IDPs), a

21

term that gained legal implication, and c) a shift in assistance strategies to "assertive intervention," often at the expense of sovereignty. As the case studies show, the conflicts between the prerogative of the state and the right to exercise "assertive humanitarian intervention" have yet to be resolved.

Claudena Skran suggests an answer to the "sovereignty" vs. "assertive intervention" debate. She argues that the solution is to create a new forced migration paradigm. The new paradigm is based on the argument that sovereignty has become porous, and new players are now the "rule makers." In particular, the United Nations, especially the UNHCR, have become policy makers, rules creators, and managers of assistance and emergency operations. The new paradigm addresses these changes. It suggests overhauling the UNHCR structure, redefining the agency's mandate and authority, and broadening the UNHCR responsibilities. In addition to emergency assistance the UNHCR will be responsible for the development of programs that advance both sustainable peace and sustainable development.

UNHCR's present operations show important problems. First, "the UNHCR failed to meet the humanitarian needs of people who had problems similar to those of refugees. The repatriation and resettlement operations have to include internally displaced persons who until now have been omitted from the UNHCR mandate." Second, the UNHCR failed to address the conflict created by international humanitarian coercive operations. Skran argues that the value of individual and community human rights has to take precedent over the value of sovereignty. "By far, the most important development affecting UNHCR's operating paradigm has to do with the willingness of the international community to engage in "humanitarian intervention." The new paradigm will ensure a higher international involvement in the protection of refugee and the host countries from terrorism and rampant violence, even at the cost of sovereignty.

Skran argues that these changes are already taking place. The turning point was Bosnia, where the UNHCR broke with past traditions by acting as "lead agency" in a massive humanitarian relief effort that aided not only refugees but also IDPs. Bosnia, Afghanistan, and now Iraq prove that the international community has to consider not only the problematic cooperation with the host governments, but also the ethnic chiefs, the victims, the perpetrators, the local communities, and the international donor community. These new challenges require new approaches. Skran rejects jurist's claims that "forcible intervention in human rights situations was illegal because it violated state sovereignty."[6] She argues that the legality of such interventions became increasingly accepted due to the growing acceptance of international human rights norms world wide, and a Security Council recognition that grave violations of human rights constitute a thereat to international peace and security.[7] The new paradigm links humanitarian assistance with military intervention, and ensures neutrality, and independence in the strategies and tactics of assistance operations. It also ensures primary accountability to the refugees.

Abby Stoddard supports Skran's call for a new paradigm. She argues that most past assistance operations could not take pride in the results. First, the performance of the organizations charged with the responsibility to preempt and prevent forced migration, and support the refugees during and after forced migration occurs, should be reevaluated and revised. The primary revision should eliminate the distinction between refugees and "internally displaced persons" (IDPs). The normative aspects of the human rights regime should apply to all forced migration. The present two-tier approach should be eliminated. Assistance and protection have to be extended to all survivors of human catastrophes whether they are externally or internally displaced.

Second, both in theory and practice, the cooperation between the local government and the international assistance organizations in the resettlement of a refugee crisis is of utmost importance. The donor states, especially the largest donor, the United States, have to consolidate a clear and comprehensive assistance policy. Third, the various categories of displaced persons need to be redefined in comparatively inconsequential terms to avoid the creation of a stigma or bias. Fourth, the principle of "coercive intervention" needs to be adjusted to the post-Cold War era. Stoddard argues that the severity of the current human catastrophes legitimizes the humanitarian interventionist fashion although it is highly controversial. In summary, Part I of the book calls for a comprehensive reform in the concepts, strategies, and tactics used in the protection and support of forced migration.

Part: II
Forced Migration: Case Studies

Part II includes discussions of four case studies representatives of the Asia (Afghanistan), Europe (Yugoslavia), Africa (Rwanda), and the Middle East

(Palestinian refugees). Each case represents particular internal and external conflicts typical of the region and emblematic of the severe violent conflicts which resulted in the massive displacement of million of people. While each case represents unique circumstances, important characteristics are shared by all four case studies. First, serious attention is being given to the conflict between the state fundamental and ultimate sovereign rights, and the growing legitimacy of international coercive intervention. The case studies show that while coercive humanitarian intervention is often necessary, it is a still a highly controversial practice from both the legal and the political perspectives.

Second, refugees are both the cause and the consequence of the conflict. Thus, the protection and resolution of the refugee problem have to be an integral part of the termination of the conflict, and of every peace treaty. Third, because the refugee problem was historically viewed as a temporary, isolated-local problem, the existing legal instruments do not reflect the present reality; for example, they do not apply to IDPs. Fourth, after September 11, refugees have been seen as a security risk, posing a threat of insurgency and terrorism.[8] Consequently, forced migration is considered a strategic, not a humanitarian problem. Afghanistan is a clear case in point.

Afghanistan: The Role of Religion

Arne Strand, who spent over 15 years working in Afghanistan for a Norwegian assistance agency, attributes Afghan political-ethnic conflict to the British and Soviet colonialism that disrupted the delicate ethnic balance between the Pashtuns (50 percent of the population) and the various other Afghan tribes. In addition to the harmful colonial heritage, massive external interventions from neighboring Iran and Pakistan destined the fate of modern Afghanistan. Pakistan and the Islamic Republic of Iran became harbors to millions of Afghan refugees who fled the Soviet invasion. However, humanitarian assistance was provided only in exchange for loyalty to the Islamic cause or to the regime. The Mujahideen parties frequently had all their members living in refugee camps. Soon, Afghanistan became a lawless state experiencing brutality, mass arrests and mass murder by the successive governments. Both Iran and Pakistan did not favor international assistance operations. "Due to Iran's controversial regime, hardly any NGO established a presence in the Afghan refugee camps in Iran." Only the UNHCR maintained a presence there.

Afghan refugees did not return home after the Soviet withdrawal as was expected. The main reason was Pakistan's strong objection to repatriation. Only in 1992, two years prior to the Taliban emergence in Kandahar, one and a half million refugees spontaneously left Pakistan and returned home. Because the UN failed to predict the massive repatriation and was not technically and politically prepared, the returnees did not receive any international support. The lack of international support resulted in some of the worst violations of human rights. These atrocities generated new waves of refugees, in a vicious circle that only ended in 2002.

Strand argues that the Taliban recruited most of their supporters from the refugee population, mainly from refugee religious schools. When the Taliban emerged as the victors, they were received as a "long awaited alternative to the hated warlords," which explains their swift campaign. However, UN imposed sanctions (1999-2000) on Afghanistan in response to terrorism and massive drug production caused more people to flee. Additional waves of forced migration followed the military campaign of 2001-2002 and the disintegration of the Taliban regime. Repatriation, however, began soon after the overthrow of the Taliban, and millions of refugees from both Iran and Pakistan returned to their homes. The refugee camps were finally dismantled. The success of the 2001-02 massive repatriation campaign was due to two major factors: first, many family members of Afghans in exile remained back home to look after their property, and second, most houses and property were returned to the original owners. In addition, resettlement was supported by two traditional Islamic and Afghani practices: Zakat and Hijrah. Zakat is one of the five "Pillars of Islam," and it requires every provider to make contributions to the poor. Hijrah is a migration tradition based on the famous escape of the Prophet Mohammad and his followers from Mecca. These religious traditions provided a psychological and physical support mechanism for the millions of Afghans refugees who fled to Pakistan and Iran after the "infidel" Soviet invasion, and their return in 1992. However, the success of the repatriation and the reintegration of the Afghan refugees came with a price. First, it required a military and political intervention. Second, the Muslim population often felt uncomfortable with the orthodox, religious, Christian aid organizations. "Both Western and Islamic NGOs regarded each other unisonely as either Islamic or Christian indoctrinators, exploring the vulnerable state of the Afghan refugees." Third, the aid created a harmful dependency syndrome.

In conclusion, the assistance to Afghanistan refugees was neither sufficient nor satisfactory. Strand supports Skran and Stoddard's call for a "renewed session on international humanitarian laws and conventions." The refugee issue must be addressed based on the history of the people, and the particularities of the refugee society. "Assistance operation must be removed from strategic or national interests."

Rwanda and Yugoslavia

The international responses to the Rwanda and Yugoslavia crises generate interesting comparisons. In both cases ruthless power-seeking cruel leaders manipulated the ethnic divergence and caused the civil war that lead to the refugee catastrophe. Joseph Rudolph is "casting Milosevic and his fellow Serbian ultra-nationalists as the prime culprits in the unfolding drama." A similar syndrome was identified in Rwanda. Professor Whitaker explains, "the violence was politically motivated, but given the nature of identity politics in Rwanda, it took on ethnic dimension." The Yugoslav and the Rwandan ethno-political crises have deep roots, sometimes nourished by relatively recent bloody memories.[9] The ethnic conflict ripped the two Yugoslavian and three Rwandan societies apart, each community claiming the right to rule their motherland.

The Yugoslav and the Rwanda refugee crises occurred in the early 1990s, and in both cases, an early international intervention should and could have prevented the genocide and the ethnic cleansing that was later stopped by external forces. In both cases, the international community was blamed for its misperceptions and wrong evaluation of the graveness of the situation. In early 1991, Western diplomats were under the mistaken belief that external intervention would not be required in Yugoslavia. Milosevic's preoccupation with the problems in Kosovo would force him to accept as *fait accompli* the independence of Croatia and Slovenia. In the case of Rwanda, the Western diplomats and the UN Secretary General wrongly assumed that the Arusha agreement (1993) would prevent the outbreak of the ethnic violence. In Yugoslavia, as in Rwanda, killers were intermingled with the refugee population and militias were organized for the return by force to Rwanda and Kosovo. As in Rwanda, the West was "stung by criticism that it had waited too long to respond vigorously to the carnage occurring in

26

Bosnia." In both cases, the refugee crisis spilled over to neighboring states, namely, Burundi, Congo, Tanzania, and Uganda, and in the case of Yugoslavia, to Macedonia, Croatia, Slovenia, and Albania. "The numbers of the refugees were staggering. In Yugoslavia, the consensus is that more than two million out of a population of five million were rendered homeless. By the end of 1994, up to two million Rwandan were internally displaced and nearly two million others had fled to neighboring countries."

The two conflicts created two types of refugees: refugees who crossed the border and found refuge in neighboring countries, and internally displaced persons (IDPs). Whitaker explains that in the case of Africa, NGO were in the front line of assistance. "In the Tanzania and Zaire refugee camps over a 100 NGOs set up operations, and between April and December 1994, international donors allocated nearly $1 billion to the Rwandan refugee crisis. The cost to the international community was approximately $1 million per day."

However, assistance operations remain controversial, especially repatriation operations. In the case of Rwanda, former Hutu killers took charge of the camps, controlled the distribution of food, and used the camps to recruit and rebuild their army. Assistance agencies were faced a dilemma: how to separate the killers from victims. Although facing strong criticism of its support of the killers, the UNHCR continued its general assistance operation in the refugee camps until all the refugees were repatriated.[10] Tanzania played an important mediation role, also serving as the site for the International Tribunal for War Crimes in Rwanda. The principle issue of "distinguishing between killers and victims" has yet to be resolved since most assistance agencies lack "coherent strategy for dealing with 'mixed' refugee population, i.e., those that include both victims and killers." The issue remains open, waiting for legal and political answers.

Repatriating both in Yugoslavia and Rwanda was neither simple nor coherent. First, the international peacekeeping forces could not promise the returnees a secured environment. Second, many could not return to their original homes since they were occupied either legally or illegally. Finally, in the background still loomed political problems that could hardly be separated from ethnicity. In addition to the psychological, and frequently human cost, the large volume of the relocated returnees in Yugoslavia, more than two and a half million people, created financial problems. Rudolph concludes that the answer is an early and forceful intervention. "Military powerful states and international organization now posses the legal authority as well as the physical capacity to curtail forced migration in most disintegrating states... Equally important, intervening forces should adhere to a policy of neutrality regardless of who may have been the initial aggressor or greater violator of human rights."

The Palestinian Refugee Case: Political, Economic And Legal Dilemmas

The next three chapters discuss the case of the Palestinian refugees. This asymmetric attention is due to several *bone fide* factors: a) the case of the Palestinian refugees is the oldest, most protracted, unresolved refugee problem, one that actually poses a threat to regional and global peace and security, b) the conflict is the most contested, controversial, and politically charged, c) it involves extreme and uncontrolled violence in the refugee camps which has been recently exhibited in suicide terrorism, d) it is probably the most expensive humanitarian operation since WWII, e) a complete repatriation seems to be a impossible, invoking vexing legal definitions and the application of "the Right of Return." The three essays discus these issues at length, including a discussion of the UN unique support mechanism, the United Nations Work and Relief Agency for the Palestinian refugees (UNRWA, 1948), which provides generous relief services exclusively to the Palestinian refugees.[11]

Nitza Nachmias uses the "Frustration-Aggression" syndrome to establish correlations between violence, terrorism, and displacement.[12] The model assumes aggression to be a reaction to feelings of relative deprivation and deep frustration. The Palestinian refugees, most of whom were born in the Diaspora, have developed a nostalgic narrative of Palestine as a "Paradise lost." This imagined reality causes deep frustration when juxtaposed against the despondent reality. The more circumstances became harsh and unbearable, the more retrogression became a safe haven for the refugees. Nachmias argues that political agitators and leaders of extreme nationalist organizations manipulated the frustrated camp dwellers for the purpose of inciting violence and terrorism. They played on the refugees' feelings of deprivation, loss of identity, loss of dignity, and ultimately, loss of life. Violence, and the liberation of Palestine by force were presented as the only means to redeem the refugees and end their suffering. The frustrated

Palestinian refugees were willing to give up their individual human rights in order to secure their collective rights as a community.

Rami Goldstein examines the nucleus of the legal dispute over the "right of return," questioning the Palestinian interpretation of their "Exodus" from Palestine. The Palestinians blame Israel for a carefully designed campaign to drive the Arabs out of Palestine. Israel claims that no act of forced migration took place. Rather, it was the Arab defeat in their unprovoked assault of the newly created Jewish state (General Assembly Res. A/181, 1947) that caused the exodus. Thus, the Arab states should bear full responsibility for the refugees. The refugees could have been resettled decades ago if the host Arab countries would have followed the Jordanian policy of granting them full citizenship.[13] Indeed, many Palestinians have been naturalized and acquired new nationalities, a process which usually brings their refugee status to an end. However, to date, most Arab states and the PLO reject the "resettlement option." They demand that a solution to the Palestine question should not focus on individual refugee rights, but rather on the Palestinian people as a nation. The Arab states and the PLO insist that the "right of return" is not negotiable and resettlement will never be accepted. In December 1997 this approach was reinforced when the General Assembly "reaffirmed the right of all persons displaced as a result of the June 1967 and subsequent hostilities to return to their homes or former places of residence in the territories occupied by Israel since 1967."

The status of the Palestinians refugees created a legal paradox. Because the Palestinians are protected and supported by UNRWA, they have no special claim to protection under the UNHCR or the 1951 refugee convention. Thus, the Palestinian refugees have a status that is special and unique under international law. In addition, UNRWA revised its basic definition several times, and granted legitimate refugee status and rights to all the decedents of the 1948 refugees. The "Consolidated Registration Instructions (CRI)," adopted by UNRWA in 1993, eliminated the requirements of "need" and "initial flight in 1948 to a country within UNRWA's five areas of operations. These revisions inflated the refugee population to over 4 million persons. (2003)

According to Goldstein, the PA claims that the "right of return" derives from natural law and in 1948 it existed as a customary binding norm of international law. It was reaffirmed in 1948 in the Universal Declaration of Human Rights, and the 1966 (ICCPR) International Covenant on Civil and Political Rights. Israel, expectedly, rejects these arguments and claims that the UN resolutions employ the term "should be permitted," and never required an unrestricted right of repatriation. Also, the UN lacks the authority to grant rights to "any person to enter the territory of any sovereign country at will." Goldstein concludes that since the legal argumentation provides no legitimate answers, only a mutual political compromise could terminate the conflict.

Dr. Sari Hanafi's discussion focuses on links between the refugees in the West Bank and Gaza, the Diaspora, and the nature of the Diaspora-Palestinian relations. From a broad bird's eye perspective he asks: What role has the Diaspora played during the recent Israeli-Palestinian confrontations? Did the Diaspora induce re-mobilization, disengagement, radicalization, or moderation? Hanafi's interesting analysis shows that initially, prior to the intifada, the Palestinian Territories constituted a week center of gravity for the diaspora. But this has changed with the Intifada and has had major consequences on the Palestinian "nationalism." What is interesting in his analysis is that he deals with both the poor urban refugee communities and the Palestinian elite abroad. He shows that both of them played a major role in the two uprisings (1987 and 2000 intifadas) but the latter, in keeping intense ties with the PLO leadership, and being close to the power center, the economic elite was able to play a mediator's position between the Palestinian economic and political spheres. This happened not without contradiction with the Palestinian political leadership who, by comparing them to Rothschild, tried to reduce them to a mere fund provider. Following this analogy, Hanafi illustrates that like the Zionists in the Diaspora, the Palestinian Diaspora contributed and invested in Palestine. "These subsidies especially came from the countries of the Gulf and America. The contributions and investments reached $408 million in 1996, and $ 410 million in 1997, of which 76% was in the form of investments."

However, following the outbreak of the second Intifada and the struggle against the Israeli occupation, "The absence of a direct relationship between Palestinians in the Diaspora and the Israelis reinforced the reciprocal ignorance and the dehumanization of the other." The Hamas and the Islamic Jihad assumed the leadership position and raised the Islamo-nationalist flag. The young refugee generations who have never known historic Palestine have nonetheless become as ardent in their mobilization as those who lived through the exodus of 1948. Hanafi explains how the "Right of Return" of the Palestinian refugees was circulated: "From the beginning of the nineties, it was these associative organizations in Europe and America that carried the flame of the Right of Return... Then, it spread to the Arab countries, before taking root in the Palestinian Territories." The "Right of Return" became the essence of Palestinian nationalism. If the Palestinian national identity is founded on the narration of the Nakba, symbol of nostalgia and call to the fight against injustice, the ideology of the Right of Return first emerged as a credo of the Diaspora, before being propagated within the Palestinian territories.

Hanafi observes this approach and argues that the Right of Return, however, must not be confounded with the volume of return. Hanafi claims that Chairman Arafat himself once expressed support for this realistic approach saying, "We understand Israel's demographic concerns. The Right of Return must be implemented in a way that takes into account such concerns."[14] However, he criticizes the use of demographic argument by Arafat. Hanafi makes his analysis about the current debate on the return of the Palestinian refugee starting from the distinguished Palestinian scholar Sari Nusseibeh's declaration which mentions that: "In the framework of a two-state solution, the Palestinian cannot demand the return of the refugees to their homes inside the Jewish entity." While Nusseibeh's statement was not new, it was indeed a bombshell that opened a major on-going debate within the Palestinian community.

In conclusion, Hanafi suggests that the "Right of Return" should assume two distinct and separate dimensions: a *symbolic* and a *material* dimension. \The two have to be conceptually and operationally separated in order for the Israeli and the Palestinian narratives to be bridged. Israel, according to him, has to acknowledge its responsibility for the dispossession and expulsion of the Palestinian refugees, while allowing the Palestinian refugees to return to their place of origin. For him also, "Beyond the moral and symbolic value of realizing the Right of Return, this right will be a tool for the refugees to help them chose between remaining in their host countries, returning to their villages of origin, or coming to the Palestinian territories." The Right of Return will become the Right of Choice. Hanafi is confident that, as in other refugee cases, the majority of the Palestinian refugees will not choose to return to their original villages and live under Israeli rule. The majority of the refugees will prefer resettlement in their host countries to being uprooted and relocated again, especially since for four generations they have established kinships, raised families, got married, and build their homes. This approach requires conceptual and strategic revisions. Also, the operational tools have to be comprehensive, yet flexible enough to be tailored to every specific situation.

Part: III
A Look to the Future:
Possibilities and Constraints

Part III suggests some possibilities for the future, among them the "civil society" model that could serve as an important operational tool. Until the 1980s the issue of civil society rarely surfaced in practices concerning forced migration. Migrants were addressed as women, men, and children in need of food, shelter, and medical services. Stiles shifts the discussion framework from the individual perspective to the community perspective and his analysis places the sociological and political processes in front of the bureaucratic decision making processes. The influx of large numbers of refugees affects primarily the local civil society and could cause its disintegration. Thus, resettlement requires the understanding of the mutual dependence, rivalries, and cooperation that exist and affect the economy, politics, and social welfare of both the refugee and the host communities.

Stiles elaborates on the important, yet rarely discussed, economic tensions between the refugees and the host communities. It is not unusual for refugees to become economic competitors to the local society and thereby threaten businesses and jobs. Poor local communities often envy assistance aimed at the refugee community. These tensions determine whether a large refugee population can contribute to a stronger civil society or whether their presence is inherently destabilizing. " In fact, in most countries with large-scale refugee populations civil society has largely broken down or is under tremendous stress. This is especially true in cases of long-term refugee presence…it is not uncommon for refugee population numbering in the hundreds of thousands to reside in the same general area more than fifteen years."[15] Stiles argues that this unhealthy and unnatural condition is too often overlooked. Often, host states become virtually unrecognizable, given the influx of refugees over the years. Stiles explains that "As each of these more-or-less static communities adjusts to the departure, arrival, and return of the refugees, they experience significant changes— both good and bad—that relate to their long-term survival. Assistance should focus on civil society, namely, the empowerment of informal, family and village-level social and economic associations. Successful resettlement will be a blessing to both the refugees and the host states. After the initial mass influx of Angolans into Zambia in the late 1980s, the refugees who settled in the community began to grow their own food and eventually became fully integrated into the local society." Clearly, refugees bring with them certain degree of social and economic capital and can and often do make important contributions to the social, economic, and political development of their host societies.

However, we should not overlook the possible negative effects of forced migration. "When borders are poorly defended and porous, it is relatively easy for guerrillas or soldiers from near by states to simply cross over to attack their enemies ensconced in camps a few miles away." Other harmful consequences include: outbreak of ethnic tension, political turmoil, lawlessness, economic hardship, abuse of aid, and dependency and corruption, among others. Another problem is addiction to foreign aid, such as when the refugee crisis abates and the aid is withdrawn, and the former host state finds it cannot manage without the aid.

The best results are achieved when refugee communities who are in one place in large numbers and for long periods of time choose to integrate in the host community, and the two communities reach ethnic and political compatibility. These processes require the tailoring of the assistance instruments to the refugee group's needs and characteristics. Important factors include: ethnic background, political cohesion, economic and human resources, and probabilities of self-reliance.

Legal Possibilities and Constraints

A look to the future reveals both possibilities and constraints. Goldstein looks to the future from a legal perspective, and presents some alternatives for amending the system. First, it is possible and necessary to revise the 1951 Convention. A set of new obligations that should not increase the host countries' security risks should be put in place. Second, more material resources should be allocated, and IDPs and refugees should be separated from economic migrants. Third, reformulating the current national refugee regimes focusing on improving existing national bureaucratic and coordination mechanisms will result in greater operational effectiveness. Finally, Goldstein suggests reformulating the international refugee law by incorporating new legal tools in order to increase the enforceability and the deterrence powers of the international organizations.

Notes

1. The UNHCR budget for 2002 was $ 1,220 billion. Other agencies, both bilateral like USAID and Japan, and multilateral agencies like the Red Cross and the European Commission, have also invested billions in assistance to refugees.

2. The Republic of Congo has been burdened with hundreds of thousands of refugees from Rwanda while Pakistan has been burdened with an influx from Afghanistan. India was a chosen refuge to forced migrants from Bangladesh and Thailand received refugees from Burma.

3. For example, the stability of Jordan was threatened in the late 1960 following the influx of Palestinian to Jordan following the 1967 defeat.

4. The establishment of the two *ad-hoc* international tribunals (Rwanda and Yugoslavia) and the creation of the International Criminal Court (ICC) are only three examples of the change in the international community attitude to the subject.

5. This issue is clearly exhibited in the following case studies.

6. Skran, 9

7. Security Council Resolution 688 of April 1991

8. This characteristic is evident in all case studies; Afghanistan, Rwanda, Yugoslavia and the Palestinian refugee case.

9. The Palestinian case shares the same characteristics.

10. Amnesty International (1997) strongly criticized the process in both Zaire and Tanzania, arguing that it reflected a shocking disregard for rights, dignity and safety of refugees.

11. UNRWA annual budget is about $400 million (2003). The *per capita* expenditures for a Palestinian refugee are about double of a UNHCR refugee.

12. John Dollard et al. *Frustration and Aggression, (New Haven: Yale University press,* 1961)

13. Between 1948 and 1988, Jordan granted citizenship to over a million Palestinian refugees who resettled in Jordan. However, contrary to international law, the Palestinians who hold Jordanian citizenship still maintain their refugee ID card and are included in UNRWA's database as *bone fide* "refugees."

14. Arafat, *New York Times*, 3 February 2002

15. See detailed discussion of this problem in Nachmias, Goldstein and Hanafi's chapters.

Part: I

Forced Migration Revisited

Alan James

CHAPTER ONE:

Analytical Observations On Forced Migration

The term "forced migration" is often fairly unambiguous. Occasionally, for example, people migrate at what in effect is the point of a gun. If they do not go they will be killed. There is unlikely to be much dissent from the proposition that this is a migration which is forced. At other times the threat may be less precise, but sufficiently compelling to lead directly to migration, as when the members of a distinct community are singled out for brutal and perilous treatment. They too, it can hardly be doubted, have been subject to force. A third context, which may induce migration, is that of a civil war. The type of force may have been that of natural events in the context of a laissez-faire state, rather than the personal hostility of those with superior power or the impulsion to find a place of safety away from the hazards of war. But it is force, nonetheless. The concept of forced migration is therefore in the nature of a spectrum. At one of its ends the assertion that an individual or group has been "forced" to migrate will seem crystal clear; at its other such a claim may look very doubtful, and in between there could well be room for debate as to whether some migrations are properly designated as the outcome of the threat or use of force.

"Forced"

Many of those who flee during such happenings do so because they fear for their lives. They may not have been supplied with specific and credible evidence that individual or communal death is a real possibility if they remain. But with bullets flying, it would be an ultra strict semanticist who argued that such a response should not be brought within the concept of "forced." The same might be said of migration to avoid famine, where people are dying because of the failure of crops or eviction from the land. There is a real sense in which it can be said that they have been forced to go.

What, however, of those who, while conscious of the possibility of poverty and hunger or of physical danger, are also moved to migrate by the prospect of better things elsewhere? Harsh local conditions may supply an element of what many would call force to their departure. But, viewed overall, it might be thought somewhat strained to designate it simply as forced migration. Then, too, what of those who migrate to avoid non-lethal persecution, whether of a political, racial, or religious kind? Does their persecution, or its threat, constitute force? The answer may well turn on the form of persecution. The prospect of imprisonment for taking or refusing to take a certain stance is one thing, worry about the adverse economic or social repercussions of saying what one thinks in public is another, and a sense of being discriminated against in the daily affairs of life is a third. Some of these cases might well be regarded as indicating the presence of force, but all may not be. And even where force is seen as a factor in the situation, the existence of other factors might disincline some commentators from terming a resultant migration as "forced."

Another aspect of the concept of "force" has to do with its source. In some contexts the decision to migrate is taken individually in response to an impersonal but nonetheless very potent threat arising out of the situation in which people find themselves. The immediacy of fighting or hunger can be so frightening that it creates an impulsion to move to a less life-threatening area. Equally, individuals sometimes decide to go because they are deeply offended by some aspect of the regime under which they live. Here, too, the force comes from within, in this case from a person's conscience or spirit. In other contexts, however, the pressure to migrate has a more direct human origin, in the shape of hostility targeted at a particular set of people with a view to inducing them to migrate. Such enmity may be unofficial, in the sense that it is organised by communities or action groups without either the involvement or the blessing of the state. It may have a quasi-official form, where a state is in a condition of civil war or in the process of breaking up. In that situation de facto authorities—local, regional, or national—may emerge, and try to secure the expulsion of a minority whose presence is deemed undesirable. Othertimes, a forced migration may be deliberately engineered by the state, either by decrees to that effect or by some less formal indications that unless people leave their lives will at least be very miserable and maybe in danger.

"Migration"

This term "migration" is less of a problem than "forced." But it does call for comment, not least in a volume such as this. For in its predominant use, "migration" very probably refers to movement to another state, and discussion of the political dilemmas to which it gives rise at the international level could well be taken to confirm this usage. However, it needs to be remembered that migration can also take place within a state—so called "internal migration"—and that sometimes such movements certainly reflect the presence of force. A group of people may, for example, move within their state for religious reasons, or they may be so moved on punitive or security grounds. Intra-state migration may also occur within multinational states, which, de facto, are fragmenting into territorial sub-divisions of a specifically national kind.

It should also be noted that there is something which might be called "static migration." The phrase may seem contradictory, given that movement is integral to the concept of migration. But where borders are altered the concept may, in human terms, express a sharp reality. The affected inhabitants find their citizenship, or at least their country of residence, changed overnight. From the point of view of some of them this happening may certainly be forced, in the sense of being deeply unwelcome. Such people may now constitute a minority within their new state. That state could well, given the circumstances of its creation or altered shape, have a keen national pride, which could bode ill for those who do not share the heritage of the majority. In theory, physical migration is an option. But that is often easier said than done, and the initial circumstances may not be so hostile as to force it to the top of the agenda. Thus many of those concerned may stay put, and hope to come to acceptable terms with the form of static migration which they have so abruptly undergone.

"Analysis"

The attempt to understand how it comes about that people are forced to migrate may be made at two levels. In the first place, a search may be undertaken to identify the particular grounds on which individuals or communities feel obliged to move or are made to do so. It is an effort to elucidate the reasons for such migration, or the justifications for its imposition. It has to do with sources and motives. The task is by no means straightforward. There may be contentious questions of fact. An instance of forced migration may be justified on more than one ground. It may be hard to discover why an enforcing or migrating individual or group acted as they did. The investigation of motives is often a slippery business. The results of the attempt must therefore be offered with caution. This, very impressionistic, analysis suggests that forced migration may be explained on one the other of fourteen grounds, each of which may be seen as constituting a class of such occurrences. But there remains plenty of room for debate about both the aptness of the classes and the assignment of examples to them.

A second way of trying to comprehend the phenomenon of forced migration is to inquire into the broad behavioral circumstances in which it appears. This quest therefore operates at a higher level of generality than the first. It wants to know whether there is any differentiation between the overall situation, which result in people being made to move. It seeks to discover if all the instances of forced migration come, as it were, from the same political and social direction or if rather different driving impulses or causal factors are sometimes at work. It asks about the human origin of the element of force. As indicated in the earlier sections of this chapter, differences of this kind do exist. They permit the fourteen classes of forced migration to be divided into three categories, which may be called derivative, responsive, and purposive. The first includes migrations of a passive kind, where no physical movement is involved; the second, those cases where the people concerned make their own decisions to go rather than being obliged to do so; and the third, those migrations which have been consciously imposed on a particular group. It is thought that this categorizing process should not be over-controversial.

Derivative Forced Migration

This category consists of migrations which take place through the stroke of a map-making pen. In this manner people are transferred from one state to another simply as a by-product of geopolitical rearrangements. It is an example of static migration. The category contains only one class, named after the process from which it arises.

Cartography

To many, cartographic migration may be entirely welcome, in that it "moves" them to their "own" national state—that is, one mainly constituted by people of their nationality. But others could well have undergone the opposite notional journey, in that they have become strangers in a foreign land—a national minority. For them this happening will no doubt be a troubling event, perhaps very troubling, and in that sense their "migration" is indeed "forced." Those re-drawing the maps would not, it may be presumed, have set about their task with this as their main or even subordinate intent. Their minds would have been on the larger picture. But it is nonetheless an incidental, or derivative, result of their work.

Forced migrations of this type were imposed after the end of the First World War on large numbers of people who inhabited the belt of European territory running from Finland in the north to Greece in the south, with Germany to one side and the Soviet Union to the other. Here lay thirteen newly constituted or reconstituted states. The map-changing peacemakers had by and large genuinely tried to arrange things so that the new borders followed the lines of nationality. But quite apart from the fact that adjustments were occasionally made to that principle for the benefit of certain states, neat national separations were impossible to achieve. New minorities were the result. In an effort to provide them with safeguards, no fewer than sixteen states were induced to accept international obligations regarding the treatment of their racial, religious, and linguistic minorities, and to give the League of Nations the right to engage in some protective measures. But these arrangements became increasingly resented, and in time increasingly irrelevant. Correspondingly, the lot of the inter-War minorities created by the stroke of a pen were often unhappy.

After the Second World War the fate of those who found themselves subject to border changes was far worse. No new states were set up, but large alterations were made. By the victors' fiat, Poland was in effect moved to the west, the Soviet Union gaining land on one side, and Germany losing it on the other. Germany also lost her other pre-war acquisitions, and in the peace treaties accepted by or imposed on five other defeated states, further territorial adjustments were made. Now, however, those who thereby became minorities generally had little incentive to stay, nor even —often—the opportunity, as the passions aroused by the War were vengefully expressed. Millions moved, as will be noted below.

Responsive Forced Migration

This second category consists of migrations which are, in a real sense, voluntarily undertaken. Those concerned may or may not be willing or happy to move. But they go of their own accord in that there has been no direct attempt to get rid of them. No enmity has been specifically focused on them. They are autonomously reacting to the passage of events, rather than being the intended victims of politics. To thes some feature of their situation is unacceptable to the point of being intolerable, so they respond by leaving it behind. Therein lies the element of force.

There are five grounds on which such action may be taken. Two of them give rise to what may be called inner-directed migrations—those which occur when people move primarily on the basis of their own values. Where a state does not permit certain forms of worship, or is totalitarian, some of its members may conclude that they can no longer live there. Their beliefs or personalities demand more freedom of expression, or simply more humanity, than they can presently obtain. Hence they decide to move to a place where, without subterfuge, they expect to find spiritual or political fulfilment. It is the proper thing to do. The remaining three classes reflect an impulsion to migrate arising from impersonal external circumstances which impinge acutely upon those concerned. These particular spurs are tyranny, warfare, and famine. Indiscriminately harsh and oppressive government is sometimes liable to produce a migratory response. Grave civil or international disorder may also be too much for those who find themselves in the middle of it. And cruel natural circumstances or the operation of an inhumane economic system could well induce a decision to go. None of these phenomena has been engineered with a view to inducing a people's departure. But in all cases, a concern for day-to-day mental ease, safety, and even life points compellingly towards it. Prudence dictates flight.

Conscience

Forced but self-motivated migration may emanate from conscience. If one's god tells one to go, it may be supposed that it is an order which cannot be refused. Compliance flows from one's conscience—although in the case of some gods there may also be a lively fear of the consequences of non-compliance (and if that were the most compelling motive, the case would need to be placed in this chapter's third category). Similarly, if one lives under a regime which does not allow people to worship as they wish, those who feel that this offends their deepest beliefs may be moved to seek such freedom elsewhere. This decision may be intertwined with a people's fear of the consequences of openly professing or practising their faith, and could therefore also be seen as the outcome of persecution—making it a candidate for categorisation elsewhere. But those of a profoundly religious disposition may be more concerned about following their consciences than fearful of the state's reaction to their so doing. For this reason such a matter can properly be noted here.

Two instances which may be judged to be of this kind are among the best known migrations of the ancient and modern eras. The Bible has it that two or three thousand years before the time of Christ, Abraham and his family moved from Ur of the Chaldees, near the head of The Gulf, to Haran in northern Mesopotamia (today's southern Turkey). There the Lord told him, "Get thee out of thy country...unto a land that I will show thee," which he and his descendants were to have as "an everlasting possession(Genesis 12.1 and 17.8)." Abraham obeyed, with consequences which reverberate unto the present day.

The second instance is the movement from England to "New England" in the 1620s and 1630s of about 25,000 people—the Pilgrim Fathers, as they may collectively be called. They were escaping the increasingly rigorous persecution of worship outside the Protestant Church of England, "nonconformist worship" as it was—and still is—called.. But they were probably not going simply because they were persecuted, but because they sought a home where they could do what they believed to be right. They wanted to remain Englishmen but be free of certain religious encumbrances. They were pulled rather than pushed. The establishment of self-governing English colonies on the American continent was the answer (so that technically their migration was internal).

Totalitarianism

Where the only kind of politics in a state is that which goes on within the ruling party, those who smoulder at their lack of freedom may find life unbearable or perilous, or both. This could lead them to decide that migration is the least undesirable of the options with which they are faced. Such, one assumes, were the calculations of many if not most of those who, during the Cold War, decided to leave the Soviet bloc for the West, despite the fact that the physical business of going was itself likely to be fraught with considerable danger—and that even if the escapees got away safely those of their relatives who were left behind could well find themselves in serious trouble. That there was a strong head of this sort of steam being contained within the Eastern kettle was demonstrated as the 1956 Hungarian Rising was going down to defeat: no fewer than 200,000 people took advantage of this brief opportunity to flee to the West.

Tyranny

Forced migration may also take place to escape the attentions of a tyrannical regime. Where indiscriminate oppression, arbitrariness, and brutality is the order of the day, it is not surprising that people sometimes decide that they must pick up their belongings and go. Many millions have claimed refugee status during the second half of the twentieth century. Numbers of them fled because of civil conflict (and therefore fall into another class). Others were specifically targeted because of such matters as their race, nationhood, or politics (and hence have been subjected to purposive forced migration). But there must also be many refugees who just could not bear the uncertainty and fear which was their lot. Tyrannical rule was too much.

Warfare

People do not migrate lightly. However, if they judge their lives to be in jeopardy, or their well being to be gravely threatened, these dangers could be a sufficient spur. It may be supposed that some of those who move in response to being caught up in civil (and sometimes in international) war fall into this category. In 1971, for example, as secessionists fought the Pakistani Army in East Pakistan (which was soon to become Bangladesh), nearly ten million people fled to India. Numbers of them may have feared being treated as traitors by the Army, but many others must have been simply getting away from a situation which was both chaotic and dangerous. It is less easy to be confident about what moved those who fled from the civil wars of the last decade of the twentieth century, as tribal and linguistic factors were often involved as well as political ones. But it is perhaps reasonable to assume that some of the several million refugees from Afghanistan and of the half a million or so from each of Somalia and Liberia (not the only cases which could be mentioned) were primarily motivated by their felt need to escape from an extremely hazardous situation rather than from avenging combatants. They were driven away by fear itself, rather than fear of the fighters' purpose.

Famine

Some of those who fled from East Pakistan in 1971 may also have been trying to save themselves from looming disease and famine. These are dangers which may certainly induce fear and flight. A notable instance of this in British history is the desperation of many to leave Ireland in the late 1840s, when the staple crop—potato—was virtually ruined by blight in three years out of four. People were dying by the hundreds and there was a rush to migrate, notably to the United States. In a wider timeframe the stream of emigrants was swelled by peasants who, being unable to make enough money from the land to pay their rent, were driven off it by the English landowners, and as a result faced destitution.

47

Purposive Forced Migration

The third category of forced migrations consists of those migrations which have been purposively obtained. A certain group or type of people are deliberately made to depart, or subjected to behavior which leaves them with little option but to go. They are the targeted victims of an antagonistic, hostile, or malevolent human agency, which—crucially—is in a more powerful position than them. Migration is imposed upon them. There are eight grounds which explain this frightening course of events. The first is profit, or, less respectably put, greed. It refers to the situations where the decision or pressure to make people migrate is fuelled by the hope of financial gain. The second is "culture," which on the face of it may seem somewhat out of place. But it is a word which has in the twentieth century been used to justify an activity purporting to be in the best interests of those undergoing it. People are to be improved by a process which involves their forcible movement, and as this is intended to change their values and practices, calling it a "cultural" event may possibly—albeit ghoulishly—be fitting.

The next three classes (which may be seen as constituting a sub-category) have to do with instances where forced migration is the outcome of xenophobia. People are hated or feared because there is something strange or foreign about them, or because the historical myths and memories of the superior group about the lesser one arouse such feelings. Any one or more of three grounds may be the spark which ignites this process: race, religion, and nationhood. The blaze can quickly reach horrifying proportions. The last three classes (also making up a sub-category) concern cases where people are moved because of something specific which they have done or are alleged to have done, or because of worry about what they might do. One of the classes represents the uprooting of people in the interests of the state's security (a pre-emptively inspired migration), another the imposition of punishment, and the last the taking of revenge.

Profit

The love of money is a common human characteristic, taking the form not just of direct accumulative or commercial activity but also of envy of those who are more successful at it than oneself. If those who fall into the latter category are also members of a racial or religious minority, or both, envy may the more easily merge into resentment and thence, perhaps, into a desire to dislodge the perceived offender. This may be most likely to occur if a specific branch of commerce is dominated by the minority in question, and especially so if it is felt or believed that they are taking unfair advantage of their position.

Such a case was the expulsion in 1972 of all Asian non-citizens from Uganda—which meant virtually all of the 75,000 Asians who lived there. They were largely in control of the middle and some of the higher reaches of the economy, and many Africans believed that they were exploiting them. The dictatorial President Idi Amin sought to capitalise on this mood, and in the short run his anti-Asian move won him some support (but within a few years it had had a disastrous effect on the country's economy). However, the most blatant, egregious, and long-standing instance of a connection between moneymaking and migration is the slave trade. Starting in the latter part of the sixteenth century and going on for about three hundred years, about twelve million Africans were captured and shipped across the Atlantic to be sold as slaves.

Culture

"Culture" can be broadly defined as a group's ideas and beliefs, and on that basis much of what it asserts and does—including its attitude to race or religion—is cultural. But the term may also be more narrowly conceived as a group's social and political practices. Using it in that sense, a group may decide that its culture should be improved or extended. As a specific programme (rather than a long-term hope), that sounds somewhat improbable and impracticable. But it is always possible that a state may try to persuade or push its people along a social road which is new to them. And if they are run dictatorially such attempts at uplift may even involve forcing internal migration on individuals or collectivises.

This was the fate of the people of Cambodia between 1975 and 1979 under the Khmer Rouge regime—perhaps the most bestial regime the post Second World War world has seen. The country's institutions were systematically destroyed and the currency abolished (barter taking its place). Cities and towns were forcibly evacuated, and the population was set to work in the fields. Huge numbers starved or were killed—almost certainly up to two million (almost a third of the population), and perhaps more. In a somewhat analogous way, part of China's "Cultural Revolution" of 1965-68 involved sending bureaucrats and intellectuals into rural exile and making them work on the land.

Race

The coexistence within one state of people of different races has always been a fertile source of suspicion and disharmony (just as neighboring states who differ in these respects may find their relations exacerbated by racial issues). Problems of this kind no doubt arise from the very visibility of the physical characteristics which mark off people of one race from another, especially where they are associated with other distinguishing features such as religion or language, and particularly so if one of the groups is smaller but more successful than the other. In such contexts routine differences or conflicts can easily be viewed through the racial magnifying glass, and become entwined with the emotional fall-out, which is thereby precipitated. New resentments and fears may well be created, existing ones heightened, and theories of racial superiority advanced—all of which may contribute to the phenomenon of forced migration, either within or beyond the state in question.

In the late nineteenth and the first half of the twentieth century, one notable example of this process was the treatment of blacks in the southern states of the United States. The segregation of educational, recreational, and other facilities on the basis of "Jim Crow" laws, in conjunction with the burgeoning economy of the North, led many of them to move to that part of the country. But the most horrifying instance of racially motivated migration is more recent: the hatred of Germany's Nazi regime for the Jews, which culminated in the Holocaust. From the Nazi Party's early, 1920, manifesto the writing was on the wall: Jews were to be disenfranchised. This was developed into the theory that the German master race (*Herrenvolk)* was born to rule, and other races, such as the Semites, were destined to be ruled. Once Hitler had come to power in 1933, the Jews (among others) soon found themselves discriminated against, persecuted, and tortured and, by the Nuremberg Laws of 1935, formally turned into second-class citizens, if that. Many left, often to the great cultural and intellectual benefit of the states in which they settled.

But more remained, and with the outbreak of the Second World War no longer had the option of an exit route. Virtually all of them—six million — perished in the concentration camps.

Since the War, the only acknowledged policy of racial discrimination has been South Africa's. The whites there had never hidden their belief that they were superior to blacks, and this was expressed socially and politically in a variety of ways. Then, in 1948, this approach was formalized in the policy of apartheid. Among other things it led, under the Group Areas Act of 1952, to the deportation of Africans from specified districts which, for residential purposes, were henceforth to be for whites only. However, South Africa was soon very much the odd man out, and subject to increasing international criticism and ostracism. For elsewhere, discrimination on racial grounds became, in political terms, highly incorrect, and this taboo was extended to the making of critical remarks about the race or ethnicity of another person or group. Accordingly, anyone seeking or holding high political office is most unlikely to use that kind of terminology. Even extolling the virtues of one's own racial group may be going too far for someone with a public reputation to protect or build. However, this does not mean that racial considerations are never in the minds of those who cite some other reason for criticizing a group to which they do not belong. Nor can it be assumed that any such racial message remains unrecognized, either by the supporters of those making it or by those to whom it refers. Migrations arising, at least in part, out of racial hostility may not therefore have wholly disappeared.

Religion

Religion is another long-standing source of the kind of disharmony which can lead to forced migration. Given that for many people it is basic to their lives, and that not infrequently it takes a (or at least an apparently) theologically intolerant form, it is not surprising that at certain junctures it finds expression in physical intolerance. A community which sees itself as defined by its religion may easily turn on another such nearby which says a different creed and may bow to a different god.
A notable instance of this occurred in Spain in 1492. The local Jewish community, which numbered about 200,000 (less than two per cent of the population), saw that part of the Iberian peninsula as its home, and

understandably so as its history there appeared to date back to Roman times. Its members gave no trouble to the temporal or the religious authorities. But in religious terms they were "others" within, and the Catholic authorities decreed that their presence could no longer be tolerated. The consequential edict provided that, failing conversion, they had to leave within three months. The penalty for non-compliance was death. They went.

This was perhaps a harbinger of the religious ferment and accompanying intolerance which was a major factor in Western Europe during the sixteenth and the first half of the seventeenth centuries. One famous attempt to stem the international turbulence to which it periodically gave rise was the 1555 Peace of Augsburg, the key element in which was the *cuius regio, eius religio* clause: to him who rules, to him the religion. Accordingly, each secular prince in the (largely Germanic) Holy Roman Empire could choose Catholicism or Lutheranism, and his subjects had then to conform or depart. It gave Germany peace of a sort for some sixty years. But in 1618, in what was at first a renewed conflict between Protestants and Catholics, there broke out what was to be the Thirty Years War. It caused enormous devastation in Central Europe and uprooted large numbers of people, which to some extent accounts for the dramatic drop in Germany's population: it is thought to have fallen from about twenty-one million in 1618 to not much more than half that figure by 1648.

Supposedly, that year's Peace of Westphalia ended not just the Thirty Years War but also all religious wars. The middle of the twentieth century, however, ushered in a period which included a noteworthy amount of conflict based at least in part on religion, the initial one of which involved large-scale forced migration. It took place on the Indian sub-continent. Britain had declared her intention of leaving in 1947 and splitting the spoils between what would be the two successor states of India (a secular but predominantly Hindu state) and Pakistan (officially Muslim). As always, the determination of the dividing line was a matter of intense debate and difficulty, especially in the northwest where the Sikhs were particularly incensed at the proposed division of their homeland. Upon independence inter-communal fighting and pillage broke out, and about five million people frantically trekked in the direction of the state in which they would not be a religious minority.

On an entirely different scale, religious differences have sometimes led to forced migration in Northern Ireland (part of the United Kingdom). Ever since Protestant immigration in the seventeenth century, problems have arisen between people of that persuasion and the indigenous Catholics, and since the late 1960s British troops have had to be posted there with the difficult task of trying to maintain civil order. In certain towns and cities there are very clear dividing lines (in one case a 20 foot high concrete and fencing barrier, euphemistically called a "peace line") between Catholic and Protestant residential areas. Religious "intruders" can find themselves the objects of intimidation and violence, often to the extent that they are forced to find a new place to live. The phenomenon has even been officially recognised, a scheme called the Special Purchase of Evacuated Dwellings having been set up to buy properties from people who have moved in consequence of sectarian turbulence. Moreover, no less than 1,000 people have been sent into exile during these years from Northern Ireland by the (Catholic) Irish Republican Army.

Nationhood

The above two classes of xenophobia focus on a rather specific characteristic of the group in question or upon a particular emotion aroused by its activity or presence. Of course, more than one characteristic or emotion may become relevant as animosity towards the group gathers pace. But if, as is likely, each of the grounds for action is still clearly and distinctively identifiable, the outcome is a multiple accusation rather than a broad hostility, which represents the fusion of separate sources of ill will.

Sometimes, however, groups who live close to each other develop a general rivalry, one which is of an overall kind rather than specific in point of detail. This is not uncommon between neighbouring communities within a state, although it rarely extends beyond competitive banter. But in the case of neighbouring nationalities a much more serious rivalry can occur, especially where each of them constitutes a state. The next-door state is, after all, the one with whom one is most likely to have fought; occupations may have occurred, atrocities may be alleged to have taken place, territory may have changed hands. Hence there may be ample scope for historical memories and myths to stoke an enmity of some depth and virulence about which may be further strengthened if the two nationalities are differentiated not just by the belief that each is a distinct nation but also by one or more factors of a narrower kind, such as race or religion. Each may assume in the eyes of the other the role of *the* national enemy. In these circumstances events may move in a way which precipitates forced migration.

In this connection one may cite the population movements which took place upon the ending of the Second World War. Germany's expansionist policy, racist ideology, and brutal behaviour combined to make her people much hated. When, therefore, she was defeated and her territory reduced, the future was bleak for the many Germans who found themselves subject to the phenomenon of static migration, especially if they had been associated with the process whereby Germany's domain had earlier expanded. Millions of them moved, sometimes having no option but to do so. (The latter case can be seen as a form of punitive cross-border migration, but its emphatically national focus makes it more appropriately mentioned here.) Thus three million Germans were expelled from Czechoslovakia's restored Sudetenland, and maybe ten million more expellees or refugees poured westwards from other regions which Germany had lost. On a much smaller scale there were similar movements from additional territories which had changed hands.

Instant Minorities: Instant Migration

Another series of examples of forced migration based on nationhood arose out of the break-up of Yugoslavia about so much so that the term "ethnic cleansing" ("ethnic" here being virtually a synonym for "national") seems to have arisen from, or at least to have been popularised by, the mass murders and consequential migratory events which occurred in the area. Yugoslavia was from its 1918 proclamation (as the "Kingdom of Serbs, Croats, and Slovenes") a mixture of nationalities, the relationships between some of which was not improved by internal feuds and fighting during the Second World War. One of the successor states, which emerged in the early 1990s, was Bosnia-Herzegovina, which itself contained several of the national groups of its parent state. Soon the (Orthodox) Serbs tried to rid the state of its (Muslim) Bosnians and (Catholic) Croats, in the course of which it is estimated that about two million people were uprooted. The 1995 Dayton peace accord acknowledged the problem by turning the state into a federal association of two entities: one Serbian and the other Muslim-Croat. (In practice, this has become a tripartite arrangement, with the state acting as a unit only in international matters.) In another of the successor states, Serbia and Montenegro (which until 2003 held on to the name of Yugoslavia), fighting broke out in the Serbian province of Kosovo between the majority

Kosovar Albanians and the Serbian minority. First the Albanians fled, and then, when Kosovo became a kind of NATO protectorate (which as of February 2003 it remains, with a purely formal attachment to the Serbian state), about half the Serbians were driven out. All these are instances, formally speaking, of internal migration—but ones which unquestionably were no less forced than some which have taken place across international frontiers.

But perhaps the most dramatic twentieth century example of force migration, which testified to deep national antipathies, is one which involved Greece and Turkey. The former sees herself as the birthplace and beacon of Western civilisation. She is also the representative of a long Christian tradition, as the Orthodox Church—also known as the Greek Orthodox Church—consists of those Eastern churches which, having broken with the Church in the West in the ninth century, are in communion with the Greek patriarch of Constantinople. But in 1453 that city was taken by the infidel (Muslim) Turks and thereafter Greece was under Turkish rule for getting on for four centuries. All this left such a potent legacy of reciprocal suspicion and distrust that when, in 1923, certain territorial adjustments were made between Greece and Turkey in favour of the latter, it was also provided that except for two small groups there would be a compulsory exchange of all Greeks who lived or would find themselves living in Turkey for all Turks living in Greece. (The criterion for deciding who was to go was religious.) The territories from which Greece was to withdraw were Eastern Thrace, which she had acquired just before the First World War, and the city and hinterland of Smyrna on the west coast of Asia Minor, which her army had occupied shortly after the War's end. From then roughly 1,300,000 Greeks moved westwards, about a million of them fleeing from Smyrna in advance of the agreement so as to avoid the avenging Turkish Army, and about 400,000 Turks moved eastwards from various parts of Greece.

In Cyprus, half a century later, there was a kind of post-script to this population exchange. Cyprus had for several millennia thought of herself as part of the Greek world. But latterly, for three centuries, the Ottoman Turks, who were then replaced for almost a hundred years by the British, had ruled her. During the Turkish period there had been a relatively large immigration of Turks, and the 1960 Constitution on the basis of which Cyprus became independent sought to balance the interests of the Greek majority (about 400,000) and the Turkish minority (about 100,000). But within a few years each national group's inbuilt suspicion and distrust of the other resulted in these arrangements breaking down. Inter-communal conflict and fighting erupted in 1963-64, and about a quarter of the Turks felt obliged, for their safety, to leave their homes and join their cultural compatriots in Turkish-Cypriot enclaves or villages which were scattered throughout the island. There were also some smaller comparative movements on the Greek-Cypriot side. This form of de facto partition continued for ten years. A Turkish invasion then divided the state into two, the Turks holding the north and the (Greek) Cypriot government the south. Reactively, about 200,000 Greek Cypriots migrated southwards, and about 40,000 Turkish Cypriots moved in the other direction.

In form the Republic of Cyprus remained one, as the state later promulgated in the North—the Turkish Republic of Northern Cyprus—was recognised only by Turkey. But thus far the situation in practice has been one where two nationally "pure" states exist side by side. Each of them makes much of the barbarities its people have suffered at the hands of the other, in the recent as well as the more distant past. In this unpromising context all the many efforts at a settlement of "the Cyprus problem" have been in vain. If an agreement is reached, it is likely to involve a good deal of autonomy within a single state for each of the two national entities. Given the heavy load of adverse historical baggage which each bears, their successful coexistence would demand no less.

Security

It is widely accepted that the first duty of the state is the preservation of its security, and hence that of its members: *salus populi suprema est lex*. It does not necessarily follow that any means may be used to achieve this goal, but in its pursuit statesmen do not often feel or find themselves constrained by moral considerations. The end is so important that virtually any means may be seen as justified. Accordingly, if forcing individuals or a group to migrate is deemed necessary to bolster a state's security, it is likely to be done.

Thus in time of war, enemy aliens and perhaps others with close connections to it may find themselves subject to a temporary forced migration in the shape of internment. They cannot be trusted to be left at large. In Britain, soon after the start of the Second World War, such people were hurriedly shipped to the Isle of Man (numbers of them soon being released on evidence of their British loyalties). In the United States after the attack on Pearl Harbour, many Japanese underwent a somewhat harsh and undiscriminating confinement. In civil wars, too, those deemed to be a security risk may find themselves moved to internment camps, as happened to about 800,000 Hutus in Burundi during the 1990s.

Sometimes, however, a group that is mistrusted on security grounds may find itself subject to more drastic treatment. In 1755, as part of the long-standing Anglo-French competition and conflict on the North American continent, Britain expelled about 10,000 French-speaking Acadians from Nova Scotia (which had formerly been part of the French colony of Acadie). They had, on the advice of their Catholic priests, refused to swear an oath of allegiance to the British crown and, war having again broken out (to be followed in the next year by its extension to Europe), their presence was judged to be unacceptable on security grounds. However, it has also been said that the British had their eye on the Acadians' fertile farms in the Annapolis valley—which would give this forced migration the partial character of one driven by profit. Be that as it may, they were scattered southwards, and large numbers of them perished. Of those who survived, many made their way to what later became the American state of Louisiana, which earlier had been a French possession and was then being administered by Catholic Spain. There, in an altered version of their place of origin, they became known as Cajuns. Their travails were far from over, as the New Orleans Creoles shunted them out to the swamplands and they remained poor and illiterate, and during the first half of the twentieth century suffered linguistic discrimination. But then amends were made, and now Cajun culture is something of a tourist attraction.

Another forced migration which arose from security worries will be familiar to many who have had even a small exposure to the Judaic-Christian tradition: the Babylonian Captivity of the Jews. At the start of the sixth century B.C. the small tributary states of southwest Asia had just undergone a change of overlord. Babylon (roughly coextensive with present-day Iraq) had defeated Egypt, and hence expected the fealty of those who had formerly been part of the vanquished great power's sphere of influence. However, the states concerned did not like the change, and hoped that reviving Egypt would help them throw off the new, and heavier, yoke. One of them, Judah, revolted twice. On the first occasion, Babylon's King Nebuchadnezzar (after whom Saddam Hussein is said deliberately to have fashioned himself) captured Jerusalem, Judah's capital, and took the king and his court into captivity. A further revolt ten years later led to the destruction of the city and all the people of Judah being exiled. It was famously recalled in Psalm 137 that "By the rivers of Babylon, there we sat down, yea, we wept, when we remembered Zion." They were kept in Babylon for half a century. A leading power could not accept the risk to its security presented by an insubordinate vassal people on the perimeter of its political and military reach.

In the middle of the twentieth century there was, in reverse, a not wholly dissimilar event. Two millennia earlier the Jews had been forced to migrate from Palestine, and thereafter had seemingly been eternal strangers. It was always "Next year, in Jerusalem," never this. But in 1917 the Zionist movement persuaded Britain to issue a "declaration of sympathy" for its aspiration that Jews should return to the land, which, it was asserted, had been promised them by God. As Palestine was at this time in effect taken over by Britain, some progress was made with the Zionist scheme in the inter-war period—although not without protests from the indigenous Arab (Muslim) population. Happenings in Germany before and during the Second World War greatly accelerated the migratory pressure and, correspondingly, the Arabs' determination to resist the influx of foreign people whom they suspected—on good grounds—of wanting to succeed Britain as the territory's rulers. Despairing of an agreement between the two groups, Britain threw the problem in the UN's lap and announced that she was soon to depart. The UN's partition proposal was rejected by the Arabs, and on Britain's 1948 withdrawal (and the simultaneous proclamation of the state of Israel) war broke out between the new state and her four Arab neighbours. About 600,000 Palestinian Arabs thereupon fled from land which had been assigned to Israel. Some went in response to the call of their leaders but most, perhaps, were forced to go. A number were simply evicted by Israel from areas of possible strategic significance to the new, and very insecure, state. Many others fled fearing—not unreasonably—that they would suffer as a result of being seen by Israel as a grave security risk during what was, in effect, her war of independence. But all hoped to return before long in the wake of an Arab victory. That was not to be. Instead they had to make their homes in camps, and at the end of the century more than three million of them and their descendants were registered as refugees in the areas and states surrounding Israel.

The Kurds have suffered a somewhat comparable fate. They are a Muslim people whose language is distantly related to Persian, and they must surely be the twentieth century's unluckiest nation. Promised autonomy in the 1920 Treaty of Sevres (the peace arrangement between Turkey and the victors in the First World War), the Treaty fell by the wayside under the impact of Turkey's revival under Kemal Ataturk. In the superseding Treaty of Lausanne (1923) there was nothing for the Kurds. Ever since then twenty million of them have been mainly distributed between Iran, Iraq, and Turkey, often finding themselves in difficult conditions as their secessionist impulses present a troubling security threat to their hosts. In an Iraqi campaign against rebellious Kurds which began at the end of the 1980s, almost 200,000 of them were killed, about 100,000 fled to Turkey (where they were not much welcomed), and half a million were moved from their homeland area in the north to internment camps elsewhere in Iraq. Subsequently the north received British and American aerial protection. Whether, in 2003, the Kurds will be beneficiaries of the United States-led war against Iraq remains to be seen.

Punishment

Although (as has been noted) something of the kind occurred at the end of the Second World War, forcing individuals or a group to leave a state is not often used as a punishment. An internal forced migration could be so motivated, but few states are sufficiently big to make it a practical proposition and those that are may be unwilling to contemplate such a measure. But in this, as in other regards, a harsh or totalitarian regime may not be held back by either moral or political scruples, and the extent of its domains may make such action possible. Britain sometimes sentenced criminals to be transported to her American colonies, and when, following their secession in 1776, they were no longer available for this purpose, she used the newly discovered Australia exclusively as a penal settlement for several decades. Equally, a minority group may be punished by the expulsion of many or all of its members from their traditional area to a distant part of the state. After the Second World War the Soviet Union did this to large numbers of Chechens from the Caucasus and Kalmyks from west of the Caspian Sea, despatching them to Siberia because of what was said to be their deficient patriotism. Similarly, the same state deported its 200,000 Crimean Tatars en masse to central Asia as retribution for their alleged collaboration during the War with the invading Germans. For a decade they were forbidden to use their own language, and it was only after the dissolution of the Soviet Union in 1991 that they were allowed to return, if they wished, to the Crimea.

Revenge

In theory, people may be forced to migrate without being disliked or hated by those who do the forcing. The latter, given the perceived needs or beliefs of their (more powerful) group, could be acting in no more than a spirit of regrettable necessity. But in practice, contempt for or antipathy towards the expellees will probably be present and, as old grievances are recalled or new ones created if those being pushed out engage in armed resistance, antipathy could turn to loathing. This level of emotion has been noted in the preceding section. Sometimes, however, it may appear not in the broad context of international feuds but within a state where one group has been traditionally dominated and ill treated by the other—and where the opportunity arises to turn the tables. The previously pent-up bitterness of the underdog towards the top dog could then find violent expression, which may be additionally fuelled if there is some manifest difference, perhaps of a religious, racial, or tribal kind, between the practices or physical character of the two. But such a conflict goes somewhat beyond one rooted in race or religion, or one expressive of general antagonism or envy. Additionally, it displays the distinctive phenomenon of revenge—which is, indeed sometimes said to be part of certain peoples' culture. Very specific old scores are being paid off—a process which, even if it does not have that intention, may well have the effect of forcing the now overthrown group to migrate.

A prominent case of this kind arose out of the relationship between Tutsis and Hutus in the East-Central African territory of Rwanda-Burundi, which in 1962 became the two separate states of Burundi and Rwanda. The agriculturalist Hutus were in a majority throughout the territory, but since the sixteenth century had been subject to the feudal overlordship of the tall, aristocratic, and cattle-herding Tutsis, who made up about 15% of the population. With the approach and arrival of independence things partly changed. In Rwanda (as it was to become), Tutsi power was broken in 1959, and about 100,000 of them fled. Thereafter Tutsi exiles repeatedly attempted to invade, and fighting periodically occurred within the country, with the Tutsis being aided by some moderate Hutus. In the 1990s about one million of the insurgents were massacred, but then the latter gained control and two or maybe three million Hutus were forced to leave the country. Meanwhile, in Burundi the Tutsis held on to political control in face of recurrent Hutu attempts to topple them, which led in the 1990s to about 300,000 Hutus fleeing to neighbouring states. Neither country has yet seen an end to its civil strife.

Conclusion

So far as the effects of forced migration are concerned, those who have enforced it do not usually appear to have prospered by their activity. Indeed, a number of such states have been in disarray, and one or two on the road to ruin. Many of the states from which people have voluntarily fled have also been suffering from disorder, not to say chaos. With regard to the migrants, their immediate plight evokes the utmost sorrow. Yet it must also be said that some of them unquestionably made good in the lands to which they went. In respect of those who migrated of their own accord, this is not too surprising, as a decision of that kind rather suggests a measure of resilience and entrepreneurship. But it may well be true of others, too. When opportunity beckoned, it was sometimes embraced. It is not, perhaps, an entire coincidence that two states—the United States and Israel—who have been notably welcoming to migrants (or, perhaps, in the latter case, to certain migrants) are also known for their vigour and prosperity.

More generally, four comments may be offered. The first is that forced migration seems to be a recurring feature in human history. One must not overemphasise this; it by no means dominates the scene. But time and again it crops up. This suggests, secondly, that human differences, especially those of race, religion, and nationhood, have the capacity to be an aggravating factor in political and social contexts. And now and then that capacity is rather dramatically realised. The avoidance of that sort of trouble is a large challenge to statesmanship, and to the ordinary people who make up mixed societies. Manifestly, these challenges are not always surmounted, which draws attention to the third point: that there is still plenty of bigotry and intolerance abroad in the world—sin, as some might say. Finally, much of the tale of forced migration testifies to the vitality, self-regarding character, and attractiveness of the sovereign state as a political institution. It is states which frequently initiate the forcing. They are sometimes called upon to do so by their people; and where people take it upon themselves to throw others out they are in effect saying that they want their state to be of a certain kind. The world seems likely to remain politically divided up in this way. Is there, one wonders, any ground for hope that states and their people will develop arrangements, practices, and dispositions which are conductive to greater internal tolerance and harmony than has been evident in the past?

Leon Gordenker

CHAPTER TWO:

Basic International Rules and Issues in the Treatment of Refugees

Anywhere disaster overcomes social order, some people move away from their homes. Few or many, together or individually, they usually claim that they were forced to migrate. Observers could hardly deny that coercion and danger partly impel their involuntary displacement. Migrants who took the opportunity to move for individual advantage would hardly admit that they were not driven. Prevailing estimates of forced migrants now add up to impressive totals of at least some 20 million persons.[1] "[T]hey are amongst the great survivors of the 20th century…"[2] Their presence poses questions at every level of governance from village and city to provincial and national governments and their international institutions. It also calls into action existing and spontaneous networks of charity, sympathy, and social policy. The phenomenon of forced migration has historical origins in the beginning of human society, but with modern technology and its attendant population increases, the forced migrations in the last century and this one have involved far larger numbers of people than ever before, scattered in varying densities around the globe.

Closer inspection of what may seem a simple cause and effect process of threat or use of force followed by flight discloses not only variations but differences of a fundamental nature among both forced migrants and their movements. This essay attempts to sort out concepts to distinguish these differences. After recalling their origins, it uses the legal, organizational, and policy concepts of international responses to refugees and related categories as a guide to more precise understanding. It refers to some actual practices by international organizations and by governments in order to illustrate the alteration of the concept of refugees in contemporary situations.

The Emergence of Forced Migration as a Political Issue

The association of forced migration with political decisions emerged most clearly in Western Europe where the growing strength and mutation of the state provided a pacifying response to wars of religion of the Sixteenth and Seventeenth Century. While some of the earlier forced migrations involved strife among religions—including such striking examples as the expulsion of Jews from Spain and Portugal in the Sixteenth Century and the flight of Protestants from France in the Seventeenth Century after the revocation of the Edict of Nantes—a new element was introduced following the wars of religion in Europe and the Peace of Westphalia in 1648. It was the acceptance of the modern state with its fixed boundaries and claims by governments to exclusive control of territory and their populations. This was accompanied by explicit governmental policies affecting or controlling distinct social groups and individuals. Sometimes the aim of such governmental decisions deliberately put people on the move; sometimes the movement was a by-product of a policy, such as warring against a neighboring land. To this should be added the slave trade that plucked hundreds of thousands of Africans from their homes in the Seventeenth and two succeeding Centuries. Furthermore, organized transnational humanitarian movements, including the Red Cross and anti-slavery groups, in the Nineteenth Century began to call attention to the suffering resulting from forced migration as a general issue for all governments.

Not all forced migrations resulted from political decisions. Floods, earthquakes, droughts, fires and disease have also impelled people over the centuries to move from their accustomed homes. Their dispersal, when they could not or would not return, created diasporas that in themselves could affect the surrounding population and sometimes cause enough social unrest to spur more coercion and flight. The very term "refugee," so closely associated in our time with forced migration, arose from the emigration of royalists during the French revolution at end of Eighteenth Century. It derives from the verb *réfugier,* to take shelter, and was clearly associated with the effects of the policies of the revolutionary government in Paris and its wholesale execution of its actual and presumed enemies.

Migrants generally, including those of the French Revolution, made their own ways in foreign lands. "…They were welcomed, on the whole, by the receiving community." [3] The governments, however, hardly acted as welcoming hosts, except for a few migrants who were well connected with ruling families or other elites. Instead, the *émigrés* who kept out of political (and religious) controversy and sought to resettle found ways to integrate their lives even if they suffered from friction from their neighbors. The *émigrés* were usually free to exploit their private or church connections among the host population. And if they chose to return to their places of origin, they were usually free to leave their refuges.

This governmental indifference, however, changed under the impact of both political ideas and of technology. Prominent from the time of the French Revolution, nationalism combined with the concept that emerged under the Emperor Napoleon of a legal system that applied centralized, comprehensive control to society. This system gradually strengthened and gave juridical dimensions to vaguer notions of citizenship. It implied legal, official identification of aliens. For each category, specific rights and duties were distinguished. Technological development, especially in connection with the Industrial Revolution of the late Eighteenth and early Nineteenth Century, made it progressively easier for governments to control movements of people in the territory under their jurisdiction. That very technology reduced the time required for migration and provided easier access to better information. Moreover, populations all over the world rapidly increased in part because of better medical science and food technology. Before many years, railroads, automobiles, trucks and buses replaced animal power for land transport and increased the speed and scope of migration. Eventually steamships and aircraft added rapid facilities for moving people.

The late Nineteenth Century saw unprecedented migration and eventually new kinds of controls for entrance and exits at borders that were nevertheless relatively open. Indeed, little documentation was required and passports were not in general use for private citizens traveling abroad until after World War I. When ordered, border police and troops could increasingly easily move on railroads, could communicate by telegraph and then by telephone. Migration, some of it impelled by political events such as the liberal revolutions of 1848 and the repression of Jews in Czarist Russia, included settlement in North and South America and Australia, where immigration restrictions were hardly onerous.

Not until the Russian Revolution of 1917 was forced migration understood and generally treated as an obviously international issue with clear political coloration. Then in a brief period as many as 1,500,000 Russian nationals, many of them visible and destitute, spilled and trickled across the borders in Europe in order to escape the many effects of the revolution. This included the obviously political campaign by the Bolsheviks to eliminate the old ruling class, civil war, outside military intervention, extensive famine, and breakdown of the social infrastructure. From a grander perspective, the bourgeois governments, as the Bolsheviks defined them, could hardly ignore the many *emigrés* of the Russian social and political elite they had earlier supported against the revolutionaries.

Development of International Rules and Definitions

The growing horror of modern war, meanwhile, had given birth to the Red Cross movement.[4] It developed into formally non-governmental national societies that concentrated on relief for persons involved in natural disasters. This was supplemented by international agreements intended to make warfare more humane and eventually in the collection of law-making treaties that are known as the Geneva Conventions.[5] These came to include provisions regulating the humane treatment of people in zones occupied by military forces. Private citizens in the Swiss canton of Geneva formed a unique supervisory body, the International Committee of the Red Cross.

World War I produced migrations that were documented as never before. The by-then familiar still camera and the newer motion picture showed piteous scenes of French and Belgian peasant families trundling their belongings in two-wheel carts along narrow roads choked with military traffic moving the other way. Fearing the battle and the German occupation, tens of thousands of Belgians, for instance, pushed into the neutral Netherlands where relief agencies and the state hurriedly created Spartan camps for those who had not found some other arrangement through family, church or business. Similar scenes were recorded in farmlands and cities whenever battle sites shifted. These battle-related migrations, however, only marginally resembled the Russian phenomenon, which, above all, had a direct political origin. Moreover, the resulting migration was large in comparison with earlier incidents. From capitals to the provinces, services had to be provided, safety of both the migrant and resident population had to be insured and public health protected. If only to avoid criticism and public outrage, authorities had to react to the emergency. In addition, the impulse that underlay the humanitarian organization of the earlier century now had burgeoned and stimulated the consciences of masses of more fortunate people.

Led by the humanitarian former explorer and active Norwegian politician Fridtjof Nansen, the still-new League of Nations in 1921 provided a international basis for some relief. [6] Nansen was appointed to head a League office to help Russian refugees. His office was given the authority to issue documents that permitted Russian refugees, especially those who were deprived by the new Soviet regime of citizenship and were therefore "stateless," to travel in a time when governments began sharply to restrict entry of persons without nationality or possibility of moving on to other countries. Thus by the early 1920s, most of the main elements of the contemporary refugee regime had been put into place: the political origin of some forced migrants had been recognized; the issue was internationalized; national governments retained ultimate authority about who would be allowed to stay in their precincts; and humanitarian sentiments and institutions supported protective and material action. A parallel system that could offer humanitarian relief in natural disasters also had become available, especially under Red Cross auspices but also via some reactions by the League of Nations and associated agencies.

By 1932, a decade after Nansen had won the Nobel Peace Prize for his work on Russian refugees, only a primitive international regime remained in place. It had been challenged by several older and new forced migrations, including the residual outflow of Armenians under pressure from Turkey, the expulsion of Greeks from Turkey and the subsequent exchange of Greek and Turkish populations, and above all the beginning of the persecution of Jews by the new Nazi government in Germany. Although the League of Nations and the United States government tried in a rather desultory manner to cope with the need for the German Jews to have protection from what later was recognized as genocide, little in fact was accomplished except at the level of private organizations that sought to help individuals. Thus, the application of the conceptual understanding of what was forced migration and what could be done did not necessarily lead to the political decisions required for practical measures to assist migrants and receiving governments. Whatever practical intergovernmental machinery existed had only a limited scope and capacity.

By the end of World War II, the magnifying effect of technologically based warfare alongside the familiar slogging of the infantry had forced as many as 30 million people away from their homes. Some of them were scattered to far ends of the earth, some nearby and in the path of advancing armies on their way to victory. Stranded Russian soldiers, slave laborers of the German war industry, nearly dying inmates of the Nazi concentration camps, and frightened fugitives from the actual battle—all these and more posed a immediate political issue: how would governments deal with them; from whom would they get services and asylum; would they be repatriated or settled, or passed along to some other asylum? They created an international issue. Many of them had crossed or were transported across borders, some refused to return to repressive lands or horrible experiences, and even the location of borders changed. The humanitarian aspects could not be overlooked by anyone who saw a newspaper or went to a film or, in many parts of Europe and the Far East, by a visit to any public market or a railroad station.

Building on the precedents of the 1920s and the failures of the 1930s, the United States government and its allies formed the United Nations Relief and Rehabilitation Administration (UNRRA) in 1943 to give help to areas that came under military occupation, mainly in Europe. [7] This came to include vast camps for refugees, including survivors rescued from the murderous German concentration camps. With significant help from voluntary non-governmental organizations (NGOs) [8] for administering immediate relief, UNRRA organized life-essentials for tens of thousands and helped seven million displaced persons to return to their homes or move on to another refuge. UNRRA was an international organization based on a practical and legal agreement by member governments that also contributed its financing. Its very existence signified policy decisions by governments and was related to the consolidation of the military victory. Its technical operations, carried out by an international staff, local help, and NGOs, could not avoid the additional political issues related to the future of the displaced persons. The Soviet Union, a founding member of UNRRA and an important beneficiary, demanded enforced repatriation of its displaced nationals; the European and American governments were adamantly opposed and favored voluntarily settlement in place, when possible, or resettlement in other countries. The subjects of the disputes, forced migrants, thus unwittingly brought the item of their own future to the international and national political agendas.

The United States government, which had led the way to forming UNRRA, pressed during the genesis of the Cold War for its dismantling, primarily because of the growing friction with the Soviet Union. In 1946, the United States proposed the creation by the UN of a temporary international organization, the International Refugee Organization (IRO) that was intended in a short time to clear the remaining camps of displaced persons. Without the presence of the Soviet Union and only 18 member governments, in some four years IRO largely accomplished its aim of emptying the camps in Europe of one-and one-half million persons and offered some crucial help to others stranded in the Far East, especially China. Assistance also came from the Red Cross movement. Most of the people involved were resettled as individuals in labor-short lands, such as those in Western Europe, or in expanding economies, such as the United States and Canada. Almost a million surviving Jews found or fought their way to Palestine where immigration had been closely restricted by the British administering authority.

The liquidation of almost all of the legacy of displaced persons from World War II wiped away one kind of political issue, only to leave another one. The increasing repression of the Soviet regime and its expansion into conquered territory in Eastern Europe had sent a steady stream of people into surrounding countries. As in the days after the Russian Revolution, western governments soon felt pressure to react even if the numbers who could escape Soviet exit controls was relatively small. Moreover, IRO had left a few individuals behind as they could not for one or another reason be resettled or integrated in place.

Refugees In Our Time

With plenty of precedents in place, the United States led the United Nations in formulating a new treaty, the UN Convention Relating to the Status or Refugees [9], and the establishment in 1951 of the Office of the UN High Commissioner for Refugees[10] to supervise and promote the convention, which soon had enough ratifications to constitute legal obligations on the member governments.[11] The new Convention added an important set of new elements to the perception and treatment of refugees. The first of these was a reasonably sharp definition of refugees that has come to have almost universal international support and application. Refugees were persons who were not in their own countries. This meant that persons displaced by fighting, social tension or disastrous governmental policies but who were still within the borders of their country were not refugees. What they were was not defined, but they presumably fell under the broad category of displaced persons, the term used in UNRRA days.

If the definition of refugees implicitly paid tribute to the legal scope of the state, a further provision had yet more political implications. Refugees were persons who had "...a well-founded fear of being persecuted for reasons of race, religion, nationality, membership of a particular social group or political opinion..." As understood in the West, this obviously, and deliberately, could cover refugees from Communism and many among the remaining displaced persons from World War II. It clearly implied individual treatment for its subjects, not a group definition as with the Russians in Nansen's time. At first, the geographical scope of the UNHCR was limited to Europe; a provision that neatly avoided the forced migration of Palestinians as Israel emerged from battle (see essays below by Goldstein, Nachmias, and Hanafi). The geographical scope of the Convention in 1967 was extended to the entire world but still excluded the Palestinians.[12] Above all, it was forbidden to governments to send a claimant for refugee status away into danger. This central protection usually is referred to by the French term, *non-refoulement*.

Along with these provisions, the Convention provides that as a condition of recognition as a refugee, a person's own government offered no protection. This means in practice, for example, that no consul of the person's homeland is prepared to come to his assistance, that no claims on the person's behalf are made from the capital, that hostile attitudes towards the migrant are shown or that the person involved may be understood as having left home in violation of national policy or was deprived of citizenship.[13] The definition of an individual who has a claim to be a refugee then has a partly subjective character. It is based on fear of persecution: the individuals have to believe that they had to flee, they must think they were forced out, they have to feel fear. That fear has to be "well-founded."

If the 1951 Convention looked ahead to individual treatment of refugees, it did not foresee much in the way of international operations. Indeed, the numbers of refugees who might require services was at first estimated as very low; nor would the huge camps of a few years earlier be necessary. Few people had then crossed the fortified frontiers of the Soviet Union to the West or the forbidding mountains and deserts to the south. Moreover, the Soviet authorities had repeatedly demonstrated brutal talents at keeping prospective migrants behind the Eastern borders. Accordingly, the Office of High Commissioner—the first was G.J. van Heuven Goedhart of the Netherlands—was given a tiny budget and no authority to approach governments for more money.[14]

The application of the Convention raises some practical questions. Who determines whether the expression of fear was well founded? Who discovers whether or not a claimant for refugee status might be deported into danger, that is, has a right to *non-refoulement?* Here the UN Convention in actuality bowed to the member states. No one was given a *right to asylum,* only protection from being returned into danger. The High Commissioner and his staff, initially so few as to be hardly visible, could state their opinion on individual cases if they came to know of them, but the receiving government made decisions about whether the claim that persecution lay behind an individual's appearance abroad was "well-founded."

Thus, the international definition of a refugee that puts obligations on some 100 governments that have now acceded to the UN Convention sets out the following tests persons seeking asylum:

♦ Must be over the border of their home country
♦ Must have a fear of persecution
♦ Fear must be well-founded
♦ Own government provides no protection

If the tests were satisfied, the person involved had the right to status as a

71

refugee in the country of asylum. This did not mean permanent resettlement but did signify that most normal services of the government, e.g. medical treatment, would be available. The refugee, for instance, legally could take on employment and had the right to free movement inside the host country and could decide to leave for the home country. For travel to another country and return, the refugee could obtain a special document to be used as a passport from the host government; this document had a standard format specified in the Convention. UNHCR had the obligation to protect these and other rights for the individual.

In accordance with a set of international rules, then, refugees have rights as persons once a host government admits that a convincing case has been set out. Furthermore, the growing elaboration of human rights law by the United Nations sets an overarching standard.[15] In any case, that person is supposed to be protected from immediate expulsion into danger, but until the government concerned offers a refugee status, a migrant has little claim to asylum beyond the time required to determine his status. Even then, the refugee acquires no right to settle in the place of asylum. "…[P]rotection granted to a foreign national against the exercise of jurisdiction by another State lies at the heart of the institution of asylum."[16] How to apply international guidelines which have been suggested by UNHCR as well as local laws is a matter for the receiving government to decide on the basis of its own counsel in accordance with its own immigration rules and practices. At the same time, the High Commissioner and his staff must seek permanent solutions for refugees through repatriation, settlement where they are or resettlement in third countries. Once a durable solution is found, UNHCR may continue to help and protect refugees in resettling in new homes or reintegrating in the countries to which they return.

These tests and rules make it possible conceptually to separate "refugees," who by definition assert that they are forced migrants, as a distinct category. In practice, they usually are designated as "Convention refugees." The formal rules leave no doubt that refugees are supposed to be treated as individuals, not as a category, such as, for example, all Tamils fleeing from the civil war in Sri Lanka. No such comparably elaborated and applied set of rules exists for other forced migrants although the Geneva (Red Cross) Conventions represented international humanitarian law that sometimes would apply. Nevertheless, organizational creep, practice, the sheer weight of suffering people, insufficiency of local government and the broad political aims of governments all have led to further distinctions, as well as blurring, among forced migrants. Whether all of this has produced more clarity about what is a forced migrant, what rights such a person may have, how that person is treated, whether categories of people leaving their homes are forced and whether operations of governments and international organizations are sufficient remains at least questionable.

Deeper in the Basket

Convention refugees make up one component of forced migration. UNHCR reported that in 2001 it exercised general supervision via its offices in 120 countries over some 12.1 million persons in this category. To this can be added 900,000 persons known by UNHCR to be seeking asylum, 800,000 returnees and 8.9 million stateless persons who may be at risk. Still deeper in the basket of forced migration and of concern to UNHCR are 7.3 million displaced persons still away from their homes but within the state where they normally reside. And not counted by UNHCR are the growing number of persons recognized under other international rules as refugees from Palestine.

The internally displaced category sharply highlights the expansion of the mandate given UNHCR. It results from a confluence of political and humanitarian factors. Legally speaking, it is not part of international law as specified in the Convention, but separating refugees from unfortunates whose migration did not extend over borders or whose plight could not escape notoriety has gradually led to a series of instances in which the UN General Assembly and a large number of governments agree that UNHCR should react if for no other reason than humanitarian solidarity.

This creep of the organization into new ventures grew in considerable part out of the pressures of the Cold War. In 1956, the Soviet repression of an uprising in Hungary resulted in some 200,000 persons hurriedly leaving the country. Most of them tumbled across the Austrian. Led by the second High Commissioner, August Lindt of Switzerland, UNHCR immediately invoked the experience of its actual and erstwhile staff with UNRRA and IRO, organized camps, and was even allowed to raise money to provide relief and to help coordinate host government and NGO activities. This expansion of the Office of High Commissioner gradually was solidified into long-lasting forms. It was further expanded in a whole series of dramatic, not to say savage, incidents. This enlargement included the creation of refugee camps in Pakistan and Iran for several million persons leaving the site of the Afghan-Soviet wars of the 1980s. Farther east, the Viet Nam war and the genocide that followed in neighboring Cambodia produced another displacement and flight of millions of persons to the south or to China. In all such incidents, UNHCR patched together very large (relative to the usual restrained intergovernmental practice) operational organizations, found funds to pay for the camps and supervised them to protect human rights and to promote some solution to individual needs. Especially in the Indo-China incidents massive resettlement in third countries that were willing to receive the camp residents as immigrants reduced the populations. Later in Afghanistan, large-scale repatriation followed pacification in the countries of origin.

In political and administrative aspects, UNHCR was turned by this series of operations into a relatively large, highly experienced agency and a budget largely contributed by governments that in the late 1990s hovered around $1000 million.[17] Whatever the original intentions of the General Assembly in creating the Office of High Commissioner, it was no longer a modest affair with a few thousand dollars for mainly diplomatic activity but an organization of some 5000 staff members that apparently could be rushed into service in massive human emergencies. And indeed it was engaged in a series of cases with highly political characteristics. These included much criticized services for the Kurds of northern Iraq after the UN-sponsored Gulf War; similar action for refugees from the breakdown of Yugoslavia during the 1990s; in the African lakes district after the genocide in Rwanda; and in an lengthy series of smaller disasters during the whole period. Its activities were neither without controversy nor neatly brought to a happy close. Nor for that matter did the succor of forced migrants in camps where thousands lived for four or more years in misery spare UNHCR from the criticism that it was sponsoring dependence instead of practical solutions.

At the beginning of the Twenty-first Century, UNHCR's main efforts went into operations, some of them put together in extreme haste for large numbers of forced migrants. The very masses obstructed the handling of the migrants as individual cases. Indeed, UNHCR developed a doctrine for designating refugees in a "group determination." Moreover, the inability of the host governments, as in Zaire (or Democratic Republic of the Congo in a later rhetorical transformation), to police the camps opened the way to political violence and inhumane practices. Furthermore, the execution of UNHCR programs no longer, as originally was envisaged, could be left in the hands of governments. Many of the host governments, especially some of those that became independent in the wave of decolonization in the 1950's and 1960's, had insufficient competence to deal with these situations. UNHCR could direct operations but had little capacity of its own to build shelters, fit clothing and dispense medicine. Thus, the majority of the actual operations were carried out by NGOs, including the ICRC, which had built a substantial field relief capacity. The private foreign organizations were based in various, mostly rich parts of the world and often dependent on their governments for support. Local contractors also were employed for such essential services as road transport. Consequently, organizational complexity grew with the numbers of forced migrants.

Especially in northern Iraq, in the Balkans, the Horn of Africa and in the African lakes region, UNHCR was put to work after the 1980's on relief for migrants within their own borders. These were newly labeled as persons of concern to UNHCR, because they were in refugee-like situations. But they failed an initial test as Convention refugees and furthermore were treated as a category rather than individuals. Nevertheless, the policy organs of the UN, including the General Assembly and the Security Council, either acquiesced or promoted this stretching of the original UNHCR mandate. Indeed from an operational perspective, it was logical to do so, for here was an experienced organization, manned by veterans of the humanitarian-diplomatic process, that could be put to work immediately without the tedious process of making new international law and new administrative structures.

As for financing, this remained tenuous and dependent largely on the largesse of rich governments in North America and Western Europe as well as Japan.[18] They also provided most financing for the partner international organizations, such as the World Food Program (WFP), and for some of the larger NGOs. These governments were hardly under a legal obligation to contribute funds although moral pressures and commitments usually led to positive, if frequently inadequate, responses to appeals. From the private sector, the peak contributions were less than $35 million and in 2000 less than $20 million. The UNHCR in 2002 expects to spend something like $50 per year per person on those who came into its categories of concern.[19]

By the beginning of the Twenty-first Century then, the formal rules of international law clearly distinguished Convention refugees from other forced migrants, but complementary policy decisions blurred the distinction. What were once internally displaced persons now could come within the purview of the organization for applying the UN Convention. What was intended to handle a few cases had become a vehicle for treating mass migrations. And what had been envisaged as a matter of temporary asylum in a peaceful place was in a series of incidents replaced with services in war zones or near fighting. In striking respects, it seemed that UNRRA was reborn.

Giving Concepts Practical Effect

From the point of view of an individual who meets the Convention standards, the internationally accepted concepts promise protection, assistance and an eventually regularized status either at the country of origin or elsewhere. An international institution—the United Nations and its Office of High Commissioner—supervises the application of these standards. The actuality is far from so tidy.[20] Moreover, the language of the Convention, strictly applied, excludes large numbers of forced migrants.

To begin with, the execution of the Convention is highly decentralized. The actual responsibility for making decisions about forced migrants, except in the rare cases of actually failed states, mostly remains in the hands of governments. No known government has yet explicitly placed the administration of its rules about the entry of aliens in the hands of anyone else. The terrorist attacks on September 11, 2001 led to immediate tightening of immigration in many donor and resettlement countries. Claims by some suspected terrorists that they had convention refugee status only intensified examinations. Entry and remaining on the territory of a state depend more than ever on the application of national regulations about immigration. UNHCR officials, and sometimes NGO personnel, on the spot may make remarks about the application of such laws in case of putative refugees, but they make no decisions binding host or asylum-granting governments. "Whether a State takes steps to protect refugees within its jurisdiction and, if so, which, steps are matters very much in the realm of sovereign discretion."[21] For example, the US government regards Cuban nationals who find their way into the country through informal routes, such as landing from a boat on a lonely Florida beach, as refugees. Under American law, they are invited to become permanent residents. Haitian nationals following the same route are interned, sometimes for long periods, and closely examined; few get refugee status and most are deported.[22] UNHCR has pointed out the discrepancy in handling and has urged a more generous treatment of Haitians.[23] This diplomatic persuasion has left American laws and practices unchanged.

Where immigration policies are intended to discourage even applicants for asylum, let alone migrants who have little claim to convention status, government officials attempt quickly to screen and exclude all but the most obvious candidates for refugee status. This is the situation in the 15 European Union (EU) countries that have coordinated their policies internationally under the Schengen Convention of 1990 and the Treaty of Amsterdam of 1999 and have empowered the European Commission to expand Europe-wide regulations.[24] The declared aim of the Schengen process foresees travel among the members of the European Union without visas or border formalities. This harmonization of rules led to more searching entry procedures. "European harmonization...blocks refugee access, as EU nations attempt to consolidate their refugee determination procedures, resorting to more restrictive interpretations of the refugee definition."[25] A cooperative information network among the national border police notes the country where an asylum seeker first applies and prevents once-refused persons entry into another Schengen country. As a result, the percentage of asylum seekers granted refugee status has progressively declined in the Schengen countries and elsewhere where governments use similar procedures. Asylum seekers, including possible Convention refugees, presumably try elsewhere or else seek to slip into the illegal status of unauthorized immigrants. They may use the dangerous smuggling rings that attempt to evade police control to bring migrants across borders where they either claim asylum or melt into the urban mass. If they come into the hands of the police, they are detained as illegal immigrants and then usually deported. UNHCR has repeatedly called attention to the likelihood that candidates for Convention refugee status among the so-called illegal and "economic refugees"[26] may be unjustly handled, but in the last decade, as immigration has become a political issue in most Western European countries, the Schengen practices and other exclusionary devices have only been augmented. So has the notoriety—and, no doubt, clients-- given illegal smuggling rings.

Where UNHCR has been given, or has assumed, concern over internally displaced persons or others with refugee-like character, its mandate may be as uncertain as the definition of those brought into its jurisdiction. In most instances, the persons involved have left their homes because of fighting, guerilla action or even genocide where the state apparatus has broken down or has become incompetent. Examples are the situation in Rwanda and the surrounding African lakes area and the civil war in Bosnia-Herzegovina and later in Kosovo. Here UNHCR can help organize relief operations but hardly resolve the conflict that caused displacement. And, where the governments in the region have not become party to the Convention, as in the flight from the genocide in Cambodia, when ICRC was the main operational agency, UNHCR may have little role.

In any large-scale displacement that gets organized international treatment, UNHCR is only one of many engaged institutions. Large-scale relief supplies now can be expected from the WFP, also part of the UN family. Other UN agencies may also engaged, such as the UN Children's Fund (UNICEF) and the World Health Organization, to furnish expert services. These organizations typically have only limited operational capacities in the sense that they primarily supervise the ultimate delivery of assistance. Actual distribution for the most part left to the local governing authorities, who may be overwhelmed, corrupt or even destroyed, and to some of the 500 NGOs with which UNHCR has worked; yet more may on their own initiative turn up on the spot. Moreover, wealthy governments, such as the United States and those of the European Union, may mount direct--so-called bilateral--programs. The International Organization for Migration, an intergovernmental agency not part of the UN system, may be called on to transport refugees to permanent resettlement or to their own countries. This manifold organizational engagement gives rise to friction and difficulties in coordinating both policies and operations. Even appointing a lead agency, sometimes UNHCR, does not end such difficulties but only opens a forum for discussions that could lead to coordination.

Furthermore, in the background, an unceasing demand for efficiency and long-term programs comes from governments, international agencies and NGOs. "...there is a need," says Ruud Lubbers, the latest UN High Commissioner for Refugees, "to address the issue of UNHCR's position within the UN system." Lubbers points out the many refractory organizational and conceptual issues:
"Currently, UNHCR is boxed in as a purely "humanitarian" agency. Yet UNHCR's work also relations to prevention, conflict, resolution, peace building and development. To achieve durable solutions in accordance with UNHCR's mandate requires close co-operation and strengthened partnerships with the UN's development actors, the Bretton Woods institutions and the peace and security pillars of the UN."[27] Among the people

to whom such assistance efforts are directed may be some or many who would qualify for Convention refugee status. In the confusion of humanitarian disasters, personal determinations tend to be deferred, not to say ignored. Yet the underlying terror that drives these migrations is obvious to anyone who sees pictures of the children, women and men involved. This fear may be augmented when among the migrants are soldiers and guerillas who try to escape imprisonment or prosecution by fleeing. That it is ever possible to dry such a swamp of misery redounds to the credit of the patient field operatives, the forced migrants themselves and the conviction, even if it is vacillating, of the regional governments.[28] But before that is done, many people may die of violence, malnutrition, fatigue and disease.

Does The System Need Repairing?

The gradual, crisis-driven expansion of what UNHCR takes on suggests that the present international definition of refugees no longer comes even close to fitting, if it ever did, the whole universe of forced migrants. It was, of course, never originally intended to do so. But in the course of years and after the end of the Cold War as well as a series of forced migrations, the edges of the old definition of refugees has become fuzzy and arbitrarily elastic. "Whether the people concerned are refugees, economic migrants or a mixture of the two, it has become apparent that current asylum and migration practices are to a large extent dysfunctional."[29]

One possible reaction includes demands that the whole international process of writing a new definition should be undertaken by leading governments. In 2001, UNHCR itself encouraged a discussion of the Convention. A meeting in Geneva of representatives of 156 countries capped a consultation process in every region of the world with a strong endorsement of the existing Convention.[30] This conclusion hardly suggests a revision of existing concepts. If the issues in revising the Convention were seriously set out, whether in official meetings or by analysts, they would implicitly raise questions about the broad phenomenon of international migration. Such a wide-ranging discussion has been notably absent from those arenas, such as the UN General Assembly, where it might be held. The reason for this avoidance is not far to seek. Hardly any topic penetrates to the governmental policies of controlling people and territory than this one. It raises the prospect that sovereign governments would no longer control their own immigration rules. The refusal of governments ever in the past to accept a right of asylum for refugees—rather than the weaker *non-refoulement*—highlights the taboo. When coordination of immigration rules has entered the international arena, as in the Schengen Convention, it is intended to strengthen governmental control and to exclude migrants rather than to deal with migration more generally.

If an attempt were made to revise the Convention definition of refugees, it could result in an agreement at a lower level and even more confusion about the status and definition of forced migrants. The stiffening of immigration rules may only strengthen this prospect, both before and after the terrorist attacks on the United States in 2001, in Europe and America. The argument against revision could lead to the conclusion that the system is not yet crippled to the point that it must be repaired.

That conclusion underlies the view that muddling through with the present definitions not only works well enough but also has advantages. It begins with the observation that responses to forced migration always include a large measure of improvisation. It is hardly possible to forecast precisely how such a migration will take shape, how big it will eventually become and what political consequences it will have. At least a good basis for protecting Convention refugees exists in law and practice. In view of the persuasiveness and popularity of the UN human rights standards in much of the world, the Convention definition has an even broader base than it had at the beginning of the Cold War.

Furthermore, the argument against revising the definition says that the operational capacities of the UNHCR, WFP and other international agencies and their support in the parallel NGO sphere, offer a ready and flexible structure for dealing with forced migration. The injection of UNHCR and other international agencies into situations of internally displaced persons shows that this can work much better than nothing. And beyond that, this collection of organizations has been employed with some success in combat zones.

Focusing on the concepts that define and distinguish refugees and other forced migrants leaves the causes of forced migrations in the background. Indeed UNHCR and their partners that deal with migrants as individuals offer little direct opportunity to prevent forced migrations, whatever their causes. That is left mainly to arenas where the broadest political discussions take place, such as the UN General Assembly, the European Parliament, regional agencies and national parliaments and governments. "There are no easy choices or simple solutions in this area," according to UN Secretary-General Kofi Annan in 2002. Migration and refugee flows can lead to human trafficking, disrupt settled patterns, and make the very fact of change seem threatening to many people...Politicians have a choice to make. They can embrace the potential that migrants and refugees represent, or use them as political scapegoats. I hope they will begin by "demythologizing" migration, addressing the negative myths and fears that surround migration and informing their publics of the benefits that well-managed migration can produce...[31]

If the experience of the organized international treatment of forced migrations provides clues to ameliorating the causes of forced migration, they have so far not led to much practical activity. Instead, managing migration tends usually to be treated as an inevitable concomitant of war and other fundamental disturbances of society or as matter for policing at the borders those "...with the greatest ambition to make a better life for themselves...."[32] Whether the views of the UN Secretary-General portend novel or more organized international attention to migration generally was not immediately apparent, but that the conceptual developments of the last century would continue to affect intergovernmental treatment of forced migration seems beyond doubt.

Notes

1. "Refugees and Others of Concern to UNHCR, 2000 Statistical Overview...," June 2002. This total should be regarded as indicative. It covers only those people in whom the United Nations High Commissioner for Refugees has some relationship. Other forced migrants fall outside these categories.

2. Sadako Ogata (then UN High Commissioner for Refugees), UNHCR, *The State of the World's Refugees: Fifty Years of Humanitarian Refugees* (Oxford, Oxford University Press, 2000), x

3. Saskia Sassen, *Guests and Aliens* (New York, The New Press, 1999), 10. This study offers a concise account of the relationships of migrants and authorities.

4. For an analysis of the Red Cross movement and its modern role, see David P. Forsythe, *Humanitarian Politics; The International Committee of the Red Cross* (Baltimore, Md., Johns Hopkins University Press, 1977).

5. For texts of treaties, see International Committee of the Red Cross, *International Red Cross Handbook,* 12th ed, (Geneva, International Committee of the Red Cross, etc., 1983). See also Internet page: www.ICRC.ch for later information.

6. For an account of the League's response and programs, see Louise W. Holborn, *Refugees: a Problem of Our Time,* Vol. 1 (Metuchen, NJ, Scarecrow Press, Inc., 1975), 3-20.

7. The standard account is George Woodbridge, *The History of UNRRA* (New York, Columbia University Press, 1950). It should be noted that the United Nations organization as we now know it had not yet been established and that while the UN was being formed, opinions formed in the US government that UNRRA could not cope with opposing policies in Washington and Moscow.

8. This descriptive, but vague, terminology derives from the UN Charter, which had not yet been drafted. At the time, such organizations might be called charitable agencies, voluntary agencies, and the like. The point is that they formally were private organizations and sought no profit.

9. UN Treaty Series no. 2545, vol. 189, p. 137, adopted by the UN Conference of Plenipotentiaries on the Status of Refugees and Stateless Persons on 28 July 1951. It came into force on 28 July 1951. Its scope was extended to the whole world, not just Europe, in 1966, by a protocol, (UN Treaty Series no. 8791, vol. 606, p. 267) adhering to which meant that a government also adhered to the 1951 convention. This was the route chosen by the US government.

10. UN General Assembly Resolution 428 (V), 14 December 1950, contains the statute of the office. Many of its operationally restrictive elements have been superseded in practice.

11. For an authoritative treatment of contemporary international rules regarding the Convention and refugees subsumed under it, see Guy Goodwin-Gill, *The Refugee in International Law*, 2nd. Ed. (Oxford, Clarendon Press, 1996).

12. See endnote 7.

13. In case a government no longer was willing to accept a migrant as a citizen, that person would fall into the category of "stateless," a term that had been used in the Nansen office to describe many of the *émigrés* who appeared after the Bolshevik revolution in Russia. The revolutionary government had withdrawn their citizenship.

14. For a comprehensive treatment of the history of the office, see Gil Loescher, *The UNHCR and World Politics: a Perilous Path.* (Oxford, Oxford University Press, 2001) and UNHCR, *The State of the World's Refugees: Fifty Years of Humanitarian Action* (Oxford, Oxford University Press, 2000).

15. For brief treatments, see Peter R. Baehr, *The Role of Human Rights in Foreign Policy* (London, Macmillan, 1994) and David P. Forsythe, *The Internationalization of Human Rights* (Lexington, MA, Lexington Books, 1991). Despite the obvious relationship of the concept of human rights with the protection of refugee rights, UNHCR long hesitated in drawing attention to it and working with the UN institutions that supervised a growing body of law. Recently the High Commissioners have drawn attention to the relationship. For an argument that migrations are forced by the denial of human rights, see Leon Gordenker, *Refugees in International Politics* (London, Croom Helm & New York, Columbia University Press, 1987), *passim.*

16. Guy S. Goodwin-Gill, *The Refugee in International Law*, 2nd ed. (Oxford, Clarendon Press, 1996), 173. Goodwin-Gill gives a full account of the failed attempt to create an international right of asylum. *Ibid.,* Chapter 5.

17. UNHCR, 2002 *Global Appeal*, 13. These numbers are estimates. They cannot be accepted either as absolute, all-inclusive or without overlap. But they do make clear the magnitude of human displacement, much of its forced. For a discussion of the statistical framework, see Bela Hovy, "Statistically correct asylum data: prospects and limitations," UNHCR Evaluation and Policy Analysis Unit, *New Issues in Refugee Research*, Working Paper No. 37, available at http://www.unhcr.ch/refworld/pubs/pubon.htm

18. UNHCR, *The State of the World's Refugees: Fifty Years...*, 166-67. See also UNHCR, 2002 Global Appeal.

19. Summary data can be found in UNHCR, 2002 Global Appeal.

20. My calculation from data in UNHCR, 2002 Global Appeal. Obviously the actual expenditures would vary greatly by place and case.

21. Nor do the causes of migration fit neatly into these categories, however useful they may be conceptually. For elaboration of this point, see Gordenker, especially Chapter 4.

22. Goodwin-Gill, 324. See Chapter 9, for a full treatment of the rights of refugees.

23. For a brief account of the United States laws on refugees after World War II, see Roger Daniels, *Coming to America*, 2nd ed. (New York, Perennial, 2002), Chap. 13.

24. UNHCR, *The State of the World's Refugees: Fifty Years,* 176-177. As this is written in 2002, some 200 Haitians appeared on a south Florida beach, stranded by a leaky vessel. Those who failed to escape the police were interned and presumably will be returned to Haiti.

25. A brief summary of the Schengen agreement, but hardly its application, can be found on the World Wide Web page of the European Union, http:// europa.eu.int/scadplus, under the title "The Schengen acquis and its integration into the union."

26. Laura Barnett, "Global Governance and the evolution of the international refugee regime," UNHCR Evaluation and Policy Analysis United, New Issues in Refugee Research, Working Paper No. 54, available at http://www.unhcr.ch/ publications, 13

27. This is a term used in political discussions and propaganda but has no basis in international rules.

28. Statement at the 53rd session of the Executive Committee of the High Commissioner's Programme, 20 September 2002, Geneva. The Executive Committee comprises representatives of more than 50 governments with NGO observers that meet to advise the High Commissioner on policy. It sessions accurately portray the mixture of governmental policies that bear on issues of international cooperation on refugees and displaced persons.

29. To sample the atmosphere of field operations, see Jennifer Hyndman, *Managing Displacement: Refugees and the Politics of Humanitarianism* (Minneapolis, University of Minnesota Press, 2000. This is one of the relatively few scholarly studies of handling forced migration that relies of extensive field research as well as on informed conceptual examination.

30. Jeff Crisp, "Poverty, Migration and Asylum," *Wider Angle*, 1/2002.

31. A brief account of this Global Consultation Process, sponsored by High Commissioner Ruud Lubbers, was available on the UNHCR web site, http://www.unhcr.ch., in November 2002.

32. Statement by Annan at the release of a Declaration on the Future of Refugee and Migration Policy, Nov. 22, 2002, at The Hague, UN Press Release SG/SM/8522. The Society of International Development of the Netherlands produced the Declaration. High Commissioner Lubbers also was present at the meeting.

Abby Stoddard

CHAPTER THREE:

Every One's and No One's: IDPs, Refugees, and the Politics of Aiding the Displaced

Introduction

In the international humanitarian community the special category of forced migrants known as internally displaced persons (IDPs) has been the subject of serious concern for well over a decade. Lacking the international legal definition and protected status of refugees, IDPs do not explicitly fall under the mandate of any international humanitarian agency, though their needs may be greater than those who have crossed a border. They are also more difficult to define, identify, and enumerate, and access to them is often hindered by armed conflict conditions and the complexities of sovereignty. Over the past several years an international consensus has emerged on the need for focused action and institutional reform to better protect and assist these populations. However, concrete progress has been slow to follow, and beyond the important development of normative policy frameworks in the United Nations system, there has been little real change in operations and institutions.

Throughout the IDP debate one of the major issues that had gained surprisingly scant attention has been the role of the major bilateral and multilateral humanitarian donors. Today just nine donors provide over 90 percent of the resources that drive the international humanitarian system; a cadre of Northern governments wielding considerable, concentrated influence over the international humanitarian system. The largest donor by far is the United States, which provides approximately one third of global humanitarian assistance resources annually, and whose internal structures and policies largely affect how and to whom aid resources is programmed.

The article addresses the IDP gap that has been brought to light over the past decade by internal and external studies of government aid bodies, and even championed by influential individuals, but has yet to be resolved. The refugee-IDP distinction is examined from the provider perspective, and the analysis focuses on how the international humanitarian assistance structures have reinforced the separated and unequal aid efforts. The United States, and to a lesser extent the other major donor governments have been content to follow the lead of the UN and international organizations (IOs) on the IDP issue rather than take the initiative. Their reticence stems both from the political difficulties of intervening to protect citizens within sovereign states, on the one hand, but also from the more plebian matters of resource flows and bureaucratic entrenchment of outdated humanitarian institutions, to be examined further in Chapter 11.

Comparative Data on Internal Displacements and Refugee Movements

The data on uprooted populations are notoriously soft and politically fraught. Aside from the inherent difficulties of counting populations that are often on the move, aid agencies, donors, host countries and countries of origin all have interests at different times in either exaggerating or downplaying the estimates.[1] Since the end of World War II (and the beginning of an international system to provide assistance to crisis victims) the numbers of refugees and IDPs have both increased, but IDPs have proliferated a great deal faster, and now outnumber refugees two to one across the world. The largest percentage (est. 10 million) is in Africa, with Sudan possessing an estimated four million IDPs, the largest number of any single nation. Europe and Asia are thought to have five million IDPs each, and there are an estimated two million in the Americas.[2]

Though IDPs are not recognized as a group under international law, the United Nations' 1998 *Guiding Principles on Internal Displacement*, the authoritative international document on the subject, defines IDPs as "persons or groups of persons who have been forced or obliged to flee or to leave their homes or places of habitual residence, in particular as a result of or in order to avoid the effects of armed conflict, situations of generalized violence, violations of human rights or natural or human-made disasters, and who have not crossed an internationally recognized State border."[3] While the described condition is not a new phenomenon in human history, the IDP numbers have risen steadily over the past five decades, and seemed to spike in the early 1990s with the civil wars and state failures that beset the developing world. On an individual level, it is difficult to pinpoint when IDP status begins and ends, and how to differentiate IDPs from other rural-urban or economic migrants. Because IDP populations are especially fluid, and given the lack of systematic data collection on them, some assume the true figure may be well over 20-25 million generally cited. Yet most share the assessment that, compared to refugees, IDPs are the larger problem in terms of numbers, need, and difficulty of access.

The IDP Challenge

International humanitarian law, as enshrined in the Geneva Conventions, aims to provide protection and ensure rights for all civilians during conflict situations. Refugee law was codified later in various international legal instruments, particularly Convention Relating to the Status of Refugees and provides specific legal definition, rights, and protections for this particular status of individual. International human rights law, the broadest in scope of the three, is applicable to refugees and non-refugees alike, in peace or war. Therefore, civilians who are displaced from their homes by force or fear, but do not cross an internationally recognized border, come under international humanitarian and human rights protections but are not afforded the status of refugees and the automatic response from international agencies mandated to protect them. Those IDPs who are unable to successfully merge with the local community find themselves without basic support structures, and frequently threatened by armed groups or at times the government itself, as targets in civil war, forced recruitment, slavery, and sexual violence and exploitation.

Refugees, to put it simply, are easier for the international community to assist than IDPs. Once they cross the border, they become visible and are usually simple to distinguish from others in the area. There are laws outlining the responsibilities of host governments and the international community, and at least two United Nations agencies (UNCHR and IOM) dedicated to caring for them, along with numerous other humanitarian agencies and NGOs that see to their basic sustenance, health, and psycho-social needs until repatriation or resettlement can be negotiated. It may be that they have a more emotional impact was well, as the concept of exile and statelessness resounds with the public on a different level than "simple" homelessness.

The Mandate Gap

In the international humanitarian community it is often said that when it comes to organizational mandates, IDPs belong to everyone and no one. As civilians endangered by conflict, IDPs seem a natural beneficiary group for the International Committee of the Red Cross, and indeed they represent roughly 80 percent of the ICRC's caseload, though the ICRC does not distinguish IDPs from other civilian non-combatants. Since IDPs are unrecognized by international law as a distinct group, ICRC does not maintain a separate operational category for them, and in fact until the late 1990s, the ICRC refrained from using the term IDP at all.[4] In the past few years ICRC has done a great deal more research on the issue and clarified an organizational policy on IDPs, though in substance it is not much changed from the original. Similarly, UNICEF overcame its initial reluctance to single out IDPs as a special category of victim and has since become one of the most active members of the UN system in raising awareness of the issue and supporting interagency IDP initiatives, such as operational guidelines and standards. Of course UNICEF is focused first and foremost on children, and IDPs is only one of many humanitarian issues that it grapples with under its large, crosscutting mandate.

The United Nations High Commissioner for Refugees (UNHCR) is among the largest and most active humanitarian assistance instruments in the UN system. While IDPs do not come under its official mandate, the agency generally assists them in areas where they are already operational assisting refugees. The idea of UNHCR expanding its mandate to take formal responsibility for IDPs within the UN system has been floated several times and refuses to die, though UNHCR and others have thus far resisted this approach, as will be discussed later in this chapter. The humanitarian NGOs (non-governmental organizations), working in concert with each other and with UN agencies, also serve IDPs where they are operational and when they are able to access the displaced population. In their frequent role as the implementing partners of the UN agencies and the last link of the assistance chain, NGOs are generally closest to the ground, and therefore crucial for accessing populations in distress. However, unlike the UN agencies, NGOs decide to which emergencies and beneficiary groups they will respond, given their organizational capacities and programming preference at the time. At the end of the day, not one of the major humanitarian implementers has the primary responsibility for or specializes in meeting the particular needs and vulnerabilities of IDPs, despite the widespread and growing consensus that as a group, IDPs indeed require special interventions.

Sovereignty and the Protection Dilemma

When people are uprooted by conflict within their own country, international law places primary responsibility for their aid and protection on their national government. International humanitarian assistance is designed to intervene when the authorities are unable or unwilling to fulfill this responsibility. Yet this process can be very problematic if the authorities in question are the ones responsible for their plight, or when the chaos and violence that prompted the forced displacement are ongoing in the country. It wasn't until the beginning of 1990s that most humanitarian agencies, ICRC being the exception, had access to victims within war zones. Until a negotiation with the combatants in Sudan allowed for humanitarian groups to operate within the country while the fighting continued, the typical mode of operation in conflict emergencies was to ready relief supplies and wait until refugees began streaming across the borders, where they would (ideally) be met with food, water, shelter, and health care. [5]

During the 1990s the strictures of sovereignty (at least regarding the developing world), were loosened considerably by decisions and actions of the major powers, the Secretary-General, and the Security Council, intent of rescuing populations from the crises induced by intrastate conflict. With the end of the superpower proxy contest, many developing countries lost their geo-strategic significance, and consequently their political crises and conflicts came to be framed by the international community in almost purely humanitarian terms. Francis Deng, the man appointed by the Secretary General to serve as his Special Representative on Internally Displaced Persons, approached the sovereignty issue by redefining it as one of *responsibility* of the local government to its own people, and to the international community.[6] When that responsibility is abdicated or betrayed by embattled, corrupt, or failing governments, he reasoned, it is incumbent on the international community to intervene on behalf of the victims.

Humanitarian practitioners almost universally agree that IDPs' most crucial need is for protection. They also concede that it is the one most difficult to meet under traditional aid practices and mechanisms. Roberta Cohen, an expert on displacement issues at the Brookings Institution, has observed that the only predictable international humanitarian response is to crises involving mass hunger.[7] This reflects donors' capacity, particularly that of the US, of procuring and transporting large amounts of agricultural commodities, and their willingness to engage in the relatively straightforward transfer of food aid. In comparison, providing protection is extremely difficult because freedom of operations and access to victims often depends on the acquiescence, or at least tolerance, of the local authorities, which in many cases are actively or passively colluding to cause the displacement.

International representatives, particularly UN Resident Coordinators, are typically reluctant to confront governments on the problem for fear of damaging the working relationship and jeopardizing all other programs. A US government report found that the international community fails in protection not only for the obvious political and security reasons (including a very real threat faced by international aid workers and their local staffs in some areas), but also due to the failure on the part of the agencies to provide proper training, to dedicate staff members to protection activities, and to develop of country-wide coordination mechanisms on protection. In short, the report found, the international community has not been sufficiently assertive or proactive in protection measures.[8] The report cited an ICRC source observing that no single country can be held up as a model for successful IDP protection, in many countries protection measures aren't being taken at all.[9]

The UN Inter-Agency Standing Committee for humanitarian assistance (IASC) notes in a 1999 policy paper on IDP protection, "Traditionally, humanitarian and development agencies lacking an explicit protection mandate have tended to conceive of protection for internally displaced persons as falling outside the scope of their work. Their protection role has been limited to the extent that the provision of assistance does in itself constitute a form of protection."[10] It is this type of passive or "environmental" protection that constitutes most of the protection measures currently undertaken by the humanitarian agencies. Similarly, human rights workers engage in witnessing, reporting, "public shaming", and advocacy activities aimed at "promoting respect for international humanitarian law"—also an undeniably passive role in protection.

Human rights and humanitarian assistance find their nexus in the issue of IDP protection. Over the past several years, humanitarian agencies have increasingly adopted the "rights-based approach" to providing aid, acknowledging that assistance outside a human rights context becomes mere voluntary charity rather than a human imperative, and does little to address the causes of the crisis or promote long-term solutions. Accordingly, a growing chorus of European humanitarian organizations has called for the office of the UN High Commissioner for Human Rights to play a more active, or even leading, role in IDP emergencies. But this body lacks both the financial resources and the ground-level operational capacity to meet protection needs. Furthermore, the rights based concept, much less its application in practice, has been slow to penetrate donor government policies and practices. The US humanitarian NGOs and advocacy organizations, such as Refugees International, have been much more focused on protection and what would be feasible within the current system. They have rightfully pushed for more field level partnerships between UNHCR and ICRC. At times, the political feasibility of true protection seems further and further out of reach. Given the scope and ferocity of modern civil conflict, where civilians do not merely get caught in the crossfire, but are themselves the target, the protection task may ultimately prove beyond the capacity of the humanitarian community or the UN system writ large. Observers say for example, that the MONUC force in DR Congo, for example, is "almost worse than nothing."[11] Instead of the legions of blue helmets that local populations had hoped for, the country received only 700 poorly trained and largely ineffective soldiers, reportedly spending much of their time visiting brothels.

What's in a Name: Views on the IDP Label

There are those who believe the designation "internally displaced person" is itself part of the problem. According to former US Permanent Representative to the UN Richard Holbrooke, this "sterile and bureaucratic term"[12] only serves to disqualify them from assistance that would automatically be provided to cross-border refugees. To Holbrooke the legal and bureaucratic distinction was fictitious.

Others have expressed distaste for the terms but for different reasons. As mentioned above, humanitarian agencies such as the ICRC and UNICEF in the past avoided making the distinction for fear it would lead to discrimination to civilian crisis victims who were not displaced. Notwithstanding these valid concerns, most humanitarian practitioners maintain there is a benefit to using the term IDP. Refugees International agrees that the fundamental goal is to protect civilians, rather than creating a new category of victims or agencies to help, but the reality remains that is it so much easier to identify and help refugees than IDPs that the former end up getting the bulk of the resources and the latter are too often ignored. Looking at the operational implications of delineating IDPs, one sees a case such as Sri Lanka, where UNHCR took operational responsibility for IDPs launched an effective response to their needs, vs. a case like Sierra Leone where UNHCR managed refugee impeccably, while IDP return was mishandled by a jumble of NGOs, none of whom had ultimate responsibility, and people left by the side of the road, unprotected and without assistance.[13]

Upholding protection as the fundamental objective may be prove too vague, especially when protection, as an international humanitarian function, is still in its infancy. The phenomenon of internal displacement warrants being dealt with separately. Not only are IDPs more vulnerable to all kinds of abuse than refugees, but also the record shows the lack of legal distinction and institutional responsibility for IDPs has clearly hindered the development of strategies and innovative approaches to help them.

Developments in Approaches to Forced Migrants in the International Humanitarian System

The earliest humanitarian mechanisms created within the United Nations system were designed to address two sets of needs: victims of acts of violence, i.e. refugees, and victims of natural disasters. The United Nations Relief and Rehabilitation Administration was established two years before the formal signing of the UN charter to aid wartime refugees in Europe, and assist in economic recovery. UNCHR (then the International Refugee Organization) was created in 1947 to take over the role of protecting and resettling European refugees. Other early UN humanitarian activities were designed around the natural disaster model, which emphasizes speed, efficiency, and delivery of material aid.

The IDP issue had already been a subject of discussion for some years within the international humanitarian and human rights circles when, in 1992, at the prompting of the Commission on Human Rights, the Secretary General appointed a Special representative to study and recommend action on internally displaced populations. Ambassador Francis Deng spent the next several years developing the *Guiding Principles on Internal Displacement* (1998), which remain the key international document defining the scope of the issue the definition of an IDP and a framework for action by states and humanitarian actors.

The Guidelines emphasize that IDPs must be afforded the same rights and protections as other citizens, and those that apply to cross-border refugees (such as the right to seek asylum and the principle of non-refoulement). They also state that displacement may not be used as a tool of war, oppression, or ethnic cleansing, and that while the government should have primary responsibility for protecting and aiding its own IDPs, when it cannot do so it must allow unimpeded access to humanitarian actors. It also acknowledges IDPs special vulnerabilities such as forced inscription and camp-based crimes. The Guidelines have been widely disseminated and endorsed within the international community, but are considered non-binding of states and thus lack the normative force of humanitarian and human rights law. As a focal point for international consensus, the Guidelines, at the very least, represent progress in the "evolution of international norms"[14] in the humanitarian sphere and positive steps toward constructing an institutional safety net for IDPs.

In 2000, Ambassador Holbrooke took a personal interest in the plight of the internally displaced. Returning from a trip to Angola, where he witnessed for himself the stark difference between assistance programs for refugees and those for IDPs, he called upon the international community to place the responsibility for IDPs with one agency, preferably UNHCR, which will be "predictable, accountable, universal and equipped" in meeting the needs of IDPs in crisis situations. Accountability, Holbrooke emphasized, required designating a single responsible agency, not adding further layers of coordination bureaucracy between agencies. The UN agencies, however, by and large rejected the idea, as they did when it was first floated by Francis Deng, and opted to stick with the so-called "collaborative approach" which since 1996 had formalized the concept of IDPs as a shared responsibility of the UN humanitarian bodies. Defensive in the face of Holbrooke's assertions that they had not done enough for IDPs and protective of their turf, some other humanitarian agencies strongly objected to expanding the scope of UNHCR. Later that year, at the recommendation of the UN Inter-Agency Standing Committee for humanitarian assistance, a new Internal Displacement Unit was established within the Office for Coordination of Humanitarian Affairs (OCHA) "to help promote a more effective inter-agency, operational response to internal displacement and help support the (Emergency Relief Coordinator) in his role as the coordinator of the international humanitarian response to IDPs."[15] The unit is non-operational, and focused on research and training, and to some observers serves simply as another example of meaningful institutional reform rejected in favor of continued UN-style "adhocracy." For its part, UNCHR was also reluctant to take on a new role, and despite its public statements that it intends to become more active in IDP protection, it is often absent from areas with large IDP populations, and covers only about 20 percent (5.3 million) of the estimated number of IDPs globally. In 2001, UNHCR was running protection operations in only 11 countries, less than a quarter of those with IDPs.[16]

Many US government officials also disagreed with Holbrooke on the UNHCR point. Taking on the mandate for IDPs, according to this argument would muddy UNHCR's mandate, as its effectiveness depends on the legal status of refugees and the cooperation of governments. Without those elements UNHCR would be operating out of its element and getting into ICRC territory.[17] Yet UNHCR has already expanded its programming scope well beyond its original mandate. From a temporary administrative body set up to assist with the return of refugees to specific countries in Europe after

World War II UNHCR has evolved into a large operational agency increasingly concerned with long term, development-related solutions to forced migration issues. Its current initiative, known as the "Four Rs" (for repatriation, reintegration, rehabilitation and reconstruction), aims at bridging relief and development in a holistic approach to complex humanitarian emergency response.

At first glance one might conclude that a great deal of substantive progress has been made in the UN system on IDPs, however upon closer scrutiny the accomplishments – The Guiding Principles, the Interagency Network on Internal Displacement, the Internal Displacement Unit in OCHA - are mostly on paper and in headquarters offices rather than on the ground. The norms and policies developed over the 1990s, in the words of former Under Secretary General Kenzo Oshima, have yet to be "operationalized." In the international humanitarian NGO community the IDP issue is seen as one of the biggest failures of inter-agency humanitarian coordination.[18] Recently NGOs have expressed particular dismay at the appointment of the International Organization for Migration (a much smaller agency known mostly for providing transport trucks) rather than UNHCR as lead agency for IDPs in Iraq.

Possibly the most striking feature of the international efforts on IDPs, is that the donors have largely been left out of the equation. As with other many other humanitarian issues, the discussion has proceeded as if the UN structure and the implementing agencies were the sum total of the humanitarian international. (In fact only one major aid study, the comprehensive evaluation of the Rwanda refugee crisis, included an assessment of donor behavior).[19] In addition, the Guiding Principles are directed at the implementers: local governments, combatants, and humanitarian agencies, but no mention is made of the major donor governments, whose contributions serve as the engine of the entire international aid mechanism. In point of fact, donor preferences, their bureaucratic structures and channels for assistance have everything to do with what ultimately is happening on the ground.

Conclusions

In the immediate aftermath of World War II, when the UN system was taking shape and western governments were enacting foreign assistance legislation that would serve as the basis for their donor institutions, refugees were international humanitarian priority number one. UNHCR was among the first UN agencies to be established and become operational. During the Cold War period, the emphasis was on natural disasters, economic development, and cross-border and asylum issues took on further political meaning in the context of the US-Soviet rivalry and the emigration restrictions in the communist bloc.

IDPs as an issue remained off the radar screen until the late 1980s and 1990s when conflict patterns, state failures, and increased humanitarian access first revealed the institutional gap. The post-cold War period ended abruptly with the attacks on New York and Washington and, a new uncertain period is now unfolding. The crisis of internal displacement, however, shows no sign of abating, and may more likely be exacerbated by recent political developments. US and allied security actions in "countries of concern" have the potential to create more displacement and with countries increasingly unwilling to provide asylum for refugees (even those formerly praised for their generosity such as Tanzania) IDPs stand to remain the majority of forced migrants and the least helped.

Notes

1. For a in-depth examination of the politics behind refugee and IDP data, see Jeff Crisp, "Who Has Counted The Refugees? UNHCR and the Politics of Numbers" Working Paper No.12 in *New Issues in Refugee Research,* (Geneva: UNHCR, 1999).

2. Roberta C. Cohen, R. lecture, "Masses in Flight: People Under Assault in the Own Countries." (Lecture at University of Missouri, (January 16, 2001).

3. United Nations, *"Guiding Principles on Internal Displacement"* (New York: United Nations) 1998.

4. Catherine Phuong, "Improving the United Nations Response to Crises on Internal Displacement," *International Journal of Refugee Law*, Volume 13, Issue 4 (2001): 491-517, p. 506

5. Interview with William Garvelink, Assistant Administrator, Bureau for Democracy, Conflict, and Humanitarian Assistance, USAID, April 22, 2002.

6. Roberta Cohen, "Masses in Flight: People Under Assault in the Own Countries.". Lecture at University of Missouri, (January 16, 2001.)

7. Cohen, Lecture, p. 10-11.

8. US General Accounting Office, *Foreign Affairs: Internally Displaced Persons Lack Effective Protection*, GAO Report 17 August 2001, http://www.gao.gov/new.items/d01803..pdf), 10.*n.* GAO Report 17 August 2001 http://www.gao.gov/new.items/d01803.pdf (1 April 2003)

9. US GAO, 12.

10. Inter-Agency Standing Committee, *Protection of Internally Displaced Persons,* Policy Paper (New York: United Nations, December 1999), 5.

11. Interview with Joel R. Charny, Vice-President for Policy, Refugees International, April 1, 2003.

12. *Statement by Ambassador Richard C. Holbrooke, United States Permanent Representative to the United Nations, Cardozo Law School, New York, March 28, 2000,* USUN Press Release # 44 (00) March 28, 2000 http://www.un.int/usa/00_044.htm (11 February 2003), 2.

13. Interview with Joel R. Charny, Refugees International, April 1, 2003.

14. Larry Minear, *The Humanitarian Enterprise* (Bloomfield, CT: 2002), 87.

15. Kenzo Oshima, UN Emergency Relief Coordinator, letter dated 7 August 2001, Appendix V, "Comments from the United Nations" US General Accounting Office, 56.

16. US GAO, 17.

17. Interview with Anita Menghetti, USAID, April 1, 2003.

18. Interview with James K. Bishop, Director, Humanitarian Policy and Practice, InterAction, February 25, 2003.

19. Joanna Macrae, et al., *Uncertain Power: The Changing Role of Official Donors in Humanitarian Action,* . HPG Report (12 December 2002) London: Overseas Development Institute. 12 December 2002.

Claudena M. Skran

CHAPTER FOUR:

New Paradigms In Refugee Assistance

O ne of the most important developments in refugee assistance since the end of the Cold War concerns the changing role of the United Nations High Commissioner for Refugees (UNHCR). In Iraq, Bosnia, Kosovo and elsewhere, UNHCR has found itself in uncharted waters and has often responded by steering a course away from its traditional policies. After the Persian Gulf War, instead of insisting that it could only help Iraqi Kurds once they had left their home country as refugees, UNHCR accepted responsible for aiding them within Iraq in the UN declared "safe haven." In the Bosnian conflict, UNHCR broke with past traditions by acting as "lead agency" in a massive humanitarian relief effort that aided not only refugees but also displaced people within Bosnia and "war-affected" populations who never moved. This effort also required UNHCR, a civilian agency, to co-operate to an unprecedented degree with military forces, specifically the United Nations Protection Force (UNPROFOR) and to co-ordinate the activities of a multitude of NGOs. In Kosovo, UNHCR found itself struggling with a mass exodus of refugees, an unintended consequence of NATO's air strikes on Serbia. In this case, UNHCR, usually the main international refugee agency, found itself by-passed as military actors from NATO countries and national NGOs raced to assist these highly important refugees.

Despite these dramatic changes in UNHCR's role and an increased salience of refugee issues worldwide, UNHCR's new role in world politics has not been fully explored. To truly understand this new role, one must understand both the parameters of the old paradigm for refugee assistance and of the new one. The backdrop of Cold War politics and the aftermath of European colonialism in the developing world shaped UNHCR's old paradigm. In response to this situation, UNHCR saw itself as a neutral and humanitarian agency that largely assisted people outside their home countries with minimal direct involvement in conflicts that produced refugees. Since the end of the Cold War, UNHCR has had to adapt to a politically charged environment created by international intervention in ethnic and communal conflicts, faced increasing numbers of both refugees and internally displaced people, and shared its humanitarian work with military actors. These changes have generated challenges for UNHCR's traditional role in refugee work and the need for a new paradigm. In this chapter, both the legacy of UNHCR's old paradigm and the emerging dimensions of a new one will be explored. UNHCR's role in both Bosnia (1992-95) and Kosovo (1999) will be highlighted because these cases best show the direction of change.

The "Old" Paradigm:
UNHCR as a Neutral, Humanitarian Agency

Created after the Second World War, UNHCR was designed as a non-political, humanitarian agency with a mission: the protection and assistance of refugees. In establishing the agency, the UN gave the High Commissioner the responsibility for carrying on the work for refugees originally begun by the League of Nations and continued by the International Refugee Organization (IRO). UNHCR's mandate covered refugees—defined as people who were outside their country of nationality and had a "well-founded fear of being persecuted"[1]—but did not extend to the needs of people who were internally displaced within their own country. Initially, the 1951 Refugee Convention principally applied to refugees produced by the Second World War in Europe, but UNHCR's mandate was extended so that the agency could meet the needs of refugees from Hungary in 1956. UNHCR also gradually took on responsibility for the refugees created by colonial and post-colonial conflicts in Asia and Africa, a fact that was recognized when the 1967 Protocol to the Convention removed any geographic or time restrictions on its legal mandate.[2] Although the agency occasionally provided some support to the internally displaced, they would largely stay outside the parameters of UNHCR's refugee work.

Unlike the IRO, an agency that had focused on the expensive task of resettlement,[3] UNHCR's first task was that of the legal protection of refugees. Non-governmental organizations and host governments were to be the primary providers of refugee aid. This was possible in the 1950s because both Europe and the United States were willing to provide asylum to refugees from East bloc countries on a permanent basis. For example, about 200,000 Hungarian refugees were resettled in a short two-year period, primarily in Western European countries, Canada, and the United States.[4] Over time, UNHCR's focus shifted to the developing world, and its role in directly assisting refugees grew. The agency became more concerned with both the provision of relief supplies in refugee emergencies and the provision of durable solutions, such as repatriation, integration, or resettlement, over the longer term. In the 1960s and 1970s, UNHCR activities particularly focused on Africa; beginning in 1965, the region surpassed Europe as the place where the greatest amount of UNHCR's expenditures was made.[5] In the 1980s, UNHCR offered assistance to the Vietnamese boat people, the Afghans uprooted by the Soviet invasion, and refugees from civil wars in Central America. Although the refugee groups of concern to UNHCR changed over time, the agency was guided by the principle that it should be a non-political, independent agency that primarily responded to the needs of people in exile who were outside their home countries.

In carrying out its mandate for refugee assistance, the UNCHR earned a reputation as a neutral and humanitarian agency. In doing so, it strove to apply humanitarian principles in international politics that affirm the belief in the fundamental worth and dignity of all human beings and require that human needs be met in an apolitical, non-discriminatory way through non-military means. The legal foundation of UNHCR's neutrality can be found in its statutes, which state that "The work of the High Commissioner shall be of an entirely non-political character; it shall be humanitarian and social…"[6] The posture of humanitarian, non-political work was also embedded in the history of international assistance to refugees. The very first High commissioner for Refugees, Fridtjof Nansen, started this tradition when he delivered aid to both Greek and Turkish refugees after the 1922 Greco-

Turkish war, even though most Europeans were more sympathetic to the Greek position.[7] In the 1950s, UNHCR's posture of neutrality differentiated it from the IRO, an agency that the Soviets viewed as a tool of the United States because it promoted resettlement of Eastern European refugees rather than their repatriation.[8] In the Hungarian refugee crisis, High Commissioner Auguste Lindt found support within the socialist bloc for his role and was able to arrange the repatriation of about 18,000 Hungarian refugees, despite initial opposition from Western countries.[9] The acceptance of High Commissioner's work by both West and East was manifested in voting on General Assembly resolutions related to UNHCR. Although the USSR and its close allies initially voted against resolutions related to refugee work, beginning in 1954, they began to abstain in votes on refugee-related matters. In 1956 and again in 1958, they even supported the election of Lindt as High Commissioner by acclamation.[10]

In the developing world, especially in Africa, UNHCR had to steer a neutral course by aiding refugees from politically charged colonial conflicts, including those from colonies still under Portuguese control such as Angola, Guinea Bissau, and Mozambique, or from white-dominated countries in Southern Africa. UNHCR also aided refugees from newly independent states that were experiencing instability or ethnic violence. Some of the best known of these movements were Ewe refugees from Ghana, Tutsi refugees from Rwanda, Hutu refugees from Burundi, refugees in the Zairian civil war (Congo), Eritrean refugees from Ethiopia, and Asian refugees from Uganda. For UNHCR, providing aid in a non-political manner was made easier because people were usually helped outside their country of origin.[11] This policy, in turn, was possible because of the willingness of newly independent countries to accept refugees fleeing ongoing colonial conflicts. African governments officially realized that " 'the granting of asylum is a humanitarian act and not an unfriendly one' toward the country of origin."[12] Although UNHCR dealt with the internally displaced on an ad hoc basis, they largely remained outside its sphere, thus keeping UNHCR from direct involvement in conflict zones. In the 1960s, High Commissioner Prince Sadruddin Aga Khan, stressed the importance of donor countries using multilateral agencies such as UNHCR because "bilateral aid ... is sometimes suspected of perhaps not being free from self-interest" while multilateral aid was more acceptable both to the governments of the country of origin and of asylum.[13] One measure of the perception of UNHCR as a non-political actor in dealing with African refugee issues was the widespread support for its work within the General Assembly from the Eastern, Western, and G-77 voting blocs. In 1968, for instance, the Assembly accepted the High Commissioner's annual report unanimously.[14]

During the Cold War period, the person filling the position of High Commissioner was key to maintaining UNHCR's independent position. An international agency that particularly reflects the personality and style of the High Commissioner, UNHCR has been called "a man and his staff." When it was first established, UNHCR followed the "Nansen" tradition, begun in the League period, of appointing a dynamic individual from a country that was not a Great Power as the High Commissioner.[15] As the first High Commissioner, Nansen, a Norwegian polar explorer, scientist, and Nobel Peace Prize winner, often acted as an outspoken advocate for refugees. When the first United Nations High Commissioner, Gerrit Jan van Heuven Goedhart of the Netherlands was appointed, controversy ensued; "the fact that he was not the candidate of the US – and his passionate and vocal support of refugee interests – created tensions in the early years."[16] Other men from non-major powers, especially Switzerland, Denmark, and Norway, would later fill the job. In 1990, the appointment of Sadako Ogata, a Japanese academic and first female High Commissioner, continued the tradition of having a chief refugee administrator outside the military powers.[17]

One important limitation on UNHCR's independence was its reliance on voluntary contributions from Western governments. In particular, the United States made the largest financial contributions; in recognition of this, the Deputy UNHCR was typically been a citizen of the United States. [Note: I'm still gathering data on this and will produce a chart showing financial contributions, 1951-1990.] UNHCR tried to compensate for its dependence on Western funding by diversifying its sources but it could not, however, escape the confines of the Cold War entirely. UNHCR's largest programs flowed to refugees of interest to the West. For example, most of UNHCR's aid to refugees from Afghanistan, example, went to pro-Western Pakistan, which hosted 2.9 million people, rather than to neighboring Iran, which hosted 3.2 million refugees.[18]

The End of the Cold War and the Need for a New Paradigm

Although the end of the Cold War removed from UNHCR the pressure to take sides in the struggle between East and West, it also brought dramatic changes that required UNHCR to rethink its operating paradigm. The first of these changes had to due with increasing numbers of internally displaced people, defined by the UN as people "who have been forced or obliged to flee or to leave their homes or places of habitual residence in particular as a result of, or in order to avoid the effects of, armed conflict, situations of generalized violence, violations of human rights or natural or human-made disaster, and who have not crossed an internationally recognized state border."[19] Until 1984, the number of refugees either approximated or exceeded the number of displaced people. By the early 1990s, however, the gap between the groups grew so that, by 1996, one study estimated that there were twice as many internally displaced as refugees.[20] As the number of internally displaced people escalated, UNHCR's traditional policy of aiding only refugees became increasingly problematic because it failed to meet the humanitarian needs of people who had problems similar to those of refugees.

A second change that undermined UNHCR's old operating paradigm concerns the renewal of mass population movements within Europe. As late as 1990, only 5% of refugees and others under UNHCR's mandate were located in Europe. By 1995, almost 25% were located there as conflicts within the former Soviet Union and Eastern bloc countries generated mass migrations.[21] In 1992, just one year after the breakup of the Soviet Union, 700,000 refugees and 2.3 million internally displaced people made their homes within the 12 members of the Commonwealth of Independent States.[22] Among the largest of these groups were those uprooted by conflict between Armenia and Azerbaijan over Nagorno-Karabakh (1.6 million displaced), civil war in Tajikistan (600,000 displaced and 250,000 refugees), and the independence war for South Ossetia (36,000 displaced and 120,000 refugees).[23] In the former Yugoslavia, ethnic conflict generated as many as two million refugees and displaced people.

During the Cold War, the trickle of political dissidents and others who managed to flee the Soviet bloc usually found asylum easily. In the early 1980s, only about 10,000 asylum seekers made their way from Eastern to Western Europe each year. By 1987, this figure had grown to 50,000; by

1991, it had multiplied five times to almost 250,000.[24] People fleeing as part of a mass movement encountered a difficult asylum climate within Europe as governments erected a system of national and regional laws that some have called "Fortress Europe." The Schengen Accord, officially in force for seven of the EU member states by 1995, helped make travel easier for people from EU countries easier even as it increased controls on the entry of non-EU citizens. Some of the measures associated with the Schengen Accord undermined established elements of international refugee law. For instance, it required that commercial airline personnel, rather than government officials, check travel documents for their validity. This effectively moved "the decision of whether a person will have the chance to apply for asylum into the hands of the personnel of a commercial carrier company," in violation of established norms in refugee law.[25]

Changes in the immigration and asylum policies of particular countries also became more restrictive. Germany the country that had had the most liberal asylum laws during the Cold War, amended the Basic Law in 1993 so that it would allow "the rejections of the asylum claims filed by persons entering Germany through neighboring countries considered safe." As a result of this legislation, the number of asylum applicants in Germany fell by half, from 322,800 in 1993 to only 127,000 in 1994.[26] In the United States, as well, anti-immigration sentiments and lack of Cold War imperatives meant this country was less willing to receive refugees. The old paradigm for refugee assistance heavily depended on the willingness of countries to accept refugees; in the era of ethnic conflict and mass migrations in Europe, less willingness existed.

UNHCR responded to the growing problem of internal displacement by changing its "unsystematic and ad hoc" method of dealing with the internally displaced.[27] Breaking with its tradition of helping refugees only in exile, first for Iraqi Kurds and then in the former Yugoslavia, the UNCHR took responsibility for both refugees and displaced people; 60% of the people of concern to UNHCR there were either internally displaced or "war affected" populations.[28] As early as 1993, UNHCR set up guidelines to identify circumstances under which it would assist the internally displaced, including those in which the internally placed "are present in or going back to the same areas as returning refugees," or when they are "living alongside a refugee population and have a similar need for protection and assistance." In Bosnia, UNHCR's rational for extending services to the internally displaced was that "in situations where the same factors have given rise to both internal and external population movements, and where there are good reasons for addressing those problems by means of a single humanitarian operation."[29] UNHCR, however, declined to take account of all internally displaced populations, meaning its aid efforts for two of the largest populations, in Sudan and Columbia, would be strictly limited.[30]

The Challenge Of Humanitarian Intervention

By far the most important development affecting UNHCR's operating paradigm has to do with the willingness of the international community to engage in "humanitarian intervention." An early example of this practice can be found after the Persian Gulf War when the United States, Great Britain, and France set up a "safe haven" for Kurds in northern Iraq. Other internationally sanctioned interventions of the 1990s would include the UN and NATO in the Bosnian civil war, France's Operation Turquoise in Rwanda, and NATO's involvement in Kosovo. Although the concept of humanitarian intervention, defined as "external interference with the internal affairs of a country with a view to ending or at least reducing the suffering caused by such events as civil war, genocide and starvation."[31] was not an entirely new one, it attracted new attention after the collapse of the USSR. During the Cold War, humanitarian intervention was considered unacceptable and intervention itself was associated with the "dictatorial interference" of one state in the affairs of another.[32] For example as late as 1974, the distinguished jurist Ian Brownlie strongly maintained that "forcible intervention in human rights situations" was illegal because they violated state sovereignty. He argued that there was no consensus on their acceptability within the United Nations and no record of state practice.[33] In the post-Cold war era, however, the legality of such interventions became increasingly accepted for two major reasons. With the discrediting of the Soviet system and the growth of democratic regimes, there was a growing acceptance of international human rights norms worldwide. Moreover, there was international recognition that such violations constituted a threat to international peace and security. A shift toward this new view could be seen as early as January 1992, when the UN Security Council made a departure from traditional notions of security and recognized that "'the non-military sources of instability in the economic, social, humanitarian, and ecological fields have become threats to peace and security."[34] Such recognition paved the way for legally sanctioned interventions if they had the purpose of protecting people from gross violations of human rights.

In one respect, intervention to protect human rights represents a sharp departure from the historical practice of intervention for reasons of political or economic gain by Great Powers. In another respect, however, the humanitarian interventions of the post-Cold War world show striking similarities to earlier interventions. In order to be strictly legal, humanitarian interventions need to be sanctioned by the UN Security Council, which rather than being a democratic body, is dominated by the Great Powers and gives the five permanent members – the US, the UK, France, Russia, and China – a veto over any actions. In Iraq and Somalia, the major Western powers on the Security Council pushed for intervention and the targets were clearly less powerful states. The intervention in Iraq after the Persian Gulf War has been compared to Allied actions in Germany after the Second World War; they were "the sort of action one would expect in the aftermath of a war in which the victors could claim military rights to intervene in the territory of the defeated states, independent of any humanitarian justification."[35] In the case of Kosovo, a coalition of NATO countries led by the United States, the world's lone superpower, intervened against a much weaker European state, Serbia. In addition, it appears that a Great Power, especially a nuclear one, is still an unlikely target for humanitarian intervention. One need only consider the treatment of Russia on the issue of Chechnya to see this difference in treatment.

In this new era of humanitarian intervention, governments also departed from traditional understandings of national security. They acknowledged that human rights violations could endanger national security, particularly if they generated massive refugee flows, a point made by John Vincent much earlier in his work on human rights and foreign policy.[36] These same governments, however, proved themselves unwilling to fully commit to humanitarian interventions if immediate interests were not threatened, despite the severity of the human rights violations. A case in point is the international response to the genocide in African countries compared to the response to ethnic cleansing in Europe. In Rwanda, the US government declined to intervene, citing Presidential Decision Directive 25 (PDD 25) which said that the "United States would not become involved unless American interests could be advanced at an acceptable risk."[37] In Bosnia, the UNSC launched a large peacekeeping force with some peace enforcement functions under Chapter VII. It fell short, however, of a full-scale intervention, however, despite evidence of brutal murders, concentration camps, and mass rapes. In Kosovo, NATO intervention was justified on both humanitarian and security grounds. U.S. President Bill Clinton argued that if the conflict continues, "it will push refugees across borders," "draw in neighboring countries" and "undermine the credibility of NATO on which stability in Europe depends."[38] Prime Minister Tony Blair made a similar point when he argued, "when oppression produces massive flows of refugees which unsettle neighbouring countries they can properly be described as 'threats to international peace and security.'"[39]

The increasing number of interventions for humanitarian purposes posed major challenges for UNHCR's paradigm as a non-political, humanitarian agency. In the Cold War, UNHCR almost always aided refugees outside of zones on conflict. In the post-Cold War era, UNHCR redefined its humanitarian mission so that it could take responsibility for internally displaced and war affected populations, often in conjunction to UN peacekeeping efforts or some other forms of international intervention. In doing so, it put itself in the center of conflict zones and operated in an environment where the other saw the very act of aiding one side as hostile. In such a situation, UNHCR's traditional concept of neutrality became highly problematic. In Iraq, Somalia, and Bosnia, the traditionally civilian functions of aid distribution became closely linked to military activities; in Kosovo they were literally taken over by military forces. In deciding when and how military forces would be used, the strong influence of national governments could be evident, calling into question UNHCR's independence and neutrality at the operational-level. Under these circumstances, how could UNHCR act as an independent agency in the interests of refugees when humanitarian interventions tend to be dominated by states using military and other means to advance their national interests? As an agency, UNHCR, faced three major challenges: (1) maintaining neutrality between conflicting parties; (2) staying independent from the major powers in operational decision-making; and (3) being primarily responsive to refugee interests rather than national interests. All three of these challenges can be illustrated with respect to UNHCR's role in Bosnia from 1992 to 1995 and in Kosovo in 1999.

The Bosnian conflict presented UNHCR with one of the most severe refugee emergencies of the early post-Cold War years. Over a three-year period, over half of Bosnia's pre-war population of 4.4 million was uprooted;

another 1.4 million in Bosnia were labeled "war affected." After three years of fighting, 1.3 million people were displaced within Bosnia and another 800,000 had sought refuge in other countries (400,000 to Serbia and 400,000 to other European countries).[40] UNHCR's role in the Bosnian civil war can only be described as one of the most massive humanitarian efforts ever launched. From 1992 to 1995, UNHCR delivered 950,000 tons of food to 2.7 million people. A key part of this aid delivery system was maintaining over 250 trucks, which could be run by convoy teams. In addition, UNHCR was responsible for coordinating the activities of 3000 personnel from over 250 organizations.[41] The humanitarian aid airlifted into Sarajevo constituted more supplies than the allies did in the Berlin airlift of 1948-49. [42]

UNHCR's involvement in the former Yugoslavia began in 1991, when it first responded to refugees from Croatia, uprooted by the outbreak of ethnic violence.[43] At the request of the Secretary-General, UNHCR began helping refugees and displaced people from the Bosnian civil war in 1992. UNHCR took on the job of "lead agency" in the conflict, coordinating the efforts of other UN specialized agencies and NGOs. What is particularly remarkable about UNHCR's response is that the agency went beyond its traditional mandate and assisted refugees from Bosnia, displaced people within Bosnia; and "war affected" people within Bosnia who never moved. Tom Weiss and Amir Pasic have pointed out that "what was especially vital about UNHCR's actions in the former Yugoslavia was the expansion of its mission beyond refugees to aid all those with well-founded fear of persecution."[44] Many others have praised UNHCR's role in the conflict. According to one analyst, "the relief effort in Bosnia was a success by humanitarian standards. It helped to avert starvation, provided emergency health and medical care, and supported civilian living condition. As UNHCR officials have often remarked, no one starved during the war in Bosnia."[45]

Although UNHCR has been widely praised for delivering much needed aid to displaced people and others who did not fit the traditional—and rather narrow—definition of a refugee, its role was not without controversy. As soon as UNHCR became heavily involved in aiding internally displaced people, issues of neutrality were raised because of the agency's relationship with UNPROFOR and the UN's policy in general. Under the terms of UNSC Resolution 776,[46] UNHCR aid convoys were to be protected by UNPROFOR forces. Indeed, the very reason for the UNPROFOR peacekeepers, which reached 23,000 in number by Dec. 1994, was to protect humanitarian aid supply routes. In Bosnia, the UN adopted some functions traditionally associated with impartial peacekeeping: arranging cease fires, placing themselves between opposing sides during ceasefires, and helping in the delivery of humanitarian aid. The Security Council, however, went beyond traditional peacekeeping norms and also mandated UNPROFOR to take on peace enforcement functions by using "all available means" to deliver supplies, to use force to defend safe areas, and to cooperate with NATO air strikes against the Serbs.[47] Moreover, the UNSC had ordered both an arms embargo on all parties and comprehensive mandatory sanctions against the FR of Yugoslavia for intervening in the Bosnian civil war.[48] In the summer of 1995, punishing NATO air strikes were added to the enforcement mechanisms available to back up UNSC resolutions.[49] This combination of peacekeeping and peace enforcement functions required by communal conflicts proved difficult for the UN system, including UNHCR, to reconcile.[50]

In authorizing UNHCR to get involved in food aid, the UN Secretary-General stressed that "delivery of relief must be seen by all parties as a neutral humanitarian act."[51] Initially, UNHCR resisted a greater role for the military in providing aid. As the conflict progressed, UNHCR officials on the ground deemed it necessary to save lives.[52] This contrasted with some NGOs, particularly the ICRC, which shunned UN protection for their convoys. Resolution 776, which authorized UNPROFOR to protect aid convoys, specifically avoided evoking Chapter VII of the UN Charter.[53] But relying on the consensual nature of a traditional Chapter VI, peacekeeping operation in an ongoing civil war was difficult. In Bosnia, this was especially true because convoys had to get permission from Serb forces to deliver aid, resulting in the diversion of up to half of all aid to military sources.[54] For UNHCR, " to continue to be seen as impartial was hard if not impossible."[55] According to leading experts on peacekeeping, "every action taken by outsiders in a civil war situation affects the local balance of power." Humanitarian intervention especially favors the side that is behind or the side that needs the most use of time to gather resources.[56] Moreover, in a conflict such as Bosnia where civilians were primary targets and creating ethnically homogeneous areas was a main war aim, aid is likely to be considered a weapon of war.

One measure of the perception of UNHCR by the parties to the conflict is the treatment of its workers. In the Bosnian conflict, more than 50 UNHCR workers died,[57] some of them have been deliberately targeted as aid workers. For instance, in June 1993, Serb forces targeted a UNHCR convoy attempting to reach the town of Maglaj, then blockaded by Serbian and Croatian troops.

As a result two Danish drivers and their interpreter died. On August 14 of 1993, while driving in a UNHCR vehicle, a UNHCR interpreter was shot in the town of Vitez in Central Bosnia.[58] An important study of the Bosnian civil war comments on the inability of UNHCR to be non-political: UNHCR was "unable to operate in a non-political fashion. In Bosnia and Herzegovina, the humanitarian activities of UN agencies were undoubtedly tainted by association with the UN's military and political wings."[59]

Despite the difficulties mentioned above, UNHCR did not abandon its commitment to distributing aid in as impartial a way as possible. Throughout the conflict, UNHCR managed to distribute aid in regions controlled by both Bosnian Muslims and Serbs. Indeed, in Serb-controlled regions they were one of the few outsiders allowed to operate.[60] Moreover, UNHCR also distributed aid in surrounding countries. David Owen praises UNHCR's role, saying that "a rare encouraging feature of the whole tragedy was that refugees in Montenegro and Serbia were well looked after, mainly in people's own homes under UNHCR supervision, throughout the war."[61] By the end of 1993, for instance, UNHCR provided assistance for 350,000 refugees in FRY, including 150,000 from Croatia and 200,000 from Bosnia.[62] Beginning in 1993, UNHCR was also one of the only sources of support for "socially vulnerable" non-refugees in the FRY; at the end of 1994, some 75,000 people were aided in this way.[63] Overall, Serbia received less international aid, but this was primarily because few NGOs operated in the country; only 12 NGOS had programs there in 1993, while more than 250 operated in Bosnia.[64]

Added to the difficulty of being impartial in a civil war is the issue of being independent from the major powers. In policies related to UNPROFOR, the British and French had particularly dominant voices because they contributed the most troops to the operation. French support for the operation grew from 2500 soldiers in February 1993 to a high of 4500 in April 1994, giving it the largest national delegation. Over the same period, British contributions grew from 2600 to 3400 troops, making them the second largest force in UNPROFOR. By contrast, Germany and the United States did not contribute to UNPROFOR with peacekeepers.[65] As key members of the EU and permanent members of the UNSC, Britain and France had a unique role in policy formation for UNPROFOR.[66]

In the Bosnian conflict, High Commissioner Ogata tried to stop the manipulation of aid deliveries by all parties to the conflict. On Feb. 17, 1993, the High Commissioner suspended aid operations throughout most of Bosnia. But this suspension was to be short lived. Both General Philippe

Morillon, Commander of UNPROFOR in 1993, and Secretary General Boutros Boutro-Ghali were surprised and annoyed by the decision. Two days later, the Boutros-Ghali ordered UNHCR to resume aid deliveries.[67] In the words of one commentator "This hardly helped her [Ogata's] claims to independence."[68] During the negotiations over the Vance-Owen plan, moreover, UNHCR threatened to pull out of Bosnia because of the deteriorating climate there. High-level negotiators for the British-backed peace plan convinced them to stay in Bosnia and to continue to co-operate with their efforts.[69]

In struggling to steer an independent course, UNHCR faced this question: to what extent should UNHCR provide aid when that aid could be used as a cover for political inaction by Western governments? Susan Woodward has written of the "false humanitarianism" of the Western governments: "Channeling moral concerns into humanitarian relief while refusing to confront the political causes of the conflict … was creating more war, more casualties, and more need for humanitarian assistance."[70] David Reiff, in his critque of Western policy toward Bosnia writes that "The West … chose to do anything but intervene. Instead, they mounted one of the largest and most heroic humanitarian relief efforts in modern history, under the aegis of the United Nations High Commissioner for Refugees, all the while pursuing decidedly unheroic diplomatic negotiations."[71] UNHCR was not unaware of this problem. In the words of High Commissioner Ogata, "Humanitarian action became a fig leaf for political and military inaction."[72] According to a high level UNHCR official in the former Yugoslavia, "It is not simply that the UN's humanitarian efforts have become politicized; it is rather that we have been transformed into the only manifestation of international political will."[73] UNHCR clearly made the decision that saving lives in the short run was their highest priority. Berg and Shoup have argued that humanitarian intervention alone did not deter a stronger military-political response because other factors stood in the way.[74]

In Bosnia, the problem of acting in the interests of refugees rather than to those of major donors was brought to the fore by ethnic cleansing. Ethnic cleansing, or the deliberate liquidation of an ethnic minority from a region, was to characterize the Bosnian civil war and create many of the displaced people and refugees. In dealing with this issue, UNHCR faced a difficult dilemma, or what Myron Weiner has called a conflict between humanitarian norms.[75] Should UNHCR act to evacuate ethnic minorities from an area likely to be "cleansed" in an attempt to save their lives, knowing that in doing so it would facilitate the process of ethnic cleansing? Or, should it maintain the "right to remain" of ethnic minorities and participate in the creation of "safe areas" for them? Any decision by UNHCR would be complicated by the willingness—or unwillingness—of neighboring states to accept more refugees. In the early 1990s, many European countries adopted more restrictive immigration and asylum policies making it more difficult for Bosnians to find places of refuge outside their home country.[76]

UNHCR confronted the practice of ethnic cleansing very early in the Bosnia conflict as minorities were pushed out of their homes in ethnically mixed areas. In mid-July 1992, for instance, UNHCR negotiated for four days with the mayor of Bosanski Novi as he threatened to legally expel the Moslem population. When negotiations failed, UNHCR evacuated 7000 people to Croatia.[77] Although UNHCR officials initially resisted such evacuations, they eventually adopted this policy as the best way to save lives in the short run. According to UNHCR Special Envoy to the former Yuguosalvia, Jose-Maria Mendiluce, "…it is my responsibility to help them [people threatened with ethnic cleansing], to save their lives. I cannot enter any philosophical or theoretical debate now. …"[78] According to an important study of the Bosnian conflict, UNHCR should be given credit for saving "thousands of people who were trapped, whether by negotiating cease-fires, assisting and protecting them where they were, or evacuating them."[79]

In Bosnia, UNHCR also faced a similar predicament in relationship to the creation of "safe areas," particularly those in eastern Bosnia, including Srebrenica. When Srebrenica was first threatened by approaching Bosnian Serb forces in early 1993, UNHCR warned of deteriorating conditions there: "They are surviving on the chaff from wheat and roots from trees. Every day people are dying of hunger and exhaustion." In a letter to the UNSC, High Commissioner Ogata outlined two options for those trapped within Srebrenica: (1) turn the enclave into a UN protected area with much greater assistance and an enhanced UNPROFOR force; (2) require a "large-scale evacuation of the endangered population" with sufficient resources devoted to UNHCR to make the evacuation safe.[80] What Ogata outlined was a policy of "preventative protection," a policy designed to keep people in their homes and so they could exercise a "right to remain." Although critics of this policy have argued that it reflected donor interests rather than refugee needs,[81] preventative protection would allow, in theory, UNHCR to deal with the root causes of refugee movements. In practice, however, UNHCR lacked the resources to make such a policy effective. In 1993, for instance, it had only 25 protection officers in the whole of Yugoslavia.[82]

In Srebrenica, UNHCR pursued a two-track approach rather than one of only preventative protection. UNHCR's Mendiluce emphasized its role was "to save as many people as we can." The organization evacuated 15,000 refugees from Srebrenica, with an emphasis on the wounded, elderly, and women with small children. Muslim political leaders outside the enclave objected to further evacuations because they did not want to give up the territory. When these evacuations stopped despite UNHCR's support, UNHCR continued to ship food aid into the town.[83] Shortly afterwards, on April 16, 1993, the UNSC declared Srebrenica a "safe area."[84] Srebrenica then became even more of a haven for Muslim refugees. The tragedy of Srebrenica is that, despite UNPROFOR protection, Serbian forces took the town in July 1995, killing over 7000 men in "Europe's worst massacre since World War II."[85]

UNHCR, NATO and Kosovo, 1998-1999

In Kosovo, NATO launched its first extended use of armed force in its history and engaged in "the first major bombing campaign intended to bring a halt to crimes against humanity being committed by a state within its own borders." This "humanitarian war" created a refugee emergency of staggering proportions.[86] Before the NATO bombing began on 24 March 1999,[87] the number of uprooted people reached 460,000, including 260,000 within Kosovo and 200,000 elsewhere in Yugoslavia or in other countries. NATO's 78-day bombing campaign precipitated a massive attack on the ethnic Albanian population by Serbian forces, uprooting 90 percent of this population and causing nearly 900,000 refugees to flee the country. An estimated 447,000 went to Albania, 245,000 to Macedonia, and 70,000 to Montengro. As part of a Humanitarian Evacuation Program (HEP), some 91,000 refugees were airlifted to third countries.[88] What distinguishes this mass exodus from others is the relatively short time that the Kosovar Albanians spent in exile. Following the peace agreement of June 1999, an estimated 600,000 refugees quickly returned to Kosovo.[89]

In Bosnia, UNHCR had difficulty maintaining neutrality between conflicting parties. In cases of humanitarian intervention by states, such as that performed by the NATO countries in Kosovo, neutrality became impossible. UNHCR began its involvement in Kosovo in 1992 and aided people there throughout the Bosnian civil war. When violence grew worse in 1998, UNHCR increased its presence, concentrating on aiding the ever increasing number of displaced people. In planning for the winter of 1999, UNHCR estimated that there were 175,000 internally displaced people within Kosovo.[90] Prior to the NATO bombing of Serbia, High Commissioner Ogata was increasingly critical of the activities of the Serbian forces, which were producing Kosovar refugees.[91] In Nov. 1998, for instance, she made a speech calling attention to the "indiscriminate shelling and excessive use of force by government security forces."[92] By March 1999, UNHCR was running a $28 million dollar program for 400,000 people.[93] Once the conflict began, UNHCR suspended its operations because the Serbian government blamed the agency for causing the air strikes.[94]

After March 24, the first day of the bombing, UNHCR shifted its focus to aiding refugees produced by the conflict. In the middle of April, negotiations between High Commissioner Ogata and NATO's Secretary General Javier Solana set up arrangements whereby NATO recognized "the leading role of UNHCR." In return, UNHCR accepted the help of NATO in key "support tasks" such as constructing camps, providing logistics, transporting refugees, and repairing roads. When UNHCR accepted field cooperation from NATO troops in the Kosovo crisis, the agency effectively "took sides" with the NATO authorities against the Serbian government. Once this choice was made, the agency found it impossible to maintain its position as a neutral, non-political agency in the traditional sense. According to one study of UNHCR's role in Kosovo, "some aid personnel viewed the agreement as signaling NATO's co-opting of UNCHR. ...Others viewed the agreement as shattering any pretense of humanitarian neutrality and independence by UNHCR and its associated UN and NGO partners."[95]

In Kosovo, the NATO powers exerted strong influence over the response to refugees. For them, refugees from Kosovo were what "U.S. prisoners of war had been to American leaders during the final years of the Vietnam war: rather than causing the war, the war had caused their existence; but, as the war progressed, resolving their fate became one of the principal aims of the war."[96] The importance of the refugees was heightened even more because in Kosovo, the very purpose of the war was "humanitarian" and yet the war itself had created the refugees. According to one report on UNHCR's role in the crisis, the "UNHCR had little leverage and was rapidly marginalized by more powerful actors."[97] NATO forces became the main providers of refugee relief. In Macedonia and Albania, NATO troops built refugee camps, reception centers, and emergency feeding stations. They also conducted a humanitarian airlift and moved aid on the ground.[98] UNHCR distributed only a small fraction of the total aid. This contrasts with the refugee emergency in Rwanda where funds from the European Union were chiefly distributed through UNHCR.

In Kosovo, the overwhelming preference of the NATO powers was to set up their own refugee camps and staff them with their own NGOs. The Italian government, for instance, donated only $800,000 to UNHCR at the peak of the crisis. At the same time, they put unprecedented sums into bilateral projects, constructing the first camp in Kukes, northern Albania.[99] Other governments constructed their own camps and competition grew up among them so that aid distribution had "all the elements of a popularity contest." Differences in services "were not lost on the refugees, who shopped around" for the best conditions. In one Italian camp, refugees received three hot meals a day while in an American one they received only one "ready-to-eat" meal.[100] Even pro-UNHCR governments such as that of Norway considered setting up their own national refugee camps.[101] In other refugee emergencies, UNHCR has typically exercised a kind of supervision that resulted in greater uniformity in services.

Without adequate resources, the power of independent decision-making diminishes. Even though UNHCR was officially the "lead agency" in the crisis, it was often behind the game in the distribution of aid. UNHCR was "often among the last to know about a new program or camp."[102] In Kosovo, UNHCR was subjected to "unprecedented attacks for being unprepared, disorganized and inefficient."[103] While poor staffing decisions and underestimates of the magnitude of the refugee flow partially account for UNHCR's performance, there were other important issues involved. UNHCR delayed making decisions because it was unwilling simply to turn its operations over to NATO. For instance, UNHCR has been criticized for delaying cooperation with NATO while refugees waited to get into Macedonia.[104] The delay was caused by a dispute over who would build refugee camps. In the early stages of the crisis, NATO and the government of the FYR Macedonia wanted NATO's military forces to build the refugee camps. High Commissioner Ogata, in keeping with traditional notions of humanitarian action, wanted civilians to construct the camps. After appeals from the UN Secretary-General, the Secretary-general of NATO, and the US embassy, however, UNHCR agreed to construction of the camps by NATO forces.[105] UNHCR's problems with NATO were compounded by the difference between the "military culture" and that of humanitarian organizations. The military valued discipline, hierarchy, and accountability while the humanitarian organizations valued participation in decision-making and advocated a "no frills" approach. These cultural differences made the day-to-day working relationships between the two groups more difficult.[106]

In the Kosovo crisis, UNHCR struggled to make refugee protection the first priority of policy decisions. As the crisis developed, it became clear that one of the chief goals of the Western European states was to avoid mass refugee flows into their own countries. From 1997 to 1998, the number of asylum seekers from the former Yugoslavia had already increased 200 percent; the majority of these were Kosovo Albanians. At a meeting of Western European governments on the eve of the air strikes, March 23, concerns were raised that "Europe had already absorbed hundreds of thousands of refugees from the previous wars in the former Yugoslavia; it could take no more."[107] This position was particularly taken by the Italian government, which developed "Operation Rainbow," a plan by which Italy transported refugees to special camps in Albania.

Partly in response to governmental concerns, UNHCR's developed the Humanitarian Evacuation Program (HEP), which was designed to transfer refugees from Macedonia to third countries willing to host them on a temporary basis. Speaking to the UNSC during the Kosovo crisis, High Commissioner Ogata emphasized that the HEP had "no precedent in UNHCR's history."[108] Eventually, the program transferred 92,000 refugees from Macedonia to 29 other countries. As a country, Macedonia was a reluctant host to Kosovar Albanians because its government feared that they would upset the ethnic balance of the country. The USA, the leading military power in the intervention, took the side of the Macedonian government because it wanted its support for the air campaign.[109] UNHCR, in contrast, focused on the obligation of states of first asylum to accept refugees and on the need to establish regional solutions. The agency was also concerned that eventual repatriation would be difficult if Kosovars were sent far from the region.[110]

UNHCR reluctantly agreed to sponsor the HEP which, according to Nicholas Morris, "would have happened anyway."[111] Afterwards, criticism was showered on UNHCR from all sides. Human rights advocates accused it of being "too timid" for not pressing the government more while some NATO members criticized it for putting "too much pressure" on the government.[112] The HEP program, although it appears to be in keeping with the burden-sharing norm of the international refugee regime, actually represented a departure from previous efforts at third country resettlement.[113] While governments agreed to take the Kosovars, most fell short of giving them full refugee status within their home countries. Germany, the country that accepted the largest number of Kosovars (15,000), only gave these refugees a special temporary protected status for people from war zones.[114] In the Netherlands, host to at least 4000 Kosovars, refugees were denied "A" designation, a status that confers all the rights set out in the 1951 Refugee Convention. Instead, they were given "F" status, which confers temporary protection for one year (renewable twice) but initially without full employment and education rights.[115] Although the HEP did safely remove people from a crisis point and ensure the openness of the Macedonian border, it may have undermined universal standards of refugee assistance. It is unlikely that governments would launch a similar program in a less politically charged situation.

Toward A New Paradigm

The problems faced by UNHCR in Bosnia and Kosovo—maintaining neutrality, independence, and responsiveness—were not unique to these particular crises. Instead, they are inherent in any humanitarian action conducted through coercive means. These problems are likely to be repeated in any future interventions that the international community might embark on in the future. While such interventions are presented as solutions to human rights violations and mass refugee flows, they, in turn, generate new problems for actors involved in refugee assistance. These problems have led UNHCR toward a new paradigm in its refugee assistance programs. In Bosnia, UNHCR attempted to meet its humanitarian imperatives by expanding the beneficiaries of its assistance to include the internally displaced and war-affected populations but found its neutrality called into question by its association with military forces sponsored by major powers. Although co-operation with UNPROFOR seemed a reasonable way to carry out its humanitarian mission in a conflict zone, in doing so UNHCR compromised itself. In other words, in Bosnia, UNHCR had to choose between being "humanitarian" and being "neutral" but it could not be both.

UNHCR's refusal to take full responsibility for all displaced people is important in understanding the emerging paradigm for refugee assistance. In the mid-1990s, proposals circulated within the UN system about transferring responsibility for all internally displaced peopled to a single agency. Because of its work in Bosnia and elsewhere, the obvious agency to take on this job would have been the UNHCR. Although feasible, the High Commissioner for Refugees opposed such a change. Other UNHCR officials were known to do so as well because of the fear "that greater involvement with the internally displaced will change the character of the organization and distract it from its primary responsibility."[116] This refusal indicates that UNCHR was not willing to fully abandon the old paradigm. Under an emerging paradigm, UNHCR would take on a broadened humanitarian mandate, even if it meant sacrificing neutrality, but only in the limited circumstance when movements of refugees and displaced people were closely connected.

UNHCR's independence was also tested by the practice of international intervention. In Bosnia, UNHCR found that its discretion to take controversial actions, such as stopping aid distribution, to be limited by UNPROFOR's leadership. In Kosovo, major military powers dominated UNHCR's policy even more. UNHCR reluctantly joined the NATO camp, but was dwarfed by the other actors involved. Not until the immediate military crisis had passed did UNHCR take on an expanded role. Similarly, UNHCR found that the pressure to develop policies that reflect refugee interests to be more difficult during a humanitarian intervention. Unlike many other actors, UNHCR had to think beyond the current refugee emergency to the implications for future ones. While the HEP might have been the best policy in a particular instance, the evacuation could have set unwise precedents for future refugee emergencies.

Since humanitarian intervention, as practiced in the post-Cold War period, is a fusion of both military intervention and humanitarian action, the "space" for neutral, humanitarian actors has become smaller as military actors have taken over some of their traditional functions. This same fusion, however, has also created new opportunities for UNHCR as an agency and the High Commissioner for Refugees as an individual to expand their influence on refugee matters. For instance, frequent requests from the UN Security Council for "briefings" in high profile emergencies gave Mrs. Ogata a public forum to advocate for refugee interests. Mrs. Ogata first gave such a briefing in 1992 and would conduct 12 by the time she finished her tenure as High Commissioner. These briefings allowed High Commissioner Ogata to address the Security Council at critical times, including during the Bosnian civil war, the Rwandan exodus, and the Kosovo intervention.[117] These frequent appearances stand in sharp contrast to the Cold War period when a great distance was kept between the High Commissioner and the Council. They have given the High Commissioner a unique forum to present an independent view and to exercise moral authority, one of the important assets available to the executive head of a humanitarian agency. But, more than this, they have also placed the UNHCR closer to the center of decision making on security and refugee issues. Thus, although changes brought by the end of the Cold War have, in some circumstances, limited UNHCR's independence and forced it to choose between its neutrality and humanitarian mission, they have also offered the agency new opportunities to fulfill its mission as an independent refugee agency is world affairs.

Notes

1. Article 1 of the 1951 Convention Relating to the Status of Refugees adds that a person be outside his country of nationality because of events in Europe occurring before 1 January 1951. The definition also gives five grounds for persecution: race, religion, nationality, membership of a particular social group, or political opinion.

2. UNHCR, *The State of the World's Refugees 2000: Fifty years of Humanitarian Action* (New York: Oxford University Press, 2000), 53.

3. On the IRO, see John Stoessinger, *The Refugee in the World Community* (Minneapolis: University of Minnesota Press, 1956); Louise Holborn, *The International Refugee Organization: a Specialized Agency of the United Nations, its History and Work, 1946-52* (London: Oxford University Press, 1956), Gil Loescher, *Beyond Charity: International Cooperation and the Global Refugee Crisis* (New York: Oxford University Press, 1993), 49-51.

4. Loescher, 69-70.

5. Louise Holborn, *Refugees: A Problem of our Time, The Work of the United Nations High Commissioner for Refugees*, 1951-1972 (Metuchen, N.J.: 1975), Vol. II, Annex 50.2.

6. United Nations, *Statute of the Office of the United Nations High Commissioner for Refugees*, Chapter I, Paragraph 2 [HCR/INF/1/Rev.3].

7. Claudena Skran, *Refugees in Interwar Europe* (Oxford: Clarendon Press, 1995), 159.

8. Loescher, 50.

9. *Ibid.*, 70-71.

10. Loescher, 68. Holborn, *UNHCR*, Vol. II, Annex—Epilogue.1, "UN General Assembly Resolutions Relating to the UNCHR."

11. Holborn, *UNHCR,* Vol. II, 830-831.

12. *Ibid., UNHCR,* Vol. II, 843.

13. *Ibid., UNHCR,* Vol. II, 840.

14. Holborn, Annex—Epilogue.1, "UN General Assembly Resolutions Relating to the UNHCR."

15. Fridtjof Nansen of Norway served as the first High Commissioner for Russian Refugees, 1921-29. See Claudena M. Skran, "Profiles of The First Two High Commissioner," *Journal of Refugee Studies*, Vol. I, No. 3 / 4, 1988, 277-296.

16. Holborn, UNHCR, Vol II, 103.

17. The position of UNHCR has been held by van Heuven Goedhart (Netherlands), 1951-56; Auguste R. Lindt (Switzerland), 1956-60; Felix Schnyder (Switzerland), 1960-65; Sadruddin Aga Khan (Iran), 1965-77; Poul

Hartling (Denmark), 1978-85; Jean-Pierre Hocke (Switzerland), 1986-89; Thorvald Stoltenberg (Norway); 1990; Sadako Ogata (Japan), 1990-2000. On the role of each High Commissioner, see Gil Loescher, *The UNHCR and World Politics* (Oxford: Oxford University Press, 2001).

18. Ray Wilkinson, Cover Story, *Refugees*, Vol. 3, No. 230, 2000, 10.

19. For a discussion about the debate on the definition of "internally displaced people" see Roberta Cohen, "Recent Trends in Protection and Assistance for Internally Displaced People," in *Internally Displaced People: Ag Global Survey* by the Norwegian Refugee Council and the Global IDP Survey, Jamie Hampton, ed. (London: Earthscan, 1998), 4-5.

20. Susanne Schmeidl, "Comparative Trends in Forced Displacement: IDPs and Refugees, 1964-96," in: *Internally Displaced People*, 27.

21. UNHCR, *The State of the World's Refugees 1995: In Search of Solutions* (Oxford: Oxford University Press, 1995), 35.

22. Hania Zlotnik, "International Migration 1965-96: An Overview," *Population and Development Review*, Vol. 24, 3 (Sept., 1998): 449.

23. *State of the World's Refugees: 1995*: 24-25.

24. Loescher, 98 and 112. In 1983, 9600 asylum seekers from Central, Eastern, and Southern Europe sought asylum in Europe.

25. Andrew Convey and Marek Kupiszewski, "Keeping up with Schengen: Migration and Policy in the European Union," *International Migration Review*, Vol. 29, Issue 4 (Winter, 1995): 940, 942-43, and 945.

26. Zlotnik, 442.

27. Cohen, 25.

28. UNHCR, *State of the World's Refugees 1997-98: A Humanitarian Agenda* (Oxford: Oxford University Press, 1997), 103.

29. *State of the World's Refugees: 1997-98*, 117.

30. David Korn, *Exodus Within Borders: An Introduction to the Crisis of Internal Displacement* (Washington, D.C.: Brookings Institution Press, 1999), 35-36.

31. Bhikhu Parekh, "The Dilemmas of Humanitarian Intervention: Introduction," in *International Political Science Review* (1997), Vol. 18, No. 1: 5.

32. S. Williams & A. Mestral, *An Introduction to International Law*, (1987), pp. 47-48, printed in Weston, Falk, d'Amato, *International Law and World Order* (St. Paul, Minn: West, 2cd ed.), 868.

33. Ian Brownlie, "Humanitarian Intervention," in *Law and Civil War in the Modern World*, 217-218 (1974) printed in Weston, Falk, d'Amato, 886-889.

34. UNHCR, *The State of the World's Refugees: 1997-98* (Oxford: Oxford University Press, 1997), 12.

35. Robert H. Jackson, "International Community beyond the Cold War," in *Beyond Westphalia?:* 79-80.

36. R. J. Vincent, *Human Rights and International Relations* (Cambridge: Cambridge University Press, 1986).

37. Thomas G. Weiss and Cindy Collins, *Humanitarian Challenges and Intervention* (Boulder, Col.: Westview, 1996), 91.

38. "Clinton Voices Anger and Compassion at Serbian Intransigence on Kosovo," *New York Times*, 20 March 1999: 7.

39. Tony Blair, "Doctrine of the International Community," quoted in Adam Roberts, "NATO's 'Humanitarian War' Over Kosovo," *Survival* 41, No. 3, Autumn 1999: 102-123.

40. United States Committee for Refugees, *World Refugee Survey: 1996* (Washington D. C. : Immigration and Refugee Service of America, 1996).

41. *State of the World's Refugees: 2000:* 225.

42. Steven L. Burg & Paul S. Shoup, *The War in Bosnia-Herzegovina: Ethnic Conflict and International Intervention* (London: M. E. Sharpe, 1999), 199.

43. On the Bosnian conflict, see Susan L. Woodward, *Balkan Tragedy: Chaos and Dissolution After the Cold War* (Washington, D.C.: Brookings, 1995); Misha Glenny, *The Fall of Yugoslavia: The Third Balkan Wa*r (London: Penguin, 1996); Laura Silber and Allan Little, *Yugoslavia: Death of a Nation* (London: Penguin, 1997); Richard H. Ullman, ed., *The World and Yugoslavia's Wars* (New York: Council on Foreign Relations, 1996).

44. Weiss & Pasic, 46.

45. Burg & Shoup, 399.

46. UNSC Res. 776 of Sept. 14, 1992.

47. Berg and Shoup, 199.

48. UNSC Res. 757 of May 30, 1992.

49. John Tessitore and Susan Woolfson, eds., *A Global Agenda: Issues Before the 51st General Assembly of the United Nations* (New York: Rowman & Littlefield: 1996), 15-16.

50. Adam Roberts, "Communal Conflict as a Challenge to International Organization," in Alex Danchev and Thomas Halverson, eds., *International Perspectives on the Yugoslav Conflict* (Great Britain: MacMillan, 1996), 199.

51. *State of the World's Refugees: 2000:* 226.

52. S. Alex Cunliffe and Michael Pugh, "The Politicization of UNHCR in the Former Yugoslavia," *Journal of Refugee Studies*, Vol. 10, No. 2, 1997: 144.

53. John Tessitore and Susan Woolfson, eds., *A Global Agenda: Issues Before the 50th General Assembly of the United Nations* (New York: UPA, 1995), 13.

54. Tessitore and Woolfson estimate that up to one-third of all aid was diverted, p. 13. Woodward estimates that up to one-half was diverted, p. 319. Weiss estimates up to one-half of all aid was diverted in 1994. Thomas G. Weiss, *Military-Civilian Interactions: Intervening in Humanitarian Crises* (New York: Rowman & Littlefield, 1999), p. 121. In this sense, the Bosnian conflict was not unlike other complex emergencies, including Biafra and Somalia; in Somalia, up to 80 percent of food aid was stolen. See John J. Stremlau, *The International Politics of the Nigerian Civil War* (Princeton, NJ: PUP, 1977); Enrico Augelli & Craig N. Murphy, "Lessons of Somalia for Future Multilateral Humanitarian Assistance Operations," *Global Governance* 1 (1995), 347.

55. *State of the World's Refugees, 2000:* 211.

56. William J. Durch and James A. Schear, "Faultlines: UN Operations in the Former Yugoslavia," in William J. Durch, ed., *UN Peacekeeping, American Politics, and the Uncivil Wars of the 1990s* (New York: St. Martin's, 1996), 229 and 253.

57. *State of the World's Refugees, 2000: 225.*

58. U.S. Committee for Refugees, *World Refugee Survey: 1994* (Washington D.C.: Immigration and Refugee Services of America, 1994), 121.

59. Cunliffe and Pugh, 137.

60. *State of the World's Refugees: 2000:* 222.

61. Owen, 115.

62. U. S. Committee for Refugees, *World Refugee Survey: 1995* (Washington D.C.: Immigration and Refugee Services of America, 1995), p. 172. By 1994, this figure had been reduced to 196,000 (170,000 in Serbia and 26,000 in Montenegro) and an estimated 100,000 refugees were not officially

registered or receiving assistance. By the end of 1995, the UNHCR was again assisting about 330,000 refugees. *World Refugee Survey: 1996:* 179.

63. *World Refugee Survey, 1995*: 172.

64. Weiss, 117.

65. Durch and Schear, 239.

66. James Gow, "British Perspectives," pp. 87-99 and Oliveir Lepick, "French Perspectives," 76-86 in Dancheve and Halverson.

67. *World Refugee Survey: 1994*: 123.

68. Francoise Hampson, "Law and War," in Dancheve and Halverson, 163.

69. Owen, 196.

70. Woodward, 325.

71. David Rieff, *Slaughterhouse: Bosnia and the Failure of the West* (New York: Touchstone, 1995), 13.

72. "We are living in a world of revolutionary change...Interview with Sadako Ogata," *Refugees*, Vol. 3, No. 120, 2000: 23.

73. Francois Fouinat, Coordinator of the UNHCR Task Force for the former Yugoslavia, quoted in *State of the World's Refugees: 2000*, 220.

74. Berg & Shoup, 400.

75. Myron Weiner, *The Clash of Norms: Dilemmas in Refugee Policies* (Cambridge, Mass.: The Inter-University Committee on International Migration, Dec. 1998). *Working Paper #2* in the Rosemarie Rogers Working Papers Series.

76. See *Journal of Refugee Studies*, "Special Issue: Changing Asylum Policies in Europe," Vol. 13, No. 1, March 2000.

77. Sadako Ogata, "Statement of the United Nations High Commissioner for Refugees to International Meeting on Humanitarian Aid for Victims of the Conflict in the Former Yugoslavia in Geneva, 29 July 1992," available at www.unhcr.ch/refworld/unhcr/hcspeech/29jul1992.

78. *State of the World's Refugees, 2000*: 222.

79. Larry Minear, Jeffrey Clark, Roberta Cohen, Dennis Gallagher, Iain Guest, and Thomas G. Weiss, *Humanitarian Action in the Former Yugoslavia: The UN's Role, 1991-1993*, Occasional Paper No. 18, (Providence, R.I.: Watson Institute, 1994), 23 quoted in Weiss, 115.

80. Jan Willem Honig and Norbert Both, *Srebrenica: Record of a War Crime* (London: Penguin, 1996), 82 and 92-93.

81. Cunliffe and Pugh, 146.

82. Weiss, 115.

83. Jan Willem Honig and Norbert Both, *Srebrenica: Record of War Crime* (London: Penguin, 1996), 92- 93.

84. Res. 819, April 16, 1993.

85. David Rhode, *Endgame: The Betrayal and Fall of Srebrenica: Europe's Worst Massacres Since World War II*, (New York: Farrar, Straus and Giroux, 1997).

86. For a discussion of the legal and strategic concept of "humanitarian war," see Adam Roberts.

87. A chronology of NATO's role can be found in "NATO's role in Kosovo: Historical Overview," available at www.nato.int/Kosovo/history.

88. Official UNHCR statistics give a total of 848,100 ethnic Albanian refugees. *Refugees*, Vol. 3, No. 116, 1999: 11. USCR gives slightly higher figures: 465,000 to Albania, 360,000 to Macedonia, and 70,000 to Montenegro. United States Committee for Refugees, *World Refugee Survey: 2000* (Washington, D.C.: Immigration and Refugee Service, 2000), 289.

89. Fernando del Mundo and Ray Wilkinson, "A Race Against Time," *Refugees*, Vol. 3, No. 116, 1999: 11.

90. *Refugee Reports*, Vol. 19, No. 11, Nov. 1998, cover page. At the same time, the Mother Theresa Society estimated that there were over 300,000 IDPs.

91. UNHCR, "The Kosovo Refugee Crisis – an independent evaluation of UNHCR's emergency preparedness and response," para #70. Available at [www.unhcr.ch/refworld]. Hereafter referred to as *Report on Kosovo*.

92. Sadako Ogata, UNHCR, "Statement to the Humanitarian Issues Working Group of the Peace Implementation Council," Geneva, 20 November 1998, www.unhcr. ch/ refworld/unhcr/hcspeech/981120.htm

93. del Mundo and Wilkinson, 10.

94. *Report on Kosovo*, para. #73.

95. Larry Minear, Ted van Baarda, and Marc Sommers, "NATO and Humanitarian Action in the Kosovo Crisis," *Occasional Paper #36* (Providence, RI: Thomas J. Watson J. Institute for International Studies, 2000), 14-17.

96. Bill Frelick, "Humanitarian Evacuation from Kosovo: A Model for the Future?" *World Refugee Survey: 2000*: 32.

97. *Report on Kosovo*, para #188.

98. Minear, et al., *Kosovo,* 6.

99. del Mundo and Wilkinson, 13.

100. Minear, et al., *Kosovo*, 34-35.

101. Interview with Official of the Norwegian Refugee Council, Oslo, Norway, June 2000.

102. del Mundo and Wilkinson, 13.

103. *Report on Kosovo*, para #48.

104. *Report on Kosovo*, para. #78.

105. *Report on Kosovo*, paras. #173-#176.

106. Minear, et al., *Kosovo*, 57-73.

107. *Report on Kosovo*, para. #40.

108. UNHCR, "Briefing by Mrs. Sadako Ogata, UNHCR, to the Security Council," 5 May 1999, available at www.unhcr.ch/refworld/unhcr/hcspeech/990505.htm.

109. *Report on Kosovo*, para. #58.

110. *Refugee Reports*, Vol. 20, No. 5, May 1999, 3.

111. Nicholas Morris, "Origins of a Crisis," *Refugees*, Vol. 3, No. 116, 1999, p. 19. Morris was the UNHCR Special Envoy in the Balkans in 1993-94 and again in 1998 until April 1999.

112. *Report on Kosovo*, paras. #446-#468. A similar sentiment is express by del Mundo and Wilkinson, p12: "At Blace, for instance, while UNHCR was criticized in some quarters for its alleged timidity, at least one government insisted behind the scenes that the agency tone down its publish statements and even asked for the recall of one of its spokespersons."

113. Frelick, 38.

114. Wolfgang Bosswick, "Development of Asylum Policy in Germany," *Journal of Refugee Studies*, Vol. 13, No. 1, 2000: 49.

115. Joanne Van Selm, "Asylum in the Netherlands: A Hazy Shade of Purple," *Journal of Refugee tudies*, Vol. 13, No. 1, 2000: 77-78.

116. David A. Korn, *Exodus Within Borders* (Washington, D.C.: Brookings Institution Press, 1999), 36.

117. High Commissioner Ogata addressed the Security Council on these dates: 11 March 1993, 28 June 1996, 25 October 1996, 28 April 1997, 21 April 1998, 5 May 1999, 13 January 2000, 10 Nov. 2000. High Commissioner Redd Lubbers addressed the Council on 7 Feb. 2002.

Part: II

Case Studies In Forced Migration

Arne Strand and Petter Bauck

CHAPTER FIVE:

Afghan Refugees: Victims Of Shifting Politics

"How can a small power like Afghanistan, which is like a goat between these lions (Britain and Tsarist Russia), or a grain of wheat between two strong millstones of the grinding mill, stand in the midway of the stones without being ground to dust?" (Abdur Rahman Khan, 1900, II, 280)

A large number of Afghans have now been refugees for more than 23 years. Some have never seen their homeland and some have repeatedly been forced to leave it. Indeed, Afghanistan has moved from being a Cold War proxy for the then two superpowers, via a pawn in a regional power struggle, to its current position as the battle arena for the "War on Terror." The Afghan people have endured repeated rounds of warfare and forced migration, war-related destruction and a lack of development. Afghanistan is by nature a disaster-prone country, and the continued war has increased its vulnerability. Paradoxically, these intermittent conflicts have forced Afghans to become more resilient and adaptive.

The interference of a range of state and non-state actors in Afghan affairs has contributed to the prolongation of the conflict. Humanitarian needs and threats to Afghan forced migrants have frequently been used as a justification for military and political interventions. However, such arguments for international involvement have often been based less on a concern for the Afghan migrants and more on the self-interest of the various states involved in the conflict. Not only have Afghan forced migrants, as elsewhere in the world, been denied their basic human rights. In many cases, due to their vulnerable status in neighboring countries, they have been deliberately used to further external interests.

In Afghanistan, international powers, neighboring states and Mujahideen groups (holy warriors) regarded the refugee population as a resource for continued fighting, either for the liberation of Afghanistan or for furthering their own tribal, ethnic, religious or economic interests. This was the case prior to and during the Soviet invasion when the Mujahideen parties operated from across the Pakistani and Iranian border in the 1990s, with the Taliban recruiting their Talibs[1] among the refugee population in Pakistan and recently with the Coalition forces recruiting commanders among the Afghan Diaspora in Europe and the US. To succeed, such a policy requires that the external powers apply the necessary level of control over the refugees and regulate their ability to express their discontent or to become a political opposition to the at the time preferred Afghan government or opposition. In this process the international humanitarian agencies became important instruments, both to ensure that support was upheld for families of those venturing back to fight or to convince people to remain inside Afghanistan.

In general, political and strategic concerns, largely induced by Cold War rhetoric, overshadowed concerns for the rights and actual needs of the Afghan refugees. As long as Afghanistan remain a hotbed for international and regional forces in their struggle for influence and/or struggle against terror, the Afghan refugees remain a useful tool. A forced repatriation policy might further destabilize Afghanistan and certainly add to the challenges facing the new Afghan Government and the international humanitarian community. The task of assisting the 3.4 million Afghan refugees residing in Pakistan and Iran by late 2003, on top of the assistance needs among the estimated 25 million Afghan populations, is extremely difficult and demanding.[2] The chances of "solving" the largest refugee challenge in the modern world will remain meager if not accompanied by a massive rehabilitation and development effort and by the establishment of a more representative Afghan government. An aggressive and forced repatriation strategy might rather increase the number of internally displaced persons inside Afghanistan, notably in the major cities.

For political and humanitarian players the experiences from Afghanistan over more than 20 years call for a renewed discussion of how international humanitarian laws and conventions are applied. International actors responsible for safeguarding the rights of forced migrants, including the UN agencies, have not fulfilled their mandate towards the Afghans. The international support provided to Afghanistan was neither sufficient nor satisfactory. And that is not only a problem of the past. Indeed, since September 2001, civil rights have been routinely violated, blocked or overlooked by neighboring countries and the international Coalition forces.

Afghanistan's role as a proxy in the Cold War resulted in a partial breakdown of the political and social fabric of Afghan society, and a promotion of armed groups over traditional leaders and structures. The solution to the refugee problem will have to be found while taking this into consideration, and the international community will need to stand by and protect those civil society groups and political parties that now are gradually starting to voice their concerns and advocate for their rights. The international community should listen to the Afghan refugees when they develop their assistance policies and projects. The refugees' experiences are crucial in understanding how to meet future political and humanitarian challenges. Another important consequence is that the humanitarian actors need to shift their assistance strategy and focus from a short-term emergency engagement to a more long-term development approach with greater emphasis on the protection of human rights and civic education. Such a shift would provide Afghans with a better prospect of taking control of their own development. The fact that only a handful of the more than one thousand six hundred NGOs engaged in Afghanistan involve themselves in the promotion of human rights and the advocacy of peace building is an indicator of how low a priority such issues have among humanitarian agencies.

For the major powers, which are today in the forefront of the struggle against terrorism, it might be worth reflecting on their own role in assisting radical Islamic movements in gaining ground in Afghanistan in the aftermath of the 1979 Soviet invasion. The bulk of the financial and material support for the Mujahideen that came from the US and Saudi Arabia was delivered through Pakistan to groups that today are defined as terrorist organizations and a threat to international security.

Afghanistan is a country formed by the "great game" between Tsarist Russia and the British Empire during their expansionist era, and was assigned the role of buffer between the two. As a result Afghans often have their kin on the other side of the border, e.g. the Pashtuns in Pakistan, the Uzbeks in Uzbekistan. Afghanistan has been one of the most important "road crossings" in world history, not least due to its strategic location at the entrance to Central Asia. People have moved continuously from one continent to another, major key trade routes have passed through, major religious movements have settled. And world-renowned conquerors have come and gone, e.g. Ghengis Khan and Alexander the Great. These historical events have had a strong impact on today's Afghanistan.

In modern historical times a balance of power was established in Afghanistan. The Pashtuns, making up about 50 percent of the population, seized power in Kandahar in 1747, and later enforced their rule all over Afghanistan (by the death of king Abdur Rahman, in 1901.[3] They remained in charge of the royal title and the capital Kabul, but allowed a degree of self-rule for the other ethnic groups. The central power in Afghanistan was never strong. With continual internal struggles between the tribes and the various ethnic groups, this induced both neighboring and world powers to try to increase their influence in this barren but strategically important country.[4] Consequently, between 1891 and 1893 the struggle waged by Kabul against the Hazaras residing in the central parts of Afghanistan left thousands of Hazaras refugees, who fled across the border into what is today the Baluchistan province of Pakistan, where they settled. Up to the present, the province has remained an important base for exile Hazara organizations. During the same period Abdur Rahman forced Pashtuns to migrate to the core territories of the other ethnic groups with the aim of strengthening his grip on power Following the 2001-2 war, however, ancestors of these Pashtuns were forced to flee from northern Afghanistan to the south.

A political "earthquake" took place in Afghanistan during and following the 1978 Saur revolution and the 1979 Soviet invasion, and the subsequent Western and Islamic support for the Mujahideen. With weapons and money in hand and with the establishment of armed resistance organizations, often tribal or ethnically based, the previous balance between the ethnic groups in Afghanistan was drastically disrupted. The key role of the Pashtuns was questioned by many of the minority groups as they gained larger organizational and military influence and power.

An additional factor that may play a crucial role in any understanding of the battle of Afghanistan is the long-term and persistently hostile relations between the Afghan government and the state of Pakistan. Disagreement over the border, the so-called "Durrand line" established in 1893 by the

British, resulted in Afghanistan voting against Pakistan becoming a member of UN in 1947. Since that date Afghanistan has annually marked the "Pashtonistan Day" to keep alive their claim to unite all Pashtuns, equally divided between Afghanistan and the Baluchistan and North West Frontier Provinces of Pakistan.[5] It is not without reason that all Pakistani governments since the establishment of the state have viewed it as crucial to have a reasonable influence in power circles in Kabul. This adds to their long lasting conflict with India, since both countries have competed for influence in Kabul.

Political Awakening-
Internal and External Refugees:
A Shift from West to East

In the 1960s a political awakening emerged between the Afghan middle class and the students. The new constitution presented in 1964 opened the way for a revitalization of political life.[6] Political parties and politically affiliated newspapers were established[7] and became a channel for voicing discontent as the king did not fulfill previous promises to allow full political and civil rights. Kabul University became central in the political struggle from the mid 1960s onward.[8] In addition to the more traditionalist and royalist groups, equally large groups of Islamists, the Soviet-supporting communists and the Maoists battled for influence. Within this rather small group of educated Afghans emerged those who later became the leaders of the Afghan resistance, the Mujahideen, and the Soviet-backed Afghan Government. The Maoists lost out as both the other groups saw them as a threat, and those who were not assassinated either left the country or went underground.

The late 1970s were a turbulent time in Asia. In Iran the US-supported regime of the Shah fell in an Islamic revolution (1979), while in Afghanistan a Soviet-backed communist party staged a coup d'etat against President Mohammad Daoud (1978 – Saur revolution). President Daoud had himself overthrown his cousin King Zahir Shah in 1973, and his persecution of Islamic opposition groups caused them to flee to Pakistan and establish a military presence there. The period prior to the Soviet invasion in December

1979 was marked by superpower competition, while Afghanistan tried its best to maintain a degree of neutrality, or a "bi-tarafi" (without sides) position, as President Daoud described it.[9] This failed as the United States shifted its policies in 1972 and withdrew funding for development projects after completion of the Kabul-Herat highway, several irrigation and hydropower projects and the Kandahar airport. [10]A larger Soviet influence was the end result.

By the late 1970s the pro-Soviet camp was in strong opposition to President Daoud as he continued to try to avoid Soviet domination by orientating Afghan foreign relations towards Iran and Saudi Arabia, as an alternative to the US. Meanwhile, the Islamists initiated military insurgency activities from bases in Pakistan. Although regarded as a military failure, not least as they lacked support from within the Afghan population, connections were established in Pakistan with politicians, religious groups and the Army, in particular the Inter Service Intelligence agency (ISI). The official figures for Afghan refugees in Pakistan between 1973 and early 1978 was only 1500,[11] while in Iran at this same period Afghans, being part of an official labor migration scheme (Rubin 1996), numbered as many as 600 000. Afghans who started to flee their homeland after the Saur revolution in 1978 used the networks of these two migrant groups, that were established in the neighboring countries. Likewise the descendants of the Hazaras that fled to Baluchistan as early as 1891-93 established the base for their political and military force. [12]

Exodus: Pakistan A Preferred Partner

The Afghan Government was overthrown in what was termed the Saur revolution in 1978, a coup d'etat that had its base in pro-Soviet circles, including in the army. The aim was to foster a rapid change of the backward Afghan society by introducing several "socialist" slogans, e.g. land reform and means to ensure equality between men and women. More traditionalist forces, in particular in the countryside, were in uproar and mobilized substantial segments of the population for resistance against the "infidels."[13]

As armed opposition to the government increased, Afghans continued to flee to Iran and Pakistan in large numbers, with an estimated 3.2 million going to Pakistan and 2.3 million to Iran.[14] The decision on which country to flee to was influenced by their networks and what was the shortest and safest way to cross a national border. Moreover, their choice between Iran and Pakistan was influenced by their Muslim orientation (Sunni or Shia) and whether they spoke mainly the Pashto or the Dari language. Interestingly, if the number of forced migrants can be taken as an indication, access to humanitarian assistance in the asylum country seems to have played a minor role, as this was only provided on a larger scale in Pakistan. Due to the international tension and Iran's controversial regime under Ayatollah Khomeini, only the United Nations High Commissioner for Refugees (UNHCR) established a presence there. All non-governmental organizations (NGOs) ventured to establish their offices in Pakistan. And, as with the humanitarian community, the military and political actors favored collaborating with the Pakistani General and President Zia-ul-Haq over Ayatollah Khomeini.

During the Cold War period the Soviet invasion of Afghanistan was met with equal opposition in the West and in the Islamic world. While the West feared a Communist expansion towards the Indian Ocean, Islamic countries mobilized for a Holy War (Jihad) against an "infidel" invasion of a Muslim country. Although their justification was different they agreed to support the Afghan Mujahideen forces, and to channel their funding and military supplies through the Pakistani Army and the ISI. An agreement was made between USA and Saudi Arabia for equal funding. Additional assistance was also provided from a number of governmental and private sources favoring various Afghan groups or funding the military activities of Islamic volunteers in the Jihad.

To organize and control both the military and humanitarian assistance to Afghanistan, the Pakistani government decided to approve only seven Afghan parties out of the more than 100 groups that had established offices in Pakistan by the early 1980s.[15] This laid the foundation for a "refugee-warrior" arrangement in Pakistan,[16] as refugees had to register with one of the approved parties to be entitled to refugee assistance from UN agencies or NGOs.[17] While making humanitarian assistance conditional upon membership of one particular military party was a blatant violation of the international refugee conventions, the international community did not challenge the arrangement due to the strong political support that existed for the Afghan cause, overriding humanitarian and refugee legal concerns. This could happen, it seems, mainly because, as Baitenmann (1990) has documented, several NGOs agreed to deliver politically and military oriented assistance from Western intelligence agencies to the Afghan Mujahideen groups.

The extent of Afghan warrior activities can be illustrated by the gender distribution among Afghan refugees in Pakistan and Iran. Whereas in Iran there was a large majority of adult men, exceeding 60 %, the number was 25 % in Pakistan.[18] The Iranian figure was influenced by the high number of male work migrants who joined the refugees in their settlement along the Iranian border. In contrast, Afghan refugees in Pakistan were able to return to Afghanistan for longer periods of time to fight. This arrangement was organized through the various Mujahideen parties, which frequently had all their members living in the same refugee camps or in designated parts of a larger camp. In this way the party apparatus could protect the family of the refugee warrior and ensure that they continued to receive humanitarian support during the absence of the male family members. On the other hand this arrangement gave the particular party leverage over their soldiers as they knew that their families might suffer if they avoided fighting, or if they were tempted to join other Mujahideen groups that made attractive offers to the warriors to shift their loyalty.[19]

The Internal and the External Fronts

Another aspect of the resistance movement in Afghanistan was the distinct difference between the "internal" and the "external" front.[20] The "internal" resistance was established locally in the countryside based on a tribe, an extended family, a specific ethnic group and/or a religious network. An example is one of the main ethnic Pashtun tribes, the Gilzays, the population of the remote Nuristan area and the religious Deobandi Madrassa network. Its base for mobilization was partly religious (against the "infidels"), partly historical (against the intruders and in favor of the previous government). Roy estimates that before the Soviet invasion in December 1979, three-quarters of the country were in a state of rebellion due to unpopular reforms imposed by the People's Democratic Party of Afghanistan (PDPA) government. During the early years of the war against the Soviet invasion, there were several examples of different internal groups that had developed broad co-operation in the southern and eastern parts of the country. One typical example was the coordinated action instigated by a network of Maulawis and Mullahs (religious leaders) to assassinate educated people, especially teachers, because they assumed these were indoctrinated by the new communist ideology.[21] It is, however, worth noting the great differences throughout Afghanistan regarding where and when local resistance was initiated.[22] Likewise, it is important to remember here that the brutality, mass arrests and mass murder committed by successive PDPA governments during this period heightened the desire for revenge of the resistance groups.[23]

The "external" resistance was established in exile and in particular in Pakistan, although the fundamentalist Sunni parties and the Shia parties established offices in Iran as well. The Sunni parties were heavily dependent on Pakistan and in particular the USA and Saudi Arabia as the main suppliers of military and financial resources. Without these resources, the external leaders would hardly been able to sustain their support inside Afghanistan. The internal resistance had to establish close relations with the external organization. For several years internal groups shifted their loyalties from one external party to another, or ensured that members of a clan or a larger family associated themselves with different groups. It is, though, according to Roy, possible to see some trends in the affiliations. The so-called "traditionalist" parties led by Nabi, Galilani and Mujadiddi had their main following in the tribal Pashtun areas in the southern parts of the country. The Shi'ite Hazara population joined the Shi'a parties with headquarters in Quetta in Pakistan and in Iran. In regions where the spoken languages were Turkish and Persian the resistance joined mainly Jamiat-i-Islami.[24] During the entire period of resistance against the Soviet Union, co-operation between internal groups belonging to different external organizations was often seen. The same was true of armed conflicts between the external groups as they competed for influence and a larger share of the external military assistance.

Pakistan the "Kingmaker" and Afghanistan-Base for the "International Islamic Brigades"

This close involvement and supervision of the Afghan resistance was, to a great extent, motivated by Pakistan's wish to be the "kingmaker" in Kabul.

This was to assure that an Afghan regime would not pose a threat to the unity of Pakistan or side with India and thus challenge Pakistan on two fronts. For both Western and Islamic intelligence the use of Pakistan and the Pakistani Army for organizing the Afghan resistance and channeling supplies to the Mujahideen was an effective way to pursue their own foreign policy goals. It was furthermore direct support to and a bolstering of the military apparatus in Pakistan, a perceived pro-Western and Sunni Islamic country in a region where Iran had turned into a radical Shi'ite Islamic state and India maintained strategic relations with the Soviet Union.

For Afghanistan and the Afghans, the outcome of this policy was doubtful and proved, in retrospect, to be very negative. The external resistance leadership thereby established had, in reality, very little standing among the Afghan population. Many disliked their relationship with radical Islamic groups in other parts of the world and the fact that Afghanistan as a result became a training field for an "International Islamic Brigade". As a part of this violent and aggressive continuum, in the mid 1980s the US actively supported the strengthening of extreme Islamic groups in Central Asia, as another counter-measure and a pressure on the Soviet Union. These two strategies led to an increased influx from a number of Muslim countries into Afghanistan of Islamists who later became refugees themselves.[25] They were left with very few options for asylum, and had to remain in Afghanistan, in the Tribal Areas[26] of Pakistan or become "volunteers", engaged in military actions with militant Islamic groups in other countries, e.g. Bosnia and Herzegovina and Chechnya.

Afghanistan Divided

During the early 1980s the Mujahideen groups gradually gained control over the countryside, while the Government maintained its grip on the largest cities and the main roads. Various military campaigns forced new groups of the village population into exile, often following systematic destruction and mining of the irrigation systems. At the same time, quite a large number of Afghans moved towards the larger cities. Here they saw possibilities for higher education, job opportunities for women, fewer war activities and a much more liberal and modern lifestyle. The population of the capital Kabul increased from 0.5 to over 2 million during the 1980s. [27]

Following the UN-brokered Geneva Accord, signed on 15 May 1988, the Soviet Union accepted a full withdrawal from Afghanistan, which was completed by May 1989. However, the Soviet Union, together with the US and the Islamic countries, continued to support their respective clients under a "negative symmetry" agreement.[28] The failure of the Mujahideen to gain complete military control despite massive external assistance can be attributed to their internal differences, which resulted in considerable time and energy being spent on battling each other and allowed the Kabul Government some success in its attempts to forge a national reconciliation consensus. Furthermore, the sharp differences between the external front being funded by the international community and the internal front gaining its support from the population weakened the Afghan resistance movement as a whole. Even the establishment of a Pakistan-based Afghan Interim Government in 1988, with massive external support and pressure, did not improve intra-Mujahideen relationships.

Repatriation

However, neither the Soviet withdrawal in 1989 nor the Mujahideen control over large parts of the countryside led to any massive repatriation to Afghanistan. The collapse of the Soviet Union in December 1991 resulted in the discontinuation of Soviet support for the Kabul Government. This caused the Kabul government to collapse in April 1992, just as the UN was working on a plan for holding a Loya Jirga (national council) and an evacuation of President Naqibullah[29] and his family. Groups within the military, the militia and the Communist party formalized their links with the Mujahideen groups, mainly along ethnic lines. In a swift move Kabul was divided between these groups and the deposed Afghan President had to seek protection with the United Nations.[30] Hectic negotiations among the Pakistan-based Mujahideen parties led to the formation of an Afghan Government, requiring the Presidency to be rotated among the leaders of the major Afghan Sunni parties. The first president was Mujaddedi, and the last president was Rabbani.

A spontaneous repatriation to Afghanistan from Pakistan and Iran occurred immediately after the Mujahideen parties took control of Kabul in 1992. About 1.56 million refugees returned within a short time span. The UN was not prepared for such a massive repatriation, and many of those returning did so without any support. The Mujahideen parties in Pakistan were not pleased with the repatriation movement as they lost their control over the refugee population and their recruits now escaped back into Afghanistan. Among the most vocal opponents of the repatriation movement were the more fundamentalist parties, the Hezbi-e-Islami (Hekmatiar), and Ittehad-e-Islami.

During this period the urban elite, many of whom were affiliated with the PDPA or who had been governmental employees, left Afghanistan. During the years 1991–93 as many as 80,000 Kabulis were registered entering Pakistan, and a large number reportedly also left for India, the former Soviet republics in Central Asia, or to the West. A major battle in Kabul, commencing on 1 January 1994, led to another wave of internal displacement and a new outflow of people from the city.[31] After the Pakistani government closed its border with Afghanistan, the migrants were confined inside the country, with as many as 300,000 internally displaced persons (IDPs) residing for almost a year in tent camps outside the city of Jalalabad. A number of migrants tried to enter Iran, but as the Iranian government closed its border with Afghanistan, many opted for temporary settlement in Herat (NCA 1994).

These events coincided with the expulsion of Afghans from Iran back into Afghanistan, which began in 1994. The forced repatriation was formalized through a tripartite repatriation program that was established between UNHCR and the Afghan and Iranian governments.

Warlords

However, as these events were taking place, a war was waged for control over Kabul. The countryside was carved up between different warlords competing for power and influence while extorting money and goods from travelers. Commanders controlling strategic trading routes were then in a position to generate substantial income to maintain their private armies and expand their areas of influence as external military support subsided. Regional state and non-state actors took advantage of the decreased international interest in and support for Afghanistan following the end of the Cold War. The local warlords increased their pursuit of power due to the growing support they received from the regional actors. This was influenced by different dynamics, for example, internal conflicts such as the one in Tajikistan, regional conflicts such as the long-lasting conflict between India and Pakistan, and illegal financial interests such as those in drug production and trade.[32]

During the 1990s some of the worst violations of human rights occurred in Afghanistan, setting aside the frequent occurrence of military attacks on the civilian population. Abduction at ransom, systematic sexual offences against men and women, kidnapping, random killing and extensive ethnic cleansing were daily occurrences, not least in Kabul where the different Mujahideen and militia groups had divided the city among themselves.[33] These violations, in addition to the fear of forced recruitment by warlords and the general lack of rehabilitation and development activities due to the continuing warfare, initiated a new wave of people fleeing Afghanistan. This time it was largely young men seeking job opportunities in the Middle East and the black labor markets of western countries.

The Taliban

It was in such an environment that the Taliban emerged in Kandahar in the summer of 1994 as a political and military force. They quickly gained control over the Pashtun heartland in the south of the country, hardly encountering any major military opposition. The young Islamic warriors moved swiftly towards the Western city of Herat in September 1995, before capturing Kabul in September 1996. Among the war-weary Afghani population, the Taliban were received as a long awaited alternative to the hated warlords. This is the reason for their swift campaign. But when they gained control over the cities and imposed their rural lifestyle on the urban population, protests started to emerge. Their strict gender segregation, refusal to allow women to hold jobs with the Government, UN and NGOs except where health related, and the closure of most schools for girls enraged both Afghans and international agencies.[34] By late 1999 they controlled as much as 80 % of Afghanistan, but three countries only recognized their government. On the other hand, the ousted Rabbani government (the last of the Mujahideen-based governments established in 1992) retained broad international recognition and occupied Afghanistan's seat at the UN. Among the neighbors only Pakistan supported the Taliban government. Turkmenistan traded with both sides in the conflict, while other neighboring countries, including India and Russia, supported the opposition to the Taliban.

The Taliban drew their supporters from different ranks. Many of the Talibs were recruited from religious schools for refugees in Pakistan ("madrassas"), established during the 1980s by the Mujahideen parties and Pakistani religious groups. However, many of the commanders had fought with Afghan traditionalist parties. From the very beginning the Taliban organization was supported both by Pakistan, through the army, and by Afghan traders. The traders were greatly encouraged by the Taliban disarmament strategy, under which the carrying of guns was banned, and all kinds of weapons were confiscated. Consequently, travel and road transport became safer and cheaper as different commanders no longer demanded "road tax."

There are several instances during the Taliban period, as had also been observed under the Mujahideen, of Pakistani military personnel being actively engaged in Afghanistan.[35] At the same time, their opponents, who became known as the Northern Alliance, received support, training and military advice from Iranian and Indian military forces. Thus, the continued warfare in Afghanistan saw a shift from a Cold War superpower conflict to a regional power struggle. For Pakistan, an alternative force to influence Kabul was urgently needed as during the 1990s the different Afghan commanders further divided Afghanistan and not least as Pakistani strategies for securing political support and trade partnership in Central Asia did not materialize. The Taliban could well have been that force, but there was not one common Pakistani policy during this period. ISI, for example, maintained its contacts with and support for commanders from all parties, including those belonging to the Northern Alliance.

While the Taliban was primarily a Pashtun movement, attempts were made to broaden their ethnic representation and in some cases, as in Hazarajat, they left the governance of the areas to the local Hazara commanders. In a historical perspective the Taliban was just one more conqueror of Afghanistan by force, thereby causing widespread migration. Throughout the last century a range of military campaigns and natural disasters have left Afghans with little choice except to flee for shorter or longer periods of time, as is illustrated to the right.

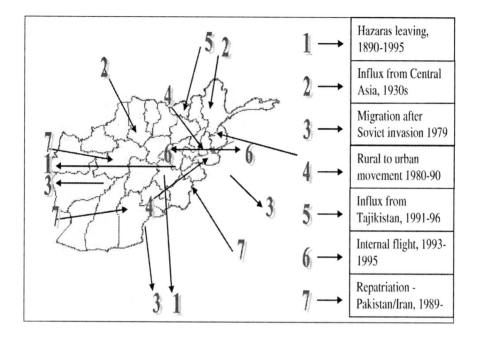

Figure 1: Historical Migration Patterns
Source: Strand, 1999

The Taliban and Terrorism

The issue of the Taliban's housing of terrorists emerged after the attacks on US Embassies in Africa in 1998, which were attributed to Osama Bin-Laden's organization Al Qaida. Ironically, it was not the Taliban that invited Bin-Laden back to Afghanistan in 1995, after he was expelled from Sudan, but elements in the Northern Alliance with whom he resided until Kabul was captured by the Taliban in late 1996.[36] Having been a firm supporter and financier of the Mujahideen parties during the Jihad period, Bin-Laden and his entourage were warmly invited to stay in Afghanistan.

The presence of various Islamic groups defined as terrorist, combined with massive drug production and violations of human rights, particularly the rights of women, caused the UN to impose sanctions on the Taliban regime in late 1999 and to prolong these sanctions in 2000. It should be mentioned that these sanctions hurt mainly the weak and the most discriminated against sections of Afghan society. The UN sanctions came into force despite documentation of increasing humanitarian suffering and protest from the UN Humanitarian Coordinator. [37]

All of this took place during a period where a number of major natural disasters struck Afghanistan, namely, a number of earthquakes and a severe drought that gradually affected larger parts of the country. By 1999, despite continuing military confrontation, a much higher number of people became internally displaced or refugees due to natural disasters than due to war. Male labor migration to Pakistan, Iran and countries in the Middle East increased as well, as people felt forced to seek source of income outside Afghanistan. The Taliban ban on poppy cultivation added to this increase in migration, as it sharply reduced the availability of seasonal labor opportunities. Simultaneously, more Afghans sought the services of professional smugglers to bring them to Europe and the USA, many borrowing as much as 10 000 US dollars from family and friends to pay for their travel. Given the uncertainty about Afghanistan's future, families prioritized the sending of young men to get jobs (often on the black market) and support their families back home in Afghanistan.[38] By the late 1990s there was a shift towards sending boys under the age of eighteen, as these could more easily obtain asylum and later family reunification.[39]

A combination of limited warfare and severe drought caused new migration patterns, as illustrated on the map below, including major internal movements as people sought protection and jobs in larger cities such as Kabul and Herat.

In the Aftermath of September 11, 2001

The September 11 attack greatly affected political, social and economic conditions in Afghanistan. Because Al Qaida was held responsible for the terrorist attack, a military campaign against the Taliban and Afghanistan commenced in October 2001. The international coalition forces created an alliance with the Taliban opposition, using the Northern Alliance as their proxy force, while neighboring countries closed their borders and refused access for Afghans fleeing the military campaign. In addition to the war on terror the international coalition made use of humanitarian arguments for their military engagement, or a "bombs and butter strategy" (a USA definition). The strategy of establishing military supply lines in the North and dropping yellow food packages over large parts of Afghanistan was heavily criticized by humanitarian agencies.[40] According to Leslie and Johnson, arguments asserting the urgency of addressing humanitarian needs in Afghanistan through military means were largely unfounded.[41] A number of Afghans still managed to cross the border, either passing through unguarded border crossings or through the use of bribes or paying smugglers to take them across. It is estimated that the total number of refugees admitted to new UNHCR camps between October 2001 and February 2002 was some 300 000.[42] The quick disintegration of the Taliban regime and the prompt return of their rank and file to their villages helped to make the war a short one. The military operations that followed the collapse of the Taliban regime have all had a rather limited scope and have not led to any major migration movements.

However, again the refugees were mobilized for the fighting as old commanders from the war against the Soviet Union were rearmed and brought back from exile in USA and Europe where most of them were living by September 2001.[43] A flood of weapons and cash was brought into Afghanistan and distributed together with satellite telephones among those expressing willingness to oppose the Taliban. Thus, the end result was the re-establishment of the old commander network in the countryside. The Northern Alliance group secured considerable military and political influence in the Afghan Interim Administration established by December 2001 through the Bonn Agreement. This agreement was heavily influenced by US strategic and political interests and cannot be termed a fully-fledged peace agreement. One important element missing in the agreement was how disarmament of the various military groups should be pursued.[44] However, it provided a direction and a framework for the development of a more peaceful Afghanistan, and defined the role of the United Nations in this process.

After the War:
Internal Migration and Remigration

The establishment of the Afghan Interim Administration (and later the Afghan Transitional Administration) and the commitment made by the international community in early 2002 to support Afghanistan's rehabilitation with 4.5 billion US dollars in aid over a five year period, led to a massive voluntary repatriation from Iran and Pakistan. Repatriation picked up during the spring and summer of 2002, reaching 1.8 million returnees in the year as a whole. Just fewer than 50 % of these returned to Kabul,[45] where they expected to find jobs and protection against violence as the city was guarded by soldiers from the International Security Assistance Force (ISAF).

Fears have, however, been raised within the aid community about a too rapid pace of repatriation and the extent to which it may become an enforced repatriation. A fragile national political environment, the long lasting negative effects of the drought, generally reduced agricultural production and severe environmental damage is given as reasons for Afghans to postpone their return. Added to that could be the limited job opportunities so far generated in Afghanistan, reducing the opportunity to secure a reasonable income. The trend during winter 2002/03 has been towards a gradual movement of Afghans out to neighboring countries as neither the job opportunities in Afghanistan nor the degree of expected assistance have materialized.[46]

An unexpected upsurge of internal migration occurred from 2000 onwards when Pashtuns living in the North were forced to leave their land and property in revenge for past Taliban atrocities. Not allowed into Pakistan, the Pashtun IDPs were moved by the UNHCR from the border to camps in the Zhare Dasht district in Kandahar Province. As the winter approached reports emerged of high death rates and the UNHCR admitted that it had "received considerable criticism for this move".[47] Another group that faced increased problems was the Afghan nomads. Since they belonged to Pashtun tribes they were subject to a similar fate. As a result of the continuing atrocities against the Hazaras, the Pashtun nomads were denied access to their traditional winter pastures in Central Afghanistan and were thereby forced either to move their herds within drought-struck areas or to sell or slaughter their animals.

The new strategy of the US-led coalition forces in early 2003 was to establish militarily protected civilian/military units in selected provinces, termed Provincial Reconstruction Teams (PRT), rather than expand the ISAF beyond Kabul. The aim was to win "the hearts and minds of the Afghans" while engaging these units in rehabilitation activities. But as CARE USA stated in one of its policy briefs, "…military engagement in reconstruction is no substitute for security."[48] A concern raised by several NGOs, for example, the UK-based Christian Aid, is a fear of attacks on humanitarian workers as there is no way to distinguish them from military personnel dressed in civilian gear. This has proved well justified, as by mid April 2003 an ICRC staff member had been executed and there were several reports of armed men searching cars for "foreigners" on the Kandahar-Herat highway. By early 2004 there were still as many as 3.4 million Afghan refugees in Pakistan and Iran, between 0.2 - 0.6 million internally displaced people within Afghanistan, and an unknown number of Afghans living legally and illegally all over the world. With many of these refugees having been away from their homes for more than two decades, one might expect that they would not be inclined to return home in the near future, if ever. Should they decide to move back to Afghanistan, they might, as we have seen during 2002 and 2003, opt to settle in the urban centers rather than the impoverished countryside from which the majority of them initially left.

A contributing factor to this development might be the strategies adopted by the international humanitarian community. It seems that a majority of the UN agencies and NGOs have established themselves in Kabul and major cities in Western, Central and Northern Afghanistan.[49] Not only does this fact deprive the areas to the south and south-east, from where the majority of the refugees originate, of highly needed assistance. Not only does this raise tension between different Afghan groups. It could furthermore be regarded as support for some of those commanders that opposed the ATA.[50] Thus, again, humanitarian assistance plays a highly political role in a very fragile political environment.

It must be assumed that the ability of the international community to assist the ATA in its efforts to initiate rehabilitation and economic development may have a large influence on the willingness of Afghan refugees to return. However, if there is no trust in the stability of the ATA and a continued fear of warfare due to the presence of allied forces hunting remnants of Taliban and Al Qaida, the remaining refugees are not very likely to risk returning to Afghanistan in the near future.

Mechanisms for Coping with the Situation

As documented above, a number of factors caused Afghans, over recent decades, to flee their homes and livelihoods, and to become internally displaced or refugees in neighboring or more distant countries.

There are, however, some particularities that need to be taken into account, and which might make Afghan refugees different from other forced migrants. First, it has been acknowledged that Afghans in exile actually have kept up a very good knowledge of the situation in their home areas. They have been aware of how their relatives and neighbors coped during the different periods of the war. In many instances some members of a family remained back home to look after their property, or land and houses were rented out to fellow villagers who frequently shared the produce with the original owners. This, combined with the men's frequent return to take part in military activities, secured them updated knowledge of the actual situation. And, contrary to common belief, many families maintained contact with family members who had opted to join the pro-Soviet Government or reside in government-controlled areas.

During the late 1980s and early 1990s there were few conflicts over property rights when refugees returned to rural areas, not least because there were traditional conflict resolution mechanisms in place to resolve land disputes. During early 2003 it appeared that the Afghan Transitional Authority was less able to handle property disputes in Kabul. Governmental positions had been distributed between warlords and corruption was on the rise. For a certain amount of money, property was sold and ownership documents prepared, causing conflicts when the original owners returned and confronted those who claimed legal right to their property.

Frequently only the men of the refugee family returned to Afghanistan and restarted cultivation of their land. Or, when a family returned, some male members remained in exile to ensure a certain degree of income for the family. The establishment of such coping mechanisms within the larger family units ensured a continuous flow of remittances that enabled people to survive during the extremely harsh conditions upon their return. Further aid came from other Muslims, who were religiously obliged to share their wealth with the poorest segments of the population. This is termed "Zakat" and is one of the five pillars of Islam, which helped ensure minimum chances of survival for the wider population. This regulation applied to people locally and to Muslims internationally, and many Islamic NGOs received much of their income from Zakat contributions. It should also here be noted that poor Afghan refugees in Iran, predominantly Sunni Muslims, benefited from Zakat contributions from their Shi'a brothers, assisting their survival in the absence of international humanitarian support.[51]

Regional Powers

It should be remembered that a number of important concerns transcend the realm of the family considerations and what are generally perceived as the duties of practicing Muslims, and influence refugees decisions to leave, stay or return. Notably, the attitude and interests of the regional powers played a major role in the politics of Afghanistan. With the emergence of new power brokers in Afghan society, including the development of more radical Islamic movements, it was clear that the refugees were used as a trade-off in the power struggle in and concerning Afghanistan. In the Cold War climate anyone perceived as holding Communist sympathies or even advocating a social democratic system in Afghanistan was seen as a legitimate target for the Islamist groups (the Afghan Mellat party is a case in point). The end result was a more passive political environment, where a number of well-educated Afghans fled from both Afghanistan and Pakistan in fear of persecution and established themselves in the West. Such a trend was repeated from 1990 onwards, as the future of the Kabul Governments started to look bleak and the second wave of educated Afghans arrived in Pakistan. Termed "Zakerbists" after a particular type of missile the Mujahideen fired towards Kabul, the refugees were mistrusted among Afghans residing in Pakistan and although well educated, they were frequently denied jobs in the humanitarian agencies.

While both Iran and Pakistan initially welcomed Afghan refugees with open arms when they arrived from late 1979, there was a significant difference in how they were treated and supported. While staying in Pakistan, the majority of the refugees were confined in camps and supported by international NGOs and UN agencies. In contrast, Iran did not establish a camp structure and refugees were freely allowed to settle after their registration, and allowed the same access to public education, health facilities and subsidized food as Iranians. In Pakistan, the different Afghan parties were set up to administer the refugee camps, and the parties were allowed wide-ranging authority, e.g. to make arrests, to torture and even to carry out assassinations of Afghans suspected of opposing the Afghan parties (and later the Taliban regime). Pakistani police and intelligence agencies used the opportunity to shift Afghan prisoners to the autonomous Tribal Area, where they could be held indefinitely. More liberal elements of the Afghan population or those opposing the Afghan parties were effectively and violently suppressed.

Liberators or Terrorists?

The Pakistani ISI played a central role in channeling external resources to the Mujahideen parties during the 1980s, and then implicitly directed the warrior activities of the refugees. Pakistan openly favored and supported the more radical Islamist groups, over those supportive of more moderate or traditional Islamic values and the re-establishment of the Kingdom. Through prioritizing younger warriors, often technocrats, over traditional leaders to strengthening the military capability of the Mujahideen, Pakistan effectively undermined the tribal structures and such elements of Afghan society as had earlier held large influence both at the local and the national level. In this way Pakistan not only effectively reduced the number of influential Afghans, but also ensured that they became largely dependent on Pakistani support to further their own private ambitions. It is, therefore, not very surprising that, in fear of losing their influence over Afghan refugees, parties led by these people attempted to block the repatriation from Pakistan that took place at the early 1990s.

Ironically, the party most frequently accused of terrorizing, kidnaping and murdering members of the Afghan opposition during the 1980s was Hizb-i Islami led by Hekmatyar, which was also the largest recipient of US assistance during this period. Groups from this party were also hired by US oil companies to protect their installations in Azerbaijan during the early 1990s[52] and the party allegedly continued to receive Pakistani support until Hekmatyar fled to Iran after the Taliban captured Kabul in 1996. Expelled from Iran, by early 2002 Hekmatyar was expressing opposition to what he regarded as a US-imposed Afghan government, and he was later accused of collaboration with the Taliban and Al Qaida in their attacks on Coalition forces. This action lead the US in early 2003 to include Hekmatyar's Hizb-i Islami on their list of terrorist organizations, an act many Afghans consider to have come 20 years too late.

International Organizations and the Role of the Media

The western media was extremely helpful in presenting the Mujahideen leaders chosen by the West and Pakistan as unquestioned heroes, totally neglecting the atrocities they committed against their own people and avoiding exposing the vision they held for how Afghanistan should be governed. As such, the media embraced people that used assassination and torture as their political tools and who advocated a medieval attitude towards women, while demonizing those that promoted more liberal values and worked for greater social justice and equal rights for women. Prominent among those media heroes was Ahmed Shah Masood, termed the "Lion of Pansjir," who was also the one that instigated massive ethnic cleansing of the Hazara minority in Kabul in 1993. [53]

The media hype was part of a larger strategy to ensure that Afghan commanders and parties were presented in a positive light. According to journalists Erwin Knoll and Mary Williams Walsh, the US Embassy in Islamabad had weekly briefing meetings for selected journalists, and a US NGO, the Mercy Fund, deliberately directed western journalists towards commanders who would provide them with "the right information".[54] By using highly inflated figures on war activities and the number of killed Soviet soldiers, a picture was created in the international media of a successful and united Afghan resistance defeating a demoralized Red Army.[55] The result of such strategies was to generate an image of a higher level of war activity and destruction than was actually the case, which in itself could discourage repatriation or motivate people to flee from Afghanistan.

International humanitarian agencies were also instrumental in shaping the political and humanitarian environment for Afghan forced migrants. First, as described above, the international community endorsed and in effect, accepted and supported the "refugee-warrior" system. Secondly, many of the non-governmental organizations that assisted the Afghan refugees were European and US-based solidarity movements that openly stated their aims as combining political advocacy work at home with practical support for a military liberation of Afghanistan. For them, provision of humanitarian assistance could ease the burden on the military organizations and possibly attract Afghans to support the Mujahideen, or allow people to remain in Mujahideen-controlled areas inside Afghanistan and thus take up resistance against the Soviet invaders.

This strategy had, however, two notable downsides. The first was that the majority of these organizations became depended on military commanders to channel their support inside Afghanistan. Most NGOs prioritized one particular party, a specific commander, or a geographical area, while some NGOs tried to divide their support among various groups and areas to avoid supporting one particular ideology or party. But in both cases it often led to the strengthening of the same commanders that the ISI and the Western media promoted, rather than to support and strengthen groups with strong local backing inside Afghanistan. And, furthermore, the high degree of secrecy that shrouded the operations resulted in many NGOs supporting the same commanders. These could then go "aid shopping" in the "relief capital" Peshawar, and later duplicate and distribute their report. The second downside was that the NGOs, as a group, were not regarded as humanitarian and neutral supporters of the Afghans. Rather, they were regarded as political actors promoting particular interests and groups within Afghan society, most notably the most radical Islamist groups. Only a few NGOs chose to support smaller Afghan groups or community organizations, and were then immediately labeled as "communist" supporters, with death threats following against their staff.

How politicized the aid environment was might best be illustrated by two examples. The first was related to a rift within a Western NGO, and the second was the high degree of non-collaboration and active competition that existed between Western and Islamic NGOs operating from Pakistan. In the first example the International Assistance Mission (IAM), whose staff were seconded from various Churches worldwide, had been operating in Afghanistan since the early 1970s, with among other things eye hospitals in different parts of the country in collaboration with the Afghan Ministry of Health. Following the Soviet invasion they came under heavy pressure from some of their member churches and their American donors to leave Kabul and relocate to Pakistan. Arguing against such a move on humanitarian grounds, that people in the various parts of Afghanistan might be in just as high need of assistance as refugees in Pakistan who had the assistance of the entire world community, the IAM decided to remain with its head office in Kabul. The result was that an American part of the organization cut its relationship to IAM and established a separate NGO in Peshawar, "Shelter Now," which immediately received US funding.[56] The CIA and other intelligence agencies also used a number of NGOs as front organizations for the provision of assistance for commanders, and even for intelligence gathering.

As for the second example, both Western and Islamic NGOs regarded each other respectively as either Islamic or Christian indoctrinators who exploited the vulnerable state of the Afghan refugees. The establishment in 1985 of the first NGO coordinating body, the Islamic Coordination Council, was partly to counter what were seen as attempts at Western indoctrination of Afghans through education programs and specific projects targeting women. The best example of the sharp division between these two NGO groups was the establishment of two separate camps for Internally Displaced Persons (IDP) at Hesar Shahi outside Jalalabad in 1994. Only a four meter wide road separated the camp run by UN and Western NGOs and the one run by Islamic NGOs, and the only real difference between them was the mosque in the Islamic camp. Separate systems were established for food and water distribution, and there was no contact or collaboration between the two camp administrations. More energy and funding went into competition and flag hoisting than actually ensuring the best possible assistance for people displaced by the fighting in Kabul.

Dependency Syndrome

A dependency syndrome is another feature of the prolonged refugee exile that Afghans have endured in camps in Pakistan, although a nuanced view is required to avoid the stigmatization of the entire refugee group. Although many Afghans became dependent on regular handouts from the international humanitarian organizations, a large number earned their living through trade and business or casual labor. Indeed, in the North West Frontier Province they almost entirely took over the transport trade during the 1980s. But, until the end of the 1980s, there would be some sort of NGO or UN assistance available in all camps. In Iran, however, all refugees were forced to secure their own livelihood and income. Surveys carried out by NGOs in Afghanistan show clearly that the demand for foreign support differed dramatically according to the degree of previous contact and experience with aid agencies. While discussing possible local contributions towards proposed rehabilitation projects, those who had been refugees in Pakistan, and were used to free aid distribution, most frequently claimed that "they had nothing to contribute". In more remote areas, by contrast, notably Central Afghanistan where most refugees had been in Iran, the population usually enumerated what they had planned to do and asked the external agency whether they had something to contribute in addition.

Conclusion

Based on the above discussion, there are a number of conclusions to be drawn from the Afghan refugee experience:

♦ It is evident that the present day refugee challenge in Afghanistan is closely linked to the history and the particularities of the Afghan society. Without an extensive understanding of these factors, no real understanding of the situation today can be reached.

♦ The response of the international community, including the international organizations, was from the outset of the conflict in Afghanistan guided by their strategic interests as defined by the Cold War. Moreover, the overall response to the refugee problem was influenced by events that took place in the political context of the Cold War. This practice seems to have continued during the "war on terror" and greatly affects the resettlement of the refugees.

♦ Refugees who left Afghanistan since 1978 have been treated in a political rather than a humanitarian context. Severe breaches of international conventions have occurred, and only to a limited extent have the rights of the refugees, according to these conventions, been secured.

♦ During more than 20 years there has been continuing change in reasons why new (and old) groups of refugees feel forced to leave or return to Afghanistan. A single model for explaining Afghan migration trends is therefore not sufficient.

♦ Through the highly politicized support provided for the refugees, the base for continued political and military infighting in Afghanistan has been nourished. Uncritical support of "partners" in the fight against a common enemy has led to the development of new groups that pose a threat to Afghan and international security.

♦ In summary, given the weak governance and administrative structures established in the "new Afghanistan" and the fragile security situation, an immediate forced return of the remaining refugees might actually further destabilize the country. The already long-suffering Afghan refugees may again find themselves victims of the rapidly changing agendas of the international community.

Notes

1. From the Arabic "Talib," meaning student, and often used in connection with the Taliban in Afghanistan, who were referred to as "religious students" because many were recruited from religious schools (from Arabic: "Madrassa") established for Afghans in Pakistan.

2 .There is no accurate figure on the size of the Afghan population; it has been adjusted upwards from an estimated 17 million in the late 1980s to a UN figure of 25 million in 2002.

3. See Louise Dupree, *Afghanistan* (NJ: Princeton, Princeton University Press, 1980.)

4. For example, the British three times tried to gain control of Afghanistan (1839-42, 1863-80, 1919-20).

5. From 1951 till 1989, with the exception of 1987, Afghan stamps to commemorate "Pashtonistan Day" have been issued at the end of August or beginning of September.

6. Nighgat Mehroze Chishti. *Constitutional Development in Afghanistan*, (Karachi: royal Book Company, 1998), 105.

7 . Louise Dupree, *Afghanistan,* 1980.

8. Oliver Roy, *Islam and the Resistance in Afghanistan.* (Cambridge: Cambridge University Press, 1985), 73-74.

9. Louise Dupree 1980, 511.

10. Ludwig W. Adamec, *Historical Dictionary of Afghanistan.* (NJ: Metuchen, Scarecrow Press, 1991), 282.

11. Pierre Centlivres. "A State of the Art Review of Research on Internationally Displaced," Refugees and Returnees from and in Afghanistan, (London: *The Fourth International Research and Advisory Panel Conference on Forced Migration)*, 1993.

12. Hassan Poladi, *The Hazaras.* (Stockton, California, Mughal Publishing Company, 1989), 257.

13. Terms such as "traditionalist" and "fundamentalist" were frequently applied to the different Afghan resistance groups. The first was used to describe followers of more traditional and village-based Islam while the latter were proponents of more radical and universal Islamic ideas.

14. Asger Christensen, *Aiding Afghanistan: The Background and Prospects for Reconstruction in a Fragmented Society.* (Copenhagen, Nordic Institute of Asian Studies, 1995).

15. The approved parties were Hizb-i-Islami (lead by Gulbuddin Hekmatyar), Hizb-i Islami (Mawlawi Younus Khalis), Jam'iyyat-i Islami (Burhanuddin Rabbani), Harakat-il Inqilab-i Islami (Muhammad Nabi Muhammadi), Jabha-yi nejat-i milli (Sebghatullah Mujaddidi), Mahaz-i Islami (Pir Sayyad Ahmad Gaylani) and Ittehad-i Islami (Abul Rasul Sayyaf). (Roy 1985: 128-137).

16. Aristide Zolberg, , Astri Suhrke and Sergio Aguayo, *Escape from Violence: Conflict and the Refugee Crisis in the Developing World.* (New York: Oxford University Press, 1989).

17. Raja, Anwar,. *The Tragedy of Afghanistan: A First Hand Account*, (London, Verso, 1988). 238

18. Centlivres 1993, 14-17.

19. This last observation is based on discussions with refugees and Mujahideen residing in camps close to Peshawar.

20. Roy, 1985, 127-138.

21. When criticised for their random killing, one religious leader from the Ghazni Province is quoted as having replied that "...if they were communists we did a good deed, if they were good Muslims they will anyhow come to heaven."

22. Roy 1985, 102.

23. One Afghan interviewed in April 2003 explained that during this period he had been put on death row for 9 months in the Pul-e-Sharqi jail, just because he had at that time been a classmate of the son of a person seen as being in opposition to the PDPA government.

24. Roy 1985, 110-118.

25. Many of those who survived the war in Afghanistan were, after the fall of the PDPA government in 1992, when they regarded their Islamic mission as completed, refused re-entry to their home country, such as Egypt.

26. The "Tribal Areas" in Pakistan are a limited area along the Afghan-Pakistan border in Pakistan, and are not fully under Pakistani jurisdiction. Their establishment came when the border between Afghanistan and British India was drawn in 1893.

27. Barnett R. Rubin. *Afghanistan: The Forgotten Crisis*, (Country Papers, 1996).

28. Full text of the agreement is available at http://www.forisb.org/afghan_docs/afghanistan_documents.html

29. Naqibullah was the last president under PDPA rule in Kabul, and was ousted when the Mujahideen parties seized power in April 1992.

30. President Naqibullah was killed by Taliban forces who entered the UN compound in Kabul in September 1996.

31. During the period January 1994 to mid 1995 the United Nations estimated that half of the Kabul population of 1.5 million were either internally displaced within the city, or moving back and forth to areas least affected by the war.

32. Some used their former contacts in the Soviet Union to secure continued printing of the Afghan currency, the Afghani, which they then used to pay their supporters.

33 . Amnesty International 1995.

34. In some areas, such as Jagori in Hazarajat, the local population negotiated an agreement with the Taliban to keep the girls' schools open.

35. Ahmed, Rashid. *Taliban: Islam, Oil and the New Great Game in Central Asia*, (London, I.B. Tauris, 2000).

36. It was a plane from the official Afghan airline, Ariana, controlled at that time by people close to Ahmed Shah Masood, that brought Osama Bin-Laden's family from Sudan to Jalalabad, where they were settled.

37. UNCO, 2000.

38. This is based on information from Afghans residing in the UK and in Austria.

39. Many of the youngsters that arrived in Norway were related to central members of various Afghan political and military groups (interview with Afghan Human Rights NGO, Peshawar, 1999).

40. Medicins Sans Frontieres claimed that the US simultaneously dropped yellow cluster bombs.

41. Chris Johnson, and Jolyon Leslie. "Afghans have their Memories: A Reflection on the Recent Experience of Assistance in Afghanistan," *Third World Quarterly,* Vol. 23, No. 5, (2002): 861-874.

42. UNHCR 2002: 9.

43. Dr. Shah Jan, a commander from the Jagatu area of the Ghazni province, related in an interview that he was running a small petrol station in the US when just after 11 September 2001 he was approached by US officials offering him financial and logistical support to re-establish an army of 1000 men.

44. For a broader discussion of the Bonn agreement see Suhrke, A., Strand, A and Harpviken, K.B. (2002) After Bonn: Conflictual Peacebuilding, Third World Quarterly, Vol 23, No 5, p 875-891.

45. UNHCR 2002: 17

46 . David Turton, and Peter Marsden. *Taking Refugees for a Ride? The Politics of Refugee Return to Afghanistan*, (Kabul, AREU, 2002).

47. UNHCR 2002: 9.

48. CARE International, 2003.

49. The number of NGOs registered with the Afghan Ministry of Planning in Kabul had reached over 1600 by November 2003, up from approximately 250 in mid 2001.

50. Arne Strand. *Aid Coordination in Afghanistan*, (Bergen, CMI, 2002).

51. This was documented through Strand's Doctoral research project "Who's Helping Who? NGO Coordination of Humanitarian Assistance," DPhil thesis, University of York

52. This information emerged through interviews with commanders from the Nangarhar province in 1991.

53. Amnesty International 1995.

54. The CIA direction of the media in the Afghan war is discussed in detail in The Progressive, Vol. 54, No 5, May 1990.

55. An Afghan commander commenting on these figures to the author dryly noted that if they had been correct there would not have been any Russians alive in Afghanistan.

56. Information based on interview with former IAM staff member, York, November 2002.

Works Cited

Adamec, Ludwig W. *Historical Dictionary of Afghanistan*, Metuchen, Scarecrow Press, 1991.

Amnesty International, *Afghanistan: International Responsibility for Human Rights Disaster*, London, Amnesty International, 1995.

Anwar, Raja. *The Tragedy of Afghanistan: A First Hand Account*, London, Verso, 1988.

Baitenmann, Helga. "NGOs and the Afghan War: The Politicization of Humanitarian Aid," *Third World Quarterly,* Vol.12, No.1, (1990): 6

CARE International. *A New Year's Resolution to Keep: Secure a Lasting Peace in Afghanistan*, Kabul, CARE International, 2003.

Centlivres, Pierre. *A State of the Art Review of Research on Internally Displaced, Refugees and Returnees from and in Afghanistan*, London, The Fourth International Research and Advisory Panel Conference on Forced Migration, 1993.

Chishti, Nighgat Mehroze. *Constitutional Development in Afghanistan*, Karachi, Royal Book Company, 1998.

Christensen, Asger. *Aiding Afghanistan: The Background and Prospects for Reconstruction in a Fragmented Society*, Copenhagen, Nordic Institute of Asian Studies, 1995.

Dupree, Louise. *Afghanistan*, Princeton, NJ, Princeton University Press, 1980. Johnson, Chris and Jolyon Leslie. "Afghans have their Memories: A Reflection on the Recent Experience of Assistance in Afghanistan," *Third World Quarterly*, Vol. 23, No. 5, (2002): 861-874.

NCA. *NCA Afghanistan Program: Annual Report 1993*, Peshawar, Norwegian Church Aid, 1994.

Poladi, Hassan. *The Hazaras*, Stockton, California, Mughal Publishing Company, 1989.

Rashid, Ahmed. *Taliban: Islam, Oil and the New Great Game in Central Asia*, London, I.B. Tauris, 2000.

Roy, Olivier. *Islam and the Resistance in Afghanistan*, Cambridge, Cambridge University Press, 1985.

Rubin, Barnett R. *Afghanistan: The Forgotten Crisis*, Writenet Country Papers, 1996.

Strand, Arne. *Aid Coordination in Afghanistan*, Bergen, CMI, 2002.

Strand, Arne. *Who's Helping Who? NGO Coordination of Humanitarian Assistance*, DPhil Thesis, York, University of York, 2003.

Suhrke, Astrid, Arne Strand and Kristian Berg Harpviken, "After Bonn: Conflictual Peacebuilding," *Third World Quarterly*, Vol. 23, No.5, (2002): 875-891.

Turton, David and Peter Marsden. *Taking Refugees for a Ride? The Politics of Refugee Return to Afghanistan*, Kabul, AREU, 2002.

UNCO. *Vulnerability and Humanitarian Impact of UN Security Council Sanctions in Afghanistan*, Islamabad, Office of the UN Humanitarian Coordinator for Afghanistan, 2000.

UNHCR. *Return to Afghanistan 2002*, Geneva, UNHCR, 2002.

Zolberg, Aristide, Astri Suhrke and Sergio Aguayo. *Escape from Violence: Conflict and the Refugee Crisis in the Developing World*, New York, Oxford University Press, 1989.

Beth Elise Whitaker

CHAPTER SIX:

Between Victims and Killers: Dilemmas of the International Operation for Rwandan Refugees

In July 1994, television screens around the world were filled with images of Rwandans streaming across the border into eastern Zaire (now the Democratic Republic of Congo) and subsequently dying by the thousands as the result of a cholera outbreak. Dramatic headlines sought to capture the extent of the human misery: "Cholera the New Fear for Pitiful Rwandans,"[1] "Disease Now Stalks Refugees,"[2] "Horror Rises at Way-Stations to Death."[3] The extensive media coverage prompted an outpouring of sympathy in Western countries and growing pressure on governments to take action. Within days, a massive airlift operation was underway to provide clean water, food, and medicine to roughly one million Rwandan refugees.

Based on the media's portrayal, a casual observer could have been forgiven for assuming that the refugees were victims of the genocide in Rwanda that had been the focus of international attention just two months earlier. In fact, quite the opposite was true; among the Rwandans who fled to Zaire were senior government officials and military personnel who had been involved in organizing and perpetrating the genocide. As rebels approached and eventually seized Kigali, elements of that regime blended in with legitimate refugees fleeing the violence. But the media tended to gloss over this fact in their coverage of the crisis, generally portraying the refugees as victims of an ethnic (or "tribal") war for which no further explanation was needed. In their effort to raise funds for the relief operation, international aid agencies similarly focused on the extent of the suffering rather than the composition of the refugee population.

Attempts to downplay the presence of killers in the camps were perhaps understandable given the precarious nature of funding for relief operations. The international refugee regime,[4] which depends almost exclusively on voluntary contributions from individual states and private donors, is premised on the assumption that refugees are victims. In order to raise the funds necessary for its field operations, the Office of the United Nations High Commissioner for Refugees (UNHCR) must appeal to the humanitarian sympathies of policymakers and their constituents in donor countries. That is difficult even when the refugees in question are clear victims of violence; it becomes still more complicated when the refugee population includes elements that have participated in the violence. Thus, there are obvious incentives for aid agencies to publicly downplay refugees' involvement in conflict. At the same time, however, the agencies are generally very aware of the ethical dilemmas involved in assisting such populations.

In central Africa, the international community encountered a situation in which killers were intermingled with the refugee population and militia were organizing for a return to Rwanda by force. This fact had implications for relief efforts throughout the period of the refugee operation. Although the presence of "refugee warriors" is certainly not new,[5] the Rwandan crisis provides a useful example through which to explore the dilemmas faced by international relief organizations in such cases. After presenting an overview of the Rwandan crisis, this chapter examines the difficult decisions that aid agencies were forced to make in the initial stages of the refugee operation, then again as the situation lingered from months to years, and eventually during the complicated and chaotic repatriation to Rwanda.[6] In the end, it becomes clear that the international community has yet to develop a coherent strategy for dealing with such refugee populations. As a result, UNHCR and other aid organizations will likely continue to find themselves caught between assisting victims and abetting killers.

The Crisis In Rwanda

The immediate story leading up to the refugee crisis began in 1990, when a well-organized group of Rwandan exiles whose families had been living in Uganda since the 1960s launched an attack into northern Rwanda.[7] A movement had been growing in the 1980s within the Rwandan exile community advocating a massive and imminent return to their home country.[8] This sentiment was strengthened after 1986, when Rwandans who helped Yoweri Museveni come to power in Uganda soon realized that they were not going to find a permanent home there. The invasion of exiles into Rwanda in October 1990 sparked a civil war between the Tutsi-led Rwandan Patriotic Front (RPF), as this group was known, and the Hutu-dominated government under President Juvenal Habyarimana. Very quickly, Rwandan politics once again became polarized along ethnic lines. Government forces targeted Tutsi within the country as alleged RPF sympathizers and a climate of violence and insecurity prevailed.

In October 1993, an agreement was reached in Arusha, Tanzania, between the Rwandan government and the RPF. The accords called for a transitional government in which the two sides would share power, along with other opposition parties, and the integration of their armies. Implementation of the agreement was stalled, however, due mainly to resistance among Hutu extremists who believed the government had conceded too much. In April 1994, Habyarimana traveled to a regional meeting where he finally bowed to international pressure to speed up the implementation process. As he was returning home on April 6, his plane was shot down near the Kigali airport, killing everyone on board. Although the government blamed the incident on RPF forces, most people believed that Habyarimana's own presidential guard shot down the plane under pressure from hardliners who opposed the power-sharing agreement.

Within hours, a massive campaign of calculated terror began in the capital. The violence was politically motivated, but given the nature of identity politics in Rwanda, it took on an ethnic dimension. Hard-line Hutu who opposed the power-sharing agreement targeted prominent Tutsi and moderate Hutu who supported its implementation. Extremists soon projected the violence to the countryside, using media messages and terror to coerce Hutu farmers to attack their Tutsi neighbors. What followed in the coming months was a shocking genocide in which nearly 800,000 Tutsi and moderate

Hutu were killed.[9] Suddenly, this little-known central African country was on the front pages of newspapers and magazines around the world.

Although some Tutsi fled Rwanda in early April 1994, the massive refugee exodus did not begin for several weeks. Ironically, when it did, it was Hutu rather than Tutsi who fled; they feared reprisals by advancing RPF forces. In late April and May, as the RPF moved south, more than 400,000 Rwandans crossed the border into western Tanzania. Those numbers were soon dwarfed, however, by the arrival in mid-July of more than one million refugees in Goma, Zaire. The civil war ended in late July when the RPF seized power in Kigali, but the exodus of refugees continued. Included among them were government officials and troops from the defeated regime. By the end of 1994, up to two million Rwandans were internally displaced and nearly two million others had fled to neighboring countries.

In response to the refugee crisis, various UN bodies and international aid agencies flocked to western Tanzania and eastern Zaire, where they launched massive relief operations. The extent of the response in Goma was particularly overwhelming, due largely to extensive media coverage; roughly 100 NGOs set up operations there, including multiple national chapters of several international organizations. The agencies established systems to provide food, water, health care, and other services to the sprawling refugee camps. Between April and December 1994, international donors allocated nearly $1 billion to the Rwandan refugee crisis.[10] Once beyond the emergency stage, according to UNHCR sources, the regional refugee operation continued to cost the international community approximately $1 million per day.

From the beginning, officials of the defeated Rwandan regime took charge of the camps and established systems favorable to their authority. They controlled the distribution of food and relief resources, allowing them to reward loyalty and punish dissent. They convinced civilian refugees to fear repatriation, recruited from the camps to rebuild their army, and taxed relief supplies to finance its mobilization.[11] The situation was worse in Zaire than Tanzania, largely due to the presence of senior leaders from the former Rwandan government.[12] In addition, aid agencies in Tanzania were more successful at conducting elections for new refugee leaders and thus breaking the militants' hold on power. In both contexts, though, it was clear that the refugees were preparing for an eventual return to Rwanda by force.

As a result of these dynamics, the international community was effectively supporting massive refugee camps run by elements of a defeated genocidal regime who were transforming those camps into bases from which to re-start the war. Few would deny this portrayal, and many have criticized UNHCR for its role in furthering the political and military objectives of Hutu extremists. But the point here is that representatives of UNHCR and other organizations were not ignorant of the situation. They were fully aware that their resources were being used for less than humanitarian purposes, and thus consistently faced dilemmas about their operations. Aid workers were forced to make difficult decisions about the approach they would take to refugee assistance, the relative importance of separating civilian refugees from killers, and the role they should play in the eventual repatriation. Each of these dilemmas is examined in the following sections. While individual agencies and employees responded to the dilemmas in different ways, it seems clear that they did so only after great deliberation, caught as it were between their desire to do good and their hope not to cause greater suffering.

The Approach To Refugee Assistance

In the early days of the Rwandan refugee crisis, UNHCR and host governments favored immediate repatriation. They anticipated that such a large refugee population would be difficult to sustain for any significant length of time. The emphasis was therefore on making the refugee situation as temporary as possible. In both Zaire and Tanzania, refugees were settled in densely populated camps just miles from the Rwandan border. In Tanzania in particular, unlike previous influxes, refugees were allocated tiny plots of land and agriculture was officially discouraged. Strict rules were placed on the movement of refugees beyond their camps. While authorities were aware of the obvious security risks, they hoped that this close proximity to home and the difficulty of life in the camps would tempt the refugees to repatriate spontaneously.

The magnitude of the influx certainly influenced this approach to refugee settlement, but the guilt of some refugees was also a factor. Vincent Parker, a UNHCR spokesperson in Tanzania, explained: "The Rwandans who came in 1994 were perceived as murderers, so the [Tanzanian] government wanted to limit their movement and try to get rid of them as soon as possible. The international community also had this view."[13] In Zaire, in September 1994, the minister of justice vowed to disarm the Rwandan militia in order to facilitate repatriation by the end of that month.[14] Despite hopes for a quick repatriation, however, aid workers and government officials soon settled in for a longer operation than originally expected.

As it became clear that the camps had been taken over by Hutu extremists, many agencies started to have doubts about their involvement in the relief effort. Aid workers worried that relief resources were making the situation worse rather than better by sustaining the former Rwandan government and its military. Continued protection of these groups by the international community was allowing them to mobilize for an attack back into Rwanda, a possibility that threatened the security of the new RPF regime in Kigali. This dangerous combination increased the likelihood of further conflict, which could only worsen human suffering in the region.

Faced with this realization, in late 1994, two organizations—Médicins Sans Frontières (MSF)-France and the International Rescue Committee (IRC)—decided to withdraw from the Rwandan camps in Zaire. In a recent book, Fiona Terry, director of research for MSF and an employee in the region in 1994, defends her organization's decision.[15] She argues that aid agencies should give more consideration to the option of pulling out, and is critical of the logic of institutional preservation that compels agencies to continue their operations regardless of the implications. She holds the organizations that stayed in the camps responsible for sustaining the genocidal regime, thus contributing to the subsequent Rwandan attack and war in Congo (discussed below). Of course, because these agencies stepped in to fill the void left by MSF-France and IRC, the decision to withdraw had little effect on the actual relief operation.

Although confronting a similar dilemma, most other aid agencies chose to continue their operations in the Rwandan camps.[16] To many, the option of not assisting innocent civilians was worse than that of providing assistance that indirectly fueled a war effort. No one knew exactly how many *génocidaires* were among the refugees, but estimates suggested they represented about 10 percent of the camp population.[17] The majority of the refugees consisted of men, women, and children who were under the influence of the militant few but were not themselves guilty of genocide. In such cases, Gerald Martone argues, the withdrawal of relief services is a "cruel and uncreative way" to protest human rights violations.[18] He accuses those who withdrew from the Rwandan camps of violating key humanitarian principles:

By withholding or even withdrawing life-sustaining assistance to refugees of Hutu ethnicity on the basis of an untested generalization of culpability in the Rwandan genocide, were humanitarian agencies being partial? Without a trial, a verdict had been rendered on the basis of ethnicity. Is this not precisely the sort of prejudice and ethnic generalization that had caused the conflict in the first place?[19]

Martone proposes instead that aid agencies develop innovative ways to prevent the diversion of aid resources to military causes, an effort that was not always successful in the Rwandan case. Even when their organizations chose to stay, individual aid workers often faced personal dilemmas about assisting a refugee population that included suspected *génocidaires*. In 1995, after a refugee registration process in Tanzania, the head of the World Food Programme office there asked a volunteer, "So how does it feel to feed a bunch of killers?" Most people dealt with this dilemma by assuming innocence until proven otherwise, which was an effective way to avoid the moral quandary since few *génocidaires* in the camps were brought to justice. After employing this approach for two years, the director of a British NGO was devastated to learn that a senior refugee employee had admitted involvement in the genocide. Over time, even when they tried to avoid the issue, aid workers could not help but wonder which refugees were guilty. As a senior Tanzanian official explained, "suspects of genocide were there in the camps, [but] as time went on, they were all seen as killers."[20]

In the early stages of the Rwandan operation, therefore, the perceived guilt of people among the refugee population affected the nature of settlement and the focus of the relief operation. Aid agencies and individual employees were forced to make a difficult choice: "Should they cease their humanitarian work and put at risk the lives of innocent refugees, or accept the fact that they must hand over millions of dollars in supplies to the perpetrators of Rwanda's recent holocaust, who hope to use the camps as headquarters for rekindling a bloody civil war?"[21] While most opted to continue their operations in the camps, they did so with the knowledge that relief resources were being diverted to other causes. The international refugee regime is thus open to criticism for its role in fueling a war effort, but the difficulty of the choice faced by decision-makers at the time should not be underestimated.

Focusing on the "Intimidators"

As time went on, Rwandan refugees in Zaire and Tanzania started building more durable dwellings, developing small businesses, and planting little gardens; it was clear that few were planning to return home any time soon. Host governments and relief agencies thus started to suggest new policies designed to facilitate the repatriation process. By early 1995, Tanzanian officials were championing the idea of "safe zones" within Rwanda where civilian populations would be assisted and protected under the same UN organs as the external refugee camps.[22] The idea was based on the establishment in the early 1990s of similar safe areas for Kurds in northern Iraq, essentially to protect Turkey from a massive refugee influx. At regional summits in January and February 1995, leaders of Kenya, Burundi, Rwanda, Tanzania, Uganda, Zambia, and Zaire agreed to support the establishment of safe corridors from refugee camps to the border and of safe zones within Rwanda. Despite its popularity among regional leaders, the idea never gained much support in the broader international community.[23]

In addition to the safe zones proposal, host governments started actively promoting the principle advocated by the new Rwandan government that suspected perpetrators of genocide and intimidators within the camps should be separated from "innocent refugees."[24] There was significant support for this idea among aid workers in the camps. As long as militant elements were in control, they reasoned, ordinary refugees would be prevented from returning to Rwanda on their own. Although extremists' control of camps in Zaire was seen as particularly strong, intimidation was also a factor in Tanzania. On several occasions, officials there reported, individual Rwandan families who registered with UNHCR for voluntary repatriation found their homes destroyed and belongings looted before they could leave the camps.

As the situation persisted, according to UNHCR representative Henrik Nordentoft, relief agencies became "increasingly convinced that people were holding refugees hostage through intimidation and forcing them to stay."[25] Indeed, the perception of the refugees as hostages was widespread. It is not entirely clear, however, the extent to which physical intimidation and violence were necessary to prevent the refugees from returning home; persuasion and cajoling (some might say brainwashing) may have been just as effective. Informal discussions with Rwandan refugees over a period of several years revealed that many truly believed—rightly or wrongly—they would be killed upon returning to Rwanda. Whether this mindset was the result of militants' public relations strategies or well-founded fears based on the experience of civil war is difficult to know. In any case, throughout 1995, regional governments and relief agencies increasingly focused on the importance of separating the intimidators from the refugees in order to facilitate repatriation.

While the principle of separation was widely accepted, international support to make it happen was not forthcoming. It was clear that international relief agencies did not have the capacity or the enforcement power to identify and arrest war criminals in the camps. As one UNHCR protection officer explained, "We couldn't do it. It was too hard to distinguish the innocent from the *génocidaires*."[26] Nor were host country police and military units equipped to capture killers in the camps, especially those that enjoyed protection from civilian followers. In September 1994, the arrest by Tanzanian police of an official from the former Rwandan government led to three days of violent protests in the camps. Several months later, attempts by Tanzanian officials to arrest a European man accused of genocide were repeatedly thwarted as refugees rioted and protected the suspect.

Officials in Zaire repeatedly pledged their commitment to separating intimidators, but in actuality did nothing to facilitate it. This was the result of a split within the Zairian government. Although ordered by the prime minister and minister of justice to disarm refugee warriors, the army answered only to President Mobutu, who was less interested in such a strategy.[27] In fact, as an ally of the former Rwandan regime, Mobutu gave suspected *génocidaires* freedom of movement rather than arresting them and allowed militia to mobilize and train near the camps. He permitted and even facilitated the procurement of weapons for these groups, despite an international arms embargo, and played a crucial role in the establishment of a Rwandan government-in-exile on Zairian territory.[28] In August 1995, Zaire suddenly expelled 15,000 Rwandan refugees (but did not specifically target militant groups) and demanded the others leave by the end of the year. Despite continued rhetoric about the importance of separation and repatriation, Mobutu had a somewhat different approach.

In November 1995, another meeting of regional leaders was held in Cairo to establish clear plans for repatriation. Facilitated by former U.S. President Jimmy Carter and South African Bishop Desmond Tutu, the summit ended with an agreement to facilitate the safe and voluntary repatriation of all Rwandan refugees at a rate of roughly 10,000 per day.[29] Yet again, Zairian and Tanzanian delegates agreed to disarm and remove *génocidaires* and intimidators from the camps. But still, separation did not happen and massive repatriation did not begin. In early 1996, more than half a million Rwandan refugees remained in western Tanzania and more than one million continued to live in eastern Zaire.

According to senior UNHCR officials, a primary reason for the failure of repatriation efforts was the lack of international support to separate intimidators and former soldiers from refugees in the camps.[30] The international community continued to seek a diplomatic solution through which they could avoid having to deploy peacekeepers or other armed units to central Africa. In the absence of such support, and lacking their own capacity, relief agencies and host governments had to settle on information campaigns and cross-border exchanges to encourage massive repatriation. Such efforts had little effect. Even though international attention was focused on the guilt of some people among the refugee population, therefore, the lack of will among key actors prevented anything from being done.

The Approach To Repatriation

Throughout 1996, as the Zairian government repeatedly threatened to close camps within its borders, international negotiations continued to seek a resolution to the Rwandan refugee crisis. In the middle of the year, key donors hinted that they would no longer be willing to support the refugee operation, thus intensifying the diplomatic push for repatriation. In October 1996, at a meeting of UNHCR's executive committee in Geneva, regional and UN representatives agreed that there would be all-out measures to promote voluntary repatriation and that refugees would be informed about the climate of donor fatigue. But diplomatic discussions about repatriation were soon to be rendered irrelevant by events in the region.

On October 9, 1996, armed men attacked a hospital in eastern Zaire where Rwandan refugees were being treated. At first, the incident appeared to be a local uprising, but it later emerged that the Rwandan government and its Ugandan allies were backing the rebels. In subsequent days and weeks, rebels systematically attacked the network of refugee camps along Zaire's eastern border. Hundreds of thousands of refugees fled, and aid agencies evacuated their staff from the area. Many refugees congregated in Mugunga camp, west of Goma, where their fate was unknown for several weeks. Finally, on

November 15, rebels stormed Mugunga and sent the refugees running. Within days, roughly 600,000 refugees returned to Rwanda. Another 300,000, many of them suspected *génocidaires*, headed west into the forests of central Zaire, where many were subsequently massacred by advancing rebel and Rwandan troops. Others reached the Republic of Congo, Angola, and Zambia, where new refugee sites were established.[31]

As events unfolded in eastern Zaire, aid workers in Tanzania watched closely. Refugees in the camps were glued to their radios, listening for news on the fate of their compatriots. To many Tanzanian officials, the repatriation from eastern Zaire represented a timely opportunity for Rwandans in Tanzania also to return home. While President Mkapa reiterated his government's commitment to voluntary repatriation, local authorities set about to convince refugees it was time to leave. Then, on November 21, 1996, an envoy from Rwanda met with the Tanzanian president. Although no details about the meeting were released, the significance of the encounter became clear through subsequent events. Rwandan authorities viewed the refugee camps as a threat to their security, and thus had acted to disband the camps in eastern Zaire. They were prepared for the refugees to return from Tanzania, even without the separation of intimidators, and assured Mkapa that the refugees would be protected. In light of this exchange, Tanzanian officials saw conditions as ripe for repatriation.

On December 2, 1996, UNHCR and the Tanzanian government issued a joint statement requiring all Rwandan refugees to leave the country by the end of the month. The order also suspended economic interaction, travel, and agriculture in and around the camps. Within days of the announcement, refugees started fleeing eastwards, refusing to return to Rwanda. In response, the Tanzanian military moved into the region and pushed half a million refugees along the road for anywhere from twenty to 220 kilometers until they crossed the border into Rwanda. By December 28, the repatriation operation was officially finished. Through military aggression and strong-arm diplomacy, therefore, the Rwandan government had managed to achieve in just two months what the international community had failed to accomplish in two and a half years: disbanding the militarized camps along its borders and repatriating most of the refugees.

Just like earlier periods during the relief operation, aid agencies were again obliged to make difficult choices during the repatriation process. They had perhaps less of a dilemma in Zaire, where the military nature of the situation forced most to simply evacuate. In Tanzania, on the other hand, aid agencies faced a tough decision: they could participate in what amounted to a forced repatriation or they could refuse to participate and risk their other activities in the country. For a variety of reasons, some related to the perceived guilt of the refugee population, most chose to assist as the refugees were marched down the road to Rwanda.

In the case of UNHCR, the agency both issued the joint statement with the Tanzanian government and provided financial and logistical assistance for the operation. It gave the Ministry of Home Affairs more than $1.5 million toward related equipment and personnel expenses. UNHCR also provided trucks to transport refugees and established way stations along the roads at which high energy biscuits and water were distributed. Although the agency's support was reportedly based on government assurances that force would not be used, UNHCR continued to provide these and other forms of assistance even after it became clear that the military was involved (and largely in control).

Even while UNHCR as an organization facilitated the repatriation exercise, individual field staff continued to be strong voices for refugee protection. Several UNHCR expatriate employees were ordered off the road during the repatriation for challenging the army's conduct, and at least one was expelled from the country altogether. "UNHCR was split," Tanzanian refugee scholar Bonaventure Rutinwa argued. "The decision was approved by Geneva but the field staff were still following the rule book."[32] In the long run, the official UNHCR position seemed to be to support the massive return of refugees to Rwanda while questioning, if not fully criticizing, the use of the military.

To some extent, UNHCR's support for the repatriation exercise was influenced by the increasing difficulty it faced raising funds for the Rwandan relief operation. Its two primary donors—the United States and the European Union—were hesitant to pump more money into the refugee camps. With the exception of France, a close ally of the former Rwandan regime,[33] Western governments largely accepted the argument that peace and stability had been restored to Rwanda, and thus that the refugees should return home. This view was pushed strongly by the RPF government, which was embarrassed that refugees were not repatriating voluntarily. Donors argued that aid funds would be better spent on reconstruction efforts within Rwanda, and were swayed in part by the underlying assumption that the refugees had blood on their hands. Because they supported the goals of the repatriation exercise, therefore, the U.S. and other Western powers remained silent about the involuntary nature of the process.

Other relief agencies also opted to participate in the repatriation operation. Privately, aid workers expressed concern about possible human rights violations, but publicly their organizations said little. Most of the agencies that were active in western Tanzania also had projects in other areas of the country for which they needed to maintain good relations with the government. In addition, at the international headquarters level, many international organizations were split on the issue of repatriation. While staff in Tanzania expressed concern about the operation, staff members in Rwanda supported the move and wondered why the refugees had not been forced to return home sooner.[34] Given these pulls and pushes, international NGOs seemingly decided that silent cooperation was the best approach.

In contrast to the complicity of relief organizations, human rights groups condemned the repatriation operation, attacking the government and especially UNHCR for its role. Amnesty International strongly criticized the process in both Zaire and Tanzania, arguing that it reflected "a shocking disregard for the rights, dignity and safety of refugees."[35] Human Rights Watch accused UNHCR of having "shamefully abandoned its responsibility to protect refugees," and derided others for their tacit approval: "The international community has barely disguised its satisfaction at seeing the refugee camps around Rwanda forcibly disbanded."[36] Human rights activists were thus quite critical of the repatriation process, though their influence on regional policymakers was limited.

During the repatriation from Zaire and Tanzania, therefore, international groups were faced with a dilemma about how to handle the situation. Because some refugees were accused of participating in the 1994 genocide, aid workers, government officials, and even the media seemed to have a different attitude toward the population as a whole. There was little sympathy for the Rwandans and general frustration with their continued presence in camps, where they were seen as hiding from justice. This issue of guilt may help explain the relative silence about the forced repatriation. In fact, Amnesty International, one of the few organizations to publicly criticize, was seen by some as siding with the *génocidaires*. Thus, the same agencies that earlier opted to continue assisting the Rwandan refugee camps, despite the intermingling of victims and killers, subsequently chose not to protest when those refugees were forcibly sent home.

Conclusion

Throughout the Rwandan refugee crisis in the mid-1990s, the international refugee regime faced a series of dilemmas. At the root of each was the fact that the refugee population included both victims and killers. For a regime that is premised upon the idea that refugees are inherently victims, the possibility that relief assistance could be used to protect killers and even fuel further violence created a difficult moral quandary. In the early stages of the operation, many aid agencies debated their role, and some even chose to withdraw rather than see their resources support military causes. As time went on, consensus developed around the need to separate killers and intimidators from ordinary refugees, but the will was lacking among key international actors to make this idea a reality. Eventually, when the Rwandan government took matters into its own hands, international groups had to determine whether to participate in a forced repatriation operation. Recognizing that there was little sympathy for this particular refugee population, most participated willingly and moved on to other emergencies.

Perhaps more than anything else, the Rwandan crisis demonstrated that the international community has yet to develop a coherent strategy for dealing with "mixed" refugee populations—i.e., those that include both victims and killers. For most relief organizations (but not all), the idea of denying assistance to these populations is not a desirable option. Such an approach is seen as punishing real refugees and is not guaranteed of resolving the problem or preventing further violence. At the same time, however, it seems unrealistic for aid agencies to assist mixed refugee populations just as they would any other. This is essentially what happened in the Rwandan case, with tragic consequences for the region as a whole.

In order to deal more effectively with such refugee populations, therefore, alternative strategies must be developed that openly recognize the political implications of assistance and the possible consequences for aid agencies. Approaches should be tailored to each specific context, with an understanding of the historical roots of the conflict informing the relief plan. Ultimately, though, the ability of the refugee regime to deal with mixed populations will be determined by the will of the international community. If UNHCR and host governments are provided with the resources and support necessary to identify and apprehend war criminals and militants within the camps, these elements can be removed and relief efforts focused on the remaining refugee population. This may require the commitment of international peacekeepers or specially trained police units. If such assistance is not forthcoming, however, aid workers will continue to face difficult dilemmas as they struggle to assist legitimate refugees without inadvertently furthering the political and military objectives of killers within their midst.

Notes

1. *Toronto Star*, "Cholera the New Fear for Pitiful Rwandans," 21 July 1994, A16, final edition.

2. Glenn Burkins, "Disease Now Stalks Refugees," *Philadelphia Inquirer*, 21 July 1994, A1.

3. Chris Mcgreal, "Horror Rises at Way-Stations to Death," *The Guardian (London)*, 23 July 1994, 13.

4. This term refers collectively to the various intergovernmental, international, and national organizations involved in refugee aid and protection around the world.

5. Aristide R. Zolberg, Astri Suhrke, and Sergio Aguayo, *Escape from Violence: Conflict and the Refugee Crisis in the Developing World* (New York: Oxford University Press, 1989).

6. The international community also faced considerable debate over the question of whether to intervene in the Rwandan genocide itself. That issue has been the subject of a large body of literature but is not the focus here.

7. The more important historical background is covered extensively by other authors, including René Lemarchand, *Rwanda and Burundi* (London: Pall Mall Press, 1970), Filip Reyntjens, *Pouvoir et droit au Rwanda: Droit public et évolution politique, 1916-1973* (Tervuren: Musée Royal de l'Afrique

Centrale, 1985), Catharine Newbury, *The Cohesion of Oppression: Clientship and Ethnicity in Rwanda, 1860-1960* (New York: Columbia University Press, 1988), and Gérard Prunier, *The Rwanda Crisis: History of a Genocide* (New York: Columbia University Press, 1995), among others.

8 .C.P. Gasarasi, "The Mass Naturalization and Further Integration of Rwanda's Refugees in Tanzania: Process, Problems, and Prospects," *Journal of Refugee Studies* 3, no. 2 (1990).

9. The most complete account of the Rwandan genocide is found in Alison Des Forges, *Leave None to Tell the Story: Genocide in Rwanda* (New York: Human Rights Watch, 1999).

10. Joint Evaluation of Emergency Assistance to Rwanda, *The International Response to Conflict and Genocide: Lessons from the Rwanda Experience* (Copenhagen: Steering Committee of the Joint Evaluation of Emergency Assistance to Rwanda, 1996).

11. Howard Adelman, "Chaos in the Camps," *Bulletin of the Atomic Scientists* 58, no. 6 (2002).

12. Informal discussions revealed that the refugees in Tanzania tended to await signals from "our leaders" in Zaire.

13. Personal interview with author, 21 October 1997.

14. Thalia Griffiths, "Zaire urges Rwanda refugees to go home by end of the month," *Independent* (London), 2 September 1994, 12.

15. Fiona Terry, *Condemned to Repeat? The paradox of humanitarian action* (Ithaca: Cornell University Press, 2002).

16. MSF-Spain opted to pull out of the Rwandan camps in Tanzania in early 1995.

17. Adelman, "Chaos in the camps"; Augustine Mahiga, "The United Nations High Commissioner for Refugees' Humanitarian Response to the Rwanda Emergency," Paper presented at the International Workshop on the Refugee Crisis in the Great Lakes Region, Arusha, Tanzania, August 16-19, 1995.

18. Gerald Martone, "Relentless Humanitarianism," *Global Governance: A Review of Multilateralism and International Organizations* 8, no. 2 (2002).

19. *Ibid.,* 153.

20 .Personal interview with author, 4 August 1998.

21. *Time,* "Collusion with killers," 7 November 1994, 52.

22. Bonaventure Rutinwa, "Beyond Durable Solutions: An Appraisal of the New Proposals for Prevention and Solution of the Refugee Crisis in the Great Lakes Region," *Journal of Refugee Studies* 9, no. 3 (1996).

23. There were several key differences between central Africa and northern Iraq, of course, not the least of which was the perceived geopolitical importance of each region.

24. See, for example, "Communique of the Regional Summit on Rwanda, Nairobi, 7 January 1995," State House, Nairobi, Kenya.

25. Personal interview with author, 4 August 1998.

26. Personal interview with author, 4 August 1998.

27. Adelman, "Chaos in the camps."

28. Human Rights Watch, *Rearming with Impunity: International Support for the Perpetrators of the Rwandan Genocide* (New York: Human Rights Watch Arms Project, 1995).

29. Douglas Jehl, "Pact Reached on Return of Rwandans," *New York Times,* 30 November 1995, A6, late edition.

30. Ray Wilkinson, "Cover Story: Heart of Darkness," *Refugees* Magazine issue 110 (1997).

31. The flight and massacre of these refugees, and subsequent attempts by the international community to investigate, are important to understanding

complex regional dynamics but are beyond the scope of this analysis. For more information, see Human Rights Watch, *Democratic Republic of the Congo: What Kabila is Hiding: Civilian Killings and Impunity in Congo* (New York: Human Rights Watch/Africa, 1997) and René Lemarchand, "Genocide in the Great Lakes: Which Genocide? Whose Genocide?" *African Studies Review* 41, no. 1 (1998), among others.

32. Personal interview with author, 16 February 1999.

33. France's complex role in the Rwanda crisis continues to be the subject of intense critique. Many observers have accused the French intervention into Rwanda in July 1994 (*Opération Turquoise*) of allowing perpetrators of genocide to slip out of the country unpunished rather than protecting humanitarian interests. For a critique of the French role in Rwandan politics from an insider's perspective, see Prunier, *The Rwanda Crisis.*

34. Even before the repatriation, researchers noticed a division between aid workers in Tanzania and those in Rwanda. While the former were very interested in cross-border cooperation, the latter believed that all of the refugees were guilty of genocide and questioned why their organizations were assisting them. For more information about these divisions, see Adrian Keeling and Carolyn Makinson, "Cross-Border Communications between the Camps for Rwandan Refugees in Tanzania and Programs in Rwanda," Background paper for the International Rescue Committee (1995).

35. Amnesty International, *Great Lakes Region Still in Need of Protection: Repatriation, Refoulement and the Safety of Refugees and the Internally Displaced* (London: International Secretariat, 1997).

36. Human Rights Watch, "Tanzanian Government and UNHCR must respect international law regarding refugees," Press release, 17 December 1996.

Works Cited

Adelman, Howard. "Chaos in the camps." *Bulletin of the Atomic Scientists* 58, no. 6 (2002): 88-93.

Amnesty International. *Great Lakes Region Still in Need of Protection: Repatriation, Refoulement and the Safety of Refugees and the Internally Displaced.* London: International Secretariat, 1997.

Barber, Ben. "Feeding refugees, or war? The dilemma of humanitarian aid." *Foreign Affairs* 76, no. 4 (1997): 8-14.

Burkins, Glenn. "Disease Now Stalks Refugees." *Philadelphia Inquirer*, 21 July 1994, A1.

"Communiqué of the Regional Summit on Rwanda, Nairobi, 7 January 1995," State House, Nairobi, Kenya.

DesForges, Alison. *Leave None to Tell the Story: Genocide in Rwanda.* New York: Human Rights Watch, 1999.

Gasarasi, C.P. "The Mass Naturalization and Further Integration of Rwandese Refugees in Tanzania: Process, Problems, and Prospects." *Journal of Refugee Studies* 3, no. 2 (1990): 88-109.

Griffiths, Thalia. "Zaire urges Rwanda refugees to go home by end of the month." *Independent (London)*, 2 September 1994, 12.

Human Rights Watch. *Rearming with Impunity: International Support for the Perpetrators of the Rwandan Genocide.* New York: Human Rights Watch Arms Project, 1995.

_____. "Tanzanian Government and UNHCR must respect international law regarding refugees." Press release, 17 December 1996.

_____. *Democratic Republic of the Congo: What Kabila is Hiding: Civilian Killings and Impunity in Congo.* New York: Human Rights Watch/ Africa, 1997.

Jehl, Douglas. "Pact Reached on Return of Rwandans." *New York Times*, 30 November 1995, A6, late edition.

Joint Evaluation of Emergency Assistance to Rwanda. *The International Response to Conflict and Genocide: Lessons from the Rwanda Experience.* Copenhagen: Steering Committee of the Joint Evaluation of Emergency Assistance to Rwanda, 1996.

Keeling, Adrian and Carolyn Makinson. "Cross-Border Communications between the Camps for Rwandan Refugees in Tanzania and Programs in Rwanda." Background paper for the International Rescue Committee, 1995.
Lemarchand, René. "Genocide in the Great Lakes: Which Genocide? Whose Genocide?" *African Studies Review* 41, no. 1 (1998): 3-16.

_____. *Rwanda and Burundi.* London: Pall Mall Press, 1970.
Mahiga, Augustine. "The United Nations High Commissioner for Refugees' Humanitarian Response to the Rwanda Emergency." Paper presented at the International Workshop on the Refugee Crisis in the Great Lakes Region, Arusha, Tanzania, August 16-19, 1995.

Martone, Gerald. "Relentless Humanitarianism." *Global Governance: A Review of Multilateralism and International Organizations* 8, no. 2 (2002): 149-154.

Mcgreal, Chris. "Horror Rises at Way-Stations to Death." *The Guardian (London)*, 23 July 1994, 13.

Newbury, Catharine. *The Cohesion of Oppression: Clientship and Ethnicity in Rwanda, 1860-1960.* New York: Columbia University Press, 1988.
Prunier, Gérard. *The Rwanda Crisis: History of a Genocide.* New York: Columbia University Press, 1995.

Time. "Collusion with killers." 7 November 1994, 52.

Toronto Star. "Cholera the New Fear for Pitiful Rwandans." 21 July 1994, A16, final edition.

Terry, Fiona. *Condemned to Repeat? The paradox of humanitarian action.* Ithaca: Cornell University Press, 2002.

Reyntjens, Filip. *Pouvoir et droit au Rwanda: Droit public et évolution politique, 1916-1973.* Tervuren: Musée Royal de l'Afrique Centrale, 1985.

Rutinwa, Bonaventure. "Beyond Durable Solutions: An Appraisal of the New Proposals for Prevention and Solution of the Refugee Crisis in the Great Lakes Region." *Journal of Refugee Studies* 9, no. 3 (1996): 312-325.

Wilkinson, Ray. "Cover Story: Heart of Darkness." *Refugees* Magazine issue 110 (1997).

Zolberg, Aristide R., Astri Suhrke, and Sergio Aguayo. *Escape from Violence: Conflict and the Refugee Crisis in the Developing World.* New York: Oxford University Press, 1989.

Joseph Rudolph Jr.

CHAPTER SEVEN:

Military Intervention and Forced Migration: The Case of Yugoslavia

Dominating the town square in Kraljevo in central Serbia is the statue of a soldier, erected to honor those Serbian troops who fought in four wars between 1912-1918. A few miles away, another type of memorial can be found. It is a refugee camp of Serbs driven from their homes in Kosovo in 1999 and now living without heat or electricity in hand-me-down dwellings whose exterior walls are splashed with anti-Milosevic graffiti. Many of these displaced people carry "before and after" photos of the homes they left behind to be torched or occupied by the armed Kosovo Albanians streaming home from their refugee camps in Albania when NATO's air offensive against Belgrade's control of Kosovo concluded. All wonder what is to become of them next – an anxiety they share with the Romany refugees from Kosovo living in their make-shift camps outside of Podgorica in Montenegro, the internally displaced people still encamped outside Banovici in Bosnia, and others uprooted by the communal conflicts which meandered violently through the former Yugoslavia between 1991 and 2002.

Their plight is not unique. All wars produce casualties and, because they are often the most powerless, refugees are usually among any war's greatest victims. Their condition worldwide at once supports the view of Plato's crusty old warrior, Thrasymachus, who millenniums ago argued that "justice is nothing else than the interest of the stronger," and the power-centered, *Realpolitik* theories of international politics. On the other hand, considering the history of the various categories of Yugoslav refugees, the displaced Serbs in Kraljevo and the Romany in Montenegro can be forgiven for believing that in the world of the powerless, some are more equal than others.

Yugoslavia: A Fragile, Multinational State

When the 1984 Olympics were held in Sarajevo, that city was displayed to the world as a symbol of multinational harmony. In fact, from the outset the desires of Yugoslavia's national minorities for autonomy if not independence had clashed with its Serbian majority's desire to use the state as a means of achieving the Greater Serbia of which Serbian nationalists had dreamed from even before Serbia and Montenegro obtained independence from Ottoman rule. Nor did the passage of time soften that clash, albeit circumstances frequently forced the country's majority and minorities to adhere to their marriage of convenience. Pointedly, the country's last official (1981) census made it clear that in this "land of the Slavs" only 5.4% of the population thought of themselves as ethnic Yugoslavs. Elsewhere, the peoples of Yugoslavia continued to see themselves as ethnically and nationally distinct. They were Serbs (33+%), Croats (19.7%), Muslim Slavs or Bosniaks (8.9%), Slovenes (7.8%), Albanians (7.7%), Macedonians (6.0%), Montenegrins (2.6%), etcetera, including Hungarians (1.9%).[1] Alexei G. Arbetov, The Kosovo Crisis: The End of the Post-Cold War Era (Washington, DC: Atlantic Council Occasional Paper, 2002), 7-8. Heightening inter-ethnic tensions, many of these ethnonational communities were territorially intermingled throughout the Federal Republic of Yugoslavia (FRY). (See Chart)

Pre-breakdown distribution of the peoples of Yugoslavia [1]

REPUBLIC	Majority Group	% Serbian	Population
Bosnia-Herzegovina	Slovenes (39.5%)[2]	32 %	4.1 million
Croatia	Croats (75.1%)[3]	11.5%	4.6 million
Macedonia	Macedonians (67%)	2.3%[4]	1.9 million
Montenegro	Montenegrins (68.5%)	3.3%[5]	600,000
Serbia (Overall)	Serbs	85.4%	9.3 million
Kosovo Region	Albanians (77.4%)	13.2%	1.6 million
Vojvodina Region	Hungarians (19%)	54.4%	2.0 million
Slovenia	Slovenes (90.5%)	2.2%	1.9 million

1. All figures are pre-conflict. Most are based on 1981 census materials, reported in Glenn E. Curtis, editor, *Yugoslavia: A Country Study* (Washington: Library of Congress, 1992), 293. Population estimates in the final column were as of 1991.

2. An additional 7.9% of the population in Bosnia-Herzegovina identified themselves as "Yugoslavs."

3. An additional 8.2% in Croatia identified themselves as "Yugoslav." Outside of Bosnia-Herzegovina, Croatia, Serbia (4.8%), and the smaller areas of Montenegro (5.3%) and Vojvodina (8.2%), only 1% or less claimed "Yugoslav" as their national identity.

4. The Albanian minority was 19.8%.

5. Montenegro also has a 13.4% Muslim minority.

State-Making

Throughout Yugoslavia's relatively brief (1918-1992) history as a unified state, the recurrent refrain was Serbian-Croat conflict. Yet, the long tale leading to the country's last years begins elsewhere, with fall of the last great Serbian empire during the middle ages. In 1389, at Kosovo Polje (the Battle of Kosovo), the Ottoman Turks defeated the Serbs in the cradle of the Serbian nation and began the process of radically restructuring Kosovo's history. The ancient streets of Pristina, the region's capital, still reflect nearly five centuries (1389-1878) of Ottoman rule. More importantly, the population living throughout Kosovo altered considerably during that time. Once the Albanian peoples to the south embraced Islam, Kosovo's Turkish rulers encouraged them to migrate to Kosovo to dilute the Serbian presence there. They did, and by the time of the Kingdom of the Serb, Croats and Slovenes was formed after World War I, Kosovo already contained a sizeable Albanian Muslim minority.[2]

World War II further affected the province's population. Although the principal impact of German occupation was to intensify Croat-Serbian animosity by creating a puppet Croatian government that persecuted the Serbs under its control, Germany also allowed the Albanians in Kosovo to oppress the Serbs there. By the war's end, they had driven as many as 100,000 Serbs from Kosovo and the Albanian and Serbian populations had become approximately equal.[3] Ironically, it was Belgrade rule during Tito's postwar presidency which completed the virtual Albanianization of Kosovo. A Croatian by birth, Tito (*nee* Josip Broz) was committed to making the FRY a workable, multinational communist state. Towards that end, to downgrade Serbian influence in Yugoslavia (as well as isolate the hardline communist Albanian regime to his south) Tito encouraged further Albanian migration to Kosovo and increased Kosovo's political autonomy inside Serbia. By the time of his death (1980) Albanian Muslims constituted approximately 90% of Kosovo's population.[4] Also by that time, most of Yugoslavia's modern history had already occurred:

♦ Serbian nationalism had developed during the 19th century in a Greater Serbian mode, with Serbian nationalists laying claim to Serbia, Montenegro, Macedonia, Bosnia, and large parts of Croatia and Albania, while Croatian and Slovene nationalists were stressing the distinct nature of their respective territories and ways of life. [5]

♦ Serbia, the most politically advanced of the Slavic lands, had achieved independence in 1878.

♦ Austrian Archduke Ferdinand had been assassinated in 1914 in Sarajevo on the anniversary of the Battle of Kosovo by a Serbian nationalist, triggering World War I.

♦ The peacemakers at Versailles, in the name of national self-determination, had created the Kingdom of Serbs, Croats and Slovenes out of the ruins of the Austrian-Hungarian and Ottoman empires that ended the war on the losing side.

♦ Ethno-political violence had continued to haunt the region during the inter-war period as those in favor of a strong central government (mostly Serbs) squared off against those favoring a more peripheral, federal allocation of political power.

♦ King Alexander had renamed the state Yugoslavia, banned all symbols of ethno-regional identity, and assumed near dictatorial powers (1929), only to be assassinated in a joint Croat-Macedonian separatist operation in 1934.[6]

♦ Germany's wartime occupation had deepened inter-ethnic tension in the state, but also brought resistance fighters from all communities together against the German invaders and produced in Tito a wartime hero and postwar leader capable of ruling the country for thirty-five years.

The Final Years

Tito's strategy for holding his country together revolved around four elements. The first was Tito himself, the country's symbol of unity and leader of its government and party. Secondly, to ease fears of Serbian domination, the country was given a federal structure, which permitted its Slovene, Croat, Montenegrin and Macedonian peoples to be in a majority in a union republic of their own. In Bosnia-Herzegovina (hereafter Bosnia) the Croats and Bosnian Muslims, combined, constituted a solid majority. Leaning against the centrifugal tendencies inherent in this design was the third element: the Communist Party of Yugoslavia. Because it enjoyed a monopoly over political power at the center and in the union republics, it had a vested interest in the state's survival. Finally, there was external factor: the fear that if Yugoslavia split apart its peoples would be absorbed into the Soviet Union's Central European empire.

Even before Tito's death, a piece of this mosaic was eroding. Tito's efforts to ease minority concerns of Serbian domination by giving them a measure of autonomy under Yugoslavia's 1948 constitution and, later, a share of the rotating executive established for the state in 1974 antagonized Serbian nationalists without neutralizing the nationalist ambitions of the minority communities.[7] Thus, two years after Tito dismantled Yugoslavia's repressive secret police network in 1966, Albanian nationalists in Kosovo began openly demanding more autonomy. Three years later, Croat nationalists were demanding the same for Croatia.[8] With Tito's death, the unraveling process gained momentum. Widespread economic dislocations swept the country at the same time that factional power struggles inside its communist party undermined the party's ability to provide strong leadership.[9] Given these developments, the growing tension between the country's ethno-national communities would have been difficult to contain under the best of circumstances. When the threat of Soviet aggression dissolved along with the Soviet Union in the early 1990's, these conflicts grew out of control and single party rule collapsed throughout the state.

The final countdown began with the Albanian nationalist protests in Kosovo in 1988-1989 in response to Belgrade's decision to rescind that province's autonomy, and the emergence of the fervent Serbian nationalist, Slobodan Milosevic, as the country's leader. Factionalism inside the governing communist party increased sharply along ethno-national lines, and in 1990, when the Slovene and Croatian delegations walked out of the Party's 14th Congress, the party reluctantly abandoned its monopoly over political power in Yugoslavia.[10] With Tito gone, the party in disarray, and the threat of Soviet invasion vanquished, the union republics became contentious. Early in 1990, Slovenes voted the communists out of office and installed a separatist-minded cabinet. A few months later the Croat majority in Croatia elected a parliament committed to establishing a confederate relationship with Belgrade in which most power would be in the hands of the union republics. In response, the approximately 600,000 Serbs living in southern Croatia held a referendum of their own in which 99% of the voters demanded regional political autonomy inside Croatia and began to form para-military groups to secure it by force if necessary. The next year Yugoslavia exploded.

The Conflicts

Contemporary explanations of ethnic political mobilization and conflict generally fall under three broad, and not necessarily mutually exclusive headings. To simplify, one set of explanations views ethnic conflict as essentially spontaneous; that is, the result of tensions lying within the differences which separate one community from the "otherness" of another and which explode when they periodically reach a boiling point or are triggered by outside elements. A second set of theories revolve around the ebb and flow of the diverse sources of segmentation affecting communities in today's world; for example, gender, age, territorial location and social class. Where ethnic differences are cross-cut and softened by other lines of societal stratification, conflict is less likely to ensue; where territorial and/or social differences reinforce and exacerbate ethnic differences, ethnic conflict is more likely to occur. Finally, there are the "manually-operated" theories, which view ethnic conflict as the result of individuals mobilizing communities for political action – and sometimes violence – on the bases of the differences separating them.[11]

The United States Department of State still favors the third set of theories in explaining the breakup of Yugoslavia, casting Milosevic and his fellow Serbian ultra-nationalists as the prime culprits in the unfolding drama(s). So, too, do many of the international organizations (including the United Nations) and non-governmental actors (NGOs) deeply involved in trying to mitigate conflict in a world of multinational states.[12] In fact, though, support for all three of these explanations of ethnic mobilization and conflict can be found in the story of Yugoslavia's disintegration. Moreover, in the case of those conflicts shaping its final moments outsiders often played nearly as important a role in contributing to its violent breakup and the forced migration its diverse national groups as the political leaders of those communities.

Meltdown:
The Wars in Slovenia, Croatia, and Bosnia

At their core, the conflicts, which ripped Yugoslavia apart in 1991-1992, were thus ethno-political conflicts with deep roots (sometimes nourished by relatively recent, bloody memories) between communities often claiming the same ground as their motherland and no longer finding reasons to continue the political system hatched at Versailles. In some instances economic considerations reinforced the cultural differences separating them, making it easier for political leaders to exploit inter-ethnic distrust. Thus, because Slovenia was one of the richest regions in Central Europe, with an average per capita income more than three times Serbia's, Slovene nationalists could argue that it was subsidizing its Serbian masters. Croatia, too, was a richer union republic than Serbia. Meanwhile, Bosnia and, inside Serbia, Kosovo were far poorer than Serbia – a state of affairs which their militant nationalists could attribute to Serbian indifference to their problems and/or hostility to their Muslim culture.

The role of these nationalist leaders in moving their regions towards separatism, militarized ethnic conflict, and/or civil war should not be understated. Milosevic, for example, quickly championed the cause of the Serbian autonomists in Croatia and the Serbian minority in Bosnia, thereby injecting the Belgrade into the inter-ethnic conflicts in both union republics. Ironically, though, it was the outside parties, especially the German government, whose actions pushed Yugoslavia over the edge and into wars of such barbarism that before the war in Bosnia ended in 1995, such image-evoking terms as "ethnic cleansing" would be added to the world's daily vocabulary of politics.

In early 1991, western diplomats under the mistaken belief that Milosevic's preoccupation with the problems in Kosovo would force him to accept as *fait accomplis* the independence of Croatia and Slovenia, encouraged these republics to secede.[13] When, however, they declared their independence (June 25 1991), Belgrade responded militarily to preserve the state. On the Slovene front, the war lasted only ten days, partly because Slovene units in the Yugoslav army fought in support of Slovenia's independence but also because Slovenia's location in far northwest Yugoslavia and small number of Serbs placed Slovenia out of any reasonable definition of Greater Serbia.[14] The war in Croatia lingered longer precisely because that republic's large Serbian population qualified parts of southern Croatia for membership in Greater Serbia. Indeed, fighting there did not wind down until Belgrade mounted a major offensive during the winter of 1991-2, which left it in control of a third of Croatia. Even then, with a UN-imposed cease-fire in place and Croatia as well as Slovenia and Bosnia admitted to the UN as sovereign states, the battle continued between paramilitary Serbian units in Croatia backed by Belgrade and the Croatian government in Zagreb until the Dayton Accord in November, 1995 ended this first round of civil wars in what once was Yugoslavia.

In the meantime, the center of the conflict and its ugliest phase shifted between 1992-1995 to Bosnia, where the Serbs constituted nearly a plurality of the population and had voted overwhelmingly against the referendum on independence supported by a majority of Bosnian voters in February of 1992. Very quickly extremist paramilitary units and acts of atrocity proliferated on all sides. By the time the conflict ended it is estimated that 200,000 had died and that more than a million people had been displaced by the fighting.[15] Yet, throughout, the response of the international community, including that portion of it which had encouraged the breakup of Yugoslavia, remained weak. It was not until August 1992, that the European Community (now European Union) met in London to recognize Bosnia and urge the United Nations to deploy a peacekeeping force to the region. By then, the wars in Croatia and Bosnia, combined, had already forced approximately two million people to abandon their homes and claimed the lives of 50,000, mostly civilians.[16] Nor, once it took up the Bosnia issue, did the UN fare much better—a limited peacekeeping force here, failed cease-fire agreements there, and the creation of a half dozen "safe havens" so inadequately defended that in the summer of 1995 Serbian forces were able move into one of them, Srebrenica, and execute the worse single act of carnage committed during the war despite the presence of a European Defense Force unit assembled there.[17] It was the brazenness of this attack, and the subsequent Serbian attacks on the "safe" cities of Tuzla and Sarajevo that finally prompted NATO to intervene with enough vigor to establish a peace which could be kept. By December 1995, all parties had agreed to the Dayton Peace plan, which ended the war in Bosnia and provided the legal basis for establishing self-governing institutions in Bosnia under international tutelage and returning Bosnia's displaced peoples to their homes. Even then, however, it was clear that returning the refugees to their homes was going to be a long and difficult undertaking. Two of the signatories, Croatia's Franjo

Tudjman and Yugoslavia's Slobodan Milosevic, had aggressively opposed refugee repatriation at Dayton in the hopes of keeping those territories under Croatian and Serbian control as ethnically cleansed as the wars had left them.[18]

The Meltdown Continues: Kosovo Explodes

The combustible materials in the Kosovo dispute have already been noted. On the one hand, this most Serbian of all areas had become 90% Albanian Muslim by 1990. On the other hand, although the Kosovo city of Prizren was the birthplace of 19th century pan Albanian nationalism, by 1990 the province had lost its right to self-government and found itself both poorer than Yugoslavia as a whole and under the direct control of Belgrade. In 1990, that meant the Serbian nationalist government of Milosevic, who had attained political power by promising his fellow Serbs that Kosovo would be forever Serbian.[19] Five years later, Milosevic had even less room to negotiate on the matter, having already agreed at Dayton to accept a loss of control over the Serbian population in Bosnia, Croatia and Slovenia.

On the Albanian side, the principal actor was the Kosovo Liberation Army (KLA), and it was no more inclined to compromise on the issue of Kosovo's autonomy than Milosevic. If the latter's strategy by the mid-1990's had become making life so hard on Kosovo Albanians that large numbers would chose to leave the province, the KLA's strategy involved attacking enough Yugoslav police and other officials in Kosovo to provoke Belgrade into so over-reacting that the international community would intervene on behalf of the Kosovo autonomists. Between 1994 and 1997 the conflict escalated incrementally. Then, here too, the actions of an outside party became the decisive factor in provoking an open conflict between the contesting parties. Stung by criticism that it had waited too long to respond effectively to the carnage occurring in Bosnia, in 1998 President Clinton's administration began to press Belgrade to restore Kosovo's provincial autonomy and to permit an international police force to vouchsafe the security of its Albanian populace. In point of fact, while rumors of Serbian atrocities in Kosovo were rampant, there was scant evidence to support these rumors and considerable evidence that the acts of political violence being committed there were far from one sided. Indeed, beginning in the early 1980s there were reports of arson at Serbian Orthodox churches and nunneries and maiming attacks against Serbian farmers.[20] Even the increasing deployment of Serbian police and military personnel in Kosovo in the mid-to-late 1990s and the subsequent clashes between these forces and Kosovo Albanian civilians were primarily reported as Belgrade's response to KLA attacks on Yugoslav forces in Kosovo.[21] By then, however, the inhumane nature of the war in Bosnia had been well reported, and although all sides were guilty of atrocious acts, the most infamous were associated with the Serbs. Consequently, exaggerated stories of Serbian massacres of Kosovo Albanians were given widespread credence. American criticism of Belgrade increased further in 1998-99 when the FRY's aggressive military effort to crush the KLA and its supporters generated a steady stream of Albanian refugees into neighboring countries.

There is no doubt that as the conflict escalated, violent acts *did* occur against Albanians, including those civilians who returned during the occasional cease-fires. Still, each threat of NATO involvement on behalf of Kosovo autonomy appears to have emboldened the KLA and resulted in increased demands for Kosovo's independence and further attacks against the Yugoslav police in Kosovo.[22] Throughout, though, the Clinton administration continued to place the blame on Milosevic, even as Serbs as well as Albanians fled the province to escape the conflict and mass graves were found containing civilian Serb victims of KLA action. Thus, when Milosevic refused the demand that he cede sovereignty over Kosovo to an international peacekeeping force and agree to an international restructuring of Kosovo's political relationship with Belgrade at a March 1999 summit in France, United States-led NATO forces launched (on March 24th) a 78 day air campaign against Yugoslav targets to force his compliance.

Whatever its long time success in encouraging the postwar chain of events which led to Milosevic's fall from power, in terms of its immediate goals of ending Serb attacks on Albanian civilians and the exodus of refugees from Kosovo, NATO's campaign was a tragic failure. The bombing of factories, bridges, railroads, and communications facilities in Belgrade and elsewhere in Serbia provoked the Serbian forces in Kosovo into reacting against the only targets available to them: the Muslim Albanians in Kosovo which NATO had left unprotected when it ruled out deploying ground forces as a part of its campaign. Likewise, the bombings and Yugoslav-KLA fighting inside the province led to the exodus of hundreds of thousands of refugees encompassing all ethnic communities – precisely the development NATO action was meant to prevent. And, when the war ended and Kosovo Albanian refugees were hastily returned from their camps in Albania, the absence of a NATO force in place to prevent revenge attacks on Kosovo's civilian Serbs and Romany triggered a another massive exodus as non-Albanian minorities fled into exile.[23]

Balkan Dominos:
The Conflict Reaches Macedonia

The decommissioning of paramilitary forces is one of the most difficult tasks in any peace-building process, and so it has been in Kosovo. The fact that NATO did not have a ground force in Kosovo when the conflict ended precluded disarming the KLA at that time. Two years later, that omission returned to haunt NATO when KLA militants, who had been unsuccessful in their bids to achieve political power electorally in either Kosovo's post-conflict local elections (2000) or provincial assembly election (2001), initiated fighting between the Albanian minority and the majority population in the one independent, former union republic of Yugoslavia which until then had escaped war: Macedonia.

To be sure, turn-of-the-millennium Macedonia was not lacking in conditions conducive to communal conflict. Its Albanian and Macedonian peoples intermingled throughout much of country; however, invariably the Orthodox Macedonians controlled economic and political power and enjoyed a living standard visibly better than that of Macedonia's Albanian Muslims. Even the president who led Macedonia's peaceful secession from Yugoslavia warned the international community of the explosive situation in his country when he retired from office in November 1999. Nonetheless, the fighting which raged in the mountains along Macedonia's border with Kosovo in the early months of 2001 was clearly instigated by KLA guerrillas, [24] albeit in collusion with their allies in the Albanian National Liberation Army (NLA) in Macedonia. Once started, however, the mountain conflict between the NLA and Macedonian security forces gained momentum, producing yet another release of refugees forced from a war-torn area of the former Yugoslavia until, months later, international mediators achieved an uneasy peace in the area.

The Refugees

By the time the fighting eased in Macedonia, not a single union republic of the former Yugoslavia had been spared the impact of the sudden arrival of large numbers of refugees from its former fellow republics and only Slovenia and Montenegro had managed to escape the decade-long series of conflicts without becoming major donors to the world of refugees.

Totaling the Numbers

If Yugoslavia's history is important in understanding the causes and depth of the violence, which accompanied the communal warfare which destroyed it, the number of the people forcefully displaced during those wars is important as a barometer of the scope of the conflicts. Unfortunately, the nature of the fighting in Yugoslavia makes it unusually difficult to obtain precise headcounts of the refugees and IDPs resulting from those wars.

Source of Data

The source of the data is a chronic problem faced by international organizations trying to estimate the numbers dislocated by civil disturbances. Although organizations like the United Nations Mission in Kosovo (UNMIK) may have numbers of their own at their disposal, most depend to some degree on organizations, which have a vested interest in inflating or deflating the figures they report. Agencies representing the interest of refugees will frequently estimate on the high side in the hope of mobilizing more support for their cause. Conversely, those accused of causing refugee crises have an interest in downsizing the count. On the issue of the number of Romany living as displaced persons in Serbia and Montenegro, for example, UN agencies put the number at approximately 28,000 plus, whereas the Serbian government administering programs to assist them and interested in outside subsidies estimates their number in the 50,000 range, and Romany organizations claim their number to be between 80,000 and 100,000.[25]

The Nature of the Conflict

Most civil wars, from the secession of the United States south in the 1860s to the unsuccessful effort of Biafra to secede from Nigeria and the successful separatism of Bangladesh from Pakistan in the late 1960's and early 1970's to the still on-going fighting in Tamil majority areas of Sri Lanka, have revolved around the effort of *one* region to secede. These conflicts produce two distinct categories of displaced peoples: (1) those properly known as refugees—that is, those who flee to foreign countries; and (2) internally displaced persons (IDPs) who move to other parts of the existing state. Yugoslavia's breakup was different. There, multiple secessions occurred in the early 1990's, and almost immediately the separatist regions received international recognition as independent states, thereby legally transforming the IDPs who had fled into them from neighboring union republics when the fighting began into refugees for headcount purposes. Inevitably, some of the same names ended on refugee and IDP rosters. Meanwhile, the intensity of the fighting rolled from one area to another during the 1992-1995 period, pushing people about with it, then re-ignited in Kosovo inside Serbia four years later, and finally spread to the ten year old Macedonia Republic of the former Yugoslavia. Not surprisingly, in this confused world of multiple civil wars, where cease-fires encouraged refugees to return and renewed fighting sent them away again, and where decommissioned military units would stop fighting and join the homeless, tabulating the numbers of refugees, IDP's, expellees, and others became atypically difficult.[26] Add the reluctance of the displaced Romany to register at all, or inability to do so for want of proper identification,[27] and you have an overall homeless population often estimated on a "best guess" basis.

Even so qualified, the estimates of most objective actors involved with the former FRY's homeless are depressingly high. Understandably, the largest numbers result from the longer conflict in Bosnia, where the consensus is that more than two million out of a population of five million were rendered homeless. Of these, 900,000 became refugees, with 700,000 of them finding shelter in the countries of the European Union.[28] Nonetheless, even the numbers for the conflict in Croatia are striking—an estimated 700,000 refugees[29] and a resultant reduction in the size of Croatia's Serbian minority from 12% of its population in 1990 to 3% by 1995.[30] To these numbers can be added those refugees and IDPs produced by the fighting in Kosovo and

Macedonia. At the peak of the fighting in Kosovo, an estimated 800,000-860,000 Albanians (out of 1.8 million Kosovo Albanians) had departed the province, along a hundred thousand Kosovo Serbs. Perhaps as many as another 500,000 were internally displaced inside Kosovo.[31] Then, when NATO's air operation ended and most Albanians returned, revenge attacks by the returnees led to the exodus of another 130,000-150,000 of the province's Serbs and other non-Albanian people (especially Roma), mostly into either Serbia (now hosting 90% of Kosovo's Serbian IDPs) or Montenegro (where two-thirds of the Roma fled).[32] Finally, the fighting in Macedonia, which rounded out Yugoslavia's decade long trauma, briefly produced nearly another hundred thousand refugees, most of whom went to the remnants of the FRY (Serbia and Montenegro).

Classifying the Dispossessed

Altogether, nearly 20% of the FRY's 1990 population became refugees or internally displaced people as a result of these conflicts. Yet, the assistance available to these people has had less to do with their numbers than their residential-legal status and/or their nationality.

Legal Status and Refugee/IDP Assistance

Given the nature of Yugoslavia's disintegration, the traditional dichotomization of migrants between refugees (those going abroad) and IDP's (those relocating in their country) does not provide an adequate analytical handle for treating either the nature of the populations in flight or the international response to their situation. Those best off initially were the refugees who left what had been Yugoslavia and took refuge in outside countries. During the course of the conflict in Croatia and Bosnia, they benefitted in two important ways. First, they immediately fell within the protection of an established international system erected to ease the plight of refugees and they were usually beneficiaries of relatively generous, short-term national assistance programs in the economically developed countries which received them. These refugees also acquired international allies willing to champion their cause and press for their quick return to their homes, if only to get them off their welfare rosters. Once the conflict in Bosnia ended, however, their status altered abruptly as their hosts – like Germany within a year of the signing of the Dayton Accord – moved to expel them back to their state of origin.[33] Once returned, they fell in amidst an already large number of IDPs, often at the back of the line behind those who had toughened it out during the war and earned preferred status in the post-conflict normalization process.

Secondly, there is that hybrid category of refugees who sought sanctuary in those union republics where their ethno-political community enjoyed majority status, and who would have been designated IDP's had not those areas been quickly recognized as sovereign states. These peoples fared less well during the war than those who made it into the United States or EU countries because the same magnitude of resources were simply not available to them. Typically, they have either returned to join the ranks of the other IDP's in their homeland or have remained as, technically, refugees in Croatia, Serbia, and Bosnia, but with a *de facto* condition which is essentially the same as that of a third category of postwar homeless, the IDP's who were forced to relocate within their own countries because of local threats to their security.[34]

In theory, IDPs are supposed to be better off than international refugees both emotionally, because they find shelter within their national community, and economically, because "where displaced persons belong to the state's ethnic majority, governments are more likely to stretch their resources to accommodate displaced persons."[35] In practice, the IDPs generated by the conflicts in Yugoslavia appear to be at least as badly off as the refugees. They usually lack the freedom of movement enjoyed by the citizens of the areas to which they have gravitated, are often without access to the documents they need to register for health assistance and other social services, and lack secure housing or assistance to pay for it, even when international agencies have discovered that their houses are occupied by usurpers but are unwilling to evict the latter because *they* would then have no place to go for shelter.[36] Perhaps most importantly, IDPs have found little assistance beyond, here and there, community shelters, and negligible employment opportunities because area industries are idled or damaged by war and even the local work force is suffering from extraordinarily high unemployment rates.

National Identity and Assistance Politics

The ethno-national identity of the refugees and IDPs has functioned as an even more important variable affecting the assistance available to them. To date, the Serbs and Romany have vied for the honor of being the worse off, and the Kosovo Albanians have tended to do the best. Serb refugees and IDPs suffer from a serious public relations problem which appears to have dulled the international community's appreciations of their difficulties. The origins of the problem lie in the first round of warfare. It is now clear than no national group had a monopoly on conducting inhumane warfare; however, the Serbs had the most military hardware, the ability to inflict the highest number of casualties, and a policy of ethnic cleansing which was exposed in Bosnia early in the war there.[37] Subsequently, a "they-got-what-they-deserved" mentality has heavily colored the world's view of the Serbian victims of the wars in Croatia, Bosnia, and Kosovo. Yet, they live no better than other refugee and IDP groups[38] and, in absolute terms, the total of Serbian IDP's and refugees is as large or greater than that of any of the nationalities, if only because there were more Serbs in Yugoslavia than any other group when the conflicts began and they have fought in more wars over a longer period than any other FRY nation. They also remain, in both Bosnia and Kosovo, the most frequent target of political violence by members of the other national communities.[39]

Though fewer in numbers, in terms of living conditions the Romany are worse off than the Serbs, who at least have a government in Belgrade to lobby on their behalf. A stateless people, the Romany have no such ally. For this and other reasons, including their general status as Central Europe's most despised minority, their shelter is often "makeshift scrap-metal and cardboard shacks" lacking in sanitation facilities, heat, and electricity."[40] For opposite reasons Kosovo Albanians have done the best among the dispossessed. Because the Bosnian Muslims were the greatest victims in the war in Bosnia and the United States feared that a similar devastation might befall Kosovo's Albanians, they have benefitted from both the international intervention, which suspended Belgrade's authority over them and the fortunes of war. Thus, although NATO's momentarily dislocated more than 60% of their community, the war's outcome allowed them not only to return to their homes but occupy as well the homes of many thousands of Kosovo Serbs.

Restoration Policies and Politics

When Organization for Security and Cooperation in Europe (OSCE) election monitors arrived in Montenegro to oversee the 2001 out-of-area voting of Serbian and Romany IDPs living near Podgorica, they were surprised to learn that many of the translators assigned to them were themselves Serbian refugees -- from Sarajevo in 1992. They had been trying to eke out an existence in Montenegro for nearly a decade while the international community created the conditions for their safe return to their homes. Their history is not atypical of those displaced by a decade of warfare in the former Yugoslavia.

Three years after the conflict ended in Kosovo, 231,000 non-Albanian IDP's from Kosovo were still living in Serbia and Montenegro. In fact, the numbers continuing to leave were still exceeding the numbers returning through organized efforts, who totaled less than 300 in 2001.[41] Of those who have returned, a significant number have been elderly and the vast majority have settled in existing minority enclaves. There, security is better; however, mobility is limited and job opportunities are few.[42] The same pattern of elderly returnees and enclave existence has characterized the return process in Bosnia despite some notable success there in reintegrating the returnees in a few instances.[43] Similarly, the return process there was sluggish for more than six years after the Dayton Accord was signed, with less than 5% – 100,714 people – of Bosnia's refugee and IDP communities returning to their homes between December, 1995 and August, 1999.[44] The pace of return did gather momentum in 2002, but the number of returnees remains small compared to the number still displaced.[45]

The Obstacles to Return:
Safety, Security, and Self-Sustainability

At the top of the list of those factors delaying refugee/IDP returns is an arc of security issues. The sub-topics here begin with the still on-going physical attacks against returnees, the NGO staff assisting them, and the international forces assigned to protect them. To the extent they are able to provide the returnees with a secure environment, the military force in Kosovo (KFOR) and its counterparts in Bosnia (now SFOR) have been essential parts of the restoration process. Moreover, in Bosnia they have basically succeeded in providing that security.[46] In Kosovo, however, four years after KFOR's deployment, the principle obstacle to returning the region's quarter million IDP's remained that province's "fragile" security environment.[47] In fact, the evidence indicates that homicides and assaults against minorities have both increased and continued to go unpunished by local officials.[48] It is a situation still echoed in some of Bosnia's more sensitive corridors.[49]

The physical risk of returning thus remains a powerful disincentive affecting IDP and refugee willingness to seek the services of those organizations involved in the resettlement process. So do the continued presence of armed paramilitary (KLA) forces in Kosovo, and the electoral success of militant nationalists in Kosovo and Bosnia alike. Not surprisingly, where minorities have returned to Kosovo, there is evidence that they "have grown psychologically dependent on KFOR."[50] But creating a secure environment is not the only issue here. The concept of a secure return comprises returning the displaced to their own residences, if still standing. Sorting through conflicting property claims, however, is a time consuming process, even when the original owner can prove ownership. Meanwhile, at the other end we have already noted the reluctance of humanitarian organizations to support return when there is no place to put the existing occupants, despite international guidelines which specify that the rights of original owners take precedence over even that occupancy legally conferred by local authorities. Eviction becomes even more difficult where the usurpers are politically influential; for example, judges, members of the police, war veterans and the local politicians themselves.[51]

Given these factors, the return of IDP's to Kosovo has been neither smooth nor according to design. By April, 2002, only 502 of the more than 15,000 Kosovo IDP's who had filed applications for the return of their homes had seen their cases processed, and only 138 of these had actually repossessed their property.[52] And, again, among those returning the pattern remains that of minority enclavization, with its byproduct development of segregated neighborhoods, schools, and public activities.[53] Then there is the problem of the original owner's property no longer existing or being uninhabitable. The major reconstruction programs necessary to rebuild or rehabilitate these structures have been difficult to mount, and not entirely because of local resistance. Acquiring the developmental assistance necessary to return IDPs and refugees to their homes and reintegrate them into society is also a recurrent post-conflict problem.[54] NGOs usually lack the capital necessary for the larger reconstruction projects -- housing, the re-establishment of water and electrical services, *etc.*. Nor has the promised public aid been provided, especially in Kosovo where, despite magnanimous EU promises, the United States remains the primary provider of public funding. Consequently, assistance has tended to focus on easement policies aimed at helping refugees and IDPs where they currently reside.

Finally, return strategy entails providing the returnees with the employment opportunities necessary for self-sustainability when outside support is reduced or withdrawn. Here, too, progress has lagged, in part because of the high unemployment rates (40%-50%) in the more urban areas of Bosnia and Kosovo, in part because ownership of local businesses is often as disputed as housing ownership and many firms remain closed, and in part because of widespread discrimination in hiring practices, including "giving priority to demobilized soldiers, war invalids, and the families of fallen soldiers -- classes of persons that by definition exclude those from the 'other side.' "[55]

Refugee Politics

Ethnic mathematics is an integral part of partisan politics in the multinational, democratic world. Where political power is related to a group's share of the population, even census taking can be highly contentious. So it is with the return of refugees and IDPs to the ethnically cleansed areas of the former FRY. Their return challenges the ethnic distribution of political power at all levels, especially given the democratization model, which has been implemented in Bosnia and Kosovo. Despite OSCE efforts to establish decision-making arrangements involving a sharing of power across ethno-political lines, by holding elections *before* the displaced were effectively returned, the OSCE gave local political bosses and parties rooted in a single ethnonational community a significant advantage in obtaining and consolidating political power. The return of substantial numbers of minorities directly threatens their hold on that power. Consequently, local opposition to minority returns has been a persistent obstacle to resettlement in those areas of Bosnia where ethnonational communities once were intermixed. Conversely, where minority refugees have shown little interest in returning, as in parts of eastern Croatia, elected officials have offered comparatively little opposition to the resettlement of the relatively few who have chosen to return.

Refugee mathematics is even more important in another context in Kosovo. As in Bosnia, the international actors operating there are formally committed to creating a democratic, multinational political process, which is only possible if the more than 10% of Kosovo's pre-1999 population now living in Serbia and Montenegro return. Belgrade also has a keen interest in the Serbian IDPs returning to Kosovo as a step towards fully reintegrating that province into Serbia. Belgrade's goal is consistent with the UN resolution (No. 1244) authorizing UNMIK's action in Kosovo, which recognizes Kosovo as a part of Serbia; however, it is very much at odds with the objectives of Kosovo's Albanian nationalists. The latter remain committed to achieving an independent Kosovo and fear that large numbers of repatriated Serbs and Romas will weaken their ability to secure that goal. Consequently, they remain unwilling to cooperate even minimally in an effective return process. In the meantime, Serb IDPs remain "pawns in a political game."[56]

International Guidelines and the
Road to Endless Delay

In addition to following the established international guidelines for returning refugees and IDPs to their homes, which stress the *right* of uprooted people to return safety and with dignity, UNMIK has imposed on itself a further consideration: the risk of return.[57] To be sure, UNMIK authorities emphasize that this consideration should not be construed so as to give local communities a veto over the return process. In practice, however, the attention which UNMIK and others have given to such factors as "the absorption capacity of the receiving community" and the fragile nature of the peace process in Kosovo[58] has come close to doing just that. It clearly has delayed the return process. To those refugees and IDPS who all of the bureaucratic planning involving their return has been left to outsiders, the emphasis on time tables, logistical considerations, and the reception they may face upon return appear as excuses for inaction.[59] Meanwhile, they continue to live a marginal existence where they have found refuge, aware that patience with their presence is wearing thin even in host communities inclined to be sympathetic towards their plight. In the words of one Serb IDP about to be evicted from his temporary living quarters in Kraljevo, "We cannot stay, we have no place to go."

Concluding Reflections on Forced Migration in Yugoslavia

The problems involved in relocating the more than two and a half million people displaced by the fighting in the former Yugoslavia are understandable. Once outflows of this magnitude occur, the process of returning them to their homes is not just politically sensitive but very costly—in financial terms, psychologically, and frequently in human lives. Getting beyond the memories of bloody communal wars can take generations; rebuilding domestic instruments of conflict resolution and overarching senses of identity can take even longer. There are no proven blueprints for successfully building democratic, multinational states in the aftermath of communal civil wars.

The weak response of outside actors to the conflicts themselves is less easily understood. The second half of the twentieth century is replete with examples of the human costs of partition and civil war. Yet in European capitols and Washington, and at the UN, the response to Yugoslavia's violent demise focused on managing the conflicts as inexpensively as possible. Safe havens thus became traps for IDPs lined up for the massacre at Srebrenica. Lightly armed peacekeepers futilely sought a peace to keep. Air campaigns were conducted with disregard to their impact on the non-combatants on the ground.[60] The lesson seems clear. Where migration is being forced en masse, a forceful response to ending the conflic(s) may not only be the only effective way to stem the tide of fleeing civilians but the least expensive means of doing so in the long run. Prophylactic action, however costly, is usually cheaper than restorative justice. There are, however, two problems with prescribing aggressive, preventive international intervention where multinational states are violently melting down: getting it, and reconciling it with the ideal of national self-determination on the part of the separatists, whose actions may have to be as forcefully controlled as those of governments bent on ethnic cleansing.

The Intervention Option

Militarily powerful states and international organizations now possess the legal authority as well as the physical capacity to curtail forced migrations in most disintegrating states. The conflicts in Bosnia and Kosovo have produced a set of precedents and principles of international law which provide the legal framework for such action.[61] However, if undertaken it is also clear from events in Kosovo and elsewhere in the former Yugoslavia that conflict-ending diplomatic action must be early and—if unsuccessful—backed by the introduction of unquestionably preponderant military force *on the ground.* Without that secure environment on the ground nothing else is possible in terms of post-conflict institution building or secure refugee/IDP returns.[62] Equally important, intervening forces should, as much as possible, adhere to a policy of neutrality regardless of who may have been the initial aggressor or greater violator of human rights. Relatedly, the cost-cutting method of conscripting local units who seem to be on the side of the angels to assist in conflict ending actions should be avoided. As KLA action indicates, armed paramilitaries can become an important source of insecurity to returnees at a not-so-later date.[63] Persuading international actors to undertake aggressive action, much less early in an unfolding conflict, is currently improbable. Peacemaking and peacekeeping operations are difficult, costly and open-ended, especially if peacekeeping is stretched to include institution building and rehabilitation in postwar societies.[64] For these and other reasons, peacekeeping operations still suffer from "chronic undersupport."[65]

The Self-Determination Conundrum

What the international community *can* do, and do without expending many resources, is carefully reconsider the ideal of national self-determination in the contemporary world. Until the 1990s, siding with secessionists in civil wars was something the United States had almost never done. Even when Pakistan's effort to retain East Pakistan (now Bangladesh) became horridly bloody in terms of civilian casualties and then doomed because of India's intervention on behalf of the separatists, the United States

213

backed Karachi. Likewise, throughout the Nigerian civil war France's support of breakaway Biafra was almost unique among western states. With the breakup of the Soviet Union and Yugoslavia into their former parts, however, the idea of national self-determination seems to have attained renewed popularity, even though none of those states which have emerged from the Soviet Union is ethnically homogeneous and many of them are now troubled by minority rebellions.

Reassessments of the permanency of political boundaries in Europe and the dangers of encouraging separatism have been much discussed in recent conflict management literature.[66] At a minimum, Yugoslavia's experience supports a wary view of encouraging ethno nationalists whose goal is national self-determination pushed to the point of statehood. Not only is it unfeasible given the shear number of territorially concentrated, politically self-aware minorities in the multinational states of the contemporary world, but encouraging that option discourages compromise solutions to ethno-political conflict. Territorial and non-territorial options short of independence are abundant; for example, regional self-rule of the Belgian variety, federal autonomy as in Quebec, and international guarantees of minority rights as is emerging for Ulster's communities. These should be pursued as first lines of response, even if they mean accepting for long periods the *de facto* segregation of mutually antagonist communities. Enclavization is not an attractive option, but it trumps forced migration and ethnic cleansing and it appears to be an unintended but temporarily useful outcome of international peace-building efforts in both Bosnia and Kosovo.[67] Temporary psychological satisfaction aside, it is probably also preferable to becoming an independent and permanently poor state – a Bangladesh of Europe. It might be different if those wealthy states, like Germany or the United States, who unthinkingly or irresponsibly encourage dreams of self-determination were to accept the implied responsibility of helping them achieve self-sustainability, but there is nothing in the history of Yugoslavia's meltdown to support that likelihood either. Just still millions of refugees and IDPs who are running out of time where they are and have no place to go.

Notes

1. Glenn E. Curtis, *Yugoslavia, a Country Study* (Washington: Government Printing Office, 1990), 70.

2. Alexei G. Arbetov. *The Kosovo Crisis: The End of the Post-Cold War Era.* (Washington D.C., Atlantic Council Occasional Papers, 2002) 7-8.

3. I*bid.*, 8.

4. *Ibid.*

5. Jack David Eller, *From Culture to Ethnicity to Conflict: An Anthropological Perspective on International Ethnic Conflict* (Ann Arbor, MI: University of Michigan Press, 1999), 260-61.

6. *Ibid.*, 272-75.

7. Concerning the tendency of ethnonationalism "to feed on concessions" as well as "adversity and denial," see Walker Connor, "The Politics of Ethnonationalism," *Journal of International Affairs*, 22 (1973): 1-21, at 21.

8. See Joseph R. Rudolph, Jr., "Yugoslavia: The Deconstruction of a State and Birth of Bosnia," in *Encyclopedia of Modern Ethnic Conflicts,* ed. Joseph R. Rudolph, Jr. (Westport, CT. and London: Greenwood Press, 2003), 349-357.

9. See Pedro Ramet, "Yugoslavia and the Threat of Internal and External Discontents," *Orbis*, 28 (Spring, 1984): 103-122.

10. See Jane Boulden, *Peace Enforcement: The United Nations Experience in Congo, Somalia, and Bosnia* (Westport, CT: Praeger, 2001), 82-85.

11. A more thorough summary of contemporary theories of ethnic mobilization can be found in Raymond C. Taras and Rajat Ganguly, *Understanding Ethnic Conflict, The International Dimension* (New York: Longman, 2002), 9-41.

For a lengthier explanation of the second viewpoint, see Robert J. Thompson and Joseph R. Rudolph, Jr., "Ethnic Politics and Public Policy in Western Societies: A Framework for Comparative Analysis," in Dennis L. Thompson and Dov Ronen, eds., *Ethnicity, Politics, and Development*. (Boulder, CO: Lynne Rienner, 1986), 25-63.

12. See, for example, the Final Report of the Carnegie Commission on Preventing Deadly Conflict, *Preventing Deadly Conflict* (New York: Carnegie Corporation, 1997), 29.

13. See Heinz-Jurgen Axt, "The Impact of German Policy on Refugee Flows from Former Yugoslavia," in *Migrants, Refugees, and Foreign Policy: U.S. and German Policies toward Countries of Origin, Volume II*, eds. Rainer Munz and Miron Weiner (Providence, RI: Berghahn Books, 1997), 1-34, esp. 7-15 and 25-26.

14. The small percentage of Serbs in Macedonia's population and its geographical location (between the Albanian dominated province of Kosovo and Albania itself) likewise worked to the advantage of that union republic, which was able to secede at the same time without any military response by Belgrade.

15. Dave Kopel, Paul Galant, and Joanne Eisen, "When Policy Kills: More Deadly U.N. Issues," National Review.com, January 27, 2004, accessible on line at http://www.nationalreview.com/.

16. Sabrina P. Ramet, *Balkan Babel: the Disintegration of Yugoslavia from the Death of Tito to Ethnic War* (Boulder, CO: Westview Press, 2002), 208.

17. The total dead is estimated at more than 7,500 Muslim men and boys, making the Srebrenica massacre the worst in Europe since World War II. The architect of the massacre, Bosnian Serb general Radislav Krstic, was found guilty in August 2, 2001 of genocide by the International Court established to try the war crimes committed during the wars in the former Yugoslavia, and sentenced to 46 years in prison. See Kopel *et al, op. cit.*

18. International Crisis Group (ICG), *Bosnia Refugee Logjam Breaks: Is the International Community Ready?* (Washington: ICG Balkan Report No. 95, 2000), 1.

19. On the deteriorating nature of conditions in Kosovo and the 1999 NATO action over Kosovo, see John C. Scharfen, "Yugoslavia: Ethnic Conflict and the Meltdown in Kosovo," in *Encyclopedia of Contemporary Modern Conflicts, op cit.,* 337-347.

20. See, for example, Henry Kamm, "In One Yugoslav Province, Serbs Fear the Ethnic Albanians," *The New York Times,* April 28, 1986.

21. "Serbian police attack separatists," *The Sun* (Baltimore), March 6, 1998.

22. See, for example: "Kosovo Albanian leader demands independence," *The Sun* (Baltimore), March 12, 1998; Thomas W. Lippman, "U.S. Says Milosevic Must Withdraw Police in Kosovo or Risk NATO Action," *The Washington Post,* November 21, 1998; "Kosovo rebels insist on independence amid new violence," *The Sun* (Baltimore), December 5, 1998; Peter Finn, "Squeezing Out Kosovo's Serbs," *The Washington Post,* January 4, 1999; and "Kosovo rebels insist on total independence," *The Sun* (Baltimore), January 5, 1999.

23. See especially Scharfen, *op. cit.,* and United Nations Office for the Coordination of Humanitarian Affairs (OCHA), *Humanitarian Risk Analysis No. 18 — Humanitarian Situation, Protection and Assistance: Internally Displaced Persons in Serbia and Montenegro* (Belgrade: OCHA, 2002), 5-6

24. Peter Beaumont, "Albanians wage war of race hate," *The Observer* (London), February 25, 2001.

25. *Humanitarian Risk Analysis No. 18,* 22. Conversely, concerning the number of Albanian refugees caused by the fighting in Kosovo prior to the NATO air campaign, the government in Belgrade consistently offered low figures (in the 140,000 range of " dislocated" people) versus the much higher numbers estimated by both western organizations (250,000 to 265,000) and Albanian organizations (400,000). See Ramet, *Baltic Babel,* 320.

26. I am indebted to Leah Hanlon for offering this insight.

27. On the special problems involved in estimating the number of displaced Romany, see *Humanitarian Risk Analysis No. 18, op. cit.,* 22.

28. See *Lessons Learned in Crises and Post-Conflict Situations* (New York: United Nations Development Program, 2002), 53. The United States Commission on Refugees placed the number of refugees and IDP's even higher, at more than 2.2 million. Cited in Roberta Cohen and Francis M. Deng, *Masses in Flight: The Global Crisis of Internal Displacement* (Washington, DC: Brookings Institution Press, 1998), 30.

29. Ramet, *loc. cit.*, 232.

30. *Lessons Learned in Crises and Post-Conflict Situations*, 72.

31. See *Ibid.*, 86.

32. *Humanitarian Risk Analysis No. 18*, 8.

33. See William Drozdiak, "Germany Steps Up Expulsion of Bosnian Refugees," *The Washington Post*, December 5, 1996.

34. According to the United Nations, IDP's are "persons who have been forced to flee their homes suddenly or unexpectedly in large numbers, as a result of armed conflict, internal strife, systematic violations of human rights or natural or man-made disasters, and who are within the territory of their own country." Cited in Cohen and Deng, op. cit., 16.

35. *Ibid.,. 54.*

36. *Humanitarian Risk Analysis No. 18*, 20-21.

37. Of the estimated 215,000 killed during the 1992-1995 fighting in Bosnia, 160,000 were Muslims, and all but approximately 2,000 of these were killed by Serbs. Likewise, of the remaining 55,000, it is estimated that 30,000 casualties were Croats; again all but 2,000 slain by Serbs. The Serbs also had the fewest losses, 25,000, with equal numbers of these killed by Croat and Muslim fighters. Ramet, *loc. cit.*, 239-40.

38. Only 25% of the Serbian IDP's in Serbia and Montenegro, for example, receive regular assistance in acquiring food and other material aid.

Humanitarian Risk Analysis No. 18, 2.

39. *Balkan Babel*, 282.

40 *Ibid.*, 22-23.

41. *Ibid.*, p. 2.

42. ICG, *Return to Uncertainty: Kosovo's Internally Displaced and the Return Process* (Pristina: Kosovo: International Crisis Group Balkan Report No. 139, 2002), 6. The report notes that the Romany, in particular, fit into this "enclavization" of minorities pattern in Kosovo; however, the Romany have traditionally sought living arrangements apart from their host populations throughout Central Europe.

43. See *Bosnia's Refugee Logjam Breaks: Is the International Community Ready?*, 4-6.

44. *Ibid.*, 2.

45. *Ibid.*, 3.

46. The problems associated with the returnees to in Bosnia have, since 2000, tended to be localized in four areas: the once Muslim areas of the Serb Republic; the formerly Serbian suburbs of Sarajevo; the Muslim occupied Serb homes in Bocinja; and in Mostar and Croat separatist strongholds in the east. See Nedim Dervisbegovic, "Croats Attack Bosnia Peacekeepers on Bank Takeover," *The New York Times*, April 6, 2000, "Foreign Mujahideen Fighters Leave Bosnian Village," *Bosnia Today*, September 17, 2001, and "Muslim-Croat Police Keep Low Profile in Disputed Suburb," *Bosnia Today*, April 26, 2001. *Bosnia Today* is available on line through the news services of EIN News at http://www.europeaninternet.com/bosnia/.

47. Concerning the essentiality of international peacekeepers and the risks of reducing their number, see Cohen and Deng, *op. cit.*, 282-83, and *Return to Uncertainty: Kosovo's Internally Displaced and the Return Process*, 27.

48. As this manuscript was undergoing preliminary editing in June, 2003, an elderly Serbian farmer and his family were killed and their house set ablaze

in a suburb outside Pristina, the center of the international community operations in the province. Nine months later, as the final editing was being completed, cross-communal violence had erupted throughout Kosovo and forced NATO to dispatch heavy reinforcements to quell the violence. See, for example, Daniel Williams, "Riots Spread Across Kosov, Serbia," *The Washington* Post, March 19, 2004.

49. Muslims returning to such areas as Prijedor, for example, are ten times more likely to be the victim of stoning, bombings, rape, arson, assault or murder than local Serbs. The International Crisis Group reporting this data attributes it, to a significant degree, to " the climate of impunity prevailing" in Bosnia's eastern Serbian Republic. ICG, *The Continuing Challenge of Refugee Return in Bosnia & Herzegovina* (Sarajevo: Balkans Report No. 137, 2002), 18.

50 See *Ibid.*, 19-21 on KFOR's importance to Kosovo's minorities. A similar pattern in the relationship between SFOR and "successful refugee returns" in Bosnia is discussed in *Bosnia's Refugee Logjam Breaks: Is the International Community Ready?*, pp. 12-13.

51. *The Continuing Challenge of Refugee Return in Bosnia & Herzegovina,* 9-15.

52. *Humanitarian Risk Analysis No. 18*, 20.

53. *The Continuing Challenge of Refugee Return in Bosnia & Herzegovina,* 16.

54. See Cohen and Deng, 166-67.

55. See *The Continuing Challenge of Refugee Return in Bosnia & Herzegovina*, 2 & 14. The citation is from page 14.

56. *Return to Uncertainty: Kosovo's Internally Displaced and the Return Process*, 3.

57. *Ibid.*, 4.

58. See *Ibid.*

59. On this general topic, see especially Krishna Kumar, "The Nature and Focus of International Assistance in Rebuilding Wartorn Societies," in *Rebuilding Societies After Civil Wars: Critical Roles for International Assistance*, ed. Krishna Kumar (Boulder, CO: Lynne Rienner, 1997), 15-18.

60. For a succinct discussion of the options available for dealing with conflicts spilling into the international arena, see Morton H. Halperin, David Scheffer and Patricia L. Small, *Self-Determination and the New World Order* (Washington: Carnegie Endowment for International Peace, 1992): 95-117. On the use of military force in particular, see Barry Posen, "Can Military Intervention Limit Refugee Flows," in Munz and Weiner, *op. cit.*, 273-321. Safe havens are analyzed in pages 298-305. The dangers of habitually weak United Nations responses are well critiqued in Dave Kopel, Paul Gallant and Joanne Eisen, "When Policy Kills: More Deadly U.N. Issues," *op. cit.*

61. Civil wars which are likely to cause massive flows of refugees into neighboring states can now be treated by the UN as international problems falling within the jurisdiction of its Security Council. Previously, the provision in its Charter prohibiting involvement in matters falling within the "domestic jurisdiction" of member states was interpreted to block such action.

62. See former Swedish Prime Minister Carl Bildt's "Hard-earned Lessons of Nation-Building: Seven Ways to Rebuild Iraq," *International Herald Tribune*, May 7, 2003.

63. See Posen, *op. cit.*, 297.

64. See Joseph R. Rudolph, Jr., "Intervention in Communal Conflicts," *Orbis*, .39 (1995): 259-274. Concerning the open-ended nature of peacekeeping missions, it is significant that there has never been an instance where forces deployed to control communal conflict have been completely withdrawn without the conflict resuming and that one United Nations mission, the peacekeeping force in Cyprus, has been on assignment for four decades.

65 Boulder, *op. cit.*, 130.

66. See Halperin *et al*, op. cit., 119-121, Heinz-Jurgen Axt, *op. cit.*, 22-24,

Cohen and Deng, 21, and Kumar Rupesinghe and Valery A. Tishkov, "Introduction," in *Ethnicity and Power in the Contemporary World*, ed. Rupesinghe and Tishkov (New York: United Nations University Press, 1996), 20-23.

67. See Cohen and Deng, *op. cit.,* 287-289.

Works Cited

Arbetov, Alexi G. *The Kosovo Crisis: The End of the Post-Cold War Era*. Washington: Atlantic Council, 2002.

Boulden, Jane. *Peace Enforcement: The United Nations Experience in Congo, Somalia and Bosnia*. Westport, Connecticut: Praeger, 2001.

Carnegie Commission on Preventing Deadly Conflict. *Preventing Deadly Conflict*. New York: Carnegie Corporation, 1986.

Cohen, Roberta, and Francis M. Deng. *Masses in Flight: The Global Crisis of Internal Displacement*. Washington: Brookings Institution, 1998.

Connor, Walker, "The Politics of Ethnonationalism." *Journal of International Affairs*, 22 (1973): 1-21.

Curtis, Glenn E. *Yugoslavia: a Country Study*. Washington: Government Printing Office, 1990.

Eller, Jack David. *From Culture to Ethnicity to Conflict: An Anthropological Perspective on International Ethnic Conflict*. Ann Arbor, Michigan: University of Michigan Press, 1999.

Halperin, Morton H., David Scheffer and Patricia L. Small. *Self-Determination and the New World Order*. Washington: Carnegie Endowment for International Peace, 1992.

International Crisis Group (ICG). *Bosnia Refugee Logjam Breaks: Is the international Community Ready?* Washington: ICG Balkan Report No. 95, 2000.

International Crisis Group (ICG). *The Continuing Challenge of Refugee Return in Bosnia and Herzegovina.* Sarajevo: ICG Balkans Report No. 137, 2002.

International Crisis Group (ICG). *Return to Uncertainty: Kosovo's Internally Displaced and the Return Process.* Pristina, Kosovo: ICG Balkan Report No. 139, 2002.

Kopel, Dave, Paul Galant, and Joanne Eisen. "When Policy Kills: More Deadly U.N. Issues." *National Review.com.*

Kumar, Krishn, Ed.. *Rebuilding Societies After Civil Wars: Critical Roles for International Assistance.* Boulder, Colorado: Lynne Rienner, 1997.

Munz, Rainer, and Miron Weiner. *Migrants, Refugees, and Foreign Policy: U.S. and German Policies toward Countries of Origin, Volume II.* Providence, Rhode Island: Berghahn, 1997.

Ramet, Pedro. "Yugoslavia and the Threat of Internal and External Discontents." *Orbis*, 28 (1984): 103-122.

Ramet, Sabrina P.. *Alkan Babel: the Disitegration of Yugoslavia from the Death of Tito to Ethnic War.* Boulder, Colorado: Westview Press, 2002 .

Rudolph, Joseph R., Jr., Ed . *Encyclopedia of Modern Ethnic Conflicts.* Westport, Connecticut, 2003.

Rudolph, Joseph R., Jr.. "Intervention in Communal Conflicts." *Orbis*, 39 (1993): 259-274.

Rupesinghe, Kumar, and Valery A. Tishkov, Eds.. *Ethnicity and Power in the Contemporary World.*

Taras, Raymond C., and Rajat Ganguly. *Understanding Ethnic Conflict: The International Dimension*. New York: Longman, 2002.

Thompson, Robert J., and Joseph R. Rudolph, Jr. "Ethnic Politics and Public Policy in Western Societies: A Framework for Comparative Analysis," in *Ethnicity, Politics and Development*. Eds. Dennis L. Thompson and Dov Ronen. Boulder, Colorado: Lynne Rienner, 1986.

United Nations Development Program. *Lessons Learned in Crises and Post-Conflict Situations*. New York: United Nations Development Program, 2002.

Nitza Nachmias

CHAPTER EIGHT:

Frustration-Aggression-Terrorism: The Case of the Palestinian Refugees

"Flights from home demand the surrender of everything that an individual holds dear. What prompts a man to take such drastic action? Has he suddenly lost his feelings for 'his own, his native land'? Not at all. He left only because he fully expects to return some day."[1]

Every refugee aspires to return to his home. Only rarely do these aspirations materialize. The gap between the hyped aspirations and the despondent present creates deep frustration that results in aggression. The "frustration-aggression" syndrome is the heart of the case of the Palestinian refugees and is perhaps, the microcosm of the Israeli-Palestinian conflict. Since 1948, the Palestinian frustration gained momentum and incited a violent struggle for territory as a physical matter, and for territory as a social and psychological matter. The war, the violence, the successive Arab defeats, and the tragedies that followed, have shaped the Palestinian psyche beyond the refugee community. The unresolved issue of the "Right of Return" has heightened the Palestinian frustration that incited aggression that created a continued, atrocious cycle of violence. Indeed, all Palestinians, regardless of their place of residence define themselves as "refugees," people who lost their physical, spiritual and national space. For over 100 years, Israelis and Palestinians share the same land but claim exclusivity. Both exercise mutual rejection and intermittent violence, while the international community follows with horror the tremendous spill over effect of the Palestinian-Israeli cycle of violence.

The Early Years

The 1948 establishment of Israel incited an 18 months violent Arab military campaign that had left an estimated 700,000 Palestinian refugees in the West Bank, Gaza, Jordan, Lebanon and Syria.[2] However, the seeds of the protracted Jewish-Arab conflict were planted at the turn of the 20th century, following the massive waves of Jewish immigration to Palestine that increased following the rise of Nazism in Europe. Between 1919 and 1936 an estimated 300,000 Jewish immigrants came to Palestine, bringing the total number of Jews to 404,000.[3] The Jewish Diaspora generously supported the economic development campaign, and between 1919 and 1936 Jewish investments in Palestine amounted to $ 400 million.[4] In the early 1930s, 5,600 manufacturing and industrial plants were constructed. The economic development of the Jewish community spilled over to the Palestinian community.[5] In 1936, "the Arab manufacturing had branched out from traditional textile, soap, and olive oil industries, to a variety of consumer goods. Home industries, common fifteen years before, were on the wane...growing percentage of the Arab national income was attributed to trade and transport, and by the appearance of the Palestinian community first two banks, which served as bankers to the local Arab national movement... Finally, opportunities increased noticeably in the liberal professions".[6] In fact, the notable George Antonius sought work in the British mandatory bureaucracy in Palestine. "Although most Palestinians were subsistence farmers, cultivators of communal *mushaa* land or private small holdings, Palestine as a whole rebounded after World War I with an impressive 'growth and development of indigenous production.'"[7]

The Balfour Declaration of 1917 and the division of Palestine to two separate states along the Jordan River [8] caught the Arab community by surprise.[9] Anger and frustration developed among the Palestinian community as they witnessed the dramatic demographic change. They viewed the Jewish economic development as a threat to their land, culture, tradition, and an effort "to create a wholly Jewish Palestine...the disappearance or the subordination of the Arab population, language and culture, in Palestine."[10] The extreme Islamic leadership, and in particular, Haj-Amin-al Husseini, the Grand Mufti of Jerusalem (1921 and 1948), preached ethnic hatred and violence,[11] and incited terrorist attacks against the newly established Jewish settlements.[12] The clash was almost inevitable.[13] "The threats of Zionism and Israel have historically resonated among all sectors of the Palestinian and Arab population: Muslims and Christian; religious and secular; modern and traditional."[14] The breakdown of the Palestinian traditional society corresponded with radical, aggressive, social and political movements that emerged all over the Middle East and gained strength during their anti-colonial struggle.[15] The result was a radicalisation of sentiments and an increase in violent attacks on the infidel Jews.[16] An insatiable longing to return to their homeland, or the *el awda,* strengthened the Palestinian community animosity and anger. The "Nakbah" became an individual, communal and national narrative, representing both personal and communal tragedies, and transmitted from one generation to the next.

The "The Arab Predicament"

Prior to 1948 the Palestinian leadership was limited exclusively to an oligarchy of landed gentry that was anxious to preserve the old order. By 1948, only half of the 1000 Palestinian villages had schools, and these were only 4th and 5th grade schools.[17] The disenfranchised Palestinian illiterate peasantry (fellaheen) were fed anti-Zionist propaganda[18] that blamed the Jews for all their malaise.[19] The unprovoked Arab uprisings were defined as "self defence" against this Jewish "enemy."[20] Fouad Ajami has defined the condition as: "The Arab Predicament." He explained: "The invented nationalist historiography of the Arab kind had always pointed outward: It accused others— Ottomans, Europeans, and others—of causing the ills of the Arab world."[21] Ajami continues: "The outside world intrudes, but the destruction one saw reflected the logic of Arab history, the quality of its leadership."[22] In his words: "One generation has sown the wind and the other was now reaping the harvest."[23] The Jewish-Arab war of 1947-1948, which ended with Israel's independence, left the Palestinian leadership in a moral and physical break down. Other devastating consequences included (a) the fracturing of the community into splinter groups, (b) a total economic and social dependence on the Arab states, and (c) the displacement of over half of the community from their homeland.

Dr. Zadek Jalal el Razam[24] argued that both in 1948 and in 1967, the Palestinian were manipulated to believe that the war would be "a morning stroll to Tel Aviv after which the Arabs will throw all the Jews to the sea...This belief was shared by all, the Arab media, the military officers." On 30 May, 1967, "the Jordanian Prime Minister signed a strategic agreement with Nasser claiming that the combined military force of Egypt and Jordan will conquer Israel in an easy victory."[25] The reality proved to be quite different. Dr. Razem concluded that the causes for the forced and voluntary Palestinian migration in 1948 and 1967, were: (a) fear that the Israeli occupiers will rape their women and dishonour the families, a humiliation far more important than a national defeat (b) lack of local social and political organization and leadership that could guide the people and advise them of their options and alternative courses of action, (c) the forceful Israeli military who carried out a well planned program of forced migration, (d) the Western imperial countries aided Israel in order to weaken the socialist Arab regimes (in 1967, N.N.) of Egypt and Syria.[26]

The deep discrepancy between the depressing reality and the promises of an assured destruction of Israel, and the reclaiming of their homes in Palestinian, resulted in an increased sense of frustration. "The Palestinian people and its patrimony were dismembered, and three Palestinian population groupings, vastly unequal in size and varied in structure, emerged. The largest is the Diaspora, or the refugee communities; the second is made up of Palestinian in the West Bank and Gaza, either under the Palestinian Authority or under Israeli occupation. The third, the smallest group is the Palestinian community that remained on its land inside Israel after the war of 1948. They are 'Israeli Arabs,' who received Israeli citizenship and are not defined as refugees."[27] All Palestinians, including the Israeli Arab population of over a million people, (18 percent of the population of Israel), share a national, physical and spiritual narrative that expresses their frustration and helplessness. The mythology of the Nakhbah has shaped the Palestinian psyche regardless of their place of residence. The emotionally loaded narrative laments, yet glorifies the trauma of the 1948 "Disaster" (Nakhbah); the successive Arab defeats; and the on going violent struggle against the Israeli occupation.

Beyond Interpretation: Missed Opportunities

In 1948, when it became clear that the war was going in favour of Israel the issue of the refugees first gained attention. The international community began to plan relief, education, and health care for the refugees in Jordan, Syria, Lebanon and Egypt (Gaza).[28] For different reasons, both Israel and the Arab states showed clear resistance to the resettlement and integration of the refugees, into the societies where they found refuge (probably the best solution to the problem).[29] Both shared the fear that a concentration of large groups of displaced people amongst them could become a powder keg, ready to explode at any moment.[30]

No reliable data exists concerning the number of Palestinians who are scattered around the globe, and how many of them actually are refugees receiving assistance from UNRWA. The numbers cited in this paper are also estimates.[31] The official Israeli figure is that only 520,000 persons left Palestine in 1948, while the Palestinian claim that 900,000 peasants from about 700 villages fled Palestine in 1948.[32] Another major debate concerns the Palestinian unprecedented spontaneous migration. Was the migration voluntary or was it forced? The interpretations change from an unquestionable "voluntary migration" to an unquestionable "forced migration." "The reason why the Arab residents of the new Jewish state fled has its own contemporary consequences, given that the responsibility to pay compensation is legally linked to causation."[33] Among the disputed causes:(a) voluntary migration at the request of the Arab Islamic Higher Committee, or the Mufti of Jerusalem, (b) forced migration and evictions of Palestinians by the Israelis to secure villages located in strategic areas, and (c) fear of a Zionist victory, and anxiety over stories of torture, etc. The actual answer to the question is, probably, all of the above.

In 1949, the Palestinians became refugees under Israeli, Syrian, Jordanian, Egyptian and Lebanese rule. In its efforts to resettle the

Palestinian refugees the international community created in 1949, the Palestinian Conciliation Commission (PCC), headed by Gordon Clapp, of the Tennessee Valley Authority. The PCC proposed large-scale development projects, which would have resettled the Palestinian refugees in Syria, northwest Sinai and in the Yarmuk and Jordan valleys, and would have also provided employment for them.[34] "From the beginning, the Arab host governments were offered unprecedented broad opportunities based on the refugees' rehabilitation which could help develop their countries' potential under the proposed aid programs."[35] The plan was shelved at an Arab League meeting in October 1955, when "Syria vetoed any development scheme that even implied recognition of—let alone cooperation with—Israel."[36] Other plans suggested by S-G Dag Hammarskjold (1959) also failed. "Dag Hammarskjold estimated that $1.7 billion would be required to reintegrate the refugees by 1970 and an additional $12 billion in new investment would be needed to absorb the labour force in the Arab states and Israel." He suggested that the refugees "be regarded not as a liability, but more justly, as an asset for the future...and a reservoir of manpower."[37] The vast oil revenues were assumed to finance these grand economic designs, however, due to the Arab states insistence on repatriation and their rejection of resettlement, all the projects that have been proposed, the international funds that have been provided, and the studies that were undertaken were in vain.

The international community seemed confused and divided when it was required to respond to the unexpected violence created by the Israel-Palestinian "action-reaction" tactics. Since 1969, the General Assembly accepted the approach that the Palestinian refugees problem have arisen from Israel's denial of their inalienable rights under the charter of the UN and the Universal Declaration of Human Rights."[38] This approach resulted in a myriad of non- enforceable anti-Israeli resolutions reprimanding Israel's aggressive and oppressive policies.[39] The Palestinians were encouraged by these actions and intensified their violent attacks on Israel.

The introduction of Palestinian suicide terrorism changed the rules of the game concerning the refugee's legal and human rights (See Goldstein's article). The international community has not determined whether the use of terrorism by the occupant against their occupiers, namely, whether persons who commit acts of terrorism under occupation, should lose their privileges under the Geneva Conventions. "The provisions of the Refugee Convention do not apply to any person with respect to whom there are serious reasons for considering that he has committed a crime against peace, a war crime or a crime against humanity, or a serious non-political crime outside his country of refuge, prior to his admission to that country as a refugee. Nor does the Convention apply to a person who is guilty of acts contrary to the purpose and principles of the United Nations." [40]

For decades, the international community, Israel and the Arab states took little interest in the fate of the Palestinian refugees. However, since the early 1970s, the Palestinian in the Diaspora began to demand the implementation of the "right of return," while they never demanded their right of citizenship in the Arab countries where generation of Palestinians were born. Israel continues to insist that the Palestinian refugees should be resettled throughout the Middle East, and[41] repatriation should be restricted to a limited number of refugees. The Arab community rejects resettlement program on any Arab territory other than Palestine, as well as proposals for financial compensation, considering them arrogant and imperialistic.[42] This attitude severely limited the freedom of President Yassar Arafat to sign away the refugees' rights in the Oslo peace negotiations. In fact, the Right of Return became the single most important factor conditioning and determining the Palestinian communal, social and political identities, as well as the nature of their interaction with Israel and the Arab countries.[43]

The conflicting interpretations of the "right of return" created major legal and political dilemmas. In 1988, the Palestinian National Council (PNC) officially accepted the two-state solution, and "reaffirmed the Palestinian people's right of return based on UN resolution 194 of 1948. Previously that right was always affirmed with no reference to such resolutions."[44] Israel, on the other hand, argued that no UN resolution established resettlement as the main alternative.[45] UN proposals "foresees the settlement of Palestinian refugees mostly in neighbouring Arab countries and in the West Bank with a multi conditioned possibility of returning a mere 75,000 refugees to Israel."[46]

Life as a Refugee

The Palestinian refugees demanded and have received exceptional treatment and a unique status under international law.[47] First, all Arabs who lived in Palestine two years prior to 1948 were granted refugee status although many were actually economic migrants from neighbouring Arab countries who immigrated to Palestine shortly before 1948, looking for jobs in the dynamic, vastly growing Jewish economy. Second, the Arab states denied citizenship to the Palestinian refugees and their decedents although "the 1951 Convention requires states to grant nationality to persons born on their territories who would otherwise be stateless(Article1)." It also prohibits denial of nationality on "grounds of race, religion, or political opinion"[48] for political reasons, and because the international community accepted this practice that ultimately prevented the resettlement of the refugees.

The refugee camps were constructed as transitory shelters, to be demolished once the crisis was over. A UN report of September 1951 describes the poor conditions of the 1948 refugees: "About one-third of all the refugees are living in sixty organized camps; the other two-thirds live scattered among towns and villages of the host countries...The shelter is for the greater part tents, but also other buildings... the refugees are encouraged to put up small structures for themselves not in any sense as lasting housing... these camp inhabitants represent the poorest, and the most unfortunate of the refugees."[49] They viewed the Palestinian migrants as an aggressive group, usually hostile to the host government, a threat to their stability, and a security risk.

The camps, however, became permanent residences, and the fourth generation of refugees now receives aid from UNRWA. The Palestinian refugees use conflicting adjectives to describe life in the refugee camps: "A camp is an expression of dispersion," "A camp is the concrete symbol of the Palestinian problem and the suffering of Palestinians," "It preserves my identity and independence, spreads a Palestinian climate with an abundance of big and minute details everywhere." "It is exceedingly self-contradictory place...Has a refugee camp ever been a pot to melt the Palestinians? Partly, yes. It was the basis of the Palestinian revolution."[50] UNRWA's report (1951) of the first generation of refugees could perfectly describe the life of the fourth generation: "...the victims of circumstances they are unable to grasp. Legally, humanly and economically speaking, they are little better off than they were when they first left Palestine...No government, except in Jordan, has proclaimed their right to stay."[51] Life under Israeli occupation has been unsafe, full of "jeopardy to life, physical integrity or liberty...as well as intolerable psychological pressures."[52] The refugee camps have become an enormously fertile recruiting ground for various terrorist organizations that prey on the young and desperate, and easily recruit them for violent and often suicide missions.[53]

In almost every Palestinian family the father and mother would recall his or her locality in Palestine as a matter of routine. "Thanks to my father from Toulkarem and my mother from Jaffa, we were provided with memories which shaped our consciousness."[54] The symbol of this imagined reality is an old key which is hung in front of every house in the refugee camp, a symbol of the key to the family's home in Palestine. The more circumstances became harsh and unbearable, the more retrogression became a safe haven. The idealized past served as a safe haven against the humiliating living conditions under the occupation.

> "Refugees tend to create an imagined identity...the majority of the refugees in the camps were peasants, farmers, or Bedouins...because the references in the tales or narratives or memories are not the state or the homeland in general, but the village, the natural relations between a city and the countryside is reversed. Big Palestinian cities such as Jerusalem, Haifa, Jaffa, Acre, would be looked upon through their relations to that village, the village in mind." [55]

It is in the historical continuity of the struggle that the militants place themselves."[56] Contemporary anthropologists stress the fact that Palestinian refugees living in camps have developed a higher national awareness than refugees living outside camps. Life in the camps encouraged the construction of a collective memory, a dream of return, and a narration of a homeland that transcended a territorial reality:

> "It helped rejuvenate political, educational and human activity and created a refugee mentality...Refugees started recollecting their villages, their own past in front of their families, sons and grandchildren who would sit down listening. Recollection would always be about life in pre-1948 Palestine. The goodness of life before the 1948 is viewed as Paradise lost. It would be seasons, festivals, traditions, history of the village, and their role in the 1929, 1936, 1939, and 1948 revolutions and wars. Martyrs and heroes would also be respectfully mentioned...The task of the generations born away from Palestine became to talk to their sons and grandsons about oranges in Palestine."[57]

The Politics of Assistance to the Refugees Before and After Occupation: UNRWA, a Solution or a Problem?

UNRWA's experience highlights the administrative and political limitations to international humanitarian aid operations. In fact, UNRWA may have been created mostly because of the misperception created by Folke Bernadotte, the first UN mediator in Palestine, that the United Nations caused the refugee problem. Bernadotte argued: "Both in origin and disposition the refugee problem entails a United Nations responsibility."[58] Since the Palestinians were without citizenship and were residents of a former League of Nations mandated territory, the international community is responsible for them until a final settlement is achieved.

In 1950, UNRWA assumed *de facto* exclusive administrative authority over the camps as a temporary, emergency assistant organization. A refugee camp, according to UNRWA's working definition, is a plot of land placed at the disposal of UNRWA by the host government for setting up facilities to support the refugees. "Socio-economic conditions in the camps are generally poor with high population density, cramped living conditions and inadequate basic infrastructure such as roads and sewers."[59] The plots of land on which camps were set up are either state land, or in most cases, land leased by the host governments from local landowners. The residents of the refugee camps do not own the land, but have the right to use the land for a residence. UNRWA does not own, administer or police the camps, as this is the responsibility of the host authorities.

Since it was impossible to give an absolute number of refugees and to separate them from the "fraudulent claimants," UNRWA created a unique definition for Palestinian refugees:[60] "Any person whose normal residence was Palestine for a minimum of two years before the 1948 Arab-Israeli war and who lost both home and livelihood as a result of the conflict and took refuge in one of the areas which today comprise Jordan, Lebanon, the Syrian Arab Republic and the West Bank and Gaza Strip."[61] Direct decedents of registered refugees were also eligible for UNRWA's assistance. This definition is far different from the common definition of a "refugee" that ignores the length of residence and assumes the residence to be "from time immemorial." (See Goldstein discussion). Also UNRWA's definition ignores persecution and the continued fear of death, factors that do not apply to most Palestinian migrants.[62]

Following its modest creation in 1948, UNRWA became an elaborate, expensive, bureaucratic, system employing about 110 international staff and 23,665 local people.[63] After half a century of operation, UNRWA seems to be more a part of the problem than part of the solution. UNRWA's expenditures between 1948 and 2000 are unparalleled and are estimated to exceed $ 7 billion.[64] UNRWA's local employees are eligible to retirement compensation after six months of service. The pension fund, "UNRWA Providence Fund," has total assets of almost a billion USD invested in enterprises around the globe. Clearly, such an elaborate bureaucracy would be difficult to dismantle, when and if the issue of the refugees will be resolved. The fact that the Agency honours thousands of fraudulent claims was first raised as early as 1960, when UNRWA's Director General admitted that the "Jordan ration lists alone are believed to include 150,000 ineligibles and many persons who have died... UNRWA's officials told two US senators UNRWA's relief rolls are inflated by twenty to thirty percent."[65] UNRWA's existence had perpetuated and legitimised the refugees' status, and induced a "refugee camp" lifestyle, culture and state of mind.[66] The refugee population, now at its fourth generation, and continuing to grow at a dramatic rate of about five percent per year,[67] never shed the image, status and feelings of a rootless, lost people. In fact, UNRWA turned into a "non-territorial government," providing social and civic services to refugees and non-refugees alike. The continued misery of the refugees eclipses the glitter of the multilateral support for the refugees mainly via UNRWA.

Millions on a Commitment Basis in Euro (1999-2003)

	YEARS					
Category of Expenditure	1999	2000	2001	2002	2003	1994-2003
Humanitarian Aid - ECHO interventions Food aid, injury rehabilitation. Psycho-social support, Water,	6,75	18,2	26,26	35,00	25,00	143,0
Assistance to PA + Palestinian NGOs Infrastructure, Health, Technical assistance Judiciary, Human rights, Food security, Private Sector, Risk capital, subsidies for EIB operations.	57,3	31,96	5,19	98,74	52,00	546,16
Aid to the PA Administration for urgent current expenses (In Budgetary assistance as of 2000/2001 plus budgetary austerity Administrative & financial reform	0	90	40	100,00	80,00	390,00
Peace Projects / People to People program Is Arab/Palestinian co-operation on government and civil society	21,73	22,9	0	2,85	10,00	88,88
Counter-Terrorism Program budget, training PA by security Member States agencies	0	6,19	3,81	0,00	0,00	17,20
Assistance Grants Total　　　　　:	85,78	169,25	75,26	236,59	167,00	1186,14
Support to refugees through UNRWA Contribution to UNRWA's general fund	38,3	40,24	57,25	55,00	57,75	421,24
Food Aid program with UNRWA relief & social services. Health and Education program, cash	13	16,06	17,10	35,00	20,2 8	160,75
UNRWA total:	51,3	56,3	74,35	90,00	78,03	581,99
Grants Total:	137,0	225,55	149,61	326,59	245,03	1768,188

Source: Brussels, 17 July 2003　　　Ip/03/1040

　While aid seems to be flowing, the outbreak of the second Intifadah and the September 11 terrorist act resulted in the escalation of mutual violence that had made life in the refugee camps, and beyond, unbearable. The frustrated residents of the refugee camps have developed resistance to the Israeli occupation inside and outside the "green line," and in spite of the disparity in power; they have initiated several popular uprisings.[68]

Days with Border Closures in the Occupied Territories, 1993-2000*

	Total days of border closure	Of which working days lost	Lost Days in % of Potential Work Days
1993	26	17	6.1%
1994	89	64	23.1%
1995	112	83.5	29.9%
1996	121	89.5	31.9%
1997	79	57	20.5%
1998	26	14.5	5.2%
1999	16	7	2.5%
2000	75	52	18.8%

* Estimates based on information from the PA Ministry of Labour and the Palestinian border authorities. Working days exclude weekends (i.e. Saturdays and half the Fridays) and Jewish and Muslim holidays. Potential workdays for Palestinian workers in Israel average about 277 each year.

International border closures October 2000-January 2001*

West Bank / Passenger Roads	21.43 %
Bridges/commercial	36.51 %
Gaza Strip Rafah/ Passenger	38.10 %
Rafah / Commercial	61.11 %
Gaza International Airport	51.59 %

Prepared By: United Nations documents, UNSCO, 2001

*The internal closure measures total prohibitions on movement to and from the OT including: emergency needs, medical treatment, etc. For example, partial internal closure in the West Bank during October-December 2000 was 44%. Estimates based on information from UNRWA and interviews with travellers in the West Bank and Gaza, October 2000—January 2001.

Total Palestinian Refugees in the Middle East in 1950

Country	Number of Refugees
Lebanon	106,753
Syria	80,499
Jordan	465,450
Gaza	199,789
Israel	23,507
Total	875,998

Total Palestinian Refugees Registered with UNRWA(2003)

Field	In camps	Not in Camps	Total
TOTAL	1,316,710	2,819,739	4,136,449
Jordan	307,785	1,432,385	1,740,170
Lebanon	223,956	170,576	394,532
Syria	120,865	292,962	413,827
West Bank	179,541	485,705	665,246
Gaza	484,563	438,111	922,674

The "Arab countries of first refuge adopted, as early as 1952, a series of resolutions granting Palestinian refugees residency rights and the right to work, but the application of these legal resolutions has been uneven."[69] In addition, the existence of UNRWA helped the host Arab governments to adopt an anti-refugee policy. For example, Palestinian refugees could work in the Gulf States, but could never become citizens, own property, or participate in political life. While the majority of refugees living in Jordan are Jordanian citizens and are fully integrated, UNRWA has never taken them off its entitlement list. There is no precedent to this abnormal situation. The Jordanian case shows that UNRWA has created unnecessary, parallel, and separate institutions for the refugees, exacerbating their segregation and inhibiting integration. The international law has yet to resolve this question: How can a person who has become a fully integrated citizen of a host country also maintain a status of a "stateless" refugee?[70] "Be in Lebanon, the Gulf countries, Jordan, or other Arab states, the Palestinians have received more than their share of blame...for internal instability."[71]

The Refugee Camps Under Occupation

Life under Israel occupation went through several phases. Between 1967 and 1979, Israel had placed the OT (Occupied Territories) under a military administration. The new administration issued 1,200 military orders regulating and controlling all aspects of life including: transactions of immovable property, the use of water and other natural resources, expropriating land, operating banks, managing municipal and village councils, but most importantly, the Military Administration controlled "the movement of people, issued identity cards, travel permits, driving licenses, and licenses for professional practices." [72] The military administration actually functioned as a "local civil administration" providing social and civil services, including education, health, police, etc. In 1981, Israel replaced the military administration with a Civil Administration, while maintaining and applying to the OT the Jordanian and (in Gaza) the Egyptian legal and administrative structures. "However, Jordanian laws that were adopted (in Jordan) after 1967 have not been implemented in the territories."[73] Israel also cooperated with the World Health Organization on improving health services in the territories, and health conditions in the OT have improved by 50 percent since 1967.[74] But "Despite the modest economic recovery, refugee communities remained among the poorest in Palestinian society, especially in the Gaza Strip, where an estimated 40 per cent of the population lived in poverty." [75]

Growth Estimates, Inclusive and Exclusive of the Crisis Aggregate and Per Capita, in the Occupied Territories 1999-2000 (in constant prices)

	1999	2000 In the Absence Of Crisis	2000 Inclusive of Crisis Impact	1999–2000 Growth Rate (%)
Real GDP (USD millions)	5,083	5,338	4,667	-8.2%
Real GNP (USD millions)	6,278	6.654	5,801	-7.6%
Real GDP Per Capita ($)	1,656	1,678	1,467	-11.4%
Real GNP Per Capita ($)	2,045	2,092	1,824	-10.8%

* All estimates include Jerusalem. Real GDP and GNP figures for 2000 exclusive of crisis impact are based on PA Ministry of Finance and IMF growth estimates for 2000 and estimates by the PCBS in "National Income Accounts Tables: Constant Prices, 1994 –1999." Estimates for 2000 inclusive of the crisis are based on UNSCO calculations of direct income losses for the period October– December 2000. Per capita estimates are derived using mid-year population estimates from PCBS.

The occupation instigated violent anti-Israeli actions in Palestine and abroad (e.g., the 1972 Munich Massacre), and Israel reacted with harsh counter measures, such as destruction of villages, mass detentions, and situational pressure. The late 1960 saw the commencement of Palestinian international terrorism, including hijacking of civilian airplanes. Clashes between Israel and Palestinian terrorist groups spilled over to the refugee camps, that became hubs of the leadership of the newly organized PLO and Fatah.[76] Political clashes between Israel and UNRWA became inevitable. *De facto*, UNRWA controlled the refugee camps. However, UNRWA "had no legal jurisdiction over either the territory of the camps, or its inhabitants, but the agency couldn't be subordinate to any sovereign government; conversely, no sovereign government would submit to the authority of UNRWA." [77] Thus, the refugee camps became "a no man's land." While, UNRWA had no formal jurisdiction, it demanded corporate and personal immunity for its local Palestinian employees. Israel too had no formal authority, military or civil, to manage, control or enter the refugee camps. However, when the PLO instituted in Gaza a form of conscription and recruits received military training, often at refugee camps, Israel carried out incursions into refugee camps, performing searches and seizures of documents and persons. Although UNRWA's policy was to terminate employment of people recruited by the PLO, Israel claimed that UNRWA chose to ignore PLO's operations in the camps. Israel often detained UNRWA's local employees and occasionally denied them freedom of movement arguing, "no authorization by UNRWA was requested or granted." [78] UNRWA called these operations "illegal" while Israel argued that it was a necessary security measure agreed upon in the Michelmore-Comay agreement, signed in 1967 between the Commissioner General and the Israeli government. Tension was being built up following an intense construction campaign of settlements in the Occupied Territories.[79]

In 1987, after two decades of occupation, the first major popular uprising, the Intifadah, erupted. While the territories were under Civil Administration since 1982, the situation in the field did not change much.[80] More Arab land was turned into Jewish settlements, ensuring that the Jewish settlers would not be subject to the jurisdiction of the West Bank and Gaza courts. Since many camps are constructed near or inside Palestine, the refugees could witness from just several miles away the Jewish settlements taking over their land. From 20,000 settlers in the early 1970s the settlement grew in ten years to almost 10 times that many. The 1987 Intifadah was an inevitable explosion. It was a violent expression of the refugees' latent feelings of deep frustration and severe deprivation. But, its intensity and unpredicted resilience surprised all parties involved, including the United States and the EU. The Intifadah lasted until 1990, leading to the Madrid and Oslo negotiation forums, and later to the 1993 Declaration of Principles (DOP), signed in Washington between Chairman Arafat and Prime Minister Ytzhak Rabin. The agreement marked a consolidation of Israel-Jewish control over 60% of the total expropriated land of the occupied territories and did not affirmed the "Right of Return." The unfortunate failure of Israel and the Palestinians to fulfil these agreements led to dire consequences for both sides. After a short period of cooperation and hope during the late 1990s, the second Intifada erupted in September 2000 in Jerusalem. Terrorism, guerrilla attacks, and suicide bombings became the norm and the *modus operandi* of the young Palestinians in the camps.

From Frustration to Aggression to Terrorism

Dostoevsky's remark best expresses the dilemma of terrorism and counter-terrorism: "While nothing is easier than to denounce the evildoer, nothing is more difficult than to understand him." Clearly, both Israel and the Arab states failed to see the correlation between frustration and aggression. "Frustrated adults tend to react to some degree with aggression."[81] The maltreatment of the refugees had become "a catalyst in an international conflagration, as the United Nations has recognized with respect to the situation in the Middle East."[82] Statelessness, loss of identity, loss of home, persecution and real fear of death are perhaps the most frustrating causes in adult life. If we accept the proposition that terrorists are made, not born, then we have to look for the causes that make a terrorist. It seems that an individual moves from being a potential terrorist to being an actual terrorist through a process that is psychological, physiological and political. A terrorist is "a frustrated individual who has become aroused and has repeatedly experienced the fight or fight syndrome. After these repeated arouses the potential terrorist seeks relief through an aggressive act and also seeks to remove the initial cause of his frustration by achieving the political goal which has hitherto been denied."[83] The correlation between frustration and aggression is clear in both the 1987 and the 2000 Intifadah. The 1987 uprising started in Jybalia, the largest refugee camp in the Gaza Strip (60,000 residents). While the Israeli Civil Administration had full control of the camp,[84] it underestimated the frustration and the latent aggression that loomed over the camp. A traffic accident between an Israeli truck and a Palestinian passenger car that left four Palestinian passengers dead triggered the two-year uprising that quickly spread to all of OT.

The frustration-aggression hypothesis assumes a relative-deprivation condition,[85] which is based on an existing perception of a gap between rising expectations and need satisfaction. "Much of terrorist behaviour is a response to the frustration of various political, economic, and personal needs or objectives."[86] John Dollard explains: "The occurrence of aggressive behaviour always presupposes the existence of frustration, and contrariwise, that the existence of frustration always leads to some form of aggression." [87] However, the "frustration-aggression" syndrome requires an instigator. "An instigator is some antecedent condition of which the predicted response is the consequence...The concept of an instigator is clearly much broader than that of stimulus...this condition can be a verbally reported image, idea, or motive, or a state of deprivation." Moreover, Dollard argues that "several instigators to a certain response may operate simultaneously, and their combined effect represents the total amount of instigation to the response. Instigation, therefore, is a quantitative concept and so some consideration must be given to the problem of strength of instigation. This strength is measured by the degree to which the instigated response competes successfully with simultaneously instigated incompatible responses, or...by the potency of the instigated responses."[88]

In the first Intifadah, the instigator was a group of young Islamic students who spread the rumour that the car accident was a well-planned Israeli conspiracy to kill Palestinians. A call for Jihad to avenge the murder soon followed. Men, women and children blocked roads, closed all the shops, and climbed on rooftops in order to throw stones on Israel Defence Forces (IDF) soldiers. The slogan on the street was: "It is better to die than to live as a refugee."[89] The latent anger and frustration of life without hope, a life of poverty and the denial of human right was the fuel. The mantra "Allah U Akhbar" became the symbol of the uprising.

The Frustration-Aggression syndrome assumes that the interaction of three factors instigates a frustration-aggression sequence. First, a person or a group aspires to perform certain acts or wishes to attain a goal perceived to be within their reach. Second, they are blocked by a "hostile, human intervention that blocks goal attainment. A deep feeling of goal blockage is developed. Third, the frustrated person or group identifies the cause or causes responsible for the goal blockage. The final act in the sequence is identifying the enemy."[90] Our research shows that a multitude of specific factors instigated both the 1987 and the 2000 uprisings: The trauma of the Hijra (migration) and the hardships that the refugees suffered in the camps; the refusal to believe in the finality of separation from Palestine and the loss of their homes; the poverty, the humiliating living conditions, and the sense of being "different"; being displaced and dependent on rations from UNRWA; becoming day-labourers in Israel; the oppression they suffered under Israeli occupation; and the discrimination and humiliation in the host Arab countries.[91]

The PLO offered a violent, aggressive answer to the frustrated refugees. The armed struggle thesis gave them hope and courage against both Israel and the Arab states. Moreover, the Palestinians gained a national basis that they never had before. However, with the rise in the Palestinian refugees' hope, national identity, and pride came an increase in frustration and disappointment, as well as a strong sense of relative deprivation. These feelings led to a campaign of violence against Israel and the West that was legitimised as an act of "self-defence" and a rightful struggle for self-determination.[92] The following model shows how the animosity that has been building up since 1948 has an amplification effect resulting in the escalation of violence on both sides from non-violent aggression to suicide terrorism and violent counter-terrorism. During the 1960s and early 1970, hope on both sides was high and the levels of frustration were low. The protests were non-violent, and were kept for decades on a low flame. With time, hopes for a peaceful settlement were dashed and the frustration-aggression syndrome gained momentum. A frenzy of irrepressible violence erupted, and has yet to be resolved.

"Frustration-Aggression" and its Effects on the Israeli and the Palestinians Communities

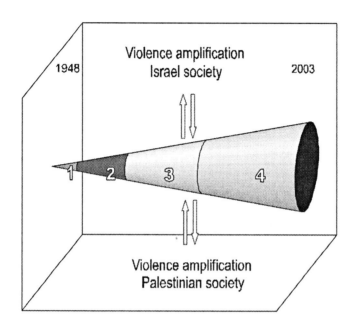

Sequence of escalation of violence:

   1: Non-violent Palestinian protest, very low repercussions.

   2: Non-lethal Palestinian violence against symbols of occupation induces non-lethal, non-violent reaction.

   3: Lethal Palestinian violence against Israeli property and people induces harsh, lethal Israeli violence.

   4: Lethal Palestinian violence against self (suicide terrorism) and innocent Israeli civilians ("enemy") induces harsher lethal Israeli reaction against Palestinian terrorists and civilians.

Growing Level Of Violence

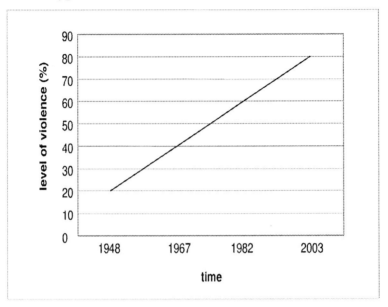

The model shows how mutual animosity has been building up from a non-violent aggression to suicide terrorism and violent counter-terrorism operations. As the vicious circle continues, both the Palestinian and the Israeli societies experience growing fear and anxiety. Our study shows the existence of frustration on both sides, which breeds violence from both sides. "Aggression is always a consequence of frustration... the existence of frustration always leads to some form of aggression."[93] The mutually increased violence is amplified across Israeli and Palestinian communities. As our study shows, the Palestinians never accepted any compromise on the issue of "the right of return," while Israel never compromised on the settlement issue. Since 1964, the PLO strategic *modus operandus* was aggression, terrorism, and violence, a strategy that was adopted officially by the Palestinian legislative bodies.[94]

Harold Lasswell elaborated on this point: "In explaining any category of response, the scientific observer looks in part at environments, which are the events impinging upon a responder while he is in a situation...That part of the environment which gets to the focus of attention of the responders is the milieu...Moreover, predispositions are the ways that participants are oriented to respond when they enter a situation."[95] The refugee camps created an environment where the link between frustration and aggression became almost inevitable. A contributing factor to the environment is the terrorist personality. Lasswell shows that mankind possesses an innate condition of human destructiveness. These are destructive impulses of two kinds: destructive practices and destructive impulses. "Practices are destructive when they express or arouse destructive impulses. Destructive impulses are the initial phases of acts which, if brought to expression, destroy congenial and creative interpersonal relations." Lasswell continued to say: "A social practice is destructive which provokes intense concentration of destructive impulses, although most of the process occurs under circumstances in which the participants neither see nor seek these results." Lasswell was perhaps too optimistic when he stated his belief that it is possible to create an environment where "men would not knowingly kill one another, whether in war, revolution, uprising, criminal violence or criminal repression. Men would not kill themselves. Human beings would not mutilate and chastise one another."[96]

In his famous letter to Sigmund Freud, Albert Einstein asks: "Is it possible to control man's mental evolution as to make him proof against the psychoses of hate and destructiveness?" Einstein continues his quest: "I am well aware that the aggressive instinct operates under other forms (than total wars) like civil wars, due to factors such as persecution of racial minorities." In his response Freud acknowledges the fact that "it is a general principle that conflicts of interest between men are settled by the use of violence." However, Freud also exhibited optimism when he said that we should create "a path that would lead from violence to right or law."[97] The community that creates the proper environment constructs the road that leads from violence to the rule of law. This is yet to happen in the Israeli-Arab conflict.

The first Intifadah (1987-89), which erupted in a refugee camp, showed that the "frustration- aggression" syndrome gains its full strength when provided with a suitable environment. The violence enjoyed social and political legitimacy as well as grass-root support. However, the devastating consequences of the first and the second uprisings proved that both Palestinian and Israeli decision-makers followed misperceptions, and did not aspire to maximize objective outcomes. They often tended to be risk-averse in the domain of gains and risk-acceptant in the domain of losses. "Moreover, strict maximization assumption does not adequately capture the actual behaviour of individuals making political or personal choices."[98] Indeed, neither Israel nor the PLO were aware of the high level of frustration and the latent aggression that was concealed under the abased surface of the refugees' despondent behaviour.[99] During the first Intifada, "over 1,283 Palestinian were killed in the West Bank and Gaza, and estimated 130,472 sustained injuries that required requiring hospitalisation. 2,533 of their homes were demolished, 481 were deported, and 22,088 have been administratively detained (never brought before a court of law), many of them tortured and beaten."[100] Displaced Palestinian children have been the most affected population, and the most frustrated. Three quarters of a million children often bear the responsibility of the day-to-day lives of their families. The high percentage of young adults among the suicide terrorists proves the correlation between their deep frustration and high level of latent and open aggression. A study done by UNICEF concluded that: "War has an all-embracing impact on a child's development, on his attitudes, his experience of human relations, his moral norms and his outlook on life. Facing armed violence on a continuous basis creates deep-rooted feelings of helplessness and undermines the child's trust in others. Socialization of children to desirable moral values is impossible in a beleaguered the social order."[101]

Since the first Arab uprising of 1921, the Palestinians define their aggression as a war of independence, while Israel defines these acts as terrorism aimed at the total destruction of the Jewish state.[102] In the early 1980s, the frustration–aggression–terrorism–suicide syndrome first appeared in the refugee camps in Lebanon and resulted in the creation of the Hezballah (Party of God). Violence in Lebanon took two forms: internal violence, mostly criminal acts of Palestinians against Palestinians, and external violence, namely, acts of violence against Western and Israeli targets.[103] The correlation between the poverty, high rates of unemployment and severe restrictions on labor and mobility placed on the refugees in Lebanon, and suicide terrorism is very clear.[104]

From a Frustrated Minority to a National Entity

Prior to 1948, the Palestinians were the majority. However, following the 1948 war, a structural demographic transformation took place in Palestine. The Arabs became a minority in their own state, while vast Jewish immigration waves of survivors of the Holocaust and Jewish refugees from Arab states and North Africa settled in Israel. The demographic transformation was a traumatic experience for the Palestinians, and the majority of the refugees chose to leave to neighboring Arab states. [105]

The Arabs who chose to stay in Israel became a minority, experiencing the traumatic separation from their past traditional clan's culture: "Life in the desert is a team effort. The clan or 'qawm' decides which lives, herds animals, fights, and makes peace together. The qawm was the effective social unit–it was, in reality, the nation-state of the Bedouin."[106]

The PLO's major success was in turning a fragmented disoriented Palestinian community into a cohesive community "in which various groups of the society could find some sense of personal and collective identity."[107] Between 1967 and 1987, the PLO dedicated their resources to: (a) raising the Palestinian refugees' national identity and consciousness and affirming their belief in the Right of Return, (b) gaining international recognition of the right of the Palestinian people to self-determination, (c) establishing the PLO as a the sole legitimate representative of the Palestinian people, (recognition awarded in 1974, regardless of the PLOs campaign of violence against Israel and the West), and (d) preparing the Palestinian people strategically, physically and emotionally to the inevitable armed struggle against the Zionist occupier.[108]

The PLO's aggressive and violent pursuit of national liberation not only challenged Israel but also threatened the Arab states, especially the traditional Arab regimes with a sizable Palestinian minority. "Thus the Palestinians in Arab host countries have been problematic minorities insofar as they have resisted subordination to the restrictions by the majority...In two instances, in Jordan and Lebanon, this dialectic led to armed conflict and civil war between the organized Palestinian communities and the Arab host."[109] It seems that the Arab states followed a two-pronged policy. While the refugees were used as a symbol in the struggle against the Jewish state, they were treated as undesirables, manual labor, but most importantly, untrustworthy. Consequently, violence against the Palestinians ebbed continuously in the host countries, and culminated in the anti-Palestinian riots and expulsion from Kuwait in the early 1990s.[110]

The host government's treatment of the Palestinians was determined by several factors: size of the host and the refugee communities, their political organization, level of hostility/support of the host government, and the strength of national ideology and beliefs. "If the Palestinian community is perceived by the host elite government as a political and economic threat, then the host state will attempt to circumscribe or suppress outright the Palestinian community... As a result, the communities have shown differing levels of political and economic involvement and contribution in support of the PLO."[111] In Jordan, prior to their expulsion (1970), the majority of the refugees were well integrated and a small number of the third and fourth generation turned into professionals, benefiting from what they called the "education revolution."[112] In Lebanon, unlike Jordan, the refugee camps were attacked brutality during the Lebanese civil war (1975-1982). In Gaza, the refugees became a cheap source of unskilled labor for Israel. In most Arab countries the Palestinians were left out of the social and political systems and were denied access to government and public positions. The Arab states' hostility and their denial of the refugees' civil rights on the one hand, and Israel's intransigence on the other hand, were major contributing factors to the rise of the aggressive, violent, Palestinian nationalism. The violence against both Israel and the Arab governments escalated from the first Intifada, humble non-lethal protests, to a massive suicide campaign.[113]

The Vicious Circle At Work

The intensification of the violence became a two-way road. The Palestinian heightened level of aggression badly hurt the Jewish community strategically, emotionally and economically. Consequently, the Israeli occupation became more violent and more oppressive. The construction of the Israeli "defense fence" is a case in point. The Palestinian community reacted with vengeance against Israeli civilians and military forces alike. The refugees perceived the Israeli harsh occupation a continuation of the uprooting and displacement that began in 1917. The Israelis perceived the Palestinian violence a continuation of the unprovoked riots of 1921, 1929, 1936 and 1948. The two communities were undergoing shattering and traumatic experiences, albeit both believing that they were engaged in a war of self-defense. The cycle of violence moved to its highest level with the introduction in the 1980s of suicide terrorism.

The crux of Palestinian violence was "to create the Palestinian national identity on the basis of an armed struggle for the liberation of Palestine."[114]

Upon the destruction of the Jewish state all the refugees will be repatriated, and an Arab, secular, democratic Moslem-Palestinian state will be established. The Jews will not be discriminated against and will be allowed to exist as a protected minority.[115] In the Diaspora, Palestinian nationalism has developed in two different directions. The PLO has been a secular political movement, while the Islamic fundamentalist movements also gained strength, e.g., the Moslem Brotherhood, the Islamic Jihad, later the Hamas, and Hezballah, among others. S.N. Eisenstadt described the above social processes: "Some of these themes of protest focussed mainly on problems of social order, and some more on those of cultural traditions–but very often they were closely related."[116] The two factions experienced strong disagreements and often clashed with each other control over the refugee camps.[117]

The rise of suicide terrorism took a high toll on the nervous Israeli society. In 2003, after three years of Palestinian uprising, the Israeli economy was declining in volume, and the GDP was lower by 3.8 percent from 2001. Actual economic losses were estimated by the Israel Central Bank to be about 18 billion NIS ($45 billion). Foreign investments declined by 14 percent, and private consumption declined by about 4 percent. Israel was experiencing its worse recession since 1983.[118] Israel was determined to combat the terrorism that was hurting all its spheres of life. Counter-terrorism measures included: (a) offensive military operations, (b) defensive military operations and, (c) punitive measures. Israel's targeted assassination practice was greatly criticized but was never abandoned. Other controversial measures included "search and seizures" in refugee camps, detaining suspects, destroying infrastructure, air force bombardments, closures, curfews, and deportations.[119]

The harsh consequences of the Intifadah only increased and heightened the Palestinian feelings of deprivation and strengthened their resolve to continue their armed struggle against Israel.[120] The violence bred violence and the vicious circle seemed to hurt both sides. Israel and the Palestinians have been experiencing deep feelings of powerlessness and frustration. Suicide terrorism and harsh military counter-measures only intensified the vicious circle.

Conclusion

Because the case of the Palestinian refugees is unique, constructive and innovative legal, operational, and political measures are required to bring the conflict to an end. The Palestinian community is partly ruled by legal authority of the PA, other parts of the community are ruled by an international administration, i.e., UNRWA, and a minority of the Palestinians are under Israeli occupation. The issue of the Palestinian refugees falls in the cracks of this strange structure, especially because the refugees' individual human rights, as they are recognized under international law, collide with the collective rights of the Palestinian community, as a nation. The Palestinian refugees believe that the entire Palestinian nation consists of forced migrants who have been stripped of their nationality as well as their land and communal life. The majority of the second, third and fourth generation of refugees is still stateless, and are rejected by both Arab and non-Arab states. Moreover, the decedents of the 1948 and 1967 refugees who were granted citizenship in countries of refuge, never relinquished their UNRWA refugee card and claim their "right of return." While UNRWA's authority as a civil administration has never been clearly defined, it continues to issue new refugee ID cards.

The five decades of statelessness have created a collective social and psychological narrative, based on anti-Jewish anti-Israeli context, that was exhibited in the active participation of the majority of Palestinian in the two violent Intifadas and the hideous campaign of suicide terrorism. The community inside and outside refugee camps is galvanized by the claim that they are entitled to benefit from precedents established in other refugee situations that have been resolved,[121] namely, it is legitimate to use violence and terrorism to achieve self-determination and the "Right of Return."

In the pre 1948 war, Palestinian nationalism was in a very rudimentary form. The nationalist narrative began to take shape as a reaction to Zionism, and it gained momentum following the Palestinian deep frustration over the loss of their land and their repeated military defeats: "When the British occupied Palestine in 1917-18, they found little evidence of any specifically Palestinian Nationalist movement."[122] The high fertility rate among the poor and the lower classes added to the frustration, poverty, and feelings of despair among the refugees.[123] The creation of the PLO in 1964 and the 1967 military defeat transformed the refugee community.[124]

The transformation of the Palestinian community followed the 1967 defeat. The tribal Arab community of 1948 moved toward structural national assertiveness, political aggressiveness and strategic violence. The process was influenced by the establishment of the PLO, the humiliating Arab defeat, the growing feelings of frustration, the continued Arab states rejection of the Palestinian refugees and the failure of the international community to budge either Israel or the Arab states from their irreconcilable positions. Especially willing to use violence have been the refugees, who insisted on "the right of return" as a non-negotiable condition.

A horrible status quo was created: the Palestinians have been using terrorism as a means to "liberate" their land, while Israel's counter-terrorism tactics involved severe human rights abuses. The Palestinian and the Israeli leaderships continued to threaten each other while the issue of the "Right of Return" loomed over both.[125] Ironically, no one asks if the "Palestinian refugees want to be repatriated, or compensated, or resettled elsewhere. Is there an international and moral consensus on the theoretical as well as the practical answers to these questions? These questions bear directly upon lives of millions of people, upon states, upon the international order."[126] There has never been a plebiscite conducted among the Palestinian refugees as to their preference. Nevertheless, "members of a community whose common experience is dispossession, exile, and the absence of any territorial homeland, the Palestinian people...have repeatedly insisted on their right to return, their desire for exercise of self-determination, and their stubborn opposition to Zionism."[127] The PLO's policy has been inconsistent and unclear. During the negotiations with Israel, the PA would agree to only a symbolic execution of the "Right of Return." However, publicly Arafat insists on full repartition.

Israel ejects repatriation and insists on a cessation of all acts of terrorism before any negotiations can take place.[128] The diametrically opposing positions of Israel and the Palestinians lead to the "frustration-aggression" syndrome, and the continued cycle of violence. The continued, uncontrolled cycle of violence is extremely frustrating for both sides. There should be substitute targets toward which the mutual aggression can be displaced, even within the conflict. The frustration should be aimed at the abysmal economic, social and political problems that both sides experience. Cooperation, confidence building, trust, and a will to compromise need to be established, as well as the resolution of the difficult issue of the refugees.

Notes

1. K.C. Cirtautas. *The Refugee*, (New York: The Citadel Press, 1963), 22

2. See data in: Moshe Efrat, "The Palestinian Refugees: The Socio-Economic Integration in their Host Countries," in Orient, No. 42, (2001) 1, (Hamburg: Deutsches Orient Institute), 47. Data is based on UN documents, September-March 1948, Doc. A/AC/25/6, 28, December 1949, p. 22

3. In 1936 The Jews constituted over 30 percent ogf the population of Palestine. Source: J.C. Hurewitz, *The Struggle for Palestine*, (New York: Schocken Books, 1976), 17

4. *Ibid.*, 30

5. Between 1919-36 the total Arab land bought by Jews was in the value $13,750,000. Quoted in Hurewitz, 31

6. *Ibid.*, 32

7. Susan Silsby Boyle, *Betrayal of Palestine,* (Boulder CO: Westview Press, 2001), 102

8. The Anglo-Jordanian treaty of 1928 recognized the Emirate as independent with some retained British powers. This treaty was replaced in 1946, when the British government awarded full autonomy to Jordan creating it as "the Hashemite Kingdom of Trans Jordan." Jordan became of member of the United Nations in 1949, after the armistice agreement.

9. Is Jordan a "Palestinians state" that should absorb all of the refugees and award them Jordanian citizenship? Perhaps an analogy can be made to Kashmir region that the British mandate left unresolved.

10. Susan Silsby Boyle, *Betrayal of Palestine*, (Boulder CO: Westview Press, 2001), 107

11. In 1925 a Jewish Yeshiva was created in Hebron for religious students and their families. In the 1929 uprising the Jewish community was attacked., and 59 unarmed students and their families were massacred. Following the attack, the Jewish community left town. In 1931 a small Jewish group tried to reopen the Yeshiva in Hebron, but they too were attacked in the Palestinian uprising of 1936.and had to leave the place.

12. In 1948 he fled to Beirut where he lived in exile until his death in 1974.

13. A British census of 1921 found that 90 percent of the indigenous population depended on agriculture. In 1948, two- thirds of Palestine's Arab population was still rural. Rosemary Sayigh, *The Palestinians*, (London: Zed Books, 1979), 6.

14. Samih K. Farsoun, *Palestine and the Palestinians*, (Boulder CO: Westview Press, 1997), 4.

15. Syria, Iraq, Egypt and North Africa experienced bloody revolutions right after the end of World War II. Only Jordan, where over a million and a half registered refugees live today, was spared the bloody transition to statehood. In 1921, the British government turned it into a stable Hashemite monarchy under the leadership of King Abdallah, son of Sharif Hussain of Arabia.

16. This feeling was clearly expressed by the Arab nationalist delegation to London in 1922, that said that they did not consider the Balfour Declaration a legally binding document, because it provided an excuse to flood Palestine with alien immigrants. *Ibid.,* 52

17. "After the Disaster, the peasant refugees were to draw a direct relationship between their lack of education and their mass eviction. Palestinians with diplomas were able to find jobs easily in the newly developing Arab countries. Palestinians without education, capital or modern skills–the mass of the peasant population–were those who filled the camps. To the marginality of being peasants, was added a new marginality of being refugees." Rosemary Sayigh, *The Palestinians,* 6

18. The landowners were either wealthy, Arab absentee owners, or the land was owned collectively by all the families of the village. About 25 percent of

the fellahin were tenant fellahin, paying over a third of their income as rent to absentee owners.

19. The Arab school system was mobilized to disseminate to children in anti-Western, anti-Jewish nationalist propaganda.

20. The appearance of an Arabic daily newspaper in 1929, helped to deliver chauvinistic messages to the literate audience. Indeed, the majority of the population was excluded from knowledge and was left out of the decision-making process both prior and following the 1948 war.

21. See Bernard Lewis, *History: Remembered, Recovered, Invented* (Princeton: Princeton University Press, 1975), 67-69. Quoted in Fouad Ajami, *The Arab Predicament,* (New York: Cambridge University Press, 1987), 3

22. Fouad Ajami, *The Arab Predicament,* 3

23. *Ibid.,* 4

24. Dr. Zadek Jalal el Razam was a professor of philosophy at the American University in Beirut, and later a professor at Aman University in Jordan. This is a quote from a book he published in Beirut, in 1968.

25. Dr. Zadek Jalal el Razam, "The cause of the Arab defeat" in: Yehoshafat Y. Harkabi, ed., *Arab Lessons from their Defeat,* (Tel Aviv: Am Oved, 1969) in Hebrew, 79

26. *Ibid.,* 79

27. The Israeli Arabs are not eligible to UNRWA's support and cannot register as refugees.

28. As early as 1949, the Israeli government with the United Nations have developed a plan for compensating the refugees in the context of an overall settlement of the Israeli-Arab conflict. In 1953 Israel suggested that it would pay a $100 million on account of the overall restitution bill. The UN Refugee Office estimated the Palestinian refugees property to be &120 million, or close to $350 million. Israel was willing to shoulder a share of the bill to the

international fund, while the Arab governments will contribute their share. However, all efforts by the Israel government to establish an international fund to resettle Palestinian refugees in Arab countries or elsewhere collectively, failed. See discussion in: Nur Masalha "The Historical Roots of the Palestinian Refugee Question," in: Naseer Aruri, ed., *Palestinian Refugees,* (London: Pluto Press, 2001), 55

29. The exception to the rule was Jordan, who until 1988 granted the Palestinian refugees legal immigrant status eligible for Jordanian citizenship.

30. During the "Black September" of 1970, King Hussein of Jordan forced out thousands of PLO members who went and established a base in southern Lebanon.

31. See data in: Moshe Efrat, "The Palestinian Refugees: The Socio-Economic Integration in their Host Countries," 45-70. Nur Masalha, "The Historical Roots of the Palestinian Refugee Question," in Naseer Aruri, ed., *Palestinian Refugees,* (London: Pluto Press, 2001), 44, argues that 750,000 Palestinians were evicted in 1948. However, N. Masalha does not mention his source.

32. The Statistical Abstract of Palestine in 1944-45 set the figure for the total Arab population living in the Jewish-settled territories of Palestine at 570,800. Don Peretz estimated the number of Palestinians who had left their homes to be 700,000. See, Don Peretz, *Palestinian Refugees and the Peace Process,* (Washington D.C.,: US Institute of Peace, 1993).

33. Donna E. Arzt, *Refugees into Citizens*, (New York: Council on Foreign Relations, 1997), 14.

34. Eric Johnston was President Eisenhower's appointee to negotiate a plan for the unified development of the water resources of the Jordan-Yarmuk River Basin.

35. *Ibid.,* 19.

36. Georege E. Gruen, "The Palestinian Question in International Politics," in George E. Gruen, ed., *The Palestinian in Perspective*, (New York: Institute of Human Relations Press, 1982), 12.

37. *Ibid.*, 12-13.

38. W. Thomas Mallison, "The United Nations and the National Rights of the People of Palestine," in Ibrahim Abu-Lughod, *Palestinian Rights,* (Wilmette IL: Medina Press, 1982), 23.

39. However, none of the resolutions, including resolution 242, was adopted under chapter VII of the United Nations charter, thus they are not enforceable. Only resolutions adopted under chapter VII of the Charter are enforceable.

40. Richard Plender, *International Migration Law,* 415.

41. See discussion in: Donna E. Arzt, *Refugees into Citizens*, (New York: The Council on Foreign Relations, 1997).

42. See discussion in Elaine Hagopian, "Preface" in Naseer Aruri, ed., *Palestinian Refugees*, viii. Perhaps the most important action was the conference organized on April 1999 at the Boston University Law School, entitled: "The right of return: Palestinian Refugees and the Prospects for a durable Peace." See *Ibid.*, viii

43. For example, the famous Security Council resolution 242, (1967), and the Declaration of Principles (DOP) signed in 1993, both avoided the refugees' "right of return," and instead talked about the humanitarian aspects of the problem.

44. Joseph Massad, "Return or Permanent Exile?" in: Naseer Aruri, *ed., Palestinian Refugees*, 106 .

45. Harvard University Program on International Conflict Analysis and Resolution, have endorsed this interpretation.

46. *Ibid*, 109.

47. Susan M. Akram, "Reinterpreting Palestinian Refugees Rights Under International Law" in: Naseer Aruri, ed. *Palestinian Refugees*, 165

48. Susan M. Akram, "Reinterpreting Palestinian Refugees Rights Under International Law," 171

49. Report of the Director of UNRWA, (A/1905), Paris, 1951, 4

50. Dr. Hamad Said Al-Mawed, *The Palestinian Refugees in Syria, Their Past, Present and Future,* (Ottawa, Experts and Advisory Services Fund, 1999), 23

51. Report of the Director of UNRWA, (A/1905), Paris, 1951, 5

52. It is also required that the persecution be committed by the state rather than by individual citizens. *Ibid.,* 417

53. The majority of the Palestinian suicide terrorists have come from refugee camps.

54. *Ibid.,* 30.

55. *Ibid.,* 31.

56. Rosemary Sayigh, *Palestinians: From Peasants to Revolutionaries,* 12.

57. Dr. Hamad Said Al-Mawed, *The Palestinian Refugees in Syria,* 30.

58. Nitza Nachmias, "The Case of UNRWA," in Nitza Nachmias and E. Belgrad., eds., *The Politics of International Humanitarian Aid Operations,* (Westport CT: Praeger, 1997), 71.

59. Nitza Nachmias "The Case of UNRWA'" in *The Politics of International Humanitarian Aid Operations,* Nitza Nachmias and E. Belgrad, eds., (Westport CT: Praeger, 1997), 71.

60. Following the UN General Assembly Resolution 194 (III) of December 11, 1948.

61. The validity of the two-year residency standard may well be questioned, given the migratory patterns of population in the Middle East. For documented migrations from Syria, Lebanon, and Jordan to Palestine before 1948, see Joan Peters, *From Time Immemorial,* (New York: Harper & Row, 1984), 4.

62. Richard Plender, *International Migration Law*, (Dordrecht: Martinus Nijhoff Publishers, 1988), 415. This issue is discussed in details in R. Goldstein's article.

63. In comparison, the UNHCR employs about 6000 workers worldwide.

64. Total of 50 years budget. For example, "The European Commission has contributed over 200 million Euro to UNRWA's activities since 2000." (EC press release, July 17, 2003)

65. Joan Peters, *From Time Immemorial*, 18.

66. UNRWA's budget for 1999 was $314 million, and it ended the FY with a deficit of $61.9 million. Report of the Commissioner General of UNRWA (A/54/13)

67. The fact that over 50 percent of the refugee population is under 15 years of age is indeed very alarming.

68. The latest began in October 2000, and is still going on.

69. *Ibid.*, 30

70. Nitza Nachmias, "The Case of UNRWA," 71

71. Elia Zureik, *Palestinian Refugees and the Peace Process,* (Washington: Institute for Palestinian Studies, 1996), 29

72. Marianne Heiberg and Geir Ovensen, *Palestinian Society*, (Oslo: Fafo, 1994), 27

73. Ironically, it was Defence Minister Ariel Sharon, in 1982, who initiated the transformation of the military administration into a civil administration.

74. Reports of the Israel military and civil administration: 1967-1971; 1972; 1985

75. UNRWA has been allocating 17% of its budget to project funding. These include: school construction, upgrading health care centres, shelter rehabilitation, etc. New projects budget contains over $ 60 million for 2000-2001. However, UNRWA's spending per refugee has fallen from a level of $ 200 per refugee in 1975, to only $ 70 per refugee in 1997. Source: *Report of the Director of UNRWA*, (A/1905), 2

76. The PLO was created in 1964, years prior to the 1967 occupation of the West Bank and Gaza

77. Nitza Nachmias, "The Case of UNRWA," 71

78. On 14, June, 1967, Israel government and UNRWA signed an agreement (the "Michelmore-Comay" agreement) affirming Israel's rights and obligations in the refugee camps. Israel agreed to honour UNRWA's autonomy in the camps, with the exception of "considerations of military security," when Israel will have the right to abridge UNRWA's control of its facilities and operations. *Ibid.,* 72

79. This involved amending Jordanian land laws that were in effect until 1967, to allow the transfer of land to foreign and Israeli companies.

80. However, the Civil Administrators were military officers, who continued to use the same tactics, policies and strategies to keep the Palestinians under confining control.

81. John Dollard and others. *Frustration and Aggression*, (New Haven: Yale University press, 1961), 84

82. Richard Plender, *International Migration Law*, 393

83. Rex A. Hudson and Marylin Majeska, *The Sociology and Psychology of Terrorism*, (Library of Congress, Federal research Division, 1999), 12

84. The Israel Civil Administration was under the full control of the Israel Defence Force (IDF) , and the head of the Civil Administration has always been a full General in active service.

85. See detailed discussion in Robert T. Gurr, *Why Men Rebel*, (Princeton University Press, 1970)

86. Joseph Margolin, "Psychological Perspectives in Terrorism," in Jonah Alexander and Symoir M. Finger eds, *Terrorism,* (New York, John Jay Press, 1977), 273-4

87. John Dollard and others. *Frustration and Aggression*, 1

88. *Ibid.,* 4-5

89. Zeev Schiff and Ehud Ya'ari, *Intifada,* (Tel Aviv, Schocken Publishing, 1990), 15 (in Hebrew)

90. *Ibid.,* 7

91. Rosemary Sayigh, *Palestinians from Peasants to Revolutionaries,* 99-100

92. The PLO tried to mobilize the legendary Palestinian leader, Haj-Amin al Husseini, who lived in exile in Lebanon, to exert his influence within the refugee ranks, to boost the refugees emotional need for an aggressive reaction, but he did not succeed in reproducing the uprisings of the 1920s and the 1930s. On the 31st of December 1964, the newly created PLO executed its first terrorist act against Israel. However, it was a minor explosive charge the did little damage.

93. John Dollard and others. *Frustration and Aggression*, 1

94. The use of violence as a strategy was incorporated in the "Palestinian Charter."

95. Harold D. Lasswell, *Power and Personality,* 105-106

96. *Ibid.,* 111

97. "Why War?" an exchange of letters between Albert Einstein and Sigmund Freud, September 1932

98. Jeffrey D. Berejikian, "Model Building with Prospect Theory: A Cognitive Approach to International Relations," in *Political Psychology*, December 2002, Vol. 23, No. 4: 759-760

99. However, the writing was on the wall. Between 1986 and 1987 there was 100% increase in anti-Israeli violence, and a 133% increase in anti-occupation demonstrations. Tire burning was increased by 178 % and in stone throwing the increase was 140%. Source: Schif & Ya'ari, 26

100. Samih K. Farsoun, *Palestine and the Palestinians*, 157

101. "Children in Situations of Armed Conflicts," Document E/ICEF/1986/CRP.2, March 10, 1986, UNICEF, para. 23.

102. "From the1960s until the PLO's November 1988 implicit recognition of Israel, the Palestinians reminded Jews that they were intended for 'transfer' not onto some other dry land but into the Mediterranean Sea." Donna E. Arzt, *Refugees Into Citizens*, 20

103. In 1982, Suicide terrorism began in Lebanon against US and Israeli targets. See the siocide attack on the Marine Barracks on November 23, 1983 that killed 235 Marines.

104. Report of the Director of UNRWA, (A/1905), 4

105. Until 1967, Gaza was under Egyptian rule and the West Bank was under Jordanian rule.

106. William R. Polk, *The Arab World*, (Massachusetts: Harvard University Press, 1980), 32

107. *Ibid.*, 32

108. The PLO tried to mobilize the legendary Palestinian leader, Haj-Amin al Husseini, the who lived in exile in Lebanon, to exerted his influence within the refugee ranks, to boost the refugees emotional need for an aggressive reaction, but he did not succeed in reproducing the uprisings of the 1920s and the 1930s. On the 31st of December 1964, the newly created PLO executed

its first terrorist act against Israel. However, it was a minor explosive charge the did little damage.

109. Samih K. Farsoun, *Palestine and the Palestinians*, 156

110. The "Black September" in Jordan, in September 1970, marked perhaps the most violent anti-Palestinian campaign, when King Hussain ordered his army to launch an all out attack on the refugee camps to suppress PLO terrorist activities threatening his rule. The PLO moved to Lebanon where they stayed until 1982, when they were expelled to Tunis.

111 *Ibid.,* 146

112. This has been the case in Jordan after the expulsion of the Palestinian from Kuwait following the Gulf war.

113. Arafat's reign of terror almost led to a civil war in Jordan in 1970, and destroyed Lebanon in a bloody civil war that began in 1975.

114. Avraham Sela, "Authority without Sovereignty- The Road of the PLO from Armed Struggle to a Political Settlement," in Moshe Maoz & B.Z. Kedar, eds,. *The Palestinian National Movement: From Confrontation to Acceptance?* 367

115. "Armed struggle is the only way to liberate Palestine. This is the overall strategy, not merely a tactical phase…the liberation of Palestine is a national (qawmi) duty…and aims at the elimination of Zionism in Palestine." *The Palestinian National Charter.*

116. S.N. Eisenstadt. *Modernization: Protest and Change,* (Englewood: Prentice-Hall, 1966), 32

117. For example, in September 1999, an armed conflict erupted in Balata refugee damp in Nablus between Fatah fighters and local residents of the camp. Arafat ordered 1500-armed militia to enter the camp and taker over.

118. "Ha'aretz" (in Hebrew), March 27, 2003

119. "Counter-terrorism, Israel Counter-terrorism activity." ITC, April 2, 2003

120. Physical damage in the OT to infrastructure, public buildings, social services, health, education, and private property has been estimated at: $ 361,363,448 (2002). Data provided by UNSCO.

121. Bosnia and Kosovo are cases in point.

122. Jon Kimche, *The Second Arab Awakening*, (London: Thames and Hudson, 1970), 239

123. The Palestinian population has increased from roughly 1.4 million people in 1948, to 6.8 in 1995, and to over 7 million in 2000. Over 50 % of the refugee population are under 15 years of age. See, Samih K. Farsoun, and C. E. Zacharia, *Palestine and the Palestinians*, 139-140

124. The 1967 war 600,000 refugees mostly in Gaza and Jordan.

125. "Armed struggle is the only way to liberate Palestine...Commando action constitute the nucleus of the Palestinian liberation war...Our aim is to restore the national rights of the Palestinian people, namely, to destroy Israel." Article 6 of the Palestinian Charter.

126. Edward W. Said, *The Question of Palestine*, 46

127. *Ibid.*, 47

128. For example, the Fatah Tanzim, and the Martyrs Al – Aqsa have taken responsibility for more than 2,000 attacks and attempted attacks, including car bombing, suicide attacks, etc. (ITC, www.itc.org.il, April 1, 2003)

Rami Goldstein

CHAPTER NINE:

Legal Dilemmas of the Palestinian "Right of Return"

Preface

The Palestinian refugee problem seems to condition and determine the status of the peace processes between Israel and the Palestinians. Since 1993 (the Oslo agreements) the complex negotiations put a growing importance on the issue but failed to address it in a constructive manner. Resolving the legal dilemmas of the "Right of Return" is imperative to the achievement of a just and comprehensive peace in the Middle East.[1]

The nucleus of the legal dispute over the controversial issue of the Palestinian refugees concerns the historical causes of the Arab exodus from Palestine during and following the 1948 war. Israel argues that (a) in 1947, the Arabs initiated a violent, ruthless and unprovoked war against Israel with the purpose of preventing the establishment of the State of Israel. Thus, Israel sees the Arabs as bearing full responsibility for creating the refugee problem; (b) Israel denounces any responsibility for the problem on the grounds that the Palestinians abandoned voluntarily their homes in obedience of the callings of their leaders and the leaders of the Arab nations;[2] and (c) the

Palestinians and the Arab states are responsible for keeping the problem alive as a political "bargaining chip."[3]

The Palestinians, on the other hand, blame Israel for leading a carefully designed strategic campaign to drive the Arabs out of Palestine and deliberately causing the refugee problem. Since the Palestinian mass flight was a direct consequence of Israel's policy, neither the Palestinians nor the Arab countries are responsible for the problem.[4] Thus, the Palestinian refugees have (a) an inherent "right of return" to their homes in all parts of the State of Israel as a right recognized under principles of international law, and (b) the right to receive compensation of their choice.

The following discussion analyzes some legal dilemmas concerning the " right of return" of the Palestinian refugees. The context of the discussion will be the policies and practices of Israel and other Middle Eastern states including the Palestinian Authority, insofar as they impinge upon Palestinian refugees. The unique case of the Palestinian refugees proves that the longer the duration of the problem, the harder it is to find a durable solution. The passage of time has created new legal issues while complicating existing ones. Moreover, the mutual blame for the refugee exodus, effects the legal questions. In the course of time, the Palestinians have hardened their position and adopted an uncompromising inflexible, ideological-strategic perspective of the problem. This intransigent perspective was rationalized by social and religious propaganda that was in and of itself, based on a categorical solution: the total liquidation of Israel and the conquest of all its territory. This ideological-strategic perspective expressed a total rejection of the other two options included in General Assembly resolution 194, namely, compensation or resettlement. The following chapter reviews the legal perspectives of these opposing claims in search of a position that will be acceptable to both sides.

The Origin of the Palestinian Refugee Problem

The causes and origin of the Palestinian refugee problem have historical, legal and practical importance. Notwithstanding, the psychological dimensions that affected the interpretation of the "right of return" also play a critical role in finding a solution to the problem.[5] Two opposing approaches explain the origin of the Palestinian exodus. The first approach attributes the problem to the General Assembly Partition Resolution (November 29th 1947),[6] and the ensuing 1948 war.[7] The second approach argues that an examination of the origins of the Palestinian exodus requires a wider historical perspective. In fact, the roots of the problem lie as far back as the end of the eighteenth century, when the Jewish immigrants perceived Palestine as "a land without a people for a people without a land."[8] This assumption instigated the Balfour Declaration.[9]

The Arab community of Palestine and the Arab states rejected the Partition Plan, which gave the Jewish community more than half of the territory, despite the fact that the Arab community was at that time the majority. In the ensuing violence between the Jewish and the Palestinian communities, the Jews seized more territory. A Jewish state was declared on 14 May 1948, and when an armistice was agreed in 1949, Israel controlled approximately three quarters of the territories that as of 1948 had been under British mandatory rule in Palestine. There is no unequivocal answer as to the causes of the exodus of the Palestinians, or if it can be regarded as forced migration. The issue remains historically controversial and raises some complex legal and political dilemmas. The first wave of Palestinians that left their homes immediately following the adoption of the Partition Resolution, were approximately 30,000 wealthy businessmen and landed gentry, who believed that a war was inevitable; an Arab victory was assure; and they will return to their homes, soon, as victors. The hostilities that erupted after the 15th of May 1948, resulted in additional large waves of refugees, most of them from the big cities, who chose to leave their homes. This plight ended in November 1948.[10]

It seems that the Palestinian exodus was as a result of several cumulative factors: (a) As in every civil war, civilians who fear their fate flee to a territory where they are part of the majority, or to regions where their religion rules.[11] Thus, one of the main reasons for the 1948 Palestinian exodus was the natural instinct of self-defense, which dictates running away from a realistic or an imaginary dangerous threat. (b) The Arab leaders organized an intensive appeal to the Palestinian people, persuading them to leave their homes. In 1950, the Lebanese Ambassador to the UN, Emil al-Ghori (a Palestinian in origin) accused the Arab leaders: "You, the Arab leaders, are guilty. You called us to leave our fields, homes and villas, asking us not to disturb our forces that will come to massacre, hang and throw the Jewish people to the sea, promising us a victory which will return us our whole land, and more Jewish loot..."[12]

There is no doubt that the intensive anti-Israeli media propaganda created an atmosphere of fear and anxiety, and induced the massive flight.[13] The rumors described in great details Israeli forces torturing and coercing the local people to flee. In contrast, Israel argued, using observers reports, that the rumors were highly exaggerated, that forced migration cases were few, and usually resulted from vicious, unprovoked Arab assaults. The Israeli government condemned all forced migration acts. This argument was supported by the report published in September 1948 by the United Nations Mediator for Palestine, Count Bernadotte, who said: "The exodus of Palestinian Arabs resulted from panic created by fighting in their communities, by rumors real or alleged acts of terrorism, or expulsion."[14]

While the rumors on the behavior of the Israeli military were mostly untrue, the civil war resulted in great suffering of the Palestinian civilian population. Prof. Shlomo Ben-Ami described the situation: "The suffering of the civilian population will always be a burden on the conscience of any nation at war. The Arab-Israeli conflict has no monopoly on this maxim. The Palestinian refugee problem was born as the land was bisected by the sword, nor by design, Jewish or Arab. It was largely the inevitable by-product of Arab and Jewish fears and the protracted bitter fighting."[15] The 1948 war left the Palestinians with a feeling of shock and defeat. More than half of the Palestinian community became minority refugees. Their military force and their political leaders vanished, their problem turned into an "international problem" and an object for political manipulations.

The Jewish community perceived the volume of Palestinian forced migration as being much smaller.[16] Dr. Yves Besson, former director of UNRWA operations in the West Bank and Jerusalem observed: "There will be no hope for a solution, given the fact that the positions are so antagonistic, unless the Palestinians somehow transacted this central reference point in the perception they have of their national memory and identity, and unless the Israelis accept revisiting their past... in so doing the Israelis might accept some sort of responsibility for what happened in 1948-1949."[17] The Arabs in general, and the Palestinians in particular, developed a high level of sensitivity to the perceived injustice that the forced migration caused them. Consequently it is imperative to recognize the importance of the emotional/ psychological dimension of the Palestinian refugee issue. This seems to be the cause of the constant, unrelenting Palestinian insistence on the full implementation of UN resolution 194.[18]

The United Nations had taken major steps to address the refugee problem.

Assistance to the Palestinian refugees was first provided by non-governmental organizations under the umbrella of the United Nations Relief for Palestine Refugees (UNRPR).[19] Later, on December 8th, 1949, the UN General Assembly adopted resolution no. 302 (iv), establishing the United Nations Relief and Works Agency for Palestine Refugees in the Near East (UNRWA)[20] as a special, temporary relief agency, responsible only for the Palestinian refugees.[21] It must be stressed that UNRWA's mandate did not include any legal responsibility, namely, UNRWA was not created to provide legal protection for individuals suffering from persecution, rather to integrate economically the refugees who fled into the surrounding Arab states.[22] The Arab states accepted UNRWA's involvement only after being assured that its establishment would not jeopardize the right of the refugees to return to their original homes, as stipulated in the General Assembly Resolution 194(3) of December 11th 1948.[23] This was clearly stated in UNRWA's founding mandate.[24] Until the Six Day War (1967), the West had hoped the Arab-Israeli conflict would wither, the refugees would be integrated in their host countries, and Arab governments would accept Israel as a neighbor. But this hope foundered following the Arab humiliating defeat of 1967, and Israel's seizure of the West Bank and Gaza, and the Golan Heights. Many Palestinians fled or were forced to migrate to Jordan, not including the West Bank, where some 210,000 persons who had not previously been refugees were now described as "displaced persons."[25]

The Arab governments opposed any resettlement plan of the Palestinian refugees in their countries as part of a general strategy to keep the refugees as "political hostages," namely, keeping alive the Israel-Palestine dispute and exercising a continuous pressure on Israel to make territorial concessions.[26] Each Arab state adopted a different tactics in pursuing its policy towards the status of the Palestinian refugees. Jordan was the only state that opted for integration, and it conferred citizenship on the Palestinians until 1988.[27] The rest of the Arab states did not award citizenship to the Palestinians. Moreover, they imposed severe restrictions and placed them under surveillance by their security services. Lebanon for example, placed the refugees in an indeterminate category, neither as foreigners nor nationals, and issued work and travel permits sparingly.[28]

The PLO leadership rejected any settlement that was less than full implementation of the "inalienable rights of the Palestinian refugees."[29] Moreover, the Arab governments and the Palestinians never abandoned their position that the founders of Israel caused the mass flights of the Palestinian civilians from the area of Mandate Palestine as a strategy, and therefore the Arab countries and the Palestinians are not responsible for the problem. The official Israeli position has been the diametric opposite. Israel claims that the Arab states ordered and encouraged the refugees to flee, in order not to interrupt the Arab armies from liberating Palestine. Thus, Israel denies any responsibility for the Palestinian refugees, and will never accept the Palestinian "right of return," especially since it would alter the character of the Jewish state.

While the resettlement of the refugees "elsewhere" rather than their repatriation to Israel seemed essential, the Arab governments and the Palestinians resisted any program of resettlement or naturalization as a way of resolving the refugee problem. Their attitude compounded the problem. Takkenberg summarized his conclusions in respect of this issue as follows:

"...The preservation of the Palestinian identity put emphasis on maintaining the Palestinian's status of refugees, so as to avoid providing Israel with an excuse to evade its responsibility for their plight. Accordingly, the Arab governments refused, as a matter of principle, to contribute to the budget of UNRWA. They argued that the United Nations created the problem and should be responsible for supporting and maintaining the refugees until their repatriation...For the same reason they resisted resettlement or naturalization as a way of resolving the refugee problem...in the view of the PLO, a solution of the Palestine question should not focus on the individual refugees, but rather on Palestinian people as a whole. It was for this reason that the PLO put emphasis on the recognition of the inalienable rights of the Palestinian people, including the right of self-determination... national independence and sovereignty."[30]

However, since 1948, the intransigence of the PLO and the Arab states created decades of strife and politico-legal arguments have clouded the basic issues and have obscured the origins and evolution of the Palestine problem.[31]

The Definition of a "Palestine Refugee"

After World War I and World War II the issue of refugees became an international problem and part of the international law. A perception developed that forced migration is not merely a humanitarian problem to be solved through humanitarian means, but a legal issue as well. The legal definition of the term "refugee" became distinct from its ordinary usage; namely, refugees are subjects of forced migration who have a special status in international law governed by the terms of the relevant international instruments.[32] International law recognizes four categories of refugees: (a) Refugees defined by the Convention Relating to the Status of Refugees from 28 July 1951[33] (hereinafter–"The 1951 convention"); (b) Protocol Refugees, who are protected by a regional agreement; (c) Refugees who fear harm as a result of serious disturbances of public order, but who are not able to invoke the protection of a special regional agreement; and (d) All persons who are forced migrants as a result of natural or man-made causes.[34] The definition used by the The1951 convention, as amended by the 1967 Protocol Relating to the Status of Refugees of 31 January 1967,[35] is the most universally acceptable definition.

The 1951 Convention defines a "refugee" as: "A person who, owing to a well–grounded fear of being persecuted for reasons of race, religion, nationality, membership of a particular social group or political opinion, is outside the country of his nationality, and is unable or, owing to such fear, is unwilling to avail himself of the protection of that country, or who not having a nationality and being outside the country of his former habitual residence as a result of such events, is unable or owing to such fear, is unwilling to return to it."[36] Article 1D of the 1951 Convention states that: "This Convention shall not apply to persons who are at present receiving from organs or agencies of the United Nations other than the United Nations High Commissioner for Refugees protection or assistance. When such protection or assistance has ceased for any reason, without the position of such persons being definitely settled in accordance with the relevant resolutions of the General Assembly of the United Nations, these persons shall *ipso facto* be entitled to the benefits of this Convention." It should be stressed that the legal interpretation of provision 1D of the 1951 Convention is controversial. Some courts and Western governments had interpreted article 1D of the 1951 Convention as intended to exclude persons who were receiving protection or assistance from United Nations organs or agencies of the United Nations other than the United Nations High Commissioner for refugees (UNHCR). Thus, a Palestinian refugee who receives aid from UNRWA does not enjoy the benefits of the 1951 Convention.[37]

A different interpretation argues that article 1D only applies to persons receiving protection or assistance from UNRWA, and if such persons cease receiving such aid from UNRWA (including cases considered as voluntary renouncement), or they were not initially entitled to receive aid from UNRWA, then they fall *ipso facto* under the provisions of the 1951 Convention.[38]

Lex Takkenberg, commenting on that article has pointed out that:

"Most states party to the convention and\or Protocol appear to be reluctant to grant Palestinian refugees access to the benefits of these instruments...In the opinion of this author it is therefore no more than reasonable that those Palestinians refugees for whom UNRWA assistance is no longer attainable, and who find themselves in countries bound by the 1951 convention, are *ipso facto* entitled to benefit from its provisions."[39]

The UNHCR approach is that the 1951 Convention does not apply to Palestinian refugees who are covered by a separate mandate of UNRWA and they are not entitled to enjoy the legal protection and the benefits of this Convention.[40] However, Palestinians who live outside one of UNRWA's five areas of operation, such as those in Iraq or Libya, are considered to be "people of concern" to UNHCR.[41] It can be therefore be concluded that the Palestinian refugees have a status that is special and unique under international law.

The Palestinian refugees could be classified into three main categories. The first includes those who were registered and were regarded as legitimate refugees by the states in which they resided, and live in one of the five areas where UNRWA provided relief (the West Bank and the Gaza Strip, Jordan, Lebanon and Syria). The second are those who reside in countries where UNRWA operates, but were not registered with UNRWA, either because they were not in economic need or missed the deadline to register. Finally, there are those refugees who could not register because they reside in countries where UNRWA does not operate, such as Egypt, Saudi Arabia, Iraq, the Gulf States, Europe, South and North America, etc. The last two categories, estimated to include about 25 percent of the total Palestinian refugee population, do not receive any assistance from UNRWA.[42]

UNRWA's original definition of a Palestine refugee was: "One whose normal residence was Palestine for a minimum period of two years immediately preceding the outbreak of the conflict in 1948 and who, as a result of this conflict, has lost his home and means of livelihood."[43] To be eligible to receive UNRWA assistance a Palestinian must be registered with UNRWA, live in an area where UNRWA operates, and be in need. UNRWA's definition was, to a large extent, an *ad hoc* definition, i.e. it developed as a result of a need for a working tool. Lacking an accepted definition of eligibility for refugee assistance, it became increasingly evident that the international community would have to be indefinitely responsible for the refugees of the 1948 war.[44] In reality, it was difficult to follow UNRWA's definition of a "Palestine refugee," because there were frequent changes in the refugees' conditions.[45]

UNRWA registration of a Palestine refugee stopped on 1 July 1952. The main criterion for being registered with UNRWA was the economic need of the refugee. However, major changes occurred in the definition of the terms "Palestine refugee" and in the refugees' statuses in the host countries. Also, the living conditions and circumstances in which the refugees live have changed over the years and often vary from country to country. These changes affected the refugees' own attitudes about their future and are relevant to prospects and plans of the various parties attempting to resolve the refugee problem.[46] Since the 1951 convention and the refugee regime do not apply to the Palestinian refugees, at least as long as UNRWA continues to provide assistance, and since the statelessness conventions do not apply to the Palestinians the consequence is a *sui generis* Palestinian refugee regime.[47]

Since 1949, UNRWA revised its basic definition of eligibility by adding to the original definition the descendents of the refugees if (a) they were registered with UNRWA, (b) lived in one of the areas that UNRWA operates and, (c) were in need. UNRWA refined its definition of a "Palestinian refugee" and the new definition stated that: "A Palestinian refugee is a person whose normal residence was Palestine for a minimum of two years preceding the conflict, lost both his home and the means of livelihood, and took refuge in one of the countries where UNRWA provides relief. Refugees within this definition and the direct descendants of such refugees are eligible for agency assistance if they are registered with UNRWA, living in the area of UNRWA operations, and in need."

This amendment was tacitly accepted without UN General Assembly approval. Although the amendment of the definition was intended only for humanitarian reasons, the original resolution, G/ 194(3), applied to those refugees who were not necessarily in need for UNRWA assistance, and were, for the time being, used as a political tool.[48] Over the years, UNRWA's criteria for "needy persons" have also been changed.[49] Many refugees whose economic situation have improved or who left one of the countries in which UNRWA operates were not required to return their refugee ID cars continued their status as registered refugees, although they were not eligible for UNRWA's assistance.[50]

Operating on the basis of its definition, UNRWA continued to refine its instructions on eligibility for "Palestine refugee" status and eligibility for specific types of assistance. The main changes were the registration of Palestinians descendants with UNRWA and the new eligibility rules issued by UNRWA in 1993.[51] The 1993 eligibility rules, known as the Consolidated Registration Instructions (CRI), eliminated the requirements of "need" and initial flight in 1948 to a country within UNRWA's area of operations. Under these rules a "Palestine refugee" is defined as follows: "(Palestine refugee) shall mean any person whose normal place of residence was Palestine during the period 1 June 1946 to May 1948 and who lost both home and means of livelihood as a result of the 1948 conflict." The 1993 eligibility rules (CRI), also address the issue of the Palestinians' descendants. Consequently, many persons who were never before registered with UNRWA were covered by the new definition.[52] UNRWA figures as for 30 June 2003 indicated some 4,082,300 registered refugees and that according to UNRWA data the 1948 refugees have more than quadrupled over five decades, and are scattered as follows:[53]

Country	1948	31 Dec. 1996	30 June 2003
Jordan	70,000	1,389,603	1,718,767
Lebanon	100,000	356,258	391,679
Syria	75,000	(c) 352,136	409,662
West Bank	280,000	538,391	654,971
Gaza Strip	200,000	731,942	907,221
Total	725,000	3,368,330	4,082,300

During the course of time, many Palestinians have acquired a new nationality. Naturalization has always been considered a step which brings refugee status to an end.[54] Former Palestinian refugees who have acquired a new nationality are expected to give up their eligibility for UNRWA's assistance since they have ceased to be refugees. However, because UNRWA never asked or tried to update its records, or attempted to conduct a census, many of the *bone fide* nationals of Europe, the United States and Jordan, among others, are still registered within UNRWA's records. The interpretation of the UNRWA definition, the question of the legality of the amendments to the definition, and the legal issue of whether Palestinian refugee status is passed from one generation to another, are key factors for the definition of a "Palestinian refugee" in any future peace negotiations between Israel and the Palestinians.[55]

The Refugees' "Right of Return": Legal Aspects and Dilemmas

The Arab states' unswerving position has been a consistent insistence on the right of the refugees, pursuant to resolution 194 (3), to either return to their homes (*Haq al-'awdah*) or to receive compensation, according to their choice.[56] Following this view, the central component of resolution 194 (3) is the return of the refugees. Since 1948, the General Assembly has recognized and periodically confirmed this right. For example, in resolution 3236 from 22 November, 1974 the U.N. General Assembly created a nexus between the Palestinians' right of return and the Palestinian right of self determination.[57]

With regard to Palestinians living in exile following the 1967 war, the General Assembly in December 1997 resolved that it "reaffirms the right of all persons displaced as a result of the June 1967 and subsequent hostilities to return to their homes or former places of residence in the territories occupied by Israel since 1967."[58] Ahmed al-Shuqieri, one of the leaders of the P.L.O., stated in one of his many speeches in the U.N.: "From December 1948 – December 1959, the return of the refugees was always the objective according to which the U.N. and its organizations acted.

U.N. resolution 194 (3) recognized the rights of the refugees to return, without referring at all to Israel's consent to such."[59] The Arab leaders clung to their goal of liquidation of Israel and argued that they will reject any settlement based on the Partition Plan. The solution of the Palestine problem cannot be found in the settlement of the refugee problem, and not even in Israel's return to the 1947 borders.[60] Any Israeli concession that will allow Israel to remain in existence will not be acceptable. Those who say that resolving the refugee problem would remove the main obstacle to a solution are mistaken. The Palestinian problem will remain as acute as ever even if each and every refugee is settled.[61] The following are several examples that will clarify the significance of the "right of return" of the Palestinian refugees.

At the Palestinian Refugee Conference in Homs, Syria, in July 1957, the following resolution was reached: "Any discussion aimed at a solution of the Palestinian problem, which will not be based on ensuring the refugees' right to annihilate Israel will be regarded as a desecration of the Arab people and an act of treason."[62] The former Egyptian President Gamal Abed-el Nasser elucidated the significance of the concept when he said, "If the Arabs return to Israel, Israel will cease to exist."[63] Naser repeated the argument that the Arab–Israeli conflict is not about the refugees and repatriation would not be the end of the conflict; the central issue is the existence of Israel: "Israel thought the ending of the refugee problem would lead to the ending of the Palestine problem, but the danger lies in the very existence of Israel."[64] The Prime minister of Lebanon, Abdullah Al-Yafi, speaking at the Lebanese Parliament, said, "The day of the realization of the Arab hope for the return of the refugees to Palestine means the liquidation of Israel."[65] The attitude of the various Palestinian terrorist organizations, headed over the years by the P.L.O., has been long known. The spokesperson for the *Al -Saika* terror organization, Hanna Batish, clearly stated: "So far, we have not achieved the strategic goal of the organization–liberation of all Palestinian land so that the camps (in Lebanon) can be liquidated and their residents returned to Palestine."[66]

The ongoing campaign to realize the "right of return" resurfaced and was presented as a central theme of the "Palestinian Declaration of Independence" of 15th November 1988. The "solution" as conceptualized by the P.L.O., includes the return of hundreds of thousands of refugees who were uprooted during the battles of 1948–them, their children and all their ancestors.[67]

The "Phased Strategy" and the "Right of Return"

After the Yom Kipur war (1973), Israel's relations with the Arab states stabilized, and attention had shifted to the Palestinian problem.[68] It was perhaps Kissinger's "Step-by-Step" political strategy that influenced the PLO to adopt the "phased strategy," or the "phased method." The basic principle was to abandon, if only for a limited time, the strategy of daring, risky violent assaults on Israel. The ultimate goal of destroying Israel will be accomplished gradually and patiently. The PLO was prepared to give up an immediate decisive war, and focus first on a partial Israeli withdrawal and the establishment of a Palestinian state. The liberation of all of Palestine, from the Mediterranean Sea to the Jordan River would be pursued in a gradual, calculated manner, while the intermittent armed struggle against Israel would be postponed to the "second stage." This political strategy required a campaign of adjustment to a gradual realization of goals, replacing the tactics of seeking an immediate realization of the entire dream. The "phased strategy" was documented and confirmed in a PLO announcement at the Tripoli conference (December 1977), sent to President Sadat: "Action will be prepared for the purpose of realizing the right of the Palestinian people to return and for self determination on every portion of Palestinian soil that will be liberated without peace, recognition or negotiation, as a progressive goal of the Palestinian revolution."[69] Within the framework of this strategy, a multitude of refugees would return to Israel to strengthen the existing Arab community. The implementation of the "Right of Return" would turn the minority Arab community to the majority, and the destruction of the Zionist entity could become a viable eventually. Moreover, the returnees would serve as the "bridge" between the two stages, accelerating and intensifying the conflict by creating an internal pressure in Israel. The "phased strategy" viewed Israeli Arabs as an inseparable part of the Palestinian people with no intrinsic difference between them and their brothers living in the West Bank and the Gaza Strip who were later conquered. Their liberation was included in the timetable of the overall plan; namely, their liberation will be postponed to the last stage.[70] Clearly, the evacuation of the territories conquered by Israel in 1948 and 1967 constitutes a corner stone and *sine qua non* for the settlement of the problem of the refugees.

The "Right of Return" and the Oslo Accords

In 1993, the PLO and the government of Israel achieved a breakthrough in their difficult and violent conflict. First, the two sides decided to recognize each other. Second, Yitzhak Rabin and chairman Yassir Arafat signed a "declaration of principles" (DOP) that provided the framework for the settlement of the Palestinian-Israeli conflict.[71] However, the DOP, which provided jurisdiction over the West Bank and Gaza to the Palestinian self-governing council, did not directly address the Palestinian refugee problem. This issue, as well as the issues of Jerusalem and the settlements, were left out to be settled in the permanent status negotiations (Article IV and Article v3).[72] Some Palestinian leaders and intellectuals have, rightfully, been skeptical of the possibility to solve the refugee problem and the Palestinian refugees' "right of return" on the basis of the agreements reached between Israel and the Palestinians at the Madrid (1991) and the Oslo (1993-4) meetings. However, the agreements had created serious hopes among all the parties involved in the conflict.[73]

Faisal al-Husaini, one of the PLO leaders who participated in the Oslo accords negotiations, stated: "The right to return to the Palestinian state is not negotiable. It's a natural right for every Palestinian to return to the Palestinian state because the very idea behind creating the state is the establishment of a homeland where the Palestinian people can feel secure, where they can fulfill their goals, hopes and national aspirations…"[74] Any proposal for less than a complete return of the refugees to their homeland was rejected by the Arab states and the Palestinians. Mr. Eli Sanbar eloquently expressed the Arab and Palestinian position in his opening remarks of the multilateral working group on refugees in Ottawa, May 13, 1992. He declared that "without the solemn recognition of the refugees 'right of return,' the refugee problem will remain unsolved. Such a recognition is also necessary to alleviate the impact of the prolonged refugee presence in the host countries, and thus to facilitate harmonious relations with the latter during the period of forced exile."[75]

Dr. Asaa'd Abd al-Rahman, a senior member of the PLO, wrote in July 1999: "The time has come…to ask ourselves why the refugees cannot return to their homes…Will we face war? Yes. Till the Russians immigrants (and their resembles) will continue to immigrate to Israel the outcome will be War."[76] A public opinion survey conducted in September 2000 in the West Bank and Gaza between 1996-1999 concluded that both Palestinians in the

West Bank and Gaza (80%), and the Arabs living in Israel (82%) agree that Palestinian refugee should be allowed to return if this is their wish.[77]

A special committee appointed by Arafat and headed by Mr. Salim Al-Zannun recommended to the Palestine National Council (PNC) alternative options regarding the Palestinian refugee problem. The recommendations were approved by the PNC in its February 2000 session, and were as follows:

♦ To cling to the context and the actual meaning of Resolution 194 and the right of return of the refugees to their homes and to receive compensation for the damages they suffered and not sign a peace treaty before achieving this goal.

♦ To reject all the resettlement attempts, notwithstanding their source.

♦ To set up a general national conference which will establish committees to follow up the implementation of the Palestinian demand of the return of the refugees who live in their homeland and the Diaspora."[78]

Clearly the PA official position after the Camp David II conference (July 2000) still remained that: (a) The universal recognition of the right of refugees to return to their homes is not only legal and moral in character; it also responds to participate necessities and considerations. (b) The return of refugees is an essential component for generating public confidence in peace. Moreover, the return of the refugees will actually generate peace. Peace will be a derivative of the return of the refugees, and (c) last but not least, it plays an essential part in validating and stabilizing the post-conflict political order. The end of a conflict is inconceivable without bringing a closure to the refugee problem. The demand that Israel must recognize the right of the Palestinian refugees to return to their homes, namely, every refugee should be permitted to return if he or she chooses to do so, requires a detailed repatriation plan that includes the modalities, timetables and numbers for a phased return of the refugees. This plan must insure the safety and dignity of return in accordance with international human rights norms."[79] Some Arab observers hold the opinion that the Palestinian refugees themselves believe that their inalienable rights *per se* cannot be negotiated between Israel and the PA. With reference to International Law they stress that agreements, which deprive civilians of recognized human rights, including the "right of return" and restitution, are null and void.[80]

The Saudi Initiative, the "Roadmap" and the "Right of Return"

On February 2002, the Saudi Crown Prince Abdullah bin Abdul Aziz announced his peace initiative, demanding a total Israeli withdrawal from all land occupied in 1967 including East Jerusalem, the Golan Heights, and the Shebaa Farms.[81] In return, a comprehensive Arab-Israeli peace would be declared, establishing normal relations between all the Arab countries and Israel.[82]

The original Saudi peace plan lacked details and did not refer directly to the refugee problem or the "right of return." After the legal and political details had been refined, the proposal was endorsed by the Arab League summit held in Beirut (27-28 March 2002). The final, revised resolution that was adopted unanimously by the Arab summit was totally different from the original initiative. The basic points were: Israel had to withdraw from all the Arab territories occupied since June 1967 in implementation of Security Council Resolutions 242 and 338, and Israel had to accept an independent Palestinian state with East Jerusalem as its capital. In return, the Arab states would establish normal relations with Israel in the context of a comprehensive peace. The Council further called upon Israel to withdraw from all the remaining occupied Lebanese territories; a just solution to the Palestinian refugee problem would be agreed upon in accordance with UN General Assembly Resolution 194. Israel had to accept the establishment of a sovereign independent Palestinian state with East Jerusalem as its capital, and consequently, the Arab countries would affirm the following.

They would consider the Arab-Israeli conflict ended, and all the states of the region would enter into a peace agreement with Israel. They would establish normal relations with Israel in the context of this comprehensive peace plan, as well as reject all forms of Palestinian repatriation which would conflict with the special circumstances of the Arab host countries.[83]

On April 30, 2003 the United States Department of State officially released an American peace initiative known as the "road map." The US "roadmap" was accepted by the European Union, Russia, and the United Nations as a three-stage plan that would lead to the creation of a Palestinian state by 2005, after a series of reciprocal steps on both sides. Only on phase three would the issues of Jerusalem, the final borders between the two states, and the resolution of the issue of the "right of return" be determined. The Israeli government continued to view the "right of return" as a menace to its existence and demanded that the "right of return" be addressed at the beginning of the process.[84] Israeli PM Ariel Sharon proposed that Israel commit itself to a two-state solution, if the Palestinians would simultaneously make concessions on the "right of return."[85]

The Religious Dispute:
Islamic Fundamentalists' Position

The Islamic fundamentalist organizations consider the Israeli-Palestinian conflict an ideological-theological dispute, not a political dispute. The "Islamic Jihad" leader, sheik Asad Bayud el-Tammimi, declared that acceptance of Israel's right of existence means abandonment of the Holy Arab territory. He emphasized that the Israeli-Palestinian conflict is not merely a political issue, but it is a battle between Judaism and Islam and no compromises can be done or accepted.[86] The other Islamic terrorist organization, the "Hamas," is a diverse, multidimensional organization with broad support in the Palestinian street. Like "Islamic Jihad," it calls for the physical destruction of Israel through a holy war (*jihad*) and the establishment of an Islamic Palestinian state from the "sea till the mountains." These organizations preach for the take over of all the Israeli territories.[87] The "Hamas" saw the land of Palestine as *Waqf* (Islamic religious endowment) and as one and indispensable unit. Thus, any concession on any part of this Holy Land is absolutely forbidden according to Islamic Law.[88] Neither the "road map" nor the Saudi initiative could satisfy the Islamic fundamentalist establishment.

Arab Main Legal Arguments on the
"Right of Return"

Arab jurists argue that Israel's grounds for rejecting the return of the refugees are purely political and not legal. Dr. Muhammad al-A'nimi and Dr. Muhammad Abd al-Hamid from the University of Alexandria claim that Israel's refusal to allow the return of the Palestinian refugees to their homes prior to reaching a final peace agreement is only a tactic, a camouflage of its recalcitrant position and its clear objection to the U.N. 194, 242 and 338 resolutions. They argue that while Israel fears that the refugees could become a fifth column, their main goal is to derail UN resolutions that Israel views as detrimental to its interests.[89]

Dr. Hammed Sultan writes in a similar vein: "Israel refused to allow the return of the refugees purely because of its own political or strategic interests, as allowing the Arabs to return to Palestine would result in a constant threat to their State." Henry Catan accuses Israel of an inhuman attitude and argues that Israel refused the return of the refugees for racist reasons, namely the policy of creating a state in Palestine that is racist, religious and exclusively Jewish.[90] The Arab states insist that a solution will not be reached by negotiations or compromises, but rather through the absolute implementation of section 11 of the General Assembly resolution 194 (3). The Arab legal arguments regarding the "right of return" were grounded both at the level of general principles of public international law, and on the concrete basis of UN resolutions. Arab jurists argue that the legal framework for the "right of return" in international law is enshrined in two basic sources: human rights law and humanitarian law.[91] With regard to general legal principles of international law, the arguments were on three main levels:

♦ The right of return derives from natural law and it existed in 1948 as a customary binding norm of international law.

♦ The right of return is based on the Universal Declaration Concerning Human Rights, from 1948 (UDCHR).

♦ The right of return is based on the international covenant on Civil and Political Rights, from 1966 (ICCPR).[92]

Arab jurists argue that the refugees' "right of return" to their homes and lives in their homeland is both an irrefutable natural legal right and a basic human right. The Egyptian jurist Dr. Muhammad A'nem says that "the Arab refugee problem is characterized by the fact that it is a problem concerning a nation whose homeland and right of self determination was stolen from it. The Palestinian refugees claim their right to return, and this is a right which is granted to them by the rules of international law."[93]

Professor Quincy Wright points out that, in this regard, Arab states have a good right of action according to international law for the return of the refugees and compensation for Arab refugees from the 1948 and the 1967 wars. The rules of war, which apply to all *de facto* acts of war, require that citizens be treated with compassion, while refusing the return of the refugees or refusing to compensate them, is in violation of these laws.[94] Arab jurists claim that the "right of return" is recognized in international law as an ancient and natural right that is self evident, and they argue further that "... the natural and inherent right of return is an acknowledged norm of international law."[95] Other arguments include the fact that the Economic and Social Council of the United Nations Commission on Human Rights had asserted the principle of the right of return in 1946, and approved in 1973 draft principles on the right of everyone to leave any country and to return to one's own country. In their opinion it proves that "the natural and inherent right of return is acknowledged norm of international law, as one of the general principles of law recognized by civilized nations."[96]   Rashid   Khalidi observes that the 1988 Palestinian Declaration marked the first time that the Palestinian National Council reaffirmed the Palestinian people's "right of return" based on UN resolutions. Previously, the "right of return" was always affirmed with no reference to the UN resolutions. In his opinion, in explicitly accepting the terms of resolution 194(3) the PLO has accepted certain crucial limitations on a putative absolute right of return.[97] Nevertheless, the idea of the "right of return" and the total liberation of Palestine underwent a major shift by 1974, and the question of the "right of return" was re-evaluated.[98] Regarding the second legal argument, Arab jurists often argue that section 13(2) of the Universal Declaration of Human Rights from 1948 (hereinafter– "The Universal Declaration") is one of the principle sources for the right of return. This section states: "Every individual has a right to return to his country."[99] According to the interpretation offered by the above Arab jurists, the Universal Declaration ensures that everyone has the right to life, freedom, liberty, security and freedom to return to their country. These principles became a legal commitment according to customary international law which prohibits countries from doing injustice to foreigners in their territory, and according to the laws of war that protect the residents of occupied territories.[100]

The Universal Declaration is presented as a legal source, confirming the argument that a "just and lasting" solution to the refugees' problem is a condition to a lasting peace. To that end, Israel must recognize its responsibility for the forced displacement and dispossession of the Palestinian people and for the subsequent prevention of their return to their homes. Besides its symbolic significance, such recognition entails Israeli responsibility for the eventual resolution of the problem. According to this approach, the principles in the Declaration have become a legal commitment pursuant to customary international law, that prohibits countries from neglecting to do justice to foreigners in their territory and the laws of war that protect people in occupied territories. Moreover, Arab jurists also often argue that in practice, resolution 194(3) embodies the principles that appear in the Universal Declaration of Human Rights. In relation to this legal argument, it must be stressed that the Universal Declaration has no binding legal validity from the perspective of international law.[101] The rights to which the Declaration refers are moral and not legal, and no country can be considered liable if it does not carry out any of its provisions.[102] There is almost a consensus in the legal literature, whereby the Universal Declaration does not constitute a binding, valid legal document.[103] In congruence to this approach the International Covenant on Civil and Political Rights of 1966 (ICCPR) is viewed as providing legal validity to numerous rights that appear in the Universal Declaration and constitutes a legal basis for the right of return. The Covenant sets out, in section 12(4), as follows: "No one shall be arbitrarily deprived of the right to enter his own country."[104] Consequently, it has been argued that "the international Covenant on Civil and Political rights of 1966 derives from the Declaration, and its status as an international treaty leaves little doubt as to its force."[105]

The Israeli Position Regarding the Return of the Refugees

Israel's objection to the full return of the refugees is based on three main reasons:

1. *Security Considerations* The return of the refugees prior to a total and durable peace is a security risk that Israel could not withstand. The refugees might constitute a hostile element in the continued battle against the Jewish state.[106] The ongoing violent hostilities, the unresolved state of war with some

Arab countries, and the on going conflicts with the Palestinian Authority do not allow any possibility of the refugees' return. The refugees never accepted the two imperative requirements outlined in resolution 194(3), namely, that they be "loyal citizens," and that they live "in peace with their neighbors." Their main intention in "returning" has been, and remains, to destroy Israel. The key point does not concern the refugees' legal right to return. The Arabs have often publicly declared their *animus belli*, and have stated that the significance of the refugees' return is, in no uncertain terms, the liquidation of the state of Israel.

2. *Social Demographic Considerations*　Israel believes that settlement of the refugees in Israel would not constitute a simple physical "return." An influx of Palestinians will alter the character of the Jewish state, turning the Jewish community into a minority group. Moreover, the refugees' separation from Arab society, and factors such as differences in language, culture, national identity and loyalty, would prevent them from merging with the Israeli society.[107] An additional consideration was that a social crisis could develop which would lead to the disintegration of Israel's identity as a Jewish State as a result of the demographic shift that would be created.

3. *Economic Considerations*　Notwithstanding its sparse resources, Israel absorbed, in the years following its establishment, about a million Jewish refugees from Arab countries. To absorb millions of Palestinians is economically unthinkable. Conversely, most Arab countries are endowed with vast economic resources and no shortage of territory, and the absorption of the Palestinian refugees would be beneficial to both.[108] Indeed, article 11 of resolution 194(3) proposed an arrangement for economic cooperation between Israel and the Arab states, but neither Israel nor the Arab states ever implement this clause.

Finally, Israel argues that resolution 194(3) is comprised of 15 articles, all of them strongly linked to each other and all directed towards the main goal of achieving a final settlement for all the existing problems in the dispute. Accordingly, it is impossible to separate any section, such as article 11, from the context of the resolution without implementing all the other articles.[109] Also, Article 11 does not include an unrestricted right of repatriation. In fact, it does not employ that term at all.

UN involvement in the issue of the refugees is also controversial. The U.N. lacks the legal ability, under its charter, to grant rights to any person to enter the territory of any sovereign country at will. Indeed, the term "right" was at first used in the draft resolution, but following objections, the term "right" was eventually deleted from the authorized version of the resolution text. The resolution employed the term "should be permitted," and the clear intention was for the relevant government, meaning the Israeli government, to decide on this issue.[110] This premise was reinforced in the mandate of the Conciliation Commission on Palestine (UNCCP) that stated that all the details concerning the refugee problem would be concluded between the governments during the final peace negotiation.[111] The disagreements concerned the interpretation of Article 11, namely, whether it allows for options other than total repatriation. Israel believes that resettlement is also offered, as well as a choice of financial compensation. Also, Article 11 did not grant the refugees an unrestricted right of return and such an expression was not used. In fact, the U.N. charter does not provide the UN with an authority to override the immigration rules of a sovereign country.[112]

It should be pointed out that during the Lausanne Conference (1949) Israel agreed to the return of 100,000 refugees.[113] Moreover, during the Camp David negotiations in December 1978 PM Menahem Begin told the US National Security Adviser, Mr. Bzezinski, that Israel would agree to the return of a reasonable number of refugees to the West Bank and the Gaza Strip.[114] Later, Prime Minister Ehud Barak (1999-2003) suggested a comprehensive and effective solution to the refugee problem, with priority given to the refugees residing in Lebanon. According to this plan, an unrestricted "right of return" would be limited to refugees returning to territories under a Palestinian rule, in the context of a Palestinian state. The proposal included a compromise allowing the Palestinians not to waive their "right of return," and not to concede their claim to repatriation. This clause would resolve the contradiction between the basic Palestinian demands for their "right of return" while, practically, there will be no return to Israeli sovereign territories. Finally, the Palestinian declaration of the "right of return" would not be legally binding on Israel.[115] This initiative was followed by a serious attempt to advance the peace negotiations with a fresh approach (President Clinton, Camp David II Conference, July 2000). Alas, both initiatives failed.

The final blow to the Oslo accords was the outbreak of the Second *Intifada* in September 2000, also known as the "*al-Aqsa Intifada.*" President Clinton's reaction to the *al-Aqsa Intifada* was another unsuccessful attempt to resolve the conflict. On 20th December 2000, President Clinton invited Israeli and PA negotiators to Washington for separate talks with the American Peace teams. On 23rd December 2000, Clinton presented his parameters for a final status agreement. Concerning the Palestinian refugees, the US proposal was build on five main elements:

♦ The solution of the refugees' problem must be consistent with the two states approach.

♦ In the implementation of the two state solutions, the general "right of return" would not include a specific right of return to Israeli territory. This, however, did not negate the aspiration of the Palestinian people to return to the area.

♦ Five possible homes for the refugees were offered: 1) The state of Palestine; 2) Areas in Israel being transferred to Palestine in a land swap; 3) Rehabilitation in present host country; 4) Resettlement in a third country; 5) Admission to Israel. In listing these options, the agreement made clear that all Palestinian refugees would have the right to enter the West Bank, Gaza Strip and area acquired in the land swap. All the options would have to be approved by the host countries. Priority would be given to the refugees in Lebanon.[116] Clinton's proposal promised to secure the internal balance of Israel as a Jewish state.

♦ Compensation to the refugees by a special international fund.[117]

♦ The parties would agree that acceptance of this proposal constitutes the implementation of General Assembly resolution 194(3), and it puts an end to all claims. The agreement would mark the end of the Israeli-Palestinian conflict. This would be confirmed by a UN Security Council resolution that noted that resolutions 242 and 338 had been implemented.[118]

On 21 January 2001 Israeli and PA officials met at Taba (Egypt). The six-day talks failed. No agreement was reached on the refugees, security borders, or Jerusalem.[119] The Palestinian rejected Prime Minister Barak's proposal to transfer approximately 94% of the areas of Judea, Samaria and Gaza to the Palestinian Authority, while approximately 6% of Judea, Samaria and the Gaza strip to be be annexed by Israel. Other Israeli proposals for territorial exchanges were also rejected. Overall, Israelsproposal, which gained the support of President Clinton, included the return of 99% of the occupied areas of Judea, Samaria, and Gaza to Palestinian control; a functional division of the city of Jerusalem; and the possibility for Palestinian refugees to return to the Palestinian territory.[120] Chairman Arafat rejected the proposal in its totality, and consequently the *al-Aqsa Intifada* continued.

Israel Main Legal Arguments Concerning the "Right of Return"

Ruth Lapidoth, a former Legal Advisor to the Israeli foreign ministry, expounded Israel response concerning the legal sources for the "right of return" under international law. With regard to the claim that the "right of return" is a natural right recognized in international law, Prof. Lapidoth said that the "right of return" is the youngest among the rights of freedom of movement and in view of the slow "hesitant development of this right" it can hardly be considered axiomatic or self-evident.[121]

Regarding the Arab claim that the Universal Declaration has obtained a status similar to that of general principals of international law as mentioned, the majority of states do not consider the Universal Declaration *per se* as binding, but only as "a common standard of achievement," as stated in the Universal Declaration itself, despite the fact that some of its provisions may have contributed to the development of customary law.[122] In summing up, Prof. Lapidoth states: "Even if the Universal Declaration did have a binding effect, it would not follow that the Palestinians have a right to return. The above right probably belongs only to nationals of the state, and at most to permanent residents. The Palestinian Arab refugees have never been nationals or permanent residents of Israel; they either fled before the establishment of the state of Israel in 1948, or in 1967. We discussed earlier that, the right of return is an individual right that does not apply to displaced masses of people."

Last but not least, the general limitation clause of article 29 of the Declaration allows for circumstances wherein the right need not be implemented; the influx of more than one and a half million mostly hostile refugees would, without doubt, violate "the rights and freedoms of others" in Israel, and it would harm "public order and the general welfare in a democratic society."[123] Don Peretz observed that the "right of return" is at best controversial: "The question of refugees' right to return to their homes is ambiguous in international law. To the extent that such a right is accepted, it usually applies to refugees returning to the states of their original nationality. Since the vast majority of Palestine refugees were never Israeli citizens this 'right' is not generally seen as applicable to them."

With regard to the ICCPR, there is no doubt that the convention has no binding force on the State of Israel. Israel did not ratify the convention into law, and the right under the convention is limited to citizens, and to permanent residents. The convention does not refer to situations of refugees, displaced persons or forced migration. Even if the Arab jurists' view is accepted, that the refugees' right of return exists by virtue of the Universal Declaration or the ICCPR, the question is asked: Why did they ignore the expressed provision included in article 4 of the ICCPR from 1966, according to which a State that is a party to a convention is entitled, in times of emergency, not to fulfill commitments it has taken upon itself? [124]

Concluding Remarks

The unsettled, fifty-year-old Palestinian refugee problem raises serious, unresolved legal and political dilemmas. Over the years, the attitudes of both Israel and the Palestinians towards the refugees' problem have changed and not for the better. The Arab states and the Palestinians cynically exploited this human tragedy and turned it to a tactical tool for gaining different strategic benefits, both during times of war and during peace negotiations. This strategy resulted in a dangerous and vicious deterioration in the relations between Israel and the Palestinians, culminating in the use of the refugee issue as an excuse for terrorism. On the other hand, Israel is responsible for avoiding tackling the issue and postponing, for decades, any meaningful discussion on the problem. Israel failed to identify the powder keg that was about to explode and ignored the serious consequences that followed this misperception. In fact, the responsibility for the protracted problem lies with all the parties involved.

In summary, any resolution of the refugee problem has to address three different disputes: first, the religious dispute, namely, Muslim-Jewish. Second is the territorial or border dispute. Third is the Israeli-Palestinian national dispute. Of the three disputes, the third one, the Israeli-Palestinian, is the most difficult, albeit most important, dispute. The Oslo accords acknowledged this fact and thus focused on the Israeli-Palestinian national conflict. Resolution of the refugee problem was a high priority item on every framework of the various peace negotiations. However, it seems that since the Palestinians had formed an ideological-strategic perspective on the problem, all serious attempts to find a durable solution to the Palestinian refugee problem failed. Israel was not ready to make the concessions demanded by the Palestinian, including the un restricted fulfillment of the "right of return," which Israel viewed as a plan to bring about the total liquidation of Israel. Israel views the Palestinian interpretation of the "right of return" as only a stage in its "phased strategy," which threatens the security and survival of Israel. The religious dimension, and the influx of hundreds of thousands (or millions, as the Palestinians demand), add to Israel's anxiety and threaten eternal ethnic rivalry.

Both Israel and the Arab countries have used international law arguments as a base for their political stances with regard to the Palestinian refugees problem. Both have brought strong arguments with maximum attention being paid to the legal implications of political acts. Our study reviewed a number of processes concerning the Palestinian forced migration problem, in the context of the Arab-Israel conflict with a focus on a number of legal dilemmas related to the heart of the dispute. The essential differences stem from the Arab's view that Israel has attempted to create a *fait accompli* by not making a serious attempt to carry out resolution 194 (3) or to accept any responsibility for the refugees' problem. In fact, Israel concentrated first and foremost on security problems, and claims that the real goal of the Arab countries and the Palestinians, which has been concealed behind political camouflage and legal constructions, has been and still is the liquidation of Israel by flooding the Jewish state with millions of hostile Palestinians.

The lack of cooperation on the part of the Arab states and the Palestinians themselves in the re-integration or resettlement of the refugees, their unwillingness to accept responsibility for carrying out rehabilitation measures, and the Israeli policy of not moving toward an agreement on the refugees problem until a durable peace is achieved have been the main causes for the duration of the problem and have thus created a complicated *sui generis* legal problem. If the Palestinians will not abandon their demand for an unrestricted repatriation and its *de facto* significance, and will not accept a symbolic fulfillment of the "right of return," it will not be possible to reach a settlement acceptable to all the parties to the dispute.

Notes

1. Yassir Arafat said on this issue: " …We seek a fair and just solution to the plight of Palestinian refugees who for 54 years have not been permitted to return to their homes. We understand Israel's demographic concerns and understand that the right of return of Palestinian refugees, a right guaranteed under international law and United Nations resolution 194, must be implemented in a way that takes into account such concerns... Left unresolved, the refugee issue has the potential to undermine any permanent peace agreement between Palestinians and Israelis." Yassir Arafat, "The Palestinian Vision on Peace" *New York Times*, 3 February, 2002.

2. Mezkin A.G., "The refugee problem in the Middle East" *Journal of Refugee Studies*, 3 (1957): 6.

3. Alon Ben Meir, *The Middle East Imperative and Choices* (New York: Decalogue books, 1975), 106. Donna E. Arzt, *Refugees Into Citizens, Palestinians and the End of the Arab–Israeli Conflict* (New York: Council of Foreign Relation books, 1996), 20. Prof. Julius Stone interesting thesis places the responsibility for the rehabilitation of the Jewish and Arab refugees on both Arabs and Jews. However, unlike the Arab states rejection of the resettlement proposal, Israel did assume responsibility for the Jewish refugees.

In time, the issue of the Palestinian refugees became a political weapon against Israel. See: Julious Stone, "Self determination and the Palestinians Arabs" in Howe and Gershman eds., *Israel the Arabs and the Middle East* (New York: Bantam books, 1972), 209.

4. Don Peretz, *Palestinians Refugees and the Middle East Peace Process* (Washington D.C: United States Institute of Peace, 1993), 5-6. Peretz emphasizes the issue of responsibility for the refugee plights that affects the many ramifications of the problem. This issue cuts across most other respects of the conflict.

5. Yves Besson, "The right of return and compensation," *Paper for conference, Resolving the Palestinians Refugee Problem: What Role for the International Community?* Warwick, 23-24 March (1998), 3-4. Joseph Massad, "Return or Permanent Exile" in Nasser H. Aruri ed., *Palestinian Refugees: The Right of Return* (London: Pluto Press, 2001), 111 quoting: Joseph Alpher and Khalil Shikaki, "The Palestinian Refugee Problem and the Right of Return," *Working Paper Series, Paper No. 98-7*, Weathrhead Center for International Affairs, Harvard University, May 1998, 20. William R. Polk, "The Arabs and Palestine" in Polk, Stamler and Asfur eds. *Backdrop to Tragedy-the Struggle for Palestine* (Boston: Beacon Press, 1957), 300.

6. GA res. 181, UN Doc. A/ 519, at 322 (1947), recommended the partition of Palestine into a Jewish and an Arab state.

7. Don Peretz, *Palestinians Refugees, and the Middle East Peace Process*, 5-6. Corm Georges, "Thoughts on the roots of the Arab-Israeli conflict," *Journal of Palestine Studies*, 21 (Spring 1992) pp.71-79. Joseph Ginat and Edward J. Perkins (ed), *The Palestinian Refugees Old Problems New Solutions* (Brighton: Sussex Academic Press, 2001), 1. The first approach was effectively described by Dr. Natanel Lorch, an Israeli military historian: "Anyone who has sought to solve the problem of the land of Israel by force, by bringing the sword to bear on its diverse mosaic – has not only felt the blood of his campaign on his forehead, but has also been responsible for the fate of the refugees gone to exile… It is the Arab leaders who resorted to force to achieve their aim: an Arab state in the undivided land of Israel. In October 1947, prior to the partition resolution… they promised… in the words of the Secretary General of the Arab League "a massacre of Jews that will be

spoken of until the end of time in the same breath as massacres by Genghis Khan." See: Netanel Lorch, *History of the War of Independence* (Tel-Aviv: Massada Press 1958), 54, (in Hebrew).

8. M.Van-Dosen "Jerusalem, the Occupied Territories and the Refugees" in: Majid Khadduri ed., *Major Middle East Problem in International Law* (Washington: AEI press, 1979), 54.

9. Bernard Lewis, *The Middle East* (Phonix: Orion Books ,1996), 391.
About the origins and evolution of the Palestine problem see: Benny Morris, *Righteous Victims a History of the Zionist–Arab Conflict 1881-2001* (New York: Vintage books, 2001). *The Origins and Evolution of the Palestine Problem 1917–1988* (part one) (New York: OPR study, United Nations, 1990). Walter Laqueur, *The Road to War: The Origins of the Arab-Israel Conflict* (London: Weidnfeld & Nicolson, 1968). On The Balfour Declaration see: Christopher Syxes, *Crossroads to Israel* (London: Collins, 1965), 15-22. For a pro-Arab view see: Thomas Mellison, "The Balfour Declaration, an Appraisal in International law" in Ibrahim Abu Lughood ed., *The Transformation of Palestine* (Evenston : Northwestern University Press, 1971), 6. Thomas Mallison and Sally Mallison, *The Palestine Problem in International Law and World Order* (England, Longman, 1986), 18-71.

10. Trence, Prittie, "Middle East Refugees" in Curtis, Neyer, Wayman And Pollack eds., *The Palestinians: People, History, Politics* (New Jersey: Transaction Books, 1975), 56. For detailed information about the Palestinians exodus see: Benny Morris, *The Birth of the Palestinian Refugee Problem 1947-1949* (New York: Cambridge University Press, 1987). There are no uniform opinions concerning the exact number of refugees, and various studies have arrived at differing results. The mediator Bernadotte estimated, on 16th September, 1948, that there were approximately 330 thousand refugees, as follows: Syria – 70,000,Lebanon – 50,000, East Jordan – 50,000, Egypt 12,000, Iraq – 3,000, the West Bank – 145,000 (including Israeli territory approximately 50,000). The acting mediator for the UN Dr Banz, (who was appointed to the position after the assassination of Count Bernadotte) numbered the refugees at 420,000, before the first stage of the war. The UN "Cluff Committee" concluded that the exact number of refugees could not be estimated, as it amounted to approximately 725,000 (which did not include 48,000 Arabs in Israel). See the breakdown of the data in footnote 53 below.

See: Mordechi Lahav, *50 Years of the Palestinian Refugees 1948 – 1999* (Tel-Aviv: Rosh Tov, 2000), pp.381-389. (in Hebrew).

11. Gabriel Ben Dor, "Change and continuity of Palestinian National Problems" in Eytan Glboa and Mordechi Naor ed. *The Arab –Israeli Conflict* (Tel-Aviv: Ministry of Defense, Israel, 1981), 166. (in Hebrew) The author draws this conclusion from similar cases of civil war as the Indian Civilian war in 1947, the Turkish-Greek confrontation in Cyprus and the Lebanese religious struggle.

12. Quoted in Gabriel Ben Dor, *Ibid.*, 167.

13. *Ibid.*, 167.

14. Lex Takkenberg, *The Status of Palestinian Refugees in International Law*, (Oxford: Clarendon Press, 1988), 14 quoting "Progress Report of the UN Mediator for Palestine" GAOR, 3rd sess., supp.11, UN doc.A/648, 14.

15 .Shlomo Ben-Ami, "The Israeli Position, Multilateral Working Group on Refugees Opening Remarks for Israel, Ottawa, November 11,1992" *Palestine Israel Journal* 2 (Autumn 1995): 115-116. (Ben Ami opening remarks, the meeting of the multilateral working group on refugees in Ottawa, November 11, 1992).

16. Gabriel, Ben Dor "*Change and continuity of Palestinian National Problems,*" 167.

17.   Yves Besson, *The Right of Return and Compensation*, 3-4.

18. Besson Yves, *The Right of Return and Compensation*, 3-4. See also Peretz, *Palestinians Refugees and the Middle East Peace Process*, 72. Artz, *Refugees Into Citizens, Palestinians and the End of the Arab–Israeli Conflict*, 15. Ben Meir, *The Middle East Imperative and Choices,* 3-33.

19. About the UNRPR see: Takkenberg, *The Status of Palestinian Refugees in International Law*, 23-24.

20. UNRWA was founded on 8 December 1949 (General Assembly Resolution no.302 [iv], 47 "yes," 0 "no" 6 abstentions.) Article 22 of the UN charter authorizes the General Assembly to establish subsidiary organs necessary to the performance of its functions. Review of UNRWA's operation see: *UNRWA:1950-1990 Serving Palestein Refugees* (Vienna: UNRWA, April 1990); also Benjamin Schiff; *Refugees Unto the Third Generation: UN aid to the Palestinians* (New York: Syracuse University Press,1995); Viorst Milton, *UNRWA and Peace in the Middle East, Reaching for the Oliver Branch* (Washington D.C.: The Middle East Institute, 1989); Jalal al-Husseini, "UNRWA and the Palestinian Nation –Building Process" *Journal of Palestine Studies* (winter 2000): 51-64.

21. The United States is UNRWA's single largest donor: Total USA contribution in 2002 was $119.25 million. UNRWA is seen by the U.S. "As a force for stability in the Middle East and is an irreplaceable partner in addressing emergency humanitarian needs in the West Bank and Gaza." Press Statement, Richard Boucher, Spokesman of the U.S. Department of State, Washington DC, September 25, 2002.

22. Howard Adelman, "Modernity, Globalization, Refugees and Displacement" in: Alistair Ager ed., *Refugees Perspectives on the Experience of Forced Migration* (London: Pinter Books, 1999), 83, 92.

23. Ga.Res.194, UN doc.a/810 at 21 (1948). General Assembly resolution 194(3) was adopted following the Bernadotte reports. It provided for the establishment of the United Nations Conciliation Commission For Palestine (UNCCP) with representatives from: the United States, France and Turkey. The UNCCP's mandate was to advise and summon the parties to the dispute in order to bring them to arrive to a final settlement on all the issues in dispute between them.

24. UN General Assembly Resolution 302(iv) on 8th December 1949.

25. David McDowall, *The Palestinians* (London: Minority Rights Group, 1998), 6. John Davies, *The Evasive Peace-A Study of the Zionist Arab Problem* (London; Murray Press, 1969), 69. For a detailed description of the Internally Displaced Persons problem (IDPs) see: Roberta Cohen and Francis M. Deng, *Masses in Flight: The Global Crisis of Internal Displacement* (Washington

D.C.: Brookings Institute,1998). Prof. George Tomeh established two main refugee categories and several intermediate refugee categories: First, the 1948 "old" refugees, and their descendants. This category includes people who lost their lands but stayed at their homes, and therefore were not included in UNRWA registration lists, (approximately 11,000 Arab citizens that were forced by Israel to emigrate from the demilitarized areas, from June 1st.1952 onwards). Second, the 1967 "new" refugees, including many old refugees, which fled from the West Bank refugee camps. See: George Tomeh, "Legal status of Arab Refugees" in Halderman J.W. ed., *The Middle East Crisis-Test of International Law* (New York: Oceana Publications, 1969), 110. In the Legal Conference held in Algeria a third category was defined: "the internal refugees," i.e. refugees that stayed in their homes during and after the 1948 war, claiming to be second degree citizens. See: Seminar of Arab Jurists on Palestine, The Palestine Question, Algiers, July 22-27,1967 p.129. (Will be referred to "Algiers Seminar").

26. Shamay Cahana, *The Claim to a "Right of Return" for the Palestinians and its Significance for Israel*, (Jerusalem: Hebrew University of Jerusalem,1993), 13-15.

27. Between 1950-1988, Jordan granted full citizenship to the Palestinian refugees residing in Jordan and the West Bank. In 1988, King Hussein severed all legal and administrative links between the two banks in the "1988 Disengagement" speech (*Fak al-Irtibat*). That, among other things, meant that the West Bank Palestinians were to lose their Jordanian citizenship. On the other hand, Jordan did not change the Jordanian nationality law, and the West Bank Palestinians actually continued to use their Jordanian passports, with some restrictions. See: Takkenberg , *The status of Palestinian refugees in International Law*, 156. For a detailed description on the Joranian-Palestinian relations see: Mustafa B. Hamarneh, Rosmary Hollis and Khalil Shikaki, *Jordanlan-Palestinian Relations: Where To? Four Scenarios for the Future* (London: Royal Institute of International affairs, 1997). Elia Zuriek, "Palestinian Refugees and Peace" *Journal of Palestine Studies* 24 (Autumn 1994): 5, 15.

28. Apart from Jordan, other Arab states granted citizenship to Palestinians, but on an individual basis. For a review of the legal status of the Palestinians in Lebanon see: Souheil Al-Natour, The Legal Status of the Palestinians in

Lebanon, *Journal of Refugee Studies* 10 (1997): 360 and Wadie Said, The Obligations of Host Countries to the Refugees under International Law: The Case of Lebanon in Aruri Nasser H. ed., *Palestinan Refugees: The right of Return* (London: Pluto Press, 2001), 123-152.

29. Since its inception, the PLO preached the elimination of a sovereign Jewish state. The "Palestine Covenant" calls for the elimination of Israel in all but six of its thirty-three paragraphs. See: Harkabi Yehoshfat, *The Palestinian Covenant and its Meaning* (London: Vallentine Mitchel,1979); David Landau ed., Shimon Peres, *Battling for Peace-Memories,* (London: Weinfild & Nicolson, 1995), 366. The "Right of Return" has been the first component in the PLO's political-Ideological trinity of the "inalienable rights": the right of return, the right of self-determination and the right of establishing an independent state. See: Menachem Klein, "From a Doctrine – Oriented to a solution Oriented Policy: The PLO's Right of Return," in: Joseph Ginat and Edward J. Perkins eds., *The Palestinian Refugees Old Problems New Solutions*, 47.

30 .Takkenberg, *The Status of Palestinian Refugees in International Law*, 132-134.

31. *The Origins and Evolution of the Palestine Problem 1917-1988* (part I) (New York: United Nations, 1990), 18.

32. Martin Suzan f., *"Forced Migration and the Evolving Humanitarian Regime,"* Issues in refugee research, (Geneva: UNHCR working paper No. 20, July 2000): 4. The author refers to the terms of the Convention relating to the status of refugees from 28 July 1951 that will be discussed later on.

33. 189 UNTS, 150. The 1951 Refugee Convention provided the definition of a "refugee." It was amended by the 1967 protocol and was adopted in article I of the Organization of African Unity Convention on Refugee Problems in Africa (1969), 1001 UNTS 45. The 1969 O.A.U. Refugee Convention, expended the definition and added: "shall also apply to every person who, owing to external aggression, occupation, foreign domination or events seriously disturbing public order in part or the whole of his country of origin is compelled to seek refuge elsewhere.". See: Goodwin-Gill, *International Law and the Movement of Persons Between States*, 140. For a comprehensive

examination of the 1951 Convention see: James Hathaway, *The Law of Refugee Status* (Canada: Butterworths,1991); Guy Goodwin–Gill, *The Refugee in International Law,* 2nd ed. (Oxford: Oxford University Press,1996).

34. Hathaway, *The Law of Refugee Status*, 27.

35. The Protocol Relating to the Status of the Refugees signed at New York on 31 January 1967, 606 UNTS 267.

36. The 1951 Convention and the Protocol Relating to the Status of Refugees of 31 January 1967 provide universal standards for the treatment of refugees. The 1951 convention establishes specific rights and prescribes certain standards for the treatment of refugees. Some observers see the 1951 Convention as the "Bill of Rights" of refugees or as the "Magna Carta" of international refugee law. See: Brian Gorlick, *Human Rights and Refugees: Enhancing Protection through International Human Rights Law,* (Geneva: UNHCR Working Paper No.30, October 2000): 7; Refugees, 50th Anniversary, The 1951 Geneva Convention, *Refugees*, Vol.2 ,No.123 (2001): 2. Although the 1951 convention defines a refugee in generic terms, the definition of a "refugee" was interpreted strictly. The burden of proof rests upon the person who claims asylum based on a well-founded fear of persecution. For a detailed discussion on the "burden of proof" in assessing claims to refugee status see: Brian Gorlick, "*Common Burdens and Standards: Legal Elements in Assessing Claims to Refugee Status*"(Geneva: UNHCR Working Paper No.68, October 2002) : 4-11. Being persecuted can be proved explicitly or implicitly. Moreover, it can be deduced from the silence or "non-response" of the government of the country from where the refugee had escaped. See: Jean Castel, *International Law* (Toronto; Butterworths, 1976), 498-499.

37. Some courts have interpreted article 1 D restrictively in a way that it only took into consideration the reason originally foreseen by the drafters of the Convention, that the convention will apply only when UNRWA would cease to function without the Palestinian question being finally resolved. See Takkenberg, *The Status of Palestinian Refugees in International Law*, 104-106, quoting a decision of the High Administrative Court of the Netherlands, from 6 Aug.1987, No. RO2.83.2767-Aen B. English abstract was published

in 20 NYIL 313(1989) and a similar view of the Refugee Status Appeals Authority in New Zeland (Refugee Appeal No. 1\92 Re SA (30 Apr.1992) 72).
38. Richard Plender, *International Migration Law*, 2nd Rev. ed. (Netherlands: Martinus Nijhof Publishers, 1988), 439. Grahl-Madsen, *The Status of Refugees in International Law*, 265. Takkenberg, *The Status of Palestinian Refugees in International Law*, 118, 96-123 quoting German Federal Administrative Court decision from 21 Jan. 1992 No.1 c 21.87, published in infAuslR 7\92,205.

38. Takkenberg, *The Status of Palestinian Refugees in International Law*, 121-122. For a legal review of the 1951 Convention and its link to the Palestinian refugee problem see: *Ibid.*, pp.86-130.

39. *UNHCR, Handbook on Procedure and Criteria for Determining Refugee Status Under the 1951 Convention and the 1967 Protocol Relating to the Status of Refugees, Re-edited version*, (Geneva: UNHCR, 1992). Hathaway, *The Law of Refugee Status*, 205-209.

40. An interview with Sadako Ogata, former High Commissioner for Refugees, 4th December 2001.

41. Najeh Jarar, *"Citizenship and Palestinian Refugees," Palestine-Israel journal* 3 (Autumn 1996): 61,63.

42. U.N gaur, 9th. Sees. Supp. No 17a, doc A/2717/add.1 during the years the definition of who was eligible to UNRWA assistance was refined and it included the direct descendants of the refugees.

43. Don Peretz, "Who is a refugee" *Palestine–Israel Journal* 2 (Autumn 1996): 22-23. The Palestinians refugees constitute the only category of refugees that is kept outside the general international refugee regime. The UNHCR is responsible for all subsequent refugees.

44. L.W. Holborn, "The Palestinian Arab problem" in: John.N. Moore ed., *The Arab-Israeli Conflict, Readings and Documents* (Princeton NJ: Princeton press, 1977), 671.

45. Don Peretz, *Palestinians Refugees and the Middle East Peace Process*, 11.

46. Susan Akram states that Palestinians refugees are entitled to a heightened protection regime. In reinterpreting the different legal instruments she concludes that the 1951 convention and the 1954 convention apply and effect the status of Palestinians as refugees and stateless persons. See: Susan M. Akram, "Reinterpreting Palestinian Refugee Rights Under International Law" in Aruri Nasser ed., *Palestinan Refugees: The Right of Return*, 165-194.

47. Lahav, *50 years of the Palestinian refugees 1948 – 1999*, 470. Over the years UNRWA used different definitions of the term "Palestine refugee." Today the vast majority of Palestinian refugees are descendants. See: Peretz, *Palestinians Refugees and the Middle East Peace Process*, 11-18.

48 Don Peretz, *The Palestine Arab Refugee Problem*, (Rand Corporation, 1969), 19.

49. Edward H Buehrig, *The U.N and Palestinian Refugees* (London: Indiana press, 1971), 39.

50. Consolidated Registration Instructions (CRI), January 1,1993. See: Takkenberg, *The Status of Palestinian Refugees in International Law*, 77 and Annex 2.

51. Takkenberg, *Ibid.*, 77, 80-81.

52. David McDowall, *The Palestinians*, 10. Notes: (a). UN estimate. (b) UNRWA figures for 31 Dec. 1996. (c). Includes 482,082 refugees (and descendants) displaced in 1967 to Jordan and 32,236 refugees displaced to Syria. The numbers include non-refugees displaced in 1967:
to Jordan 210,000 and to Syria 125,000. (d) This figure excludes 45,800 people (and descendants) who were inside Israel. The number of Palestinian refugees of 1948 is not known with certainty and is controversial. Indeed, UNRWA itself warns that its reported registration does not necessarily reflect the actual refugee population owing to factors such as unreported deaths and undetected false registration. See: Buehring, *The U.N and Palestinian Refugees*, 39. UNRWA figures as of 30 June 2003, are available from: http://www.un.org/unrwa/publications/pdf/uif-june03.pdf.

53. Hathaway, *The Law of Refugee Status*, 209.

54. Takkenberg, *The Status of Palestinian Refugees in International Law*, 77-78. Salim Tamari, *Return, Resettlement, Repatriation: The Debate on the Future of Palestinian Refugees* (Israel: Givat Habiba ,1998), 18-20, 32 (in Hebrew).

55 . Polk, "The Arabs and Palestine" in Polk, Stamler and Asfur eds. *Backdrop to Tragedy- the Struggle for Palestine*, 296.

56. GA res.3236. 29 GAOR, supp. (no.31) 4,UN doc. A / 9631 (1974). Kurt Renne Radley, "The Palestinian Refugees: The Right To Return in International Law," *American Journal of International Law* 72 (1978): 605-608.

57 . GA Res. A/RES/52/59 of December 1997.

58. *The Arab Refugees-Arab Statements and the Facts* (Jerusalem: Israel Ministry of Foreign Affairs Information Department), 1961, 17. Ahmad al-Shuqeiri was a former Syrian and an Arab League diplomat. He and was later appointed the first leader of the PLO organization. Between November 1948 – June 1967, The General Assembly adopted 23 resolutions that were variations of Resolution 194(3).

59. Y. Harkabi, *Arab Attitudes to Israel* (Jerusalem: Keter Publishing House, 1972), 27.

60. Y. Harkabi, Ibid., quoting: Walid al-Khalidi, *Middlle East Forum* 33 (Summer 1958): 22, 29.

61. *Refugees in the Middle East: A Solution in Peace*, (New York: Israel Information Services, 1967), 19.

62. *Ibid.*, 20. Quoted in *Zuricher Woche, Zurich*, September 1,1961.

63 Y. Harkabi, *Arab Attitudes to Israel*, 100 quoting president Naser's speech at the Egyptian National Assembly, March, 26, 1964.

64. *Refugees in the Middle East: A Solution in Peace*, 20. As reported in *El-Hayat newspaper*, Lebanon, 29 April 1966.

65. *Arab View, 1974*, 57. About the Al- Saiqa organization and other PLO-affiliated terrorist organizations see: Yonah Alexander and Joshua Sinai, *Terrorism: The PLO Connection*, (New York: Taylor & Francis, 1989), 37-47.

66 . Ori Stendel, *The Arabs in Israel Between Hammer and Anvi*l, (Jerusalem: Academon, 1992), 6. (in Hebrew)

67. Yoav Gelber, Historical Background, in: Joseph Ginat and Edward J. Perkins eds., *The Palestinian Refugees Old Problems New Solutions*, 18.

68. Stendel, *The Arabs in Israel Between Hammer and Anvi*l., 305-306. This strategy, known as the "policy of stages," or the "phased method," is a refined version of Habib Bourgiba's (former President of Tunisia) step-by-step proposal of 1965. See: Y. Harkabi, *Arab Strategies and Israel's Response* (New York: Free press, 1977)*, 45*. In his memories, PM Yitzhak Rabin wrote: "…the PLO leaders declares their creed, that they see such a 'mini state' merely as a first stage in obtaining what they call a 'secular democratic Palestine,' which is supposed to be built on the ruins of the State of Israel after all the Jews who immigrated to it after 1917 (or with slight amendment, after 1948) will be expelled from it." Yithak Rabin, *Duty Blotter,* Vol. .II, 2nd ed. (Tel-Aviv: Maariv Press, 1979), 583 (in Hebrew). After 1977, the PLO's focus shifted to securing the creation of an independent Palestinian state in any part of Palestine, which was understood to mean the West Bank and Gaza. See: Mohamad Hussam, "The Changing Meaning of Statehood in PLO Ideology and Practice," *Palestine-Israel Journal* 6 (1999): 8,14.

69. Stendel, *The Arabs in Israel Between Hammer and Anvil*, 305-306.

70. "Declaration of Principles on Self-Government Arrangements" Israel Information Center, Ministry of Foreign Affairs, Jerusalem, September 1993.

71. Takkenberg, *The Status of Palestinian Refugees in International Law*, 37. Although not explicitly stated, the term "refugees" in the DOP article (v3) refers to the 1948 refugees. This can be concluded from the fact that the

DOP contains a separate provision dealing with the 1967 displaced persons (Article xii).

72. Taysir Nashif, "The return of Palestinian refugees" *New Outlook* vol.33 (4) : 38-39. Zuriek, *"Palestinian Refugees and Peace,"* 16-17. Ziad Abu Zayyad, "The Palestinian Right of Return: A Realistic Approach," *Palestine-Israel Journal* 2 (spring 1994): 77. Rashid Khalidi, "Observations On the Right of Return," *Journal of Palestine Studies*, 82 (winter 1992): 29-40. Rashid Khalidi, "The Palestinian Refugee Problem a Possible Solution," *Palestine- Israel Journal* 2 (Autumn 1994): 72. Dr. Rashid Khalidi is a professor of Middle Eastern history at the University of Chicago. He was adviser to the Palestinian delegation to the Madrid and Washington negotiations from October 1991-June 1993. For the PLO different dialectics of the "right of return" see: Menachem Klein, "Between Right and Realization: The PLO Dialectics of the right of return," *Journal of Refugee Studies*, 11 (1998) : 1-19: Rashid Khalidi and Itamar Rabinovich, *Palestinian Right of Return, Two Views* (Massachusetts Cambridge: The American Academy of Arts and Sciences, Occasional Paper No. 6, October 1990); and Shamay Cahana, *The Claim to a "Right of Return" for the Palestinians and its Significance for Israel*, 56-61.

73. Faisal al-Husaini, "Interview" *Journal of Palestine Studies* 18 (Summer 1989): 7,11.

74. Eli Sanbar, The Palestinian Position, Opening Remarks for the Palestinian side of the Joint Palestinian-Jordanian Delegation Ottawa, May 13, 1992, *Palestine-Israel Journal* 2 (1994): 121,124.

75. Abd al-Rahman Asaa'd, *"The Palestinians Refugees – Problems and Proposals"* PA Doc. Gaza: Palestinian Liberation Organization- Department of Refugee Affairs, 1999, 2. Salman Abu Sitta wrote that "The example of *Intifada* 2000 shows that the Palestinians cannot simply continue to look across the barbed wire and see their homes occupied by Russians and Ethiopians while they rot in refugee camps. They must return home. This is in the Israelis' best interest in the long run. This is the long-term interest of the US. This is in the interest of peace and stability in the Middle East. This is what the whole world has affirmed year after year since 1948." Salman Abu Sitta, *"The Return of the Refugees; The Key to Peace"* (Palestinian

Development research Net (PRRN), 2001), and 6. Also available on: http://www.arts.mcgill.ca/mepp/prrn/papers/abu-sitta. Francis Boyle, a former legal adviser to the PA mission to the U.N, argues that the "State of Israel owes a prior legal obligation to resettle Palestinian refugees who want to return home before it undertakes the massive resettlement of Soviet Jewish citizens from the Soviet Union." See: Francis A. Boyle, *Palestine, Palestinians and International Law* (Atlanta, GA: Clarity Press, 2003), 69.

76. Isabelle Daneels, *Palestinian Refugees and the Peace Process- An Analysis of Public Opinion Surveys in the West Bank and the Gaza Strip* (Jerusalem: Abu Ghosh Printers, 2001), 17-18; 73-82. According to a survey conducted by the Palestinian Center for Policy and Survey Research (PCPSR) in 2003 (Jan.-June 2003), only 10 percent of Palestinian refugees dwelling in the West Bank, Gaza, Lebanon and Jordan wish to return to their homes in Palestine. The vast majority of refugees were willing to accept monetary compensation in lieu of a return. See: Ramzy Baroud, "Are Palestinian Refugees Defying Reality?" *Palestine Chronicle* 16 July, 2003; available from http://palestinechronicle.com/article.php, Interview: Khalil Shikaki on his poll on refugees' view the Right of Return, July 14, 2003 (Robert Siegel, host); available from http://www.npr.org/programs/atc/transcripts/2003/jul/030714.shikaki.html . For the full survey see results of the PSR refugees' polls in the West Bank /Gaza Strip, Jordan and Lebanon on refugees preferences and behavior in a Palestinian-Israeli permanent refugee agreement. Available from http://www/pcpsr.org/survey/pulls/2003/refugeesjune03,html.

77. PA Doc. A report of Mr. Salim Al-Zannun, Head of the Palestinian National Council to chairman Arafat, June 2000, 2. In this special committee participated the following persons. Abu al-Adib (Salim al-Zannun) as chairman, Fisal al-Hussaini, Abed al-Rahim Maluch, Dr. Samir Ghousha, Taysir Haled, and Yassir Abed- Rabu, as members.

78. Palestine Liberation Organization, Negotiations Affairs Department, Permanent Status Issues- refugees; available from http:// www.nad-plo.org/permanent/refugees .

79. *Palestinian Refugees* (Jerusalem: PASSIA-Palestinian Academic Society for the Study of International Affairs, 2001): 8. See also Edward W. Said,

The End of the Peace Process Oslo and After (New York: Pantheon Books, 2000), 24-26.

80. The original plan was first published in the New York Times. See: Thomas Fridman, "An intriguing signal from the Saudi Crown Prince" *New York Times*, 17 February 2002.

81. Neil Mac Farquhar "Arab Delegates Endorse Saudi's Mideast Peace Plan" *New York Times*, 28 March 2002. See also: *Al-Ahram Weekly Online*, 21-27 March 2002, Issue No. 578; available from http:// www.ahram org.eg/ weekly . Following Syria's objection, the term "normalization" was replaced with: "normal relations." The Arab leaders objected to the resettlement of the refugees in their countries of refuge, so the Beirut declaration used phases that had flexible interpretations concerning the principle of the Right of Return.

82. Arab Peace Initiative (full text of a Saudi- inspired plan) 28 March 2002,*Washington Post Online*; available from http: www.washingtonpost.com/ac2/wp-dyn/A30181. Palestinian officials hold the opinion that under the Saudi plan the principle of settling thorny issues like the Right of Return would be based on international law, but practical solutions would come via direct negotiations between the sides. See: *Khaleej Times-Online*, 25 March 2002 2; available from www.khaleejtimes.co.ae/ middleeast.htm. The Saudi plan followed previous Saudi peace initiatives. On August 7, 1981 Crown Prince Fahd proposed an eight points peace plan as a countermeasure to the Camp David Accords (1977). The plan called for an Israeli withdrawal from all the territories occupied in 1967, including East Jerusalem; the establishment of a UN trusteeship for the West Bank and Gaza for a transitional period of no longer than several months; followed by the establishment of an independent Palestinian State. The Fahd plan called on "all states in the region to live in peace."

83. Glenn Kessler, "Israel's Concerns May Alter Roadmap" *The Washington Post*, 23 May 2003. For the full text of the "Performance-Based Roadmap to a Permanent Two State Solution to the Israeli-Palestinian Conflict" See: http:/ /www.mfa.gov.il/mfa/go/asp.

84. Benziman Uzi, "Corridors of Power- When the Rubbles Burst" *Haaretz* 23 May 2003. (in Hebrew).

85. Kurtz, Burgin and Tal eds., *Islamic Terrorism and Israel- Hizballah, Palestinian Islamic Jihad and Hamas*, (Tel Aviv: Papirus Tel Aviv University, 1993),122. (in Hebrew). About the "HAMAS" as part of the Islamic fundamentalism see: Davidson Lawrence, *Islamic Fundamentalism* (Westfort Conn: Greenwood Press, 1998), 68-70; 109-111. About the meaning of the *Jihad* see: Shaul Mishal and Avraham Sela, *The Hamas Wind-Violent and Coexistence* (Tel-Aviv: Miskal-Yediot Ahronot Books,1999), 51-55 (in Hebrew). About the "*Islamist Terrorism*" see: Paul R Pillar., *Terrorism and U.S. Foreign Policy* (Washington DC :The Brookings Institute, 2001), 45-50.

86. Ya'acob Havakook and Saleh Shakib, *Islamic Terrorism, Profile of the "HAMAS" Movement* (Tel-Aviv: Ministry of Defense press, 1999), 73 (in Hebrew).

87. Mishal Shaul and Avraham Sela, *The Hamas Wind-Violent and Coexistence* (Tel-Aviv: Miskal-Yediot Ahronot Books, 1999), 71. (in Hebrew)

88. Muhammad Al -A'nimi and Muhammad Abd al-Hamid, *The Palestinian Problem In Light of International Law (*Alexandria: Almaarif Press, 1967), 198. (in Arabic).

89. Hamed Sultan, *The Legal Problems of the Palestine Problem* (Cairo: M'ahad Al-buhuth Wal-dirassat Al-arabia Press, 1967), 93. (in Arabic).

90. John Quigley, "Displaced Palestinians and the Right of Return" *Harvard International Law Journal*, 39 (1998): 172; 193-198. Suleiman Jaber, "The Palestinian Liberation Organization: From the Right of Return to Bantustan" in Aruri Nasser H. ed., *Palestinan Refugees: The right of Return*, 88-89.

91. Ruth Lapidoth, "The Right of Return in International Law, with Special Reference to the Palestinian Refugees," *Israel Yearbook On Human Rights*,16 (1986): 112-113. Boling Gail J., *The 1948 Palestinian Refugees and the Individual Right of Return: An International Law Analysis* (Bethlehem: Badil Resource Center, 2001).

92. Muhammad A'nem, *The Palestinian Problem In Light of The Principles of International Law* (Cairo: Almataba El ilmiya ,1965), 118. The author brings resolution 194(3) and resolutions of the Reconciliation Committee as references.

93. Quincy Wright, "Legal Aspects Of The Middle East Situation" in J.W Halderman. ed. *The Middle East Crisis-Test of International Law* (New York: Oceana Publications,1969), 20.

94. Ruth Lapidoth, *"The Right of Return in International Law, with Special Reference to the Palestinian Refugees,"* 113.

95. *The Right Of Return Of The Palestinian People*, UN Doc. ST/SG/SER.F/ 2, (New York: 1978), 6. This study has been prepared for the Committee On The Exercise Of The Inalienable Rights Of The Palestinian People, in pursuance of the GA resolution 32/408 of 2 December 1977, by the Special Unit on Palestinian Rights.

96. Rashid Khalidi, "Observations on the Right of Return," *Journal of Palestine Studies* 82 (Winter 1992): 35,36. Joseph Massad, "Return or Permanent Exile" in Aruri Nasser ed., *Palestinan Refugees: The Right of Return*, 105, 106.

97. Khalidi, *"Observations on the Right of Return,"* 33-34.

98. Catan Henry, *Palestine The Arabs And Israel: the Search for Justice (London: Longmans,1969)*, 161.

99. Quincy Wright, "The Palestine Conflict in International Law" in Khadduri Majid. Ed. *Major Middle Eastern Problems in International Law* (Washington: AEI press, 1972), 32.

100. See discussion notes 102,103.

101. Nathan Feinberg, *The Arab-Israel Conflict in International Law (A critical Analysis of the Colloquium of Arab Jurists in Algiers)*, (Jerusalem: Magness press, 1970), 106-107. Hersch Lauterpacht, "The Universal Declaration of Human Rights," *The British Year Book of International Law*,

25 (1948), pp.354-381. Peter R. Baher and Leon Gordenker, *The United Nations Reality and Ideal* (New York: Prager Publishers,1984), 101-108.

102. For example, Prof. Kelsen refers to the Universal Declaration as nothing more than a recommendation. Hans Kelsen, *The Law of the United Nations, A Critical Analysis of its Fundamental Problems* (London: Stevens, 1950), 40. According to Starke's International Law, the Universal Declaration did not purport to be anything more than a manifesto, a statement of ideas, a path finding instrument and it is not a binding international instrument. Ian. A. Shearer., *Starke's International Law*, 11th ed.(London: Butterworths, 1994), 330. Under international law no country is obliged to accept foreigners into its territory and therefore article 14 of the Universal Declaration, which specifies that "every individual has the right to freedom and to enjoy refuge from persecution in other countries" only constitutes a moral norm, but the moment a refugee has been accepted by any country, he will benefit from country's commitments to international agreements.

103. *Israel and the Occupied Territories 'Palestine Authority' The Right to Return: the Case of the Palestinians*, (London: Amnesty International, 2001); Gail J. Boling "*The 1948 Palestinian Refugees and the Individual Right of Return: An International Law Analysis*," 36-42. John Quingley, "Displaced Palestinians and a right of return," 172,201-202.

104. *The Right Of Return Of The Palestinian People*, UN Doc. ST/SG/SER.F/ 2, (New York: 1978), 5.

105. Polk, *The Arabs and Palestine*, 296.

106. About an Arab view of the demographic question see: Abu Sitta Salman, "Palestinian Right of Return-Sacred, Legal and Possible" in Aruri Nasser ed., *Palestinan Refugees: The Right of Return* , pp.195-207. The Palestinians are fully aware that there are limitations on the number of persons that can be brought to Israel and to the Palestinian Authority. See: Joseph Ginat and Edward J. Perkins, *The Palestinian Refugees Old Problems New Solutions*, 4.

107. Ben Meir, *The Middle East Imperative and Choices*, 106-107. Yoav Gelber, *Palestine 1948, War, Escape and the Emergence of the Palestine Refugee Problem*, (England: Sussex Academic Press, 2001), p.286-287.

108. *Arab Statements*, 13. Nathan Feinberg, *The Arab-Israel Conflict in Light of International Law* (Jerusalem: Rubin Mass press,1970), 83. (in Hebrew).

109. Mordechi Lahav, *50 Years of the Palestinian Refugees 1948* – 1999, 430. See draft resolution 194(3) in UN doc. A/CI (394), rev.2 Arzt, *Refugees Into Citizens: Palestinians and the End of the Arab- Israeli Conflict*, 65-66. Voluntary repatriation is considered by UNHCR, as well as by many others, the best of the "three durable solutions" to deal with refugee problem. The other two durable solutions are local integration and resettlement in third countries. See: Takkenberg, *The Status of Palestinian Refugees in International Law*, 233. Roger Zetter, "International Perspectives on Refugee Assistance" in: Ager Alistair ed., *Refugees Perspectives on the Experience of Forced Migration* (London: Pinter Press, 1999), 48. On the other hand, resettlement had proved in many cases to be a comprehensive solution. For example more than three million Sudeten Germans who fled Czechoslovakia were rehabilitated in their countries of asylum and fifteen million refugees in India and Pakistan made their place with political facts and were integrated and resettled.

110. Shabtai Rosen, "*Direction for a Middle East settlement-some underlying legal problems*," in Halderman J.W. ed., *The Middle East Crisis-Test of International Law* (New York: Oceana Publications, 1969), 66.

111. Arab Statements, 16-17.

112. Benny Morris, *The Birth of the Palestinian Refugee Problem*, 1947-1949 ,275-285. Peretz, *Israel and The Palestine Arabs*, 50. Walther Eytan, *Between Israel and Nations* (Tel-Aviv: Massada Press,1958) 56-57 (in Hebrew). At the Lausanne Conference (1949) Israel agreed that the refugee problem should be the first item on the agenda of peace discussions. It also suggested the repatriation of 100,000 refugees as part of resettlement – a proposal regarded by the UNCCP as "unsatisfactory." See: Fourth Progress Report, G.A.O.R (iv) ad hoc annexes vol. ii p.10. For an extended discussion on the Lousanne Conference, see: Neil Caplan, *The Lausanne Conference 1949: A Case Study in Middle East Peacemaking* (Tel-Aviv: Tel-Aviv University,1993).

113. Shmuel Katz, *No Valour and No Glory* (Tel-Aviv: Dvir Press, 1981),153.(in Hebrew). Shmuel Katz, who was the advisor on Arab matters to Israeli Prime Minister Menahem Begin, points out that there was American pressure on this issue, and that as early as July-September 1977 Begin's position was that the refugee problem needed to be solved – but in the countries where the refugees were situated. Also, when discussing refugees, the problem of Jewish refugees who fled Arab countries must also be taken into account. About the Camp David I accords see: Nitza Nachmias, *Transfer of Arms, Leverage and Peace in the Middle East* (Westfort Conn.: Greenwood Press,1988), 93-180.

114. Yossi Beilin, *Manual for a Wounded Dove* (Tel-Aviv: Miskal books, 2001), 195. (in Hebrew). Gilead Sher, *Just Beyond Reach, The Israeli-Palestinian Peace Negotiations 1999-2001* (Tel-Aviv: Miskal–Yedioth Ahronoth Books, 2001), 136. (in Hebrew) For a detailed discussion on the "Right of Return" and the peace process see: Justus R Weiner. "The Palestinian Refugee's 'Right to Return' and the Peace Process" 20 *B.C International & Comparative Law Review* (winter 1997): 1.

115. The Clinton Peace Plan. Available from http:// www.mfa.gov.il/mfa/ go.asp.

116. Beilin Yossi, *Manual for a Wounded Dove*, 84.

117. The Clinton Peace Plan, ibid. About the Clinton administration policy towards the Arab-Israeli conflict see William B.Quandt, "Clinton and the Arab-Israeli Conflict," Journal of Palestine studies 23 (Winter 2001): 26-41.

118. Moshe Mao'z , "The Oslo Peace Process: From Breakthrough to Breakdown" in Rothstein, Mao'z and Shikaki, *The Israeli Palestinian Peace Process, Oslo and the Lessons of Failure* (Brighton: Sussex Academic Press,2002), 142. About the Palestinian refugees and the peace process see: Rex Brynen, *"Palestinian Refugees and the Middle East Peace Process"* available from http://www.arts.mcgill.ca/MEPP/PAPERS/UNH.html .

119. Ben Caspit, *Maariv Newspaper*, 27 July 2001 (in Hebrew). About the Taba talks joint statement see: "Taba talks-Joint Concluding Statement," Saturday, January 27, 2001. Available from http://www.pna.net/peace/ taba_talks.htm

120. R. Lapidoth, *"The Right of Return in International Law, with Special Reference to the Palestinian Refugees,"*113, 125.

121. *Ibid.*, 113.

122. *Ibid.*,114. For a different view see: Takkenberg, *The Status of Palestinian Refugees in International Law*, 230-240. Takkenberg argues that the right of return has not only found its reflection in humanitarian and refugee law, but should rather be regarded, together with the right to leave, as a general principle of international human rights law. The right of return appears in most, if not all, modern human rights instruments, beginning with article 13(2) of the UDHR.

124. Fienberg , *The Arab-Israel Conflict in International Law*, 107.

Sari Hanafi

CHAPTER 10:

The Palestinian Diaspora: New Forms Of Mobilization Without Radicalization

The Palestinian diaspora comprises of between 4 and 5 million[1] people, settled for the most part in historical Palestine's neighboring countries, but also in the Arab Gulf Monarchies, the two Americas and in Europe. This diaspora maintains a fragile, relationship with the present Palestinian territories (West Bank and Gaza Strip), a tie that is spread out essentially in three main spheres: networks, ideology and cyberspace. The first sphere includes social and economic networks, especially domestically basis. My research challenges some literatures on the Diaspora that often presupposes in systematic way: (a) mechanical ties between peripheries and a center, founded on transnational social and economic networks, (b) ethnically organized economic activities (ethnic business) and, (c) a "natural" system of solidarity (help, grants, etc.). In the Palestinian case, however, these connections contrast from geographical areas to another and are far from being always obvious. Indeed, some networks have been completely torn under the weight of the structural constraints imposed by Israel or the Arab states.

The second sphere of ideology is constructed around the concept of the *Nakba* (literally "disaster," the term used since the fifties to designate the exodus of the Palestinians in 1948) and of the sacredness of the Right of Return. Finally, in the era of the Internet, the Palestinian diaspora has been developing among themselves virtual relations, that take on an increasing degree of significance. Indeed, the emergence of this medium has lead to a new era in transnational imagined communities, which are now established on the principle of free adherence.

Recently, Professor Sari Nusseibeh raised the issue of the return of the Palestinian refugees and their right of return. His main argument was that in the framework of a two states solution, the Palestinians would not be able to demand the return of the refugees into Israel. His remarks enriched the polemic concerning this issue within the Palestinian society and inspired strong mixed responses.[2] While the youth organization of Fatah issued a communiquéé supporting this position, some Palestinian scholars, among them, Salman Abu Sitta and Terry Rempel, of the Badil Resource Center, expressed negative responses. The Al Adwa network even issued a petition to Chairman Yasser Arafat, demanding the dismissal of professor Nusseibeh's from his post (in that time representative of Palestinian National Authority in Jerusalem). On the other hand, over 52 articles criticizing or supporting Professor Nusseibeh's argument was printed in Jordanian, Lebanese, and West Bank and Gaza newspapers. The issue was also highly debated in the refugee camps. However, the most important reaction was that of the Israeli government and scholars.

The major debate that sparked at the end of the year 2001 by professor Sari Nusseibeh shows that the diaspora approach to the issue of Palestinian nationalism has been an important factor in the Israeli and Palestinian discourses. The on-going debate about the Right of Return within the Oslo framework of a two-state solution and the surprising eruption of the 2000 Intifada (second Intifada), leads to two hypotheses: the first argues that at a crucial moment, the diaspora has played a crucial role in encouraging a new type of a non-radical mobilization process proven by the absence of incursions of Palestinian factions present abroad, or the near-absence of any challenges to the central leadership of the PLO and the Palestinian National Authority (PNA). The second hypothesis follows the first and underlines the 'pragmatic' shift in some Palestinian claims to the Right of Return as a result of the second Intifada.

In the context of these two hypotheses this study attempt to configure the role of the Palestinian diaspora in the Palestinian-Israeli conflict, in particular the diaspora's influence on the Palestinian economic, political and social spheres during this Intifada: was there re-mobilization or disengagement, radicalization or moderation? The study looks at the relations between center and peripheries in their historic, spatial and social setting, at the hour of the second Intifada. It highlights the pertinence of understanding the diaspora's reaction to this Intifada, and it historicizes the diaspora while showing its pattern of change at a particular time, in relation to space and time.

Two aspects of this issue are examined: first, the study compares the Palestinian and the Israeli reactions to Professor Nusseibah's proposition, in particular how the refugees view their right of return, and how they would exercise this right if it will be offered. An important part of the analysis is an examination of the different meanings of the concept: the right of return, both in symbolic and in practical terms. The article avoids the practice of an analysis of continuities and a research of similarities between first and second Intifadas. We find that analogies between the roles of the actors of the first and second Intifadas are necessarily limited, being very different in nature. As many of the objectives pursued, as well as the methods used, demonstrate that their repertoires of modes of action are different. Karl Marx was quite right to add while commenting on Hegel, who had noted that all big events and historic characters occur twice: "the first time as tragedy, the second time as farce."[3] I do not suggest that the second Intifada is a farce, but rather the discussion shows that the processes and events in the Palestinian-Israeli conflict go beyond their form and appearance.

I. The Role of the Diaspora in the Intifada: A Partial Re-centering on the Palestinian Territories?

The second Intifada made West Bank and Gaza a central node of the national struggle, a shift from the 70s and 80s, when the military strengths and the political direction of the PLO were central in the diaspora, in Beirut, then in Tunis. Clearly, the second Intifada shows that the report to this Palestinian territory (the center) is not obvious, nor, regarding its representation of the refugee's abroad, is it like a center of gravity for the Palestinian diasporas peripheries.

317

A classic diaspora is defined by a *center of gravity*, which has two functions: it channels the flux of communications between diaspora members who reside in the various peripheries, and it also provides a location where members of the group (especially family members) can meet. The first function does not necessarily require a physical site; the meeting location might be a service provider or institution such as the Jewish National Fund for world Jewry, the Tunisian Base of the PLO for Palestinians, and the PKK in Germany in the Kurdish case. With regard to the second function, a real physical geographical location is a necessity for communal and ethnic economic transactions. Thus the center of gravity has little to do with the symbolic weight that represents a mythical or real homeland, but it is rather, a center for connecting members of the diaspora belonging to the same economic and social networks. In this respect, the historical Palestine continues to weigh in the imagination of the Palestinian diaspora, although not necessarily playing a role for each person connections to members of Palestinian communities abroad. My research shows that Palestinian business people in the Diaspora[4] demonstrated the importance of a physical meeting place. A Palestinian originally from Nazareth (the city of Nazareth kept its Arab population after 1948) can have an active economic network based in Nazareth capable of drawing those from Canada, the US or Australia for meetings with Palestinians who remained in Nazareth. In contrast, Palestinians originating from Haifa (in this instance practically the almost all the Palestinian population was deported by Israeli forces in 1948) do not have access to such a network due to the absence of family members and relatives there. This inaccessibility to the territorial reference point effectively hinders the possibility of meeting. A Haifa family dispersed throughout Damascus, Montreal, Amman and Abu Dhabi would find little interest in meeting in Syria, where only one family member presently resides. Those in Arab countries may also find the cost of traveling to Canada or to the Gulf prohibitive, long before the equally daunting dilemma of acquiring a visa enters into the discussion. These "torn networks," due to the absence of a territorial reference point, are not limited to the Palestinians. This is also the case with Gypsies who migrated from Paris to New York. Williams reports that their family relationships were broken a few years after they migrated (1985).

I-1. The Diaspora's Investment and Philanthropic Activities During the Intifada

The difficulty with the Territories becoming a point of undisputed reference can be demonstrated clearly through the question of economic development and financial investments. The Palestinian economic elite (such as Hassib Sabbagh, Abdel Majid Shouman, Abdel Mohsen Qattan and Saïd Khouri) has been playing a major role in the national arena by supporting, both financially and in terms of human sacrifices, the struggle of resistance as led by the PLO over the last forty years.[5] For this reason they have now refused to turn into simple bankers in the Rothschild mold. Indeed the relations between the Palestinian National Authority (PNA) and this elite are characterized by a double specificity. First, the context of national liberation, as well as the pressure that Israel exercises on the PNA, prevents the Authority from functioning as a sovereign state. In addition, the dispersion of the Palestinian business people gives them the liberty of political and economic maneuver between the host countries and the Palestinian Territories, and puts them at a safe distance from the 'coercive' power of the PNA. This double specificity creates contradictory, ephemeral and fluctuating relations. The Palestinian business people do not all have the same position with regard to the Palestinian National Authority. For either objective or subjective reasons, some are satisfied by an economic role in Palestinian Territories, further to an economic and political role within the host countries. It is an action of type *exit*, to take the term of Albert Hirschman.[6] The others use their financial and relational funds in the service of Palestinian nationalism: a sort of political or economic commitment of type *voice* (also in the categories of Hirschman). This allows them to maintain close ties with the PLO.

The following discussion defines these 'Buffer elite', and defines them by the two following characteristics: they are close to the power center, and they have a mediator's position between the economic sphere and the political sphere.[7] Since the Oslo agreements, the relations between the PNA and this elite can be portrayed by tensions and fluctuations. But both sides tend not to break contact. Arafat compared these *compradors* to the dynasty of the Rothschild in a manner designed to reduce their importance to the economic and financial sphere, while keeping with subtlety good relations with them. Certainly, his friends from the early days of the Fatah movement were shocked by the fact that upon his arrival in Gaza he spent the first nights at the house of a Gazan business man 'Aqil Matar. But this symbolic act does not mean that Arafat trusts this group. The following incident amply illustrates this point: at the time of the conference of Casablanca in 1994, Monib Al-Masri, a businessman close to the PLO and president of the Palestinian Development & Investment Corporation (PADICO), incited Yasser Arafat to direct foreign investors having need of appraisal or in search of partners toward PADICO, because of the importance of this society, as well as its experience. Al-Masri invited 500 Palestinian and western business people for a lunch during which Arafat was supposed to introduce PADICO. Instead, however, he asked those willing to invest in the Palestinian Territories to phone him personally.

Beyond the cleavages between the different business groups, they feel, for the most part certain uneasiness as to the manner in which the Palestinian National Authority manages public affairs. They are in search of new rules of the game that can free their actions, which have long been dependent on "state" power. Unaccustomed to spending huge amounts of time in bureaucracy for doing business, especially those who came from the North America, they were obliged to wait many days in order to get an appointment with Yasser Arafat or concerned minister to settle any problem.

These complex relations with the Palestinian Territories and its leaders have permitted Jordan to play a privileged role for the diaspora. My studies of Palestinian social and economic networks show that Jordan arguably could play the role of a 'small' center of gravity. Many of the business people from North and Latin America who were confronted with the unfavorable atmosphere in Palestine itself, transferred their investments to the two countries which are the closest to Palestine, namely, Jordan and Egypt. However Egypt has maintained a negative policy regarding Palestinians living on its territory. Jordan might constitute a good candidate to be the central node of some Palestinian networks, since there is a large Palestinian community living there, and, moreover, Jordan is the only Arab country that has given citizenship to the Palestinian refugees. My study shows that among the entrepreneurs who decided not to invest in Palestine because of the political and economical situation there, some decided instead to invest in Jordan. However, this potential new ad hoc center of gravity is in certain respects weaker than the Palestinian Territories, and both are likely to become weaker still were they to compete with one another as rivals.

While the diaspora's investment contributions were not regular,[8] the financial contributions were important to help families, during the second Intifada, face economic decline due to the massive destruction created by the

Israel military incursions of spring 2002. [9] My previous studies of the important size of the diaspora's contribution during a "normal" time[10] showed that in 1996, the Diaspora's contribution in investments and philanthropic activities could be valued at $408.006 million (of which 74% was investments) and in 1997: $410.211 million (of which 76% was investments). This contribution probably represents one of the main resources of Palestinian society. Indeed, compared to the international help for the Palestinian Territories, it constituted 74% of this help ($549.414 million) in 1996, and 95% in 1997 ($432. 259 million).[11] However Sara Roy's study concludes that this contribution remains insufficient for a young community ravaged by 30 years of de-development.[12] However, the contributions were extensively below the capacity of the Palestinian diaspora business people.

It is very interesting to note that during the second Intifada some grants also came from the lower middle classes of the Palestinian communities. In Jordan, Lebanon and even in Syria, (where two million Syrian pounds equivalent to 40,000 Euro) have been collected, mainly in the refugee's camps. One can distinguish two types of transfer: the individual transfers to help the family residing in the West Bank or Gaza (impossible to accurately evaluate, as the major part of these remittances are not transferred through banks), the one-sided institutional transfers coming from the Islamic associations, Christians, or simply from pro-Palestinian solidarity groups/ organizations (which are not necessary managed by Palestinian diaspora). The *Welfare Association* constitutes the most important pole of the Palestinian diaspora, as much by its financial weight as by its symbolic authority. Gathering prominent Palestinian business people and intellectuals, the Association is a philanthropic and independent voluntary foundation established in 1983. It has earned a solid reputation as a serious organization helping to lead Palestinian development. From the start, it adopted the principle of self-sustainability. To guarantee financial durability, the Association trustees set up an endowment fund, supervised by an investment committee and managed by professional portfolio managers. The revenue is utilized to cover the Association's recurring costs. This ensures that annual dues and donations are wholly appropriated to fund grants related to Welfare Association programs and projects.[13]

Welfare fund *Al Aqsa* permitted the mobilization of a million dollars during the first months of the Intifada, while the program "Family to Family" gathers donations from the Arab and Palestinian communities in Qatar and Oman. There are other associations working in other countries but with little impact in comparison with the Welfare Association. The most important associations of this kind are probably the Islamic charities, raising their funds from Arabs and Moslems in the US, Europe and Arab countries. According to a survey conducted by Jamil Hilal and Majdi Malki, 40.9% of the funding of the Zakat Committees comes from abroad.[14] There are also Palestinian Diaspora organizations with the form of humanitarian organization and without religious color (*United Palestinian Appeal, United Holy Land Fund, Arab Palestinian Fund*).[15]

With the return of a phase of confrontation with the Israeli occupation forces, the suspicion—which has been widespread enough in the Palestinian street—that the PNA functioned as a gendarme in the service of the Israeli security forces has, to an extent, dissipated. The Authority appeared again like a political actor capable of playing the card of national resistance. For the first time in a considerable while the portraits of Yasser Arafat reappeared. The gains in terms of credibility were immediate: demonstrations shook the streets of the refugee camps of in Syria, Lebanon and Jordan, and organizations in opposition to the PLO, and in particular to Fatah, were suddenly adopting a more conciliatory approach toward the Palestinian National Authority. This change of attitude transcends a simple ephemeral process, and it reflects both the socio-urban mutation of the refugee communities and a structural change of the political elite.

I-2. Changes in the Role of the Diaspora-Periphery

Since the beginning of the second Intifada, the role of the leaders of Hamas and Islamic Jihad in the Arab countries has become secondary actors, while the real power passed to those leaders residing in the Palestinian Territories. This shift in the center of the political decision-making is not without political repercussions. From this point onward the speeches of the two Palestinian Islamo-nationalistic organizations focused on the liberation of the Palestinian Territories occupied in 1967, without explicit territorial demand beyond the Green line. At the very least, an unspoken issue exists regarding historic Palestine. 13 To assess the change, it is sufficient to compare the communiqués of the two organizations at the time of the 1987 Intifada.[16]

The header of all communiquéés included the slogan "From the river [the Jordan] to the sea [Mediterranean]," an illusion to the liberation of the whole of historic Palestine. The footer expressed the refusal of all negotiation with the United States or Israel. The change occurred prior to the 2000 Intifada, but the latter fed a sort of disenchantment that reinforced the feeling that it was impossible to ask more than the occupied territories of 1967. Concerning the Popular Front for the Liberation of Palestine (PFLP), it is the Intifada that accelerated the establishment of the power of the local people to the detriment of those in the Diaspora.

The first demonstration had been the nomination in July 2000 of Abu Ali Mustapha, originally from 'Arraba (a village in the north of the West Bank), as General Secretary of the PFLP, replacing George Habash, the historic leader based in Damascus. Muatapha was killed in August 2001 by the Israeli occupation forces, and Ahmad Saadat, a leader of the PFLP in Ramallah, took over. The PFLP took a new direction, which is more moderate, and signals a conversion to Realpolitik. Certainly, from a Foucauldian perspective, the absence of a direct relationship between Palestinian of the diaspora and the Israelis reinforces the reciprocal ignorance and the dehumanization of the other.[17] In relation to local Palestinians, those of the diaspora are incontestably more falcons.[18] This difference can be observed in the perception of the correct balance between acts of resistance and political negotiation. These political factions of the Palestinian diaspora, as with those of the Jewish diaspora, are less sensitive to the necessity of minimizing the violence between the two belligerents, because no military solution can succeed to put an end to the Israeli-Palestinian conflict. The overlap between Israeli and Palestinian territories requires certain normalization between Palestinians and Israelis. To cite an example, the operations against Israeli civilians inside the green line have been criticized by a communiquéé signed in the beginning of June 2002 by hundreds of local Palestinian intellectuals, belonging to different political sensitivities (including, the Islamic Jihad and the PFLP). This communiqué has been roundly denounced by many voices of the Palestinian diaspora, particularly those who reside in the Arab countries.[19]

It is important to note that the generational effect proves to be—to a certain extent—a determinant for political attitudes. The young generations, who have never known historic Palestine physically, are no less ardent in their mobilization than those who lived the exodus of 1948, because the daily images of the Israeli occupation distributed by the Arab and Western media reinforce their determination to resist. Such attitudes are not different in essence from those expressed by some parts of the Jewish diaspora regarding Israel.

The generational effect is also evident in the Palestinian communities of Europe and America. The young are often very little committed to Palestinian nationalism. Two main factors influence the generational effect: badly structured communities, and a will for integration (or even for assimilation, in the French case) into the host society. These political attitudes cannot be understood without referring to the socio-urban change undergone by each of the different Palestinian refugee communities. They tend to conform to patterns of distinction according to the countries where the camps are locates. In Syria and Jordan the new generations dwell more and more outside of the refugee camps, blending into the host society. (See table 3).[20] Even for those that live in the twenty existing camps, the situation has changed profoundly because the camps have been subject to an extraordinary mutation by their integration into the urban tissue of the host cities.[21] In addition, the camps have also become shantytowns dwelt in not only by the Palestinian refugees but also by the poor from all origins. This urban (and not political) "normalization" of some camps has an impact on the mode of political action, mobilization being not any more exclusively carried out by the organizations of Palestinian national struggle, but by a new type of associative structure, the non governmental organizations which are independent of the PLO.

Concerning Lebanon, the picture is very different. In this country the camp retains all its political significance, because of the isolation in which it is kept from the Lebanese state and the very strong presence of the political factions of the PLO. Moreover, the militarization of South Lebanon, due to the persistent tension with Israel, has been maintained continuously, with all of the various Palestinian movements fully armed. In Lebanon one finds associations for the defense of human rights that unite the Palestinians around the issue of violations of these rights by Israel and, also, by the authorities of the host countries. The denunciation of these violations is no longer made through the Palestinian political factions, but by the human rights organizations, such as the Palestinian Organization for Human Rights, and the Association for the Preservation of Heritage, which collects oral history from the Palestinian people. Likewise with the services; with a reduction of the subsidies for the popular organizations (like the Palestinian Red Crescent or the General Union of Palestinian Women), it is the international organizations that offer medical and social services, such as Oxfam Quebec, ANERA, etc.[22]

In conclusion, we believe that unlike the first Intifada, where the diaspora was frustrated for not being able to contribute to the struggle, a new tool—the internet—has facilitated the mobilization of the diaspora by enabling many Palestinians to experience the behavior of the Israeli occupying forces and the Palestinian resistance, via the distribution of information on the internet, while journalists were unable to cover the stories due to Israeli closures and designation of the West Bank and Gaza closed military zones. The mobilization of the diaspora was very meaningful in a war of images waged against the highly influential Western media, which is considered by many Palestinians to be unconcerned about the colonial nature of Israeli military actions.[23]

Ii. Right of Return and Sociology of Return

If Palestinian national identity is founded on the narration of the *Nakba*, symbol of nostalgia and call to the fight against injustice, as described by the Palestinian historian Issam Nassar,[24] the ideology of the Right of Return first emerged as a credo of the diaspora before being propagated within the Palestinian Territories. However, it did not at any point assume same significance, nor the same tone of gravity, among these different communities. Indeed, the commemoration of Nakba Day was recently, more important in the Diaspora that in the Palestinian Territories.[25]

From the beginning of the nineties it was associative organizations in Europe and America that carried the flame of the Right of Return. The Al-Awda network "Return" 'was founded in 1994 by a coalition of associations in the UK, Germany, Denmark, Belgium, the United States and Canada. Later it spread to the Arab countries neighboring Israel before taking root in the Palestinian Territories. This network, composed of Palestinian diaspora activists and supporters of Palestinian nationalism, has attempted to lobby Human Rights Watch and Amnesty International for positions in favor of the Right of Return for Palestinian refugees. This reflects a rare case of a Southern network undertaking the Herculean effort of influencing the policies of Northern organizations.[26] The success of the network of *Al-Awda* derives from its capacity to initiate a variety of political activities, such as meetings, peaceful demonstrations and information campaigns. By the force of this movement, many Palestinian communities in various western countries began to organize themselves.

While in the Palestinian national ideology the question of the Right of Return has always been central, it must not be confounded with its realization. We should situate the polemic in the context arising after comments by professor Sari Nusseibeh (declaring that, in the framework of a two-state solution, the Palestinians cannot demand the return of the refugees to their homes inside of Israel), and the spirited responses, initiated by scholars Salman Abu Sitta and Badil Resource Center's Terry Remple, among others. *Al-Awda* Network for example, even opened a petition to the Palestinian National Authority President Yasser Arafat, demanding professor Nusseibeh's dismissal from his post. The initial debate was critical, but it was followed by vagarious debates.[27] Clearly, the important Palestinian and Israeli debate on the right of return was inspired by Sari Nusseibeh's unprecedented declaration. It forced both sides to comprehend the concept and principle of the right of return both in its symbolic and its practical dimensions. In particular, how many refugees would exercise this right, and would they wish to return.

II-1. The Israeli - Palestinian Debate

The following discussion examines three issues: a comparative study of the Palestinian and Israeli debates following the Nusseibeh declaration; second, the various interpretations of the concept of "the right of return" from the symbolic and the material dimensions; finally the necessity to introduce to the debate the sociology of "Return," especially the volume of the refugees who would exercise this right.

First, on the level of content, Sari Nusseibeh's argument was not new. Azmi Bishara made the same point in one of his articles about the Israeli political system of apartheid.[28] However, the framework of his position is quite different. While Nusseibeh presented his argument according to the pragmatism of the Oslo framework, Bishara points out the inherent contradiction in the two-state solution, leading in a determinant way to the establishment of the apartheid system in Israel. With regard to the Palestinian establishment, people like Saeb Erekat and Yasser Abed Rabbo have recently and clearly reiterated their long-standing contention that while the Right of return should be recognized, its implementation should be flexible. Very recently also, President of the PNA Yasser Arafat clarified the PNA position: "We seek a fair and just solution to the plight of Palestinian refugees who for 54 years have not been permitted to return to their homes. (…) We understand Israel's demographic concerns and understand that the right of return of Palestinian refugees, a right guaranteed under international law and United Nations Resolution 194, must be implemented in a way that takes into account such concerns."[29] Talking about the demographic concerns of Israel in this declaration however represents a major concession towards accepting Israel as Jewish state. What is new about Sari Nusseibeh's declaration is the level of clarity relative to issues left un-addressed in other statements.

The surprising factor is not only the aggressive general Palestinian reaction to what has been regarded as a highly provocative declaration, but also the reaction on the part of Israeli intellectuals, who pretend that they have never heard such statements before. It may be useful to look in some detail at how this debate has been received by Palestinian and Israeli audiences.

II-1-a. The Israel Debate: An Enduring Syndrome

From Israeli side, responses have been couched in terms of colonial stereotypes, which characterize the colonized as a mob comprising of a very few intellectuals or voices of reason that can influence public opinion. This is, for instance, one of the messages of Zvi Bar'el in his article entitled "Separating the right from the return"[30] Danny Rubinstein, one of the columnists of Ha'aretz, summarizes the Palestinian debate: Nusseibeh's declarations "are the extraordinary that prove the ordinary."[31] Benny Morris also considers Sari Nusseibeh as "an exception." According to him "Nusseibeh's statements are putting his life in danger. He is not one of the first rank senior leadership. I never heard Mohammad Dakhlan, Jibril Rajoub, or Abu Allah and their guys saying that. Even if they will sign on such a text at one stage or another, a new generation will emerge in ten or twenty years and will argue that they had no right to give up the Right of Return."[32]

These comments show a total ignorance of the debate on the Palestinian side. Since the declaration of Sari Nusseibeh, many discussions have been held in newspapers, inside political parties and in the camps. The debate even assumed the form of an exchange of communiquéses from the Fateh Youth organization supporting Sari Nusseibeh and then a response from another faction inside Fateh, which reiterated the traditional position of the Palestinian leadership. In this respect, the dynamic of the Palestinian debate is much more weighty than the debate on the Israeli side, as carried out by the scholarly and journalist communities, as well as the politicians. Generally speaking, and especially since the beginning of the second Intifada, the Israeli media has reverted to a traditional response, paralleling the opinion of intellectuals and representatives of the military-political system. Not surprisingly perhaps, for the first time scholars like Benny Morris[33] and A. B Yehoshua have in their writings voiced a very positional discourse. This discourse, like the broader Israel discourse on this topic, relates to the question of Palestinian return with a highly emotional phobia. Mainly, it has three dimensions:

First, it is a discourse, which psychologizes the conflict: the extensive writings about Israeli "anxieties," "worries" and "nightmares"; and about "Palestinian hatred." Second, this discourse is also ethnically structured. The major concern is demography and how the return of returnees would throw into disorder the colonial legacy of ethnic cleansing. In the media, Israeli public relations campaigns have indeed worked intensively since Camp David to convince the world that there is actually even the possibility of massive Palestinian return, in order to bolster Israel's claim that return means the erasure of Israel through the destruction of its demographic balance, i.e. its "Jewish character." This perspective has been disseminated in many articles published in Israeli and Western newspapers by well-known members of the Israeli "peace camp," including Amos Oz [34] Benny Morris,[35] A.B. Yehoshua,[36] and David Grossman.[37] Such an enduring syndrome of victimization makes any serious discussion of the Palestinian Right of Return, let alone any of their other rights, impossible. Unfortunately, the Sari Nusseibeh declarations are not only able to open a debate in the Israeli side about Palestinian refugee issue but reinforce the Israeli attitude about the importance of the demographic issue in the Palestinian-Israeli conflict.

Finally this discourse is hegemonic. For example: in his article "Refugees Forever," Yossi Alpher[38] wrote that: "Israel could recognize some humanitarian rights of family reunifications, which Palestinians could label 'return' for all first generation refugees, i.e., those over fifty four who were actually born in present day Israel, who wish to return and who have relatives that could assist in their absorption. Their number would not be large, nor would they affect the long-term demographic balance, but their 'return' *could provide a degree of satisfaction for the Palestinian narrative without seriously challenging the Israeli narrative.*" (my Italics) While Sari Nusseibeh's declarations open up debate over the Right of Return and its meaning in the Palestinian polity, on the Israeli side he is used by his "peace partners" as evidence that Palestinians will yield their rights. At a rally of 15,000 organized in Tel Aviv on February 16, 2002 by Peace Now and the Beilin-Sarid "Peace Coalition," Nusseibeh demanded justice for the refugees and spoke of the need for Israel to apologize and take responsibility for the creation of the refugee problem. But the Peace Now report on the rally recorded only Nusseibeh's statement that "the path to peace is through the return of the refugees to the state of Palestine and the return of the settlers to the state of Israel." As the Israeli sociologist Lev Grinberg argued, this partial silencing of Nusseibeh reveals the game played by his counterparts. It is telling that a main slogan at the rally was: "Leave the territories and be ourselves again." The Palestinians as an occupied people have no place in this formulation.

It seems that the Palestinian discourse about the Palestinian Right of Return should move to the offensive by reworking "being ourselves" in terms of the question "what is the right of Jews?" This means that if the Jews have a right to be in this land, what form of limitations should be imposed on this right? How can it be exercised in a way that does not transform it into an ethnic cleansing project?

Yehudith Harel, sociologist, summarized the attitude of many Israeli intellectuals by criticizing one of the articles of Amos Oz, published in the British newspaper, the Guardian: "The attitudes reflected in Oz's article, even more than the political positions expressed, are the epitome of the intellectual corruption and the emotional handicap of the Israeli mainstream peace camp intelligentsia. This has generated within Israeli circles a deep-rooted, patronizing, self-righteous discourse, a lack of empathy for other people's suffering, a lack of understanding of their perspective and needs and, above all, an almost chronic conviction that the 'other' has to act in the best of Israeli interests."[39]

II-1-b. The Palestinian Debate: Openness, but Lacking a Strategic Dimension

The Palestinian debate is more dynamic than the Israeli one, though it still suffers from what I term the lack of strategic political discourse. Palestinian politics has four characteristics: *first,* is a *moral discourse* based on the justice of the Palestinian cause (with regard to refugee issues, meaning that the refugees uprooted from their land should return home in accordance with international and human rights law). The *second* is *a search for a national consensus.* Some voices from the Diaspora and the Palestinian Territories called for a "national consensus" for silencing Sari Nusseibeh and the other voices who have addressed, for the first time, many unspoken and 'unthinkable' issues in Palestinian political discourse in vigorous terms. Equally, some within the discourse of the Islamite movement have argued that specific topics are not up for discussion, due to the prevention of a violation of "God's Will" or the "contravention of the Koran."[40] But what is this "national consensus?" Is it a consensus concerning the establishment of two states, one Palestinian and the other Israeli, or one secular, bi-national state? Is it a consensus over the targeting of civilians during a national struggle? Or is it a consensus concerning the position of Palestinian refugees that await the implementation of their Right of Return? The Arab world has been more than a few massacres and human rights violations perpetrated and justified in the name of the so-called 'national consensus' in post-conflict situations. Any new idea, whether valid or invalid, is often considered a break from the national consensus, and thus tantamount to treason. Ironically, the discourse of national consensus has historically not been consensual, but used instead as a tool for dominant forces to retain their positions. In the past, the gamut of national movements have had wide interpretations for the means to an end (and even the end) of struggle during the colonial period - in Algeria, in Bosnia and in Egypt. The Zionist movement too lacked "national consensus," encompassing different political forces; some groups dominated over time, and with self-representation. Hence, the argument of national consensus, which some scholars have used against Sari Nusseibeh, is epistemologically no less metaphysical than any religious doctrine forced into the socio-political arena.

The third characteristic of the Palestinian discourse is externally oriented, based on fragments of positions usually taken under pressure in response to r specific crises. This discourse also integrates many tactical elements and differs from one constituency to another. Thus, what is lacking in the Palestinian discourse is the strategic dimension, what I label as a "strategic political discourse," based necessarily on moral premises, but taking into consideration the international political context, the balance of power in international relations, and the transmission of this understanding to the public. This requires the willingness of the political leadership to declare to its public the inability to achieve some of the past promises that this leadership has made. It is symptomatic that the Palestinian public is less interested in knowing what decisions are taken at the central committee of the PLO, or at meetings of the enlarged cabinet of the PNA. Rather, they listen to declarations made by Palestinian leaders during visits to Western capitals. Consequently, Sari Nusseibeh's declarations at the Hebrew and Tel Aviv Universities successfully created a debate on the Palestinian refugees Right of Return within the Oslo framework. This talk had a far greater general notice than Azmi Bishara's statement in the Egyptian Arabic monthly journal, *Wijhat Nazat*. There is a near- absence of Palestinian discourse at the negotiation table in comparison with the discourse in the public arena. For this reason the Palestinian political leadership was afraid to confront the public about what was negotiated at Camp David or Taba. The public had learned about the content of the negotiations from the French paper *Le Monde Diplomatique*, not from a Palestinian newspaper or a Palestinian press conference.

Nobody has had the courage, until Sari Nusseibeh, to launch a discussion about what is indeed possible and what is not in the context of the Palestinian Right of Return. Nusseibeh's declaration has two aspects: his concept of the Right of Return and the volume of refugees who would actually exercise this right.

II-2. The Material and Symbolic Meanings of the "Right of Return"

It seems that Sari Nusseibeh did not adequately evaluate the centrality of the Right of Return, even in the framework of a two-state solution.[41] Clearly, there are two dimensions to the Right of Return: the symbolic and the material. While Nusseibeh sees mainly the material aspect of return (when he speaks of the illogicality of the possibility of 4 million returnees to a 'Jewish' Israel), Edward Said focuses mainly on the symbolic aspect taking up the theme of mutual pardon or forgiveness.

In order for Israel to recognize the Palestinian Right of Return, it must not only acknowledge the refugees' rights but also redress the roots of the Israeli-Palestinian conflict and Israel's central role in the dispossession of Palestinians for the past 54 years. We can interpret the failure of Oslo process because it was willing to resolve the visible part of the conflict (the land issue) but not the invisible (the colonial nature of the Zionist project, at least after 1967).[42]

Not to sound romantic, in the history of international relations in the post-conflict era, oftentimes the symbolic order is more complicated than the material one. For example, it was easier for Germany to compensate Jewish property than to acknowledge the responsibility of German people (and not only the "Nazi Party" as formulated by Konrad Adenuer) for the Holocaust.[43] Bridging the Palestinian and Israeli narratives about this conflict does not necessarily mean achieving a uniform narrative; Nadim Rouhana[44] sees the necessity of finding a settlement to the conflict as superceding the reconciliation of the two narratives.

Irrespective of whether the concluding solution of the conflict would be two states or a one bi-national state, the refugee issue and their return cannot be considered as secondary. The current Intifada has revealed the importance of the refugees; they are social and political actors most unable to bear the impasse of the Oslo process that had begun in 1993. Beyond the moral and symbolic value of realizing the Right of Return, this right is useful in creating the framework for providing refugees with a choice between remaining in their host countries, returning to their village of origin or to settle in the Palestinian Territories (or to be in one of the attractive immigration countries). The *Right of Choice* is a necessity for those who have, for half a century, been forced to live as foreigners without basic civil rights, in miserable camps and in states that have not always embraced them with open arms. However, the Right of Return and the Right of Choice do not depend only on Israel's recognition, but also on the policies of the Arab countries, concerning the different civic, economic and political rights of the refugee population.

II-3. Toward a Sociology of Return: Volume of the Eventual Return

The starting point of the following discussion has to be a hard look at the volume of the population that might exercise the Right of Return. It seems that both Nusseibeh and Abu Sitta's perspectives are problematic in this regard. Both scholars assume the position that the implementation of the Right of return will trigger the return of a large number of refugees. While the former believes that such an influx would change the "character" of the Jewish state within the framework of a two-state solution, the latter in my opinion, has not adequately explored the potential sociology and implementation of the return once it is made possible. Thus, the main question concerns the potential manifestation of the return. What pattern of return will be realized, and by what type of returnee? Will there be a literal mass of refugees rushing in simultaneously, or a trickle of fragmented groups induced by factors greater than nationalism and identity and the experience of exile? Before delving more deeply into such issues, it is necessary to highlight the importance of Abu Sitta's work in opening the debate concerning geographic absorption in Israel. He demonstrates, after dividing Israel into three demographic areas (A, B and C) that the majority of Israeli Jews—or 68 percent of the population—is now concentrated in Area A, which makes up 8 percent of Israel. Area B is 6 percent of Israel and has a largely mixed population including another 10% of Israeli Jews (2001). Abu Sitta's seminal work has thus pointed out that the areas in and around the former Palestinian villages remain empty and unused, and could readily absorb returning refugees. For him, this empty rural area also corresponds to the peasant heritage of the Palestinian refugees. However 50 years later, are these refugees, the majority of whom dwell in metropolitan areas like Damascus, Amman, Cairo, not to mention Chicago and New York, still to be considered peasants? But the ability to absorb the refugees should not be the only factor in determining return scenarios. Irish-Americans did not return to Ireland following the end of British colonialism, few Armenians returned to Armenia after its independence, and only a small number of Lebanese returned to their country of origin following the end of the civil war. In all these cases, there was not only ample capacity, but also the political will for re-absorption. In general, United Nations High Commissioner for Refugees' data demonstrates that the number of refugees returning to their various countries of origin, once return is possible, is far less than the number choosing resettlement in the host country or partition to a third-party state. In this context, the structure of the global labor market plays a major role.

Our study of the economic sociology of this population supports the assumption that repatriation is determined by a variety of factors. Fieldwork and studies conducted in 13 countries have not uncovered a homogenous population of 4 million refugees who would exercise their Right of Return. In actuality the number is far smaller. It is impossible to estimate the exact percentage or number of returnees, and the uncertainties of the results of the Oslo process and the possible reaction on the part of the Arab states would cause such a figure to vary tremendously, in any case.

Abu Sitta, in his letter criticizing Sari Nusseibeh, refers to polls conducted in some areas (particularly within the Palestinian territories) that demonstrate a refugee "consensus" in intending to return. However, polls conducted both by amateurs and by highly professional research centers (including research based on questionnaires carried out in Arab dictatorships) revealed some salient criticism. No matter how the question is presented, responses will obviously tend towards the expression of a political position that is influenced more by the continuation of a protracted conflict, disillusionment and the prospect of possible eventual defeat, rather than the subject's actual intention.

Factors influencing the subject's decisions range from the experience and memories of exile to his or her economic situation. If the question of their desire to return is posed only in conceptual terms, interviewers might get a 100 percent positive response to whether the refugees will return. If, however, the question is narrowed, to include social, economic and political factors, such as the prospect of returning to a village under Israeli sovereignty and holding Israeli nationality, or one without guaranteed adequate employment or housing, the percentage might drop significantly.

Moreover, a Palestinian residing in Lebanon may not be able to determine his or her intention to return if the Lebanese position remains unclear. Will the Palestinians be literally thrown onto the border, as occurred in Libya, or will he or she be given the right of choice? A questionnaire may not be able to take into account the multifarious possibilities. Research of an anthropological nature is certainly more suitable for understanding such issues. If such factors often invalidate the methodology of polls and surveys, then we have to question the methodology of empirical studies. Fours years ago, I visited my family living in a Palestinian refugee camp in an Arab host country. My father refused to see photos I had taken in Haifa because, in his words, it was not "his Haifa." Haifa was now an Israeli city, he declared, and he was adamant that he could not return as long it remained under Israeli sovereignty. The very next day, however, a Swiss journalist friend of mine interviewed my father and asked him if he would return to Haifa if it became possible. His discourse became quite suddenly ideological and elegant as he announced that, "as a Palestinian, like any other, I long to return no matter the conditions."

Similarly, methodology is important. I was surprised to learn that in some cases, political actors were allowed to become involved in the collection of polling data, in particular surveying for a poll by one of the NGOs in the region. The poll results showed that 96 percent of refugees declared that they intended to return. Considering my own father's conflicting statements, I suggest that it would benefit us all to discuss the setting of standards for the research at hand.

It is important to mention these issues for the specific reason of demonstrating the necessity of conducting better research in the area of Palestinian return migration. It is not sufficient to prove that return is legally enshrined in international human rights law and humanitarian law. We must also demonstrate that recognition of return is a necessity for regional security and, in some cases, a humanitarian necessity as well. The latter would be determined by analyzing the individual right of choice of each individual refugee.

A decade after Oslo, it has become apparent that Palestinian negotiators have reached an impasse and that the debate concerning refugee return and their rights should be opened to creative discussion outside of the "sacred" discourse. I would offer the work of Mahi Abdel Hadi and Jan De Jong as an example of such creative thinking. It has been suggested by the Palestinian Academic Society for the Study of International Affairs (PASSIA), that the Palestinian territories will be extended to include the Galilee and some areas of the Negev in order to absorb portions of refugee populations (without denying the remainders' Right of Return), a solution that resolves, for them, the Israeli fear of altering the character of the Jewish state. Whatever my opinion of this position, it certainly represented an innovative response to the issue and one that sparked debate and new discourse. Abdel Hadi and De Jong went so far as to say that the Galilee communities should be annexed to a future Palestinian state, a proposal vehemently opposed by Palestinians inside Israel and one that I oppose for that very reason. At the same time, the spirit of his idea was included in the Taba talks, where Israel proposed giving up five percent of land within the 1948 borders to a Palestinian state, in exchange for 1967 land that it has appropriated with its illegal settlements. New ideas, even those that would not work, can unleash new possibilities.

There are countless issues, such as the creation of socio-economic pre-return profiles that should be researched and studied in order to better prepare Palestinian negotiators. The importance of the relationship between refugees and their host countries cannot be overlooked; as well as the study of the function of kinship networks (in Israel and the Palestinian Territories) in encouraging and facilitating return would be of great value. We must also examine current and prospective return patterns, whether definitive or alternative, en masse or individual, chosen or sudden, and the unanticipated. Finally, we must also focus on essential demographic aspects, such as natural growth and out-migration.

Distribution of Palestinian Population Worldwide

PALESTINE	
West Bank	1,869,818
Gaza Strip	1,020,813
WBGS residents living abroad	325,258
Areas Occupied since 1948	953,497
Total Inside Palestine	**4,169,386**
DIASPORA	
Jordan	2,328,308
Lebanon	430,183
Syria	465,662
Egypt	48,784
Saudi Arabia	274,762
Kuwait & Gulf area	143,274
Libya & Iraq	74,284
Other Arab countries	5,544
The Americas	203,588
Other countries	259,248
Total Outside Palestine	**4,233,637**
TOTAL Palestinian Population Worldwide	**8,403,023**

Total   Financial   Contribution   of   the   Palestinian   Diaspora
(US Dollars in Million)

Total Contribution	1996	1997
Total Investment	303.8	311.1
Expenses of Diaspora Visiting Palestine	96.4	90.9
Philanthropic Aid - Welfare Association	3.806	4.211
Philanthropic Aid - Other Associations	4.0	4.0
Total Contribution of the Diaspora	408.006	410.211
Donors' Foreign Aid	549.414	432.259

Diverse sources.

Refugees Registered With UNRWA (2001)

Field	No. of Camps	Refugees Inside Camps	Refugees Inside Camps (%)	Refugees Outside Camps	Total No. of Refugees	Refugees' proportion of local population
Jordan	10	287951	17.5	1351767	1639718	32.8% *
West Bank	19	170056	27.9	437714	607770	31.4% **
Gaza	8	460031	53.9	392595	852626	78.4% **
Lebanon	12	214728	56	168245	382973	10.7% *
Syria	10	200054	51	191597	391651	2.4 % *
Total all Fields	59	1,332,820		2,541,917	3,874,738	

Source: UNRWA in Figures, UNRWA HQ, September 2001

* Statistics of 2000
** Census of 1997

Notes

1. In 2001 4,233 million Palestinians were living abroad, constituting about half of the Palestinian population as a whole (see Table 1). *The Palestinian Diaspora and Refugee Center*, Shaml, in Ramallah.

2. See for example remarks by Hossam Khader, Palestinian legislator from Balata refugee camp who said: "Sari Nusseibah has taken himself away from the national camp."

3. Karl Marx, *Le 18 Brumaire de Louis Bonaparte*, (Paris: Mille et une nuits, 1997), 13.

4. Sari Hanafi, *Entre deux mondes. Les hommes d'affaires palestiniens de la diaspora et la construction de l'entitÙ palestinienne* (Le Caire: CEDEJ, 1997), and Sari Hanafi, *Hona wa honaq: nahwa tahlil lil alaqa bina al shatat al falastini wa al markaz (Ici et lÐ-bas. Vers une analyse de la relation entre la diaspora palestinienne et le centre)*, (Ramallah: Muwatin et Beyrouth: Institut d'Ùtudes palestiniennes, 2001). (In Arabic).

5. Various estimates of the fortune of the Palestinian Diaspora have been made, ranging between $7 billion and $100 billions, although I would hesitate to participate such guesswork.

6. See discussion in Hirschman Albert O., *Exit, voice and loyalty, responses to decline in firms, organizations and states*, (Cambridge: Harvard University Press, 1970).

7. However, the "buffer elite" do not constitute a group with homogeneous interests. Indeed, the groups exhibits various differences: between the generation of the exodus of 1948, that views itself as the victim of the Oslo process, and the generation of 1967, that enjoys the partial right of return due to family reunification; between social classes; between the small entrepreneurs and the big business people; between those that approved of the Oslo agreements and those that oppose them; between those that sustain the PLO and the partisans of Hamas or the Palestinian left.

8. The investments of the Palestinian Diaspora in the Palestinian Territories are less important than it has generally been considered. For example, my findings in the United Arab Emirates show that only a few Palestinian business people have the strong conviction that they should leave the Emirates one day and return to Palestine, even though the partial Right of Return (family reunification) now exists, albeit to a rather limited extent. They decided instead, to express their feelings of nationalism by contributing to the construction of the Palestinian entity. However, such an investment, made in a delicate economic and political situation, seems to indicate that the rationality is more than merely economic: it concerns prestige and the acquisition of status. There are 34 economic projects that have started since the launch of the Oslo process in 1993. From the 75 members of the sample selected for the survey, more than a third invested in the Territories. This is a considerable number, especially in face of the troubled Palestinian-America relations. It seems, in any case, that there is a correlation between proximity and investments. The type of investment is also related to the origin of the Palestinians. Indeed, those of 1948 territories origin (8 business people in the sample) were stakeholders in many holding companies, such as PADICO and International Salaam Company, since they do not have physical access to the Palestinian Territories. The Palestinians of West Bank and Gaza origins behave differently. They associate a relative or a friend in their projects *in locus* after paying a visit to these territories. See Table 3. For further analysis on the Palestinian diasporic economy, see: Sari Hanafi, *Business Directory of Palestinian in the Diaspora* (Jerusalem: Biladi, June 1998). (In English, Franch and Arabic) and Sari Hanafi, "La diaspora palestinienne et la conversion des capitaux issus de la rente pétrolière," *Tiers Monde*, Paris, no. 163: 623-643.

9. These subsidies came from the countries of the Gulf and the USA.

10. See discussion in: Sari Hanafi, *Business Directory of Palestinian in the Diaspora* (Jerusalem: Biladi, June 1998). (In English, Franch and Arabic).

11. MOPIC (Ministry of Planning and International Cooperation), Aid Coordination Department, MOPIC's 1997, "*Fourth Quarterly Monitoring Report of Donor Assistance*," www.pna.net, Ramallah. See table 2.

12. See detailed discussion in Sara Roy, *The Gaza Strip: The Political Economy of De-development*, (Washington: Palestine Studies Institute, 1995).

13. On the Welfare Association see: www.welfareassociation.org. Apart from such large funding, Palestinian development also involves private donors, both in- and outside Palestine. The Welfare Association (WLA) works with a wide range of them. Several donors have also entrusted the WLA with managing grants, and even increased their investments.. The WLA has been acting as an intermediary NGO since 1984 and has funded between 1983, (the date of its foundation), and 1996, 1,307 projects to over 300 NGOs, with a total budget of US$90 million; US $43 million from its own sources and US$47 million from external ones. (Tanmiya, 1997:1,2). The WLA excellent international reputation has turned into a counterpart for the donor institutions such as: The European Union and the Arab Fund for Social and Economic Development (AFSED) are used for projects in the Palestinian Territories, Israel and Lebanon. This gives an average of approximately US$6.42 million per year, of which US$3.071 million were generated from its own sources. The yearly total average for 1997—US$4.211 million—showed a decrease from the previous year, although it should be noted that the association is now totally reliant on its own sources, external funding having come to an end see: Welfare Association Brochure, Tawasol bila hodod fi da'im masiret al-tanmiyya wa al-bina' al-falastiniyyah 1983-1996, (Geneva: 1997), p.7 (in Arabic). Moreover, The Welfare Association consists of a consortium including the British Council (BC) and Charities Aid Foundation (CAF). The World Bank it manages the fund and monitors the NGO activities in Palestine (The Project Management Organization (PMO), Tanmiya, 1997:1,2) This project is a major breakthrough in aid to the Palestinians, and it constitutes a very important pole of philanthropic Palestinian activities with the ability to help beyond the first-aid small plans. Additionally, because of their financial and intellectual capacities, the members have the potential to influence the decision-making processes concerning national affairs. See also Welfare Association Brochure, Tawasol bila hodod fi da'im masiret al-tanmiyya wa al-bina' al-falastiniyyah 1983-1996, (Geneva: 1997), 21. (in Arabic)

14. Hilal Jamil, Majdi Malki & al. (1997) *Social Support Institutions in West Bank and Gaza, Ramallah*, MAS, 89 Pages. (in Arabic).

15. The United Holy Land Fund is composed mainly of business people from the United States. Founded in 1967 to help the Palestinian people, it used to support the Oslo peace process. There is also a similar organisation based in the West of the United States called the Palestine Arab Fund.

16. See, for example, the interview with Sheikh Ahmad Yassin, spiritual leader of Hamas, on Al Jazira TV, April 30, 2001. Similarly, the interview of Abdelaziz Rantissi, one of the leaders of the Hamas, Al-Jazira, January 3, 2002. Concerning Al-Jihad, in early January ,2002, Sheikh Al-Shami of Gaza, hinted, while speaking on Abu Dhabi television, that it is possible that Al-Jihad will accept a territorial compromise based on United Nations resolution 242.

17. Legrain, Jean Francois (en collaboration avec Pierre Chenard: *Les voix du soulèvement palestinien* 1987-1988, (Le Caire: CEDEJ ,1991).

18. Here I am talking about a process and this does not suggest a symmetry between occupier and occupied. On the problem of the otherness and the absence of mutual relations in a colonial context see: Vincent Romani. "Palestiniens des Territoires occupés et Israéliens: le corps enfermé de l'Ennemi," *Le Monde*, January 23, 2002.

19. It is always surprising for the Palestinian returnees to the West Bank and Gaza post Oslo to see their compatriots consuming Israeli products without compunction.

20. Opposition to this communiquéé has been expressed in some Arab newspapers: Al-Hayat (London), Al-Ahram (Egypt) and Baath (Syria). During my visits during the summer of 2002 to refugee camps in Jordan, Syria and Lebanon, I could scarcely avoid noticing the popularity of the suicide attacks, and the lack of comprehension of the critical attitudes that have emerged inside the Palestinian society in West Bank and Gaza Strip, since June 2002.

21. For a more detailed evaluation of the Palestinian Diaspora, see: Sari Hanafi, "Des réfugiés avant le H.C.R: les Palestiniens." in Michelle Guillon, Luc Legoux, Emmanuel Ma Mung L'asile politique dans l'immigration. (Forthcoming 2003; Hanafi, 2003b).

22. In the case of Jordan, see: Hanna Jaber, "Le camp de Wihdat à la croisée des territoires," in Riccardo Bocco, Blandine Destremau & Jean Honnoyer (ed.), *Palestine, palestiniens. Territoire national, espaces communautaires,* (Amman: CERMOC, 1997).

23. Hanafi, Sari, "Les ONG palestiniennes et les bailleurs de fonds. Quelques éléments sur la formation d'un agenda' in Sarah Bennéfissa et Sari Hanafi (Ed) Les associations dans le monde arabe. Pouvoir et politique," (Paris : Edition CNRS, 2002). (Hanafi, 2002a)

24. "CNN, Euronews and BBC are very biased in favor Israeli colonialism. The pictures of the summary execution of a Palestinian youngster by Israeli soldiers distributed by the agency France Press in February 2002, have not been broadcast by any of these. I found it my duty to distribute them via the Internet to my mailing list," declared a young Palestinian economist residing in Syria. One noted that, mirroring the Jewish Diaspora, the Palestinian Diaspora began to observe Western media. CNN has been monitored closely by a young Palestinian-American group.

25. Issam Nasser, "Narrating the Self: Violence and Memory in Palestine Historiography." Paper presented at *the International Conference 'Memory and Violence'* Cortina: Italy, 14-15 June (2002)

26. Interview with the sociologist Lena Jayyusi, Ramallah, March 5, 2001.

27. One can consider it like a network of a region of the South, even though it is partially implanted in the North, because in this case its leaders are the immigrants who have often been installed there quite lately.

28. For more information about the different reactions, see *Al-Awda* (petition), *Badil's* response, and Salman Abu Sitta (in English), BADIL Resource Center, http://www.shaml.org/ground/index.htm accessed 11/20/01; Gershon Baskin response, *IPCRI*, "letter to Aaron Lerner," www.imra.org/il, accessed 18 November 2001; Statement from Palestinians in UK: "The right of return is non-negotiable and cannot be annulled by time" (in Arabic), 17 November 2001; Yasser Abed Rabbo, (Palestinian Minister of Information) "On the Right of Return" *Brookings Institution* (Akiva Eldar, *Ha'aretz*, 22 November 2001); Communiquéu from Fateh Youth Organization, *Al Ayam*, Ramallah, 23 November 2001(in Arabic); Clarification from Fateh Youth Organization, *Al Quds* Newspaper: Jerusalem, 26/11/2001, (in Arabic);   The Palestinian Right of Return Coalition Report, *Second Annual International Coordinating Meeting,* BADIL Resource Center, 5 December 2001; Asad Abdel Rahman, "Letter to Sari Nusseibeh: No Right for Any Official to disregard 70% of the

Palestinian people," *Al Quds Al Arabi*: London, 4 December 2001. (in Arabic); Naif Hawatmeh to Sari Nusseibeh, *Al Quds Al Arabi*: London, 3 December 2001 (in Arabic); Benny Morris "we must not recognize the right of return" (Middle East Media Research Institute, Special Dispatch, *Yediot Ahronot*: 9 December 2001; Sari Nusseibeh: "Palestinian State Will Solve Refugee Problem" 21 December 2001; Vered Levy-Barzilai, "Sari Nusseibeh. Noblesse Oblige," *Ha 'aretz*, 29 December, 2001; Nizar Sakhnini, "An Open Letter to Prof. Sari Nusseibeh" *Al Awda,* 30, December, 2001 5:23; The Palestine Right to Return Coalition, "Palestinian Refugees have every right to return," *Al Awda,*1 January 2002; Sari Nusseibeh - "The Trojan Horse" *Yediot Ahronot*, 1 January 2002; The Issue of Refugees: A Cause not to be Desecrated, (Fateh online, Editorial), 15 November 2001; Meron Benvenisti, "The return of the intellectual," *Haaretz*, 15 November 2001.

29. Azmi Bishara states: "It is impossible to apply the right of return in the two-state framework! There is a structural contradiction between the two-state solution and the right of return for Palestinian refugees, which would change the demographic nature of the Jewish state, with the permission of the Jewish state itself. The Palestinian national liberation movement should decide whether the establishment of the Palestinian state without the right of return constitutes an acceptable historical compromise (as long as the state has sovereignty over the Haram al-Sharif and as long as the agreement allows refugees to return to inside the state's borders). If such a historical compromise is impossible from both Palestinian and Israeli points of view, we have before us a long struggle against apartheid, a struggle based on full citizenship for two peoples in one country. Israel will prefer a total war over this last option." Azmi Bishara, "Liberating the Homeland, Liberating Human Beings," *Wijhat Nazar* 23 (Cairo: al-Ahram, December 2001). [in Arabic], reprinted in Bishara, Azmi (2002, *The Site of Meaning. Essays from the first year of the Intifada*. (Ramallah: Muwatin, 2002), 80 (in Arabic).

30. *New York Times*, 3 February 2002.

31. *Ha'aretz*, 24 November 2001 (in Hebrew).

32. *Ha'aretz*, 12 November 2001. (In Hebrew).

33. *Yediot Ahronot*, 9 December, 2001.(In Hebrew).

34. Benny Morris, "The Arabs Are Responsible" *Yediot Ahronot*, 9 December, 2001 (in Hebrew).

35. Amos Oz argues that the Palestinians were rejecting "the most far-reaching offer Israel can make" by insisting "on the right of return for millions of refugees to their homeland." *The Guardian*, 5 January 2002.

36. He states: "any mentioning of the right of return is a disaster, a recipe for the destruction of the State of Israel. Even if Arafat will agree that Israel will only recognize its responsibility in creating the refugee problem while the Palestinians give up the actual right to implement it, Israel must still object to such a proposal ... If you recognize the responsibility, millions will demand their lands in return immediately thereafter. If the notion of the right of return will be recognized, there is also going to be an attempt to utilize that notion, and that will be the end of the State of Israel. [If that happens], there won't be a Jewish State here." (Yediot Ahronot, 9 December, 2001)

37. A.B. Yehoshua. See, *Liberation*, 23 July, 2002.

38. David Grossman, "No right of return," *Frankfurter Allgemeine Zeitung*, 10 January 2001: 43. "They might be the biggest population group in a state whose essence and symbols they had always rejected, and whose extinction had been their highest aim."

39. Bitterlemons.org - *Palestinian-Israeli crossfire*: "Refugees and the right of return," 31 December 2001.

40. Yehudith Harel, "Peace Now and its 'Other,' " *Al-Ahram Weekly*, 11-17 January 2001, Issue No. 516.

41. See endnote #2.

42. Ilan Pappe, "The Post-Territorial Dimensions of a Future Homeland in Israel and Palestine." Paper presented at *Solomon Asch Center* at the University of Pennsylvania, 2002.

43. Ian Lustick S., "Negotiating Truth: The Holocaust, Lehavdil, and al-Nakba." Paper presented at *Solomon Asch Center*, the University of Pennsylvania, 2002.

44. Nadim Rouhana, "Truth and Reconciliation: The Right of Return in the Context of Past Injustice" Paper presented at the conference, *Solomon Asch Center, 2002.*

Works Cited

Abu-Sitta Salman. "Un pays aboli de la carte," Farouk Mardam-Bey et Elias Sanbar (Ed.), *Le Droit au Retour. Le problème des réfugiés Palestiniens.* Paris: Sinbad, 2002.

_____. *The End of the Palestinian-Israeli Conflict. From Refugees to Citizens at Home.* London: Palestinian Land Society and Palestinian Return Center, 2001.

_____. *Palestinian Right of Return, Sacred, Legal and Possible*, Londres: Palestinian Land Society and Palestinian Return Center,.2000, 2nd edition.

Hanafi, Sari. "Les ONG palestiniennes et les bailleurs de fonds. Quelques éléments sur la formation d'un agenda" in Sarah Bennéfissa et Sari Hanafi (Ed) *Les associations dans le monde arabe. Pouvoir et politique*, Paris : Edition CNRS, 2002.

_____. "Des réfugiés avant le H.C.R.: les Palestiniens." in Michelle Guillon, Luc Legoux, Emmanuel Ma Mung *L'asile politique dans l'immigration.* 2003.

_____. *Hona wa honaq: nahwa tahlil lil alaqa bina al shatat al falastini wa al markaz* Ramallah : Muwatin, et Beyrouth: Institut d'études palestiniennes, 2001 (in Arabic)

_____. "La Diaspora palestinienne et la conversion des capitaux issus de la rente pétrolière," *Tiers Monde*, Paris, no 163, 2001b : 623-643.

_____. *Business Directory of Palestinian in the Diaspora*, Jerusalem: Biladi, June 1998b. (in English, French and Arabic)

_____. "Contribution de la diaspora palestinienne à l'économie des Territoires: investissement et philanthropie," in *Maghreb-Machrek*, no. 161 novembre 1998.

_____. *Entre deux mondes. Les hommes d'affaires palestiniens de la diaspora et la construction de l'entité palestinienne*, Le Caire, CEDEJ, 1997.

Hilal Jamil, Majdi Malki & al. *Social Support Institutions in West Bank and Gaza, Ramallah*, MAS, 1997, 89 Pages (in Arabic)

Hirschman Albert O. *Exit, voice and loyalty, responses to decline in firms, organisations and states*. Cambridge: Harvard University Press, 1970

Hoche, Marianne Christian. *Sari Nusseibéh, franc-tireur de la paix*. http://www.shaml.org/ground/Nusseibeh/index.htm. 19 November, 2001.

Jaber, Hanna. "Le camp de Wihdat à la croisée des territoires," in Riccardo Bocco, Blandine Destremau & Jean Honnoyer (ed.), *Palestine, palestiniens. Territoire national, espaces communautaires*. Amman: CERMOC. 1997.

Legrain, Jean François (en collaboration avec Pierre Chenard) *Les voix du soulèvement Palestinien 1987-1988*, Le Caire: CEDEJ. 1991.

Lustick, Ian S. « Negotiating Truth: The Holocaust, Lehavdil, and al-Nakba. » Paper presented at the conference : *Solomon Asch Center* at the University of Pennsylvania. 2002

MOPIC (Ministry of Planning and International Cooperation) Aid Coordination Department. MOPIC's "Fourth Quarterly Monitoring Report of Donor Assistance," see *www.pna.net*, Ramallah. 1997, and 1998.

Nassar, Issam "Narrating the Self: Violence and Memory in Palestinian Historiography," paper presented at the conference « *Memory and Violence* », Cortina: Italie, 14-15 Juin, 200.

Nusseibeh, Sari. Read! *Al Ayyam*, Ramallah,11.23.2001 (in Arabic).

_____. "What's Next," *Haaretz*, Tel Aviv, 24.09.2001

Pappe, Ilan. "The Post-Territorial Dimensions of a Future Homeland in Israel and Palestine." Paper presented at for the conference: *Solomon Asch Center:* the University of Pennsylvania, 2002.

Rouhana, Nadim. "Truth and Reconciliation: The Right of Return in the Context of Past Injustice." Paper presented at for the conference "*The Predicaments of Palestinians and Jews: The Meanings of Catastrophe, Historical Knowledge, and the Return of Exiles,*" Solomon Asch Center at the University of Pennsylvania, 2002.

Romani, Vincent. "Palestiniens des Territoires occupés et Israéliens : le corps enfermé de l'Ennemi," *Le Monde*, 23/1/2002.

Roy Sara. *The Gaza Strip: The Political Economy of De-development.* Washington: Palestine Studies Institute, 1995.

Welfare Association. *Brochure "Tawasol bila hodod fi da'im masiret al-tanmiyya wa al-bina' al-falastiniyyah 1983-1996,*" Geneva. (In Arabic), 1997.

Abby Stoddard

CHAPTER ELEVEN:

Donor-Driven Disparity?
The US Government's Response to
Forced Migration and
Displaced Persons

T his case study examines the institutional machinery, management structures, and financial flows of US humanitarian assistance to displaced persons and refugees. The study sheds light on the political preferences and bureaucratic history that have created and sustained the differential in response to forced migrants in international humanitarian policy. The humanitarian machinery of the US government exhibits the same mandate gap regarding Internally Displaced Persons (IDPs) that exists among the international implementing agencies it helps fund. The chapter will also discuss the implications for internally displaced assistance in countries affected by post-9-11 security environment, where US counter terror operations has unprecedented former humanitarian and development agendas.

Humanitarian assistance flows doubled during the 1990s, reaching just under $6 billion by 2000, and have continued to rise in recent years. A full third of these monies are provided by the United States, which dominates the small group of major humanitarian donor governments (UK, Canada, Japan, the Netherlands, Norway, Sweden, Switzerland, and Germany) who together account for 93 percent of official humanitarian assistance.[1] The humanitarian machinery of the US government exhibits the same mandate gap regarding IDPs that exists among the international implementing agencies US humanitarian structures to this day remain poorly positioned to address the needs of the internally displaced. Some small developments in early 2003, however, may possibly indicate the first steps of more significant progress towards the Unites States taking on a more active role.

The "Bilateralization" Trend

The severity of the problem is clearly exhibited in the growing volume of assistance. Humanitarian assistance grew as a percentage of overall official development and relief aid in the 1990s, from 5.83 percent to 10.5 percent.[2] While overall humanitarian assistance has increased in real terms, the amounts going to the multilateral UN agencies have seen a fairly modest rise, while a dramatic increase is evidenced in the amount that donors channel bilaterally, i.e. through project grants to NGOs or in earmarked UN contributions. While multilateral aid rose by 32 percent, bilateral assistance increased by 150 percent. Reasons for the so called "bilateralization" trend a rising sense of dissatisfaction with the UN's performance and concerns over transparency and accountability, a greater involvement of donors in the technical aspects of aid programming and the desire to exert more control over the process, and the opportunity to "fly the flag" and be seen as generous and relevant in international crises.

Even aside from the political complexities entailed, i.e. that assisting conflict victims within recognized borders would essentially mean intervening in the affairs of a sovereign state, IDPs present problems to donors that refugees do not. In the first place it is very difficult to get an accurate count, and donors, particularly the US, have placed increasing emphasis on quantifying aid recipients and outputs. US government donors want to know—because Congress wants to know when it votes to allocate funding—how many people are receiving US aid, the dollars spent per capita, the concrete results, and the relative cost-effectiveness of aid projects. When the crisis-affected nation is under economic sanctions, there are further obstacles to transferring aid resources into the country. Finally, because the IDPs' predicament is often invisible, public pressure to help is lacking. Crises of displacement seldom generate compelling images such as Vietnamese fleeing in boats, Rwandan refugees in camps in Goma, or weeping Kosovars arriving in Macedonia, that elicit an emotional response, and causing the public to put pressure on their governments to do something about it.

Bilateralization of humanitarian aid has expressed itself in tighter management by donors over cash flows, closer scrutiny of project management, and substantive involvement in project design. The more the donor puts its stamp on aid, the more its internal structures (and the politics behind them) are reflected in the assistance. In the United States these structures have changed little over the last four decades, and bear a distinctly Cold War character. Looking beyond the aid providers to the level of the donors, one begins to see the structural, practical, and political reasons why IDPs remain under-assisted.

The State of Aid in Aid and State

Like the UN, the humanitarian architecture of the US government reflects a mid-twentieth century conception of humanitarian response, with natural disaster assistance on the one hand, and refugee affairs on the other. The apparent underlying distinction made between the more complex political/ diplomatic issue of refugees and more straightforward matters of getting relief supplies from A to B, is embodied in the two main pillars of the US humanitarian architecture: the State Department's Bureau for Population, refugees, and Migration (PRM), and the US Agency for International Development (USAID). More specifically the split runs between PRM and USAID's Bureau for Democracy, Conflict and Humanitarian Assistance (DCHA—formerly the Bureau for Humanitarian Response). DCHA houses the Office of Foreign Disaster Assistance (OFDA), the most active and visible of the US government's assistance bodies. OFDA is mandated with non-food assistance for victims of natural disasters and internal civil strife, and channels the bulk of its resources (77 percent in 2002) through NGOs.

Other key offices in USAID/DCHA include the Office of Food for Peace, which oversees the donation of large scale food assistance for emergency relief and food security projects, and the Office for Transition Initiatives (OTI), which was established in the 1990s to promote democracy and peace building in transitional and recovery situations, and to fill the gap between relief and development assistance. The Foreign Assistance Act of 1961 reorganized existing government aid programmes that had their roots in the Marshall Plan and its successors, and established an executive agency to oversee them, USAID. OFDA was created four years later to provide rapid assistance for victims of disasters overseas. FAA has been amended over the years, but a number of attempts at more radical reform died in Congress, and so to this day provides the legislative basis of US foreign aid policy.

From the State department side, PRM serves as the channel for US relief aid to refugees, (as well as undertaking non-emergency population and resettlement activities). PRM was established by the Migration and Refugee Assistance Act of 1962, and is mandated to focus on traditional cross-border refugees resulting from armed conflict. It works mainly by providing large annual grants to multilateral organisations, the major recipients being UNHCR, IOM, and ICRC.[3]

Agency	Budget Request	Actual Budget	Shortfall Percentage	U.S. Contribution	
International Committee of the Red Cross	$671	$540	19%	$122	23%
UN High Commissioner for Refugees	930	693	25	239	34%
UN High Commissioner for Human Rights	53	44	17	7	16%
UN Development Program*	1,100	645	41	80	12%
World Food Program	2,117	1,685	20	796	47%
UNICEF**	254	149	41	110	74%

* Includes core or regular budget only

** Includes emergency budget only, U.S. contribution includes regular and emergency budget.

Source: US General Accounting Office

Since 1998 the Secretary of State has assumed direct authority over USAID, whose director formerly reported directly to the President, and is now the starting point for most government funding allocated to the agency. The difficulties stemming from the physical and administrative separation of the two bureaus remain, however, and officials complain of fairly basic communication problems. The only mechanisms for joint planning between USAID and State around individual emergencies have been informal,and some say unhelpful, often becoming bogged down in technical details. The US humanitarian mandates and institutions are now over 40 years old, and continue to reflect a 1960s reality. Routinely referred to by current USG officials as "dysfunctional,"[4] or in the words of one former OFDA Director "antediluvian and counterproductive,"[5] the bifurcated humanitarian mandate results in a US response that is inherently fragmented, uncoordinated, and reactive rather than cognitive. The disconnect hampers thinking in terms of incorporating humanitarian principles or formulating long-term strategic policy.[6]

Regarding the IDP issue, as in the UN system the IDP mandate is diffused across several different offices within USAID and State. Their activities are not coordinated, nor do they fall under a single coherent policy framework. PRM contributions go towards helping IDPS only insofar as UNHCR and the other multilateral organizations cover IDPs in their programming. Therefore PRM is known as the refugee funder and responsibility for IDPs has historically and more or less fallen to DCHA (and OFDA specifically) *de facto*, though aid to IDPs is not an area of particular focus in the Bureau, and there is no single office, unit, or staff position that addresses the needs of this group.

The issue of the IDP gap received a significant boost in 2000, when U.S. Ambassador to the United Nations Richard Holbrooke personally took up the IDP cause. Speaking as a private person and not as a USG representative, Holbrooke called for formal responsibility for IDPs to be placed with one agency, and made a case for that agency being UNHCR, as the most logical choice. Although this did not come to pass, the UN has arguably made at least conceptual strides in addressing the IDP problem, whereas, observers have noted that the US government has been "curiously unfocused in the face of the internal displacement phenomenon."[7] If US officials were slower to realize acknowledge their own IDP mandate gap, there is some movement on it now, thanks in large part to three influential reports on USG humanitarian structures, which highlighted this problem: a 1999 Brookings Institution/US

Committee for Refugees report written by James Kunder; a 2000 inter-agency review of humanitarian structures, the so-called "Halperin Report"; and a GAO report on IDP assistance undertaken at the request of the Senate Committee on Foreign Relations in 2001.

Kunder's report, entitled "The U.S. Government and Internally Displaced Persons: Present, but not Accounted For," examined the statutory basis and institutional mechanisms for a US response to IDPs and found them sorely lacking. The problem is not that no US aid is going to IDPs, but that it is indirect, unfocused, and not part of a coherent policy framework. The report makes particular mention of the absence of strategy and policy documents relating to IDPs, reflecting, as he saw it, a general lack of awareness of their special assistance and protection needs. The report concludes, "Absent focused leadership and dedicated resources from the United States and other influential governments, the institutional response to internal displacement, from both local authorities and international agencies, will be diffuse, inconsistent and inadequate."[8]

The Halperin Report (named for the Chair of the inter-agency commission, Assistant Secretary of State for policy planning, Morton Halperin) was not centered on IDPs *per se*, but on the larger issue of the State-USAID split on humanitarian response. Secretary of State Madeline Albright commissioned the report after a decidedly mixed USG response the Kosovo crisis, to study the issue and make recommendations for structural reform. Chief among the deficiencies cited in Kosovo was the failure of the various governmental actors to speak with one senior voice for U.S. humanitarian policy. Mandates overlapped, efforts were duplicated, and the coordination that did take place was achieved through personal relationships and "ad-hoc, mid-level coordination"[9] between the State Department and USAID. The report cited, as one of the most serious implications of the State-AID split, that IDPs are not formally covered by either bureau's mandate, and are a serious enough problem that they warrant a comprehensive approach.

The report presented options for improving and/or restructuring the emergency assistance functions of USAID and State, which included merging the two functions into one body to be located either in the State Department's regular administration or in USAID, or in a wholly new, separate humanitarian agency. Upon the report's release, serious discussion began around the option of merging PRM's refugee functions into USAID. (Although the report included no concrete recommendation, this was Halperin's favored option and enjoyed the consensus of most stakeholders, particularly those at USAID).[10]

The report prepared by the GAO at the behest of the Senate Foreign Relations Committee in August 2001 revisited the IDP issue, looking at both the international response overall and the US donor agencies, and reinforced many of the same critiques that were raised in the Kunder and Halperin reports. It noted, for instance that the State Department lacks policy/strategy documents on dealing with IDPs and a lead office designated to coordinate US efforts. It also highlighted informational deficiencies, observing that although IDPs are mentioned in the State Department's annual country profiles and human rights report, State has not developed any "standard definition or format for reporting on the internally displaced that would allow for systematic data gathering and analysis."[11] Having provided a candid assessment of the problem and a strong indictment of the system's shortcomings, the GAO report went on to offer some fairly limp recommendations.

"We recommend the Secretary of State and the Permanent Representative of the United States to the United Nations work to advance more proactive policies and programs to protect and assist internally displaced persons and see with other member states to strengthen international organizations and to form country-level protection working groups. We also recommend that the Secretary of State include a focus on internal displacement issues in State's annual *Country Reports on Human Rights Practices*."[12]

The reason the report did not present more far-reaching recommendations may be that it attempted to frame all options "within existing resources."[13] There seems little scope to push for increased funding from Congress for the purpose. Evidently, when Holbrooke raised the IDP issue, the State department reportedly made some preliminary projections on what it would cost for the US to fund expanded mandates, and it was a prohibitively large number.[14]

Latest Developments

If the US government is interested in improving the international response to the problem of internal displacement, it would seem to have two available avenues for action: 1) at the donor level, in restructuring its own aid architecture, or 2) at the implementation level pushing the UN system through its agency fundees to develop policies and rationalize institutional structures, (e.g. designating a lead agency). However, the government has yet to take on either task in a meaningful way. The Halperin Report created a certain momentum for restructuring after it was released, but fell by the wayside with the change of Administration in 2001 and is no longer on the table. Holbrooke's campaign in the United Nations also failed to move the bureaucracy mountain in Washington. Currently there is no discussion on merging PRM and USAID, nor is there consensus that a lead office with a formal IDP mandate is the way to go. Instead, like the United Nations humanitarian actors, the government aid agencies have focused on improved communication, coordination of activities, and clarification of funding roles between State and USAID.

In this regard, the PRM-DCHA Funding Guidelines in Complex Humanitarian Emergencies (March 2003) represent a step forward. Produced jointly by PRM and DCHA at the prodding of Deputy Secretary of State Richard Armitage, this is the first document that explicitly designates DCHA as "the lead for providing emergency relief assistance to internally displaced persons." It goes on to say that PRM will also provide funding for IDPs to the extent that its regular multilateral partners are "principal providers of assistance to IDPs." Where there is overlap or no clear DCHA leadership at the outset of a crisis, the guidelines call for the two bureaus to consult on the matter. As a result, for example, in Iraq DCHA will take lead for IDPs despite the fact that IOM is a PRM fundee. US humanitarian officials hope the guidelines will give IDPs both an institutional home and more predictable funding stream, and the quarterly meetings called for to consult and review their respective funding portfolios will serve to bridge some of the communication gaps that have plagued the two bureaus before. It also allows for dual-source funding of the same organization or program to allow one bureau to cover any gaps left by the other one's mandate. Notably, however, the inclusion of the words "emergency relief assistance" seems to deliberately preclude the funding of protection activities. Protection of IDPs, widely agreed to be their most pressing need, is not addressed in this document.

OFDA has historically shied away from protection (James Kunder points out that OFDA's operations manual states directly that it will not assume a protection role in emergencies) both because its know-how and capacity are geared toward material relief deliveries, and because of worries that Congress would balk (ironically, Congress recently called for more research into protection issue).[15] However, with the recent reconfiguration of the humanitarian response segment of USAID, DCHA and OFDA are "seriously rethinking the protection role"[16] and made some preliminary overtures to the UN High Commissioner for Human Rights to jointly explore this possibility.

The recent renaming of the Bureau for Humanitarian Response to the Bureau for Democracy, Conflict, and Humanitarian Assistance demonstrates a growing awareness within government of the centrality of conflict to modern day humanitarian emergencies, and acknowledges a need to address political and transitional issues along with providing aid. USAID's operational reality is one of failed and failing states, plagued by conflict, and often producing large internal displacements. In fact, DCHA's Deputy Director recently recalled, over the past four or five years approximately 35 of USAID's countries of operation had experienced armed conflict of some kind.[17]

State Department officials concede that still greater concerted effort between USAID and PRM is needed to effectively address the IDP challenge.[18] Even so, the funding guidelines were met with satisfaction on the part of both DCHA and PRM staff who see them as an important step forward. Refugee advocates and NGOs are less satisfied with the progress, however, arguing that ultimately the memorandum simply formalized the status quo without making any substantive improvements. For example, Refugees International has no particular preference as to which agency funds UNHCR or where money for IDPs comes from, as long as the US government has a clear strategy for trying to meet these unmet needs. It appears that no US government humanitarian body has come down squarely in favor of designating UNHCR the lead agency for IDPs in all cases. And although there is widespread consensus that a problem exists, there is little sense of urgency in Washington to promote significant systemic change, either in the UNB or in its own institutions. PRM's position is simply that the process should be more predictable, and would be amenable to assigning a lead agency on a case-by-case basis if there were clear criteria for how the decision would be made (something the UN normally doesn't do, witness the flap over giving IOM the lead for IDPs in post-war Iraq.)[19] However, the US government is satisfied with the progress made thus far in creating a management structure of IDP issues at the UN, and with the general state of the debate (which it is tracking, not leading).

How The Aid Flows

While Congress may increase (even double) the humanitarian funding it channels through USAID on any given year, depending on the occurrence of high profile emergencies, PRM's annual budget, the Migration and Refugee Assistance or MRA account, holds fairly steady year to year at around $700 million. Of this, $125 million goes to admitting and resettling refugees in the United States. Another earmark sets aside $60 million to assist Jews immigrating to Israel from developing or hardship countries (e.g. Russia and African nations, e.g.). The remainder, around $500 million, is slated for humanitarian assistance to international refugees. The MRA budget is augmented by funds from the Emergency Refugee and Migration Assistance (ERMA) account, which is a revolving pot of money of up to $100 million authorized by the President for "urgent and unforeseen" events—usually a sudden repatriation or a new emergency. Supplemental emergency funds authorized by Congress, a staple of OFDA's programming, are unpredictable and fairly rare for PRM.[20] For FY 2003, PRM requested $705 million from Congress in MRA funds, and received $787 million.

In 2002, UNHCR numbered 19.8 million "persons of concern" or targeted beneficiaries of UNHCR assistance throughout the world. This figure included 12 million refugees (or 61 percent), 940,800 asylum seekers (5 percent), 462,700 returned refugees (3 percent), 5.3 million internally displaced persons (25 percent), 241,000 returned IDPs (1 percent), and 1 million "others of concern" (5 percent). So if estimates are correct that IDPs number over 20 million around the world, and UNHCR reaches only about one quarter of this population. The State Department does not track the proportion of its funding that goes to assist IDPs, but USAID estimates that $123 million went to IDPs across 20 countries in FY 2000.[21]

Practically speaking, it is much easier to distribute emergency food rations to IDPS groups than it is to ensure their long-term security. Not surprisingly the immediate humanitarian needs of IDPs to whom the international community has access are often well met, water, sanitation, and health needs slightly less so, and protection hardly at all. At present there is no specific funding channel in the US government for protection activities. Additionally, after the initial displacement and acute phase of emergency ends, i.e. in a stable/settled IDP population, the IDPs receive a much lower standard of assistance than refugees, especially if it is a low profile emergency that is having difficulty attracting donor resources. In Liberia, for instance, a crisis affected country with unknown numbers of IDPs, only 50 percent of the consolidated interagency appeal was funded for 2002. Out of that, only 20 percent went to IDPs, which is the country's most urgent problem. Instead, the bulk of the money went to traditional cross-border refugees.[22]

USG Multilateral Disbursements for International Organizations (2000)

Migration & Emergency Refugees	USD thousands	Food Aid	Total
UNICEF	20,844		
UNRWA	97,300		
WFP	23,944	87,396	
UNHCR	240,160	--	
UN OCHA UN Office of Coordination of Humanitarian Affairs	3,206		
WHO	4,709	--	
PAHO Pan-American Health Org	506	--	
IOM	37,785	--	
TOTAL Multilateral	428,454	87,396	515,850
Bilateral (through State PRM)	259,847	--	

Source: USAID - Bureau for Policy and Program Coordination

Beyond strictly monetary resources, there is the question of staff hours devoted to addressing IDPs and the issues of displacement. In his 1999 report, Kunder made the point that neither PRM nor USAID had a staff person who devoted the majority of his or her time to IDPs. Four years later this has not changed, but the PRM response is that in fact several staff people at various regional and functional desks regularly deal with IDP issues as part of their daily work. Others have countered that addressing IDPs piecemeal, as a cross-cutting concern is not the same as taking charge of the issue, and staff hours counted this way add up to much less than the same number put in by a single officer who is held accountable for results on this particular issue.

The Politics Behind The Mandate Gap

The tortuously slow pace at which the international community has moved to address the problem of internal displacement—an issue that everyone in the humanitarian field seems to agree is of the utmost importance—speaks to the underlying ambivalence of the key donors. As the largest donor and the linchpin of the humanitarian system the US could presumably take the lead and set the terms of debate on any issue it wanted, but has dragged its feet on this one. The reasons are manifold, and include not only the daunting practical concerns of what is a very complicated undertaking (How to access IDPs? Identify them? Protect them?). These concerns go beyond simple bureaucratic inertia—and the left over Cold War institutions have proven as permanent as a fallout shelter.

A state department official expressed his own frustration in the humanitarian arena because the United States, like the UN, simply lacks the institutional tools and predictable resources to adequately and equitably address the needs of crisis victims around the world. Humanitarian officials in 2003 are working with 50 year-old mandates and definitions and a 40 year old set of institutions that do not reflect modern reality. The anachronistic framework has worked against developing new policy initiatives and making progress on some of the most intractable issues in humanitarian assistance. Jeff Crisp of UNCHR has a darker interpretation of donor motives. In a study of donor behavior vis-à-vis eastern Zaire and post-Dayton Bosnia he finds that major donors (and the US in particular) deliberately played down evidence of serious humanitarian conditions in order to "bring an early halt to longstanding humanitarian operations which have outlived their political usefulness."[23] This would seem an unduly harsh assessment, but there are undoubtedly political forces at work behind the US ambivalent stance as well. Largely invisible populations in largely forgotten emergencies do not make for public pressure on Congress and administration officials to help, and post-September 11 security concerns have changed the equation dramatically.

Post 9-11 Implications

The US-led invasions of Afghanistan and Iraq, and the Bush administration's radical new doctrine of "preemptive security" in response to the terrorist threat, have ushered in a profoundly different era of humanitarian action. Whereas in the post-Cold War period humanitarians would complain that the major powers were too disengaged from developing country conflicts and were using humanitarian assistance as a cover for their inaction, today the humanitarian agenda has been trumped almost completely by political/ security interests. In post-war Iraq the military will retain control of the humanitarian resources and dictate the terms of the response, encroaching on humanitarian space to an extent not seen before. It is too early to say for certain what effects the new security environment this will have on refugee and IDP assistance, but early indicators do not bode well.

On the one hand there is the fear that attention and funds will be sapped from countries outside the sphere of US counter-terror concern. But what of the countries that come under the spotlight? Some suggest that US strategic focus may actually benefit vulnerable populations in those countries by raising awareness of the situation and mobilizing new aid resources. However, thus far the actual assistance and reconstruction response by the US has not matched its rhetoric (witness the as yet unrealized "Marshall plan for Afghanistan.") And if the war on drugs can be taken as an example, the relatively meager $2 million in US support for displaced persons in Colombia stands in stark contrast to the $289 million it provides in anti-drug funding, although the conflict there has produced the world's fourth largest IDP population.[24]

Lastly, the issue of asylum in the post 9-11 environment represents still another blow to the cause of humanitarianism and refugees protection. The United States has US has progressively lowered its ceiling of 200,000 asylum applicants per year in the 1990s, to 120,000, to 70,000 after September 11. In 2002 only 50,000 out of the 70,000 target has been allowed entry, and as of February 2003, only 5,000 had arrived, continuing a steep downward trend.[25] The European Union startled refugee advocates in 2002 when it proposed a plan to repatriate hundreds of thousands of Afghan refugees living in Europe back to the Afghanistan before the fighting had even ceased.[26] Some have even linked the rise in IDP numbers to a waning of respect for the 1951 Refugee Convention and a tightening of border restrictions on those attempting to flee their country.[27]

Conclusion

As the preeminent humanitarian donor, the US could use its influence to drive the discussion and make progress on any issue, especially if it coordinates policy and practice with the other major donors, but on this one it has dragged its collective feet, content to remain on the sidelines of the international debate on IDPs in the role of "passive interlocutor."[28]

It is an axiom of international humanitarian assistance that domestic and foreign policy priorities determine donor behavior as much as, if not more than, humanitarian needs and principles. Yet it is also true that donors like the US government are constrained by the same bureaucratic obstacles and turf issues that plague the United Nations system. As this and my previous chapter have detailed, in both institutions the IDP issue has begun to provoke the taking down of some of the walls, though it has not been sufficient to reopen the debate for radical restructuring of the humanitarian architecture.

In other nascent but promising developments, a conference held in Stockholm in June 2003 on "Good Humanitarian Donorship" brought together the US and other major donors with key humanitarian implementers to discuss ways that donors could effect change in the system through greater coordination with each other and more effective and accountable practices. Though the conference did not achieve all that its organizers hoped for, it remains a hopeful portent for the IDP dilemma, as well as other problems that bedevil the international humanitarian system. A genuine effort to address the humanitarian crisis affecting tens of millions of vulnerable displaced persons may need to start with acknowledging that the problem of IDP protection and assistance begins and ends with the donors.

Notes

1. Europe's ECHO, acting as a single unit, is a major donor in its own right accounting for 10 percent of global humanitarian assistance. See Macrae, et al, 2002.

2. Joanna Macrae, et al, *Uncertain Power: The Changing Role of Official Donors in Humanitarian Action*, (London: Overseas Development Institute, 12 December 2002).

3. The fourth, less mentioned major beneficiary of PRM funds is UNRWA - the UN Relief and Works Agency for Palestine Refugees. Since 1992 WFP has also received PRM funds, through a less formal memorandum of understanding, with no set yearly amount.

4. Interview with Anita Menghetti, USAID, April 1 2003

5. Interview with H. Roy Williams, Center for Humanitarian Cooridnation, July 26, 2001.

6. Abby Stoddard, "Trends in US Humanitarian Policy" in Macrae, ed. *The New Humanitarianisms: A Review of Trends in Global Humanitarian Action* (London: Overseas Development Institute, 2002).

7. James Kunder, *The U.S. Government and Internally Displaced Persons: Present, but not Accounted For,* (Washington DC: The Brookings Institution and the U.S. Committee for Refugees, 1999), 2.

8. *Ibid.,* 2.

9. "Interagency Review of U.S. Government Civilian Humanitarian and Transition Programs" —available online through George Washington University at www.gwu.edu/~nsarchiv/NSAEBB

10. Interview with Morton Halperin, September 11 2001. See also Stoddard, "Trends in US Humanitarian Policy.".

11. US General Accounting Office, *Foreign Affairs: Internally Displaced Persons Lack Effective Protection*, GAO Report 17 August 2001 http://www.gao.gov/new.items/d01803.pdf, 29.

12. *Ibid.,* 34.

13. *Ibid.,* 35.

14. Interview with Douglas Hunter, April 22, 2002.

15. Anita Menghetti, April 1 2003.

16. *Ibid,*.

17. Interview with William Garvelink, Deputy Director, DCHA, USAID, April 22, 2002.

18. Interview with Scott Busby, State Department, PRM, April 1, 2003.

19. Scott Busby, April 1 2003.

20. Stoddard, "Trends in US Humanitarian Policy."

21. GAO, 30.

22. Interview with Yvonne Rademacher, West Africa Desk Officer, OCHA, United Nations, March 2003.

23. Jeff Crisp, "Who has Counted the Refugees? UNHCR and the Politics of Numbers" Working Paper No.12 in *New Issues in Refugee Research* (Geneva: UNHCR, 1999), 15.

24. Kunder, 13.

25. Advocates Urge Colin Powell to Reassess U.S. Refugee Program, 17 January 2003, and Charny interview, April 1 2003.

26. IRIN. "Afghans react strongly to EU repatriation initiative," Press release, Islamabad (21 October 2002) <http://www.irinnews.org.> (25 March 2003).

27. Nicola Reindorp, "Trends and Challenges in the UN Humanitarian System," in Macrae, ed., *The New Humanitarianisms: A Review of Trends in Global Humanitarian Action.*

28. Kunder, 13.

Kendall Stiles

CHAPTER TWELVE:

Refugees and Civil Society in the Developing World*

S tudies of forced migration in general and refugees in particular tend to focus on the causes and consequences for the refugees themselves. Studies of upheaval, distress, emergency relief and so forth typify refugee research. However, the fact of the matter is that for a large minority of refugees, what matters most about their experience is its durability. It is not uncommon for refugee populations numbering in the hundreds of thousands to reside in the same general area more than fifteen years. Well over four million Palestinians have been living in exile since the 1940s and over two and a half million Afghanis have lived as refugees since the Soviet invasion in 1979. As of 1999, nearly ten million refugees were part of twenty refugee communities that had lived in exile more than eight years.[1]

To illustrate the phenomenon of long-term refugee populations, consider the following: From the time of the Soviet invasion in 1979 until the defeat of the Taliban in 2002, as many as 6.3 million Afghans were refugees in neighboring countries and beyond (although the figure usually hovered around 4 million). Most became established members of local communities, with the result that they significantly influenced local politics. Perhaps the most famous case is that of the Afghan *mujahideen*—or Islamic freedom fighters—who took shelter in Pakistan in particular and received support from sources as different as Iran, Saudi Arabia and the United States at various times. Perhaps the most notorious provider of support was Osama bin Laden, who is now the world's most wanted terrorist. Interestingly enough, even though peace has returned to Afghanistan, a little less than half of the refugees have returned—many of them to find a shell of a country with no possibility of housing in the near future. However, this situation pales in comparison to the 4.2 million Palestinian refugees who have been living in areas around Israel and the Occupied Territories as well as overseas—some of them since the founding of the state of Israel in 1948 (although most since 1967). An entire United Nations agency was created to deal with their needs and two generations have now grown up in camps.

Not only have entire nations been uprooted for decades, some host states are virtually unrecognizable, given the influx of refugees over the years. Pakistan's political stability is in jeopardy in part because of the political ties Afghan refugees have created with local Pakistani ethnic groups, especially in the north. Armenia's population consists of seven percent refugees (roughly equal to the proportion of Americans of Mexican background), while roughly four percent of the population of Congo, Yugoslavia and Djibouti are refugees. By sheer weight of numbers, these refugee communities alter the social and political landscape of hosts. Table A presents a summary of the major long-term refugee situations through the end of 1999.

Protracted Refugee Situations, 1980-1999

(Continuous refugee presence of more than 100,000, for more than eight years)

Home County	Main Host Countries	Period	Max # / Yr.	No. / Last Yr.
Afghanistan	Pakistan and Iran	1980-99	6,326.4 / 1990	2,562.0 / 1999
Angola	Zambia, Namibia	1980-99	457.1 / 1980	350.7 / 1999
Armenia	Azerbaijan	1992-99	201.5 / 1994	190.3 / 1999
Azerbaijan	Armenia	1992-99	300.0 / 1992	13.2 / 1999
Bosnia	Neighboring countries	1992-99	893.6 / 1996	382.9 / 1999
Burundi	Rwanda, Tanzania	1980-99	871.3 / 1993	524.4 / 1999
Cambodia	Thailand, Vietnam	1980-99	192.7 / 1980	38.6 / 1999
Chad	Sudan, CAR	1980-99	234.3 / 1981	58.2 / 1999
DR Congo	Neighboring countries	1980-99	116.8 / 1980	249.3 / 1999
Eritrea	Sudan	1991-99	500.6 / 1991	345.6 / 1999
Ethiopia	Sudan, Kenya, Somalia	1980-99	2,567.4 / 1980	53.7 / 1999
Iraq	Iran	1982-99	1,322.7 / 1992	572.1 / 1999
Liberia	Guinea, Coted'Ivoire	1990-99	794.2 / 1994	285.0 / 1999
Mozambique	Malawi, Zambia	1986-95	1,344.9 / 1992	125.5 / 1995
Burma	Thailand, Bangladesh	1992-99	281.3 / 1993	127.8 / 1999
Rwanda	Burundi, Tanzania	1980-96	277.0 / 1981	467.7 / 1996
Sierra Leone	Guinea, Coted'Ivoire	1991-99	142.6 / 1992	487.2 / 1999
Somalia	Ethiopia, Kenya	1988-99	788.2 / 1992	451.5 / 1999
Sudan	Uganda, Ethiopia	1984-99	180.1 / 1984	467.7 / 1999
Uganda	Sudan, Kenya	1980-87	315.3 / 1983	111.0 / 1987
Vietnam	Cambodia, China	1980-99	344.5 / 1980	326.3 / 1999
Western Sahara	Mauritania	1981-99	165.0 / 1981	165.9 / 1999

* *Adapted from: Karen Jacobsen, "The Forgotten Solution: Local Integration for Refugees in Developing Countries." Working Paper #45 (January, 2001) Geneva: UNHCR: 30.*

In these circumstances, what may matter most is the relationship that develops between the refugees and the people living in the host nation, on the one hand, and the relationship between those still in the country of origin and those in the host state on the other. As each of these more-or-less static communities adjusts to the departure, arrival, and return of the refugees, they experience significant changes—both good and bad—that relate to their long-term survival. In particular, these refugee flows affect the institutions of civil society and social order that are central to political stability and economic development.

While there are numerous definitions and interpretations of civil society, there is general agreement that it is a voluntary component of society, characterized by associations and groups that are somewhat autonomous from the state and serve the economic, social and political needs of the members who create and join them. Civil society allows individuals, groups and firms to regulate their everyday business peacefully, as well as interact with state institutions from a position of strength. It is widely seen as the key outcome of the democratization process as well as an important ingredient in it. Likewise, civil society is usually associated with a certain level of development, and in turn promotes economic growth once in place. This said, it is not necessary to have full democracy to have civil society, so long as the state is either tolerant (or perhaps negligent). Civil society generally thrives in stable environments where states can guarantee civil rights (especially freedom of association).

Western, developed nations generally have vibrant civil societies that serve the functions described above. Communities organize block watch groups, parent-teacher associations, mothers' clubs, service clubs, boys and girls' clubs, youth sports leagues, church congregations, and so forth, as well as more ad hoc activities such as letter-writing campaigns, yard sales, neighborhood fairs, etc. Workers form unions, businesses organize chambers of commerce, professionals set up associations, and volunteers form service-oriented non-governmental organizations (NGOs). Alexis de Toqueville noted that such associations were the core of American democracy going back to the early 1800s. Radical scholars such as Habermas believe that civil society can form a bulwark against corporate exploitation of ordinary citizens by spawning social movements. Still other see civil society as a benign manifestation of the order promoted by the state (most civil society organizations are relatively supportive of the state and are not radical in nature). Finally, some view civil society as a culturally-defined phenomenon that may produce liberal institutions in one and conservative in another (note the desire of the newly-liberated Iraqi Shiites to install a traditional, Islamic regime tied to Iran). Even some radical Islamic terrorist organizations carry out important and successful community-building projects in this vein.

In developing countries, where such voluntary associations are small and local as a rule, international agencies such as the World Bank and the United Nations have taken it upon themselves to funnel aid and training to incipient civil society organizations, such as service NGOs. This is part of a "civil society empowerment" strategy that has been in place since the mid-1980s.[2] This effort has produced a proliferation of professionalized NGOs that provide numerous services to the population, although there is considerable debate over whether they are instilling democratic principles and practices. Many of these foreign-supported NGOs are administered in a top-down manner and deny their "clients"— as those receiving services are often called—any voice in shaping programs and policies. On the other hand, many home-spun NGOs are far more free-wheeling and participatory, while at the same time lacking the financial discipline foreign donors require. In the final analysis, "civil society," when active and indigenous in character, is often a very messy structure.

It is perhaps needless to say that in many countries with large-scale refugee populations, civil society has largely broken down. Where civil war or other forms of violence have come to dominate everyday business, civil society can no longer function. Likewise, chaotic situations where the state is largely absent are not conducive to civil society as described here. Finally, where one community's civil rights have been denied, one cannot speak of civil society in any meaningful way. This said, as numerous areas of unrest around the world return to a semblance of normalcy (Afghanistan, the Balkans, Rwanda and Burundi, East Timor, Eritrea), the conditions that nurture civil society are becoming more common. Refugees are in many cases responding either by returning home or by settling in more permanently in their host states—in either case they are no longer refugees. In so doing, they will play a pivotal role in developing civil society institutions and contributing to the economic, social and political maturation of whatever society they choose.

In this chapter, I will explore the effects of refugees on civil society in both the host and home state in a general way, with illustrations from across the world. An important conclusion will be that refugees can be seen as both a threat and an opportunity, depending on a variety of factors relating to the social, political and economic make-up of the refugee community and the static populations, as well as the institutional structures and supports that surround the refugee population. In particular, I will point out that in many cases, refugees do best when they are least regulated, unless the wars they left follow them in their new temporary home.

Refugee Characteristics and Civil Society

Much of the effect refugees will have on local and host civil society depends on the characteristics of the refugees themselves and their reasons for fleeing their country of origin. While it is generally assumed that refugees are innocent victims of the violent behavior of others, that they are destitute and without resources, and are "strangers in a strange land," the fact of the matter is that in many cases the reverse is true. Established, self-confident and strong refugee communities are not uncommon. Understanding the variety of types of refugee communities helps one better understand the interactions they are likely to have with host civil societies.

Refugee Characteristics That Promote Civil Society

A growing literature revisits the proposition that refugees are invariably a burden on host countries by pointing out that, even in their difficult circumstances, many refugees can and do make important contributions to the social, economic and political development of their host societies. This is even truer with respect to returning refugees. But some of this depends on the refugees themselves.

Ethnic Background

A refugee's ethnicity and nationality determine to a large extent the individual's kinship network, native language, racial background, culture and customs and even politics. While Westerners understand intuitively the importance of understanding how the ethnic and national background of a new arrival in their neighborhood will affect his or her ability to "fit in," this knowledge is often forgotten when the issue is how a refugee in the Third World will fit in to a neighboring community after fleeing unrest. The fact of the matter is that this is perhaps the most important predictor of "assimilation" into the local community, which in turns has a considerable effect on whether the local civil society will be enhanced. In many areas, roughly two-thirds of incoming refugees steer clear of formal camps and settlements set up by governments and international organizations such as the UN High Commissioner for Refugees (UNHCR) and instead move in with relatives and friends—most of whom share the same ethnic background. This is particularly true in Africa, where 51 national boundaries have little connection with the territories occupied by the more than 2000 ethnic groups and tribal networks. In Guinea, refugees from Liberia preferred to "self-settle among their kinsmen by a ratio of 4-to-1.[3] In Somalia, refugees from Somalia were welcomed in part due to their shared ethnicity (Amharic refugees were not so lucky).[4]

In Yugoslavia, where civil war during the 1990s pushed millions out of their homes, the first place people went for peace was with their relatives who lived in a neighboring state. This is true even where doing so did not necessarily get them out of harm's way. Roughly 600,000 Serbs have fled to Serbia from Croatia, Bosnia and Kosovo, of which only 50,000 are in organized camps while the rest are with relatives.[5] In still other areas, the existence of a stable refugee community creates a draw for next wave of refugees from the same region.[6]

These "self-settled" refugees who find shelter with relatives often blend into the local community, start up businesses, build homes of their own and even marry and raise families locally. The result is a complete assimilation to the host society. According to Bakewell, after the initial mass influx of Angolans [into Zambia in the late-1980s] …, refugees settled in the community, began to grow their own food and eventually became, fully integrated into the local society, their presence was seen as an asset and many are now indistinguishable from Zambians, even down to holding appropriate identity papers. From the perspective of many of the villagers, there are now no refugees."[7] Even where the blending is less obvious, kinship relations can lead to the creation of twinned towns and villages, close economic interaction and social ties that create relatively harmonious and productive relationships. This has occurred in eastern Sudan, western Zambia and western Tanzania.

Political Symbiosis

From time to time, the arrival of a refugee community or the return of former refugees is seen as a political boon to the host society and state if they can use the manpower and political capital (votes, organization) the refugees bring. In other words, incoming refugees are an asset to some elements of the local host community. They may help tip the political balance in their favor, for example, or might be recruited for this or that political campaign. In Macedonia, Albanian refugees coming from Kosovo were welcomed by local ethnic Albanians in 1999 since their numbers helped strengthen the cause of Albanian human rights in Macedonia. Shiite refugees returning to Iraq from Iran are enthusiastically welcomed by local populations since their numbers will help in the construction of a conservative Islamic state. The same is true of each of the various Iraqi refugees returning and their respective political partners within the country. In both cases, both departing and returning refugees have been offered shelter, safety and employment by the local community members who hope to forge a political alliance with them.

Many states also welcome the benefits refugees can bring with respect to foreign policy objectives generally. Tanzania was more accommodating to refugees from Burundi than Rwanda, for example, in part because of the warmer relationship between the two countries. Lebanese officials are likewise more tolerant of pro-Syrian Palestinians living in refugee camps, allowing them more freedom of movement. This stems in part from the considerable influence Syria has on Lebanese policy.[8] Still others hope to draw favorable attention from the international community (or at least avoid its opprobrium). This was true of the government of Macedonia that was persuaded to accept 400,000 Kosovar Albanians in 1999.[9]

Returning refugees represent a hopeful symbolism that the post-conflict situation may be peaceful and productive. As put by Crisp:
"Repatriation plays an important part in validating the post-conflict political order. When they choose voluntarily to go back to their homeland, refugees are, quite literally, voting with their feet and expressing confidence in the future of their country. More specifically, and as demonstrated again by the experience of Mozambique and Namibia, pre-election repatriation programs can bring an important degree of legitimacy to internationally supervised elections."[10]

In Latin America, returning refugees who had learned to make demands on local and national institutions to get the resources they needed, and they carried this assertiveness home:
"Guatemala and Peru are good examples of returns that supported the growth of new ideas about civic participation and responsibility. In Guatemala, returnees no longer saw themselves as being repressed or outcast, but came

to see themselves as both 'developers' and 'modernizers' who were active participants in a new society. This mindset positively contributes to community development initiatives aimed at strengthening civil society, which can have a stabilizing effect on the state. In Peru, returnee communities with no previous experience of local administration demanded to manage their own civil registers, elect their own judges, to be able to carry out military service within their own communities, and have greater influence over the local government budgetary process."[11]

Economic Resources

In addition to international attention, refugees attract international funds and materials. As put by Jacobsen:
"...Although international refugee assistance is usually intended for refugees in camps, it finds its way into the host community. Both food and non-food aid items are traded in local markets and further afield. In addition, many international refugee agencies deliberately make relief assistance available to local people so as to increase the receptiveness of the host community to refugees. UNHCR's [1999] Handbook for Emergencies states [on page 19] that in situations where there are tensions between refugees and the local population, one of the measures to be considered is... Benefiting the local community through improvements in infrastructure in the areas of water, health, roads, etc. ' This approach is embodied in UNHCR's Refugee Affected Areas programmes, which provide new or improved transport infrastructure (roads, bridges), health clinics and schools, both as an inducement to locals to assist refugees, and to improve the delivery of humanitarian assistance. Such programmes have been implemented in countries such as Zambia, Tanzania and Uganda."[12]

Refugees also bring a certain degree of social and economic capital with them. While many are in desperate circumstances, some are able to bring a few tools and some money with them. But more importantly, they bring the skills and energy that allowed them to survive in their homes. In Ghana, Liberian refugees in a camp took it upon themselves to provide things on their own that they lacked and made a tidy profit in the process. Long-term encampments sometimes give rise to relatively permanent structures (Palestinian camps have been in place for as much as fifty years) and thriving markets. Some of the skills the refugees bring interface with the needs and resources of their new hosts, as well as the needs of their home countries when it comes time to repatriate. For their poverty and lack of education, Tibetan refugees in India have mobilized their resources to the point that unemployment is an incredibly low 3.2 percent[13] and in Nepal they serve as a tourism magnet from which the entire Kathmandu Valley benefits. In Somalia, in spite of physical segregation, refugee and local towns have developed productive, symbiotic economic relations.[14]

Self-Reliance

Karen Jacobsen has expressed hopeful optimism that self-settlement, under favorable circumstances of relative peace, stability and relative prosperity in the host country, can be a durable solution to the refugee problem. This is because, given the resources and skills refugees bring and where the local community and state are tolerant and welcoming, refugees might become tools for development rather than burdens.
"Over time, many self-settled refugees become unofficially integrated after they have lived in and been accepted by the community, and have attained self-sufficiency. We might think of this as *de facto integration*, where the lived, everyday experience of refugees is that of being part of the local community."[15]

In spite of resources being readily available to many refugees, according to Van Damme:
"Many refugees preferred self-settlement without assistance, joining the ranks of previous refugees amongst whom they judged they had better chances of coping. Moreover, many refugees who officially registered in camps, did not permanently reside there ('ghost camp')."[16]

This scenario is well-known in Western countries, where asylum-seekers routinely find established immigrant communities that help in resettlement and employment. In the United States, certain refugee communities tend to relocate in certain principal cities, such as Iraqis in Detroit. Note that much depends on the attitude and condition of the host society. Where civil war is regionalized and endemic, or poverty and disease are widespread, it is unlikely that refugees will find a hospitable climate or opportunities to support themselves economically. Under these circumstances, either moving on or living in camps are the most practical and reasonable solutions in the short run.

Refugee Characteristics That Undermine Civil Society

To a large extent, many of the characteristics that increase the chances that refugees will contribute to the societies in which they live have a more destructive character as well.

Ethnic Tension

Refugees not only bring their kinship ties and affections to their host states, but also the animosities and rivalries that may have led to their decision to leave in the first place. It is often the case that refugees have little in common with local communities, which can lead to mutual suspicion and even hostility. A Lebanese group —the "Guardians of the Cedars"— has formed with the sole purpose of expelling the Palestinian refugees from Lebanon.[17] In many cases in Africa, refugees have little in common with local communities. In Guinea, in response to the influx of large numbers of Liberian refugees, locals found themselves forced to learn either English or the refugees' language in order to communicate with them, this because the Liberians would not learn French or the local languages.[18]

It is not unusual for refugees to become embroiled in local ethnic and tribal wars that exacerbate conflict in their new host societies. Jacobsen notes:

> A host government's regime is threatened when refugees enter regions characterized by actual or potential ethnic conflict and change the ethnic proportions in these areas. This occurred with the movement of Hutus into Burundi, of Irian Jayans into Papua New Guinea, of Laotians into the Thai-Lao areas of Thailand, and of Palestinians into Jordan. Even if refugees to not actually engage in the domestic quarrels of their hosts, governments often perceive them to be a threat and act to avoid or reduce political repercussions by imposing greater controls on refugees.[19]

As put by Crisp:

> On one hand, the movement of Rwandan Hutus into eastern
> Zaire—and to a lesser extent the movement of Burundi refugees
> into Tanzania—has contributed substantially to the
> destabilization and insecurity of the Great Lakes region as a
> whole. On the other hand, these events have played a major
> part in discrediting the humanitarian enterprise and the very
> principles of refugee protection.[20]

The influx of Afghani refugees in the wake of the Soviet invasion of 1979 pushed millions into exile in Iran and Pakistan. As of the September 11th, 2001 attacks, nearly four million were refugees. In Pakistan, the Pushtun Afghans mingled with Pushtuns in Pakistan, although not every Pushtun clan was sympathetic to the incoming Afghanis. Their presence exacerbated religious rivalry between Shiite and Sunni Muslims as well as between secular and religious politicians in Pakistan national politics."[21]

Political Threat

From time to time, refugees are not only less than innocent, they continue to act as participants in the wars that plagued their homelands. In many cases, borders are poorly defended and porous, and it is relatively easy for guerrillas or soldiers from a near-by state to simply cross over to attack their enemies ensconced in camps a few miles away. Further, some refugees are still actively pursuing the defeat of their opponents at home and are using the camps as staging points for new attacks. They also seek to recruit new combatants from the pool of bored, discouraged young men in their midst. It is estimated that as many as 90,000 Rwandan refugees are guilty of genocide, even as they receive international assistance. Efforts by local Tanzanian officials to arrest them in the camps are resisted by other Rwandans, who are then seen as co-conspirators.[22] Guerrillas are likewise known to have taken control of camps in Kenya and Mauritania.[23]

Palestinians were likely attracted to Lebanon upon their expulsion from Jordan in 1970 in part because they knew the weak and poor Lebanese government would not be able to effectively exercise authority over them. In this situation, Palestinian camps became a law unto themselves, to a large extent. The efforts by Palestinians to mobilize support for the various factions in Palestinian politics makes them a microcosm of the Gaza Strip. In 1985-87, rivalry between camps turned violent in what became known as the "Battle of the Camps."[24] The Lebanese government could do little to prevent the violence that ensued.

Some states view these refugees as potential threats to their own societies as well. The Macedonian government, mentioned above, believed that the Kosovar Albanians would become a "fifth column" that would work to destabilize the regime.[25] In Kuwait, Palestinian refugees conspired with the invading Iraqi army.[26] In numerous cases, the camps become military targets as those in power in neighboring states seek to crush opposition groups taking refuge in the camps. Israel attacked Palestinian refugee camps in Lebanon in 1982 and 1983, South Africa's apartheid government attacked ANC guerrillas in Zambia and other front-line states during the 1980s, and Afghan troops attacked camps in Pakistan in an attempt to root out the *mujahideen*.

Lawlessness

Refugee camps have earned the reputation of being cesspools of poverty and lawlessness. The cramped living quarters, limited resources and boredom have pushed many into criminal activity both within the camps and in the surrounding areas. As put by Crisp:

"...The refugee camps of Africa are becoming increasingly dangerous places. Indeed, far from finding a safe refuge in their country of asylum, the continent's refugees increasingly find that by crossing an international border, they exchange one form and degree of vulnerability for another..... [T]here is evidence to suggest that refugee-populated areas in Africa are now increasingly affected by a variety of non-military security threats, involving different forms of violence, coercion, intimidation and criminal activity."[27]

In addition to politically-motivated attacks and attempts to steal relief materials, crime of all types of rampant in many camps. All of this requires the diversion of scarce state resources to the regions where refugee populations are the greatest, which in turn increases hostility toward the refugees.

Poverty and Numbers

A well-known stereotype of refugees portrays them as huddled masses bereft of earthly possessions. In many cases this is not far from the truth. In spite of the best efforts of the international community, many arrive in their new homes and return to their old ones without property, money or skills. They become a burden on the community and the state, draining resources, particularly when they arrive suddenly in large numbers. As Jacobsen puts it:

> Fear of inundation is ... a factor that might disrupt traditional expectations [in societies with a tradition of hospitality]. In situations where the refugees differ from locals in significant ways, such as language, and where new inflows result in the number of refugees exceeding that of the local population, the latter can perceive themselves to be socially overwhelmed.[28]

Not only do some poor states resist helping incoming refugees, but even many affluent states have adopted, as a matter of policy, a restrictive approach. Perhaps China's approach of returning North Koreans when captured is the most disturbing case, but even liberal Scandinavian states, such as Denmark, have recently imposed new restrictions on asylum-seekers and refugees. For that matter, Denmark's record of accepting 15-17% of asylum seekers still compares favorably with the 1-2% acceptance rate by other Scandinavian states.[29] In the case of the United States, fear of Haitian refugees flowing into South Florida in the mid-1990s were enough to prompt the Clinton administration to invade Haiti and depose the government in order to improve local conditions and eliminate the cause of refugee flight. In general, the justifications for these measures rely on fears of inundation—if the first wave is permitted to come in, it only encourages the next wave and the next. There will come a point, it is argued, when even the wealthiest state will not be able to afford assistance.

Over-Abundance of Aid

Ironically, while poverty creates its own obvious problems, wealth and talent can also create tension with the local community. It is not unusual for refugees to become economic competitors to the local society and thereby threaten businesses and jobs. Liberian refugees entering Sierra Leone were noticeably wealthier than their hosts, for example, although the Sierra Leoneans did not let that stand in the way of hospitality. It is also not unusual for the international relief directed at refugees to put them at income levels that surpass the surrounding standards. The result can be arrogance on the part of the refugees and resentment in local communities, further undermining the formation of beneficial linkages. Zairian communities deeply resented the amount of aid flowing to Rwandan refugees.[30] At the Kakuma camp in Kenya, international relief lifted the standard of living of refugees so high above the impoverished Turkana who lived nearby that the refugees were able to hire them as childcare workers, water carriers, and so forth.[31] While this might be seen as a boon to some, it naturally causes resentment in others.

Aid has other problems attached to it, including dependency and corruption. A few states fear becoming "addicted" to foreign aid, such that when the refugee crisis abates and the aid is withdrawn, the former host state finds it cannot manage without it. Most states, on the other hand, welcome the risk of dependency, so long as they get their share while they can. In most developing countries, foreign aid is a way to create jobs and give contracts to cronies and relatives, or even line the pockets of government officials outright. Of course, what some call corruption, others call the "perks of office." The result, however, is tension between aid agencies and recipient states, at the very least.

Host Society Characteristics

Not all host societies are the same, and certain features are important in predicting whether the influx of refugees will strengthen or undermine local civil society.

Host Society Characteristics That Promote Civil Society

Past Experience

Incoming refugees do not enter a place with no history. In many cases their reception depends on the host country's past experience with previous waves of refugees. If these experiences were essentially positive, one can expect a more enthusiastic welcome and easier integration into the local community. In Zambia, where migration is routine and generally accepted, the influx of refugees changes little in the day-to-day life of local communities. Such movements are considered normal and favorably dispose the population to future refugee movements.[32]

Norms on Hospitality

Many societies in the world have strong mores regarding hospitality. By virtue of religious teaching or moral tradition, many believe it is simply immoral to reject visitors—especially those in distress. Both Arab and Muslim traditions include a strong norm of hospitality, for example, which combined to the benefit of the millions of Afghan refugees who fled Soviet occupation.[33] Conversely, some Protestant Western societies emphasize self-reliance over community support and feel less uncomfortable with letting refugees fend for themselves.

Adherence to International Legal Principles

With respect to state agencies, hospitality is a matter of law and policy. A number of international conventions and agreements are available through which states can make formal commitments to welcome refugees and other migrants. The 1951 UN Refugee Convention, its 1967 Protocol, and numerous subsidiary and regional agreements (such as the 1969 OAU Refugee Convention) have been established to protect people who have been forced to leave their own country as a result of persecution, armed conflict and other human rights violations. In general, these agreements require a direct, personal threat in order to warrant a grant of asylum. These agreements also include protocols that allow states to deepen their commitment to refugee protection. The overwhelming majority of states are adherents to the relevant legal instruments—144 have signed either the 1951 Convention or its 1967 Protocol as of 2002. Most of these states have adopted explicitly generous domestic laws that make it easy for refugees and asylum seekers to find refuge, services, funds, and even dual citizenship.

UNHCR has endeavored to promote a uniform, lenient standard of treatment for refugees by encouraging states to adopt a relaxed legal standard with respect to standards of proof of persecution and risks of returning.[34] These have been drawn up in the 1979 UNHCR Handbook on Procedures and Criteria for Determining Refugee Status. While a useful document, the Handbook assumes considerable absorptive capacity on the part of would-be host states, more in keeping with developed country standards. This may make it difficult for developing countries to adhere to international law and enforce domestic laws, no matter how sincere their intentions.

That said, as we will in the next section, the generosity of treatment of refugees is not correlated with wealth. Even when they have the capability of returning migrants, most African countries opt to allow them to remain, as a matter of regional international law. Farer points out:

"Africans actually feel either a higher degree of moral responsibility for involuntary migrants from other African countries or a much lower order of economic and social threat is at least suggested by the difference in breadth between the UN Refugee Convention's definition of refugee and the definition in the [1969 OAU Convention]."[35]

Whereas the UN language limits the refugee category to those with a well-founded fear of a religious, political or racial persecution that is personal, the OAU Convention includes those who are fleeing unrest and disturbance at home, even if they are not personally or directly threatened. The burden of proof is essentially removed, so long as there is a clear state of upheaval, whether because as a result of civil war, foreign aggression, military occupation or anything else.

Ethnic and Political Compatibility

As mentioned in connection with refugee characteristics, it is important to remember that host societies with compatible ethnic compositions and political structures and attitudes in relation to the refugees in question are likely to be more hospitable. This is usually made easier when a society is already secure in its structure and composition, such that the introduction of a new community does not threaten existing structures. This is most evident in developed nations such as Canada or the states of Scandinavia, but it is also seen in Kenya and Zambia, for example. Note that democracy is not a very good predictor of receptiveness, since it allows xenophobic groups to influence national policy. In Costa Rica, the government took a political risk to ignore local opposition to Nicaraguan refugees crossing the border during that country's civil war.[36]

Economic Opportunity

Although prosperous states are usually best able to absorb the additional cost of providing for the welfare of refugees, the fact of the matter is that some poor states have many reasons to welcome refugees for the economic lift they can provide, as mentioned earlier. Some developing countries have land and resources in abundance and lack only the manpower and skills to exploit them, and thus welcome new manpower. Still others welcome refugees who not only provide skills and manpower, but also increase demand for food, to the benefit of local farmers.[37]

Host Society Characteristics That Undermine Civil Society

The converse of some of the host country traits listed above can serve to make the arrival of refugees as disruptive, even destructive, event.

Time Factors

Many host countries, while receptive to refugees in principle, find that most refugees overstay their welcome. They assume that refugees will stay only for short periods of time and almost immediately return. The implication is that there is little sense for refugees to be given accommodations beyond the bare minimum.

"Protracted situations are characterized today by a "care and maintenance" or "warehousing" model of refugee assistance in countries of first asylum. Host governments, UNHCR, donor governments and international agencies have, with a few exceptions, been unimaginative in their response to long-term refugee populations. There is no vision that refugees and assistance programs could be a development asset to countries of first asylum, or that they could promote human security there. To quote one observer, "In a refugee context questions of development and human capabilities are put on hold – the situation is supposed to be merely temporary after all."[38]

Extended stays tax the patience of the host society. There is evidence that as fatigue sets in, local communities exert pressure on the state to remove the refugees to camps. This has been noted in Mexico, Somalia, Sudan, Guinea and elsewhere.

This said, the role of time is often a result of other factors, as will be reviewed below.

Social Unrest and Ethnic Composition

As mentioned earlier, some refugees bring their own ethnic conflicts in their wake. However, in some cases these conflicts exacerbate existing conflicts in the host country. Kosovar Albanians fleeing into Macedonia in 1999 were entering an ethnic hornet's nest as the local Albanian population, which makes up roughly one quarter of the population, have been demanding increased civil rights from Macedonian majority since independence. With their arrival, naturally resisted by the Macedonian majority since Albanian Muslims were "the very people Macedonians feared most," the Albanians' number swelled by fifty percent. Add to this the fact that international relief agencies provided only for about one-third of the refugees and the ease with which the refugees infiltrated the local Albanian communities, and one can appreciate the Macedonians' unease. The best outcome occurred, in that the Kosovar Albanians were able to quickly return home.[39]

Political Insecurity

States often respond to the unrest mentioned above with strict legal and administrative rules that make it unlikely that refugees will contribute to the local civil society. The establishment of rigid border controls, the expansion of the powers of the military and the denial of legal standing for refugees are natural responses to states of unrest that could be made worse by refugee movements. The Zambian government was perhaps the only institution that makes an attempt at controlling the porous border with Angola.[40] In the Congo, a government crackdown on Angolan refugees prompted them to flee "back to the bush."[41] As put by Jacobsen:

"An initial welcoming response to refugees can evolve into resentment and threats against them if the community perceives the refugees to be causing more problems than benefits. Partly in response to this changed attitude, some host governments have stopped allowing self-settlement (or at least turning a blind eye to it), and have begun forcing refugees into camps. This change is linked to increased security problems, but in some cases it is also because the government or local authorities seek to sustain or augment their legitimacy by adapting refugee policies to be more in keeping with the host population's unwillingness to allow the refugees to continue living amongst them."[42]

The disadvantages of camps have already been discussed earlier in this chapter.

Poverty

Naturally, societies that are poor are generally under even greater economic pressure when an influx of poor refugees arrives. Although, as we have seen, this pressure can be alleviated in certain circumstances through foreign aid, this aid often takes several months to arrive and can end abruptly. That said, it is noteworthy that poverty does not seem to be a good predictor of state policy or societal reception. Suffice it to recall that African states and societies generally have far more lenient attitudes toward refugees than advanced Western states.

Home Society Characteristics

The effects of departing refugees and returnees on the home society depend in part on the conditions in that society that gave rise to the flight of its members and their return.

Home society characteristics that promote civil society:

Stability

Naturally, the violence and unrest that gave rise to the flight of refugees in the first place should be settled in order for returnees to be able to participate in society again. Upon returning to such conditions, the refugees have the potential to establish themselves and begin making a useful contribution to the reconstruction of the society. Their return is hailed as a harbinger of better days ahead.

However, refugees who fled the country due to their own unlawful acts face a different prospect when facing the decision to return. On the one hand, while repatriation is naturally the goal of both international institutions and the host state and society, the refugee may resist the push and seek safe haven elsewhere—now as a fugitive rather than a refugee. In the case of those charged with genocide, each state has an obligation to arrest and prosecute the individual regardless of where the crimes were committed. The irony is that where repatriation of refugees is based on the assumption that they will become contributing members of society, the fact is that a few will return only to face a long prison sentence. In either case, civil society will be strengthened.

Economic Opportunity

Where unrest and warfare have damaged a country, economic opportunity may be considerable, assuming the infrastructure—both physical and institutional—is intact. There are several examples in Africa of returnees who have taken advantage of economic opportunities to initiate a revival in the regions. In Ethiopia, Eritrea and Somalia, returnees—both men and women—have been creating new businesses, forging trade ties with other regions, repopulating abandoned towns and so forth.

Home society characteristics that undermine civil society:

Instability

In a number of cases, refugees return home against their will to a society that is still in turmoil. Some returnees have become targets due to their ethnic or political identities. In East Timor, where 75% of the population was forced from their homes with 300,000 exiled in West Timor, the return to normalcy is slow, even with the proclamation of the independence of the former colony. Fifty thousand refugees remained in West Timor in 2000—many of them fearing the reception they would receive and the conditions of their homeland.[43] In 1996, Rwandans who had fled to Tanzania were forced to return to a country that was not yet ready to receive them.

Poverty

Even where the political situation is settled, the society may be in upheaval as a result of the destruction of property, the legacy of crime and violence, and uncertainty about the future. The Rwandans who returned in 1996 faced what UNHCR euphemistically called a "limited social infrastructure." In Somalia, many returnees are living in a large slum in conditions that are sometimes worse than what they knew in exile.[44]
"For the refugees who had received assistance in exile," Chad observes, "the return could be more difficult than the experience of exile itself. In place of the semblance of stability and physical security established in camps, where the major problems of survival were adequately met, a host of problems, uncertainties and dangers awaited the refugees on their return to their home country."[45]

International Influences

Most refugees are the object of multilateral attention and support which can both support and undermine their integration in civil society both at home and abroad. Several points made previously address this role.

Resources

The flow of international support, as has been noted, can both strengthen and undermine civil society. On the one hand, funding relieves pressure on the host country and might even make it financially worthwhile to welcome refugees. On the other hand, the concentration of resources in specific areas might create resentment from the local community and perhaps even make those refugee groups a target for attack. For that matter, the temporary nature of the aid means that it will likely come to an end at some point prior to the end of the need. In addition, international actors are often unable or unwilling to provide the type of political protections the refugees need most. In Rwanda, the failure to secure contributions from donors has left several UNHCR projects un-funded.

International Support for Camps

UNHCR has been a strong sponsor of the camp solution to the refugee crisis, in part to support the demands of states as well as to maintain control over the refugee population—both to ensure resources go to the right place and to help repatriate the refugees when the crisis passes. Unfortunately, this does little to help the refugees contribute to the local society or to develop and maintain the skills they will need after returning home. This explains the growing call for self-sustaining communities.

NGOs

Finally, international actors more often than not sub-contract their services to international and local NGOs. While this has certain important advantages, in that NGOs often have specialized skills, local experience, and a certain degree of impartiality, the NGOs suffer from vulnerability to state whims, sometimes become embroiled in local conflicts, and at any rate lack the capability to protect refugees from armed attack. In general, it is important to note that these relief NGOs are not a substitute for civil society. It is better to think of them simply as sub-contractors rather than autonomous agencies.

Conclusions and Implications

This discussion points to several new ways of looking at the refugee situation, particularly where refugees are in place in large numbers and for long periods of time. It becomes clear that the preference of most refugees is to integrate themselves into the host community and become productive members of that community. Even if they retain the hope of returning home some day, they often build lives and raise families in exile, to the benefit of the local society. In doing so, these refugees contribute to the institutions of civil society in substantial ways. When circumstances change at home, these refugees return voluntarily in large numbers with the hope of contributing to their old homes. This outcome typically occurs with minimal international or state intervention and benefits most from a benign and tolerant legal and social context.

This is not to say this outcome is feasible in all cases. As we have seen, there are formidable obstacles to this peaceful outcome, some of which stem from characteristics of the refugees themselves, some from the static communities and some from the international community. Some of these obstacles are probably insurmountable, but many can be addressed by careful and prudent policies—both at the local and international level.

* I would like to thank Piotr Paradewski for his able research assistance.

Notes

1. Karen Jacobsen, "The forgotten solution: local integration for refugees in developing countries." Working Paper #45 (Geneva: UNHCR). January, 2001

2. Kendall Stiles, "Civil Society Empowerment and Multilateral Donors: The Centrality of International Institutions in the Transmission of New International Norms," *Global Governance* vol. 4 #2 (May-July, 1998): 199-216.

3. Win Van Damme, "How Liberian and Sierra Leonean Refugees Settled in the Forest Region of Guinea." *Journal of Refugee Studies* vol. 12 #1 (1999): 50.

4. Karen Jacobsen, "Factors influencing the policy responses of host governments to mass refugee influxes" *International Migration Review* vol. 30, # 3 (1996): 669.

5. Philip Martin, "Comparative Migration Policies," *International Migration Review* vol. 28 #1 (Spring 1994): 164.

6. T. Faist, *The Volume and Dynamics of International Migration and Transnational Social Spaces.* (Oxford: Oxford University Press, 2000), 152-3, in Geraldine Chatelard.

7. Oliver Bakewell, "Repatriation and Self-Settled Refugees in Zambia: Bringing Solutions to the Wrong Problems," *Journal of Refugee Studies* vol. 13 #4 (2000): 369.

8. Rosemary Sayigh, "Palestinian Refugees in Lebanon: Implantation, Transfer or Return?" *Middle East Policy* vol. VIII #1 (March, 2001): 101.

9. Duncan Perry, "Macedonia's Quest for Security and Stability," *Current History* (March, 2000): 132.

10. Jeff Crisp, "Africa's refugees: patterns, problems and policy challenges." *Working Paper* #28 (Geneva: UNHCR), August, 2000: 23.

11. Alan Whaites and David Westwood, "Displacement and civil society in Peru." World Vision - Towards Peace and Justice: Discussion papers, No. 2, 1996:28, cited in Sarah Petrin, "Refugee return and state reconstruction: a comparative analysis," *Working Paper #66* (Geneva: UNHCR), August, 2002: 13.

12. Karen Jacobsen, "Can refugees benefit the state? Refugee resources and African state building." *Journal of Modern African Studies* vol. 40 #4 (2002): 581.

13. S. Bhatia, T. Dranyi, and D.Rowley, "A social and demographic study of Tibetan refugees in India," *Social Science and Medicine* ,vol. 54, #3, (2002): 420.

14. Gaim Kibreab, "Local Settlements in Africa: A Misconceived Option?" *Journal of Refugee Studies* vol. 2 #4 (1989): 476.

15. Karen Jacobsen, "The forgotten solution: local integration for refugees in developing countries." *Working Paper* #45 (Geneva: UNHCR), January, 2001: 9.

16. Win Van Damme, "How Liberian and Sierra Leonean Refugees Settled in the Forest Region of Guinea." *Journal of Refugee Studies* vol. 12 #1 (1999): 45.

17. Rosemary Sayigh, "Palestinian Refugees in Lebanon: Implantation, Transfer or Return?" *Middle East Policy* vol. VIII #1 (March, 2001): 94.

18. Win Van Damme, "How Liberian and Sierra Leonean Refugees Settled in the Forest Region of Guinea." *Journal of Refugee Studies* vol. 12 #1 (1999): 36-53.

19. Karen Jacobsen, "Factors influencing the policy responses of host governments to mass refugee influxes" *International Migration Review* Vol. 30, # 3 (1996): 673.

20. Jeff Crisp, "Africa's refugees: patterns, problems and policy challenges." Working Paper #28 (Geneva: UNHCR), August, 2000: 12.

21. Ahmed, Samina. "The Fragile Base of Democracy in Pakistan," in Amita Shastri and A. Jeyaratnam Wilson, ed., *The Post-Colonial States of South Asia: Democracy, Development and Identity.* (New York: Palgrave, 2001), 52.

22. Augustine Mahiga, "The United Nations Higher Commissioner for Refugees' Humanitarian Response to the Rwandan Emergency." Paper presented at the International Workshop on the Refugee Crisis in the Great Lakes Region, Arusha, Tanzania (August 16-19, 1995, cited in Beth Elise

Whitaker, "Changing priorities in refugee protection: the Rwandan repatriation from Tanzania." *Working Paper # 53* (Geneva: UNHCR), February, 2002: 12.

23.   Karen Jacobsen, "Factors influencing the policy responses of host governments to mass refugee influxes," *International Migration Review*, vol. 30, # 3 (1996): 587.

24. Rosemary Sayigh, "Palestinian Refugees in Lebanon: Implantation, Transfer or Return?" *Middle East Policy* vol. VIII #1 (March, 2001): 103.

25.   Duncan Perry, "Macedonia's Quest for Security and Stability," *Current History,* (March, 2000): 132.

26.   Karen Jacobsen, "Factors influencing the policy responses of host governments to mass refugee influxes" *International Migration Review* Vol. 30, #3 (1996): 672.

27.   Jeff Crisp, "Africa's refugees: patterns, problems and policy challenges." *Working Paper* #28 (Geneva: UNHCR), August, 2000: 11.

28.   Karen Jacobsen, "The forgotten solution: local integration for refugees in developing countries." *Working Paper* #45 (Geneva: UNHCR), January, 2001: 21.

29.   Bela Hovy, "Statistically Correct Asylum Data: Prospects and Limitations." *Working Paper* #37, (Geneva: UNHCR), April, 2001: 10.

30.   Jeff Crisp, "Africa's refugees: patterns, problems and policy challenges." *Working Paper* #28, (Geneva: UNHCR), August, 2000: 11.

31.   Karen Jacobsen, "Can refugees benefit the state? Refugee resources and African state building." *Journal of Modern African Studies,* vol. 40 #4 (2002): 585.

32. Oliver Bakewell, "Repatriation and Self-Settled Refugees in Zambia: Bringing Solutions to the Wrong Problems," *Journal of Refugee Studies* vol. 13 #4 (2000): 360.

33 . Karen Jacobsen, "Factors influencing the policy responses of host governments to mass refugee influxes," *International Migration Review, vol 30,* # 3 (1996): 668.

34. Brian Gorlick, "Common burdens and standards: legal elements in assessing claims to refugee status" Working Paper #68 (Geneva: UNHCR), October, 2002: 8.

35. Tom Farer, "How the International System Copes with Involuntary Migration: Norms, Institutions and State Practice." in Michael Teitelbaum and Myron Weiner, eds., *Threatened Peoples, Threatened Borders: World Migration and US Policy.* (New York: W.W. Norton, 1995), 269.

36. Karen Jacobsen, "Factors influencing the policy responses of host governments to mass refugee influxes," *International Migration Review* vol. 30, # 3 (1996): 671.

37. Karen Jacobsen, "Can refugees benefit the state? Refugee resources and African state building." *Journal of Modern African Studies* vol. 40 #4 (2002): 585.

38. Karen Jacobsen, "The forgotten solution: local integration for refugees in developing countries." Working Paper #45 (Geneva: UNHCR), January, 2001: 3.

39. Duncan Perry, "Macedonia's Quest for Security and Stability," *Current History* (March, 2000): 132.

40. Oliver Bakewell, "Repatriation and Self-Settled Refugees in Zambia: Bringing Solutions to the Wrong Problems," *Journal of Refugee Studies* vol. 13 #4 (2000): 363.

41. Gaim Kibreab, "Local Settlements in Africa: A Misconceived Option?" *Journal of Refugee Studies* vol. 2 #4 (1989): 477.

42. Karen Jacobsen, "Can refugees benefit the state? Refugee resources and African state building." *Journal of Modern African Studies* vol. 40 #4 (2002): 585.

43. Daniel Fitzpatrick, "Land policy in post-conflict circumstances: some lessons from East Timor." *Working Paper* #58 (February, 2002) Geneva: UNHCR:10.

44. Jeff Crisp, "Africa's refugees: patterns, problems and policy challenges." *Working Paper* #28 (Geneva: UNHCR), August, 2000: 20.

45. C. Watson, "The Flight, Exile and Return of Chadian Refugees." (Geneva: UN Research Institute for Social Development), 1996: 105, cited in Jeff Crisp, "Africa's refugees: patterns, problems and policy challenges." *Working Paper* #28 (Geneva: UNHCR), August, 2000: 19.

Works Cited

Ahmed, Samina. "The Fragile Base of Democracy in Pakistan," in Amita Shastri and A. Jeyaratnam Wilson, ed., *The Post-Colonial States of South Asia: Democracy, Development and Identity.* New York: Palgrave, 2001, 41-68.

Bakewell, Oliver. "Repatriation and Self-Settled Refugees in Zambia: Bringing Solutions to the Wrong Problems," *Journal of Refugee Studies,* vol. 13 #4 (2000): 356-373.

Bhatia, S., Dranyi, T., and Rowley, D. "A social and demographic study of Tibetan refugees in India" *Social Science and Medicine,* vol 54, #3, (2002): 411-422.

Chatelard, Geraldine "Jordan as a transit country: semi-protectionist immigration policies and their effects on Iraqi forced migrants." *Working Paper* #61. Geneva: UNHCR, August 2002

Crisp, Jeff. "Africa's refugees: patterns, problems and policy challenges." *Working Paper* #28, Geneva: UNHCR, August, 2000.

Faist, T. *The Volume and Dynamics of International Migration and Transnational Social Spaces*. Oxford: Oxford University Press, 2000.

Farer, Tom. "How the International System Copes with Involuntary Migration: Norms, Institutions and State Practice." in Michael Teitelbaum and Myron Weiner, eds., *Threatened Peoples, Threatened Borders: World Migration and US Policy*. New York: W.W. Norton, 1995: 257-92.

Fitzpatrick, Daniel. "Land policy in post-conflict circumstances: some lessons from East Timor." *Working Paper* #58. Geneva: UNHCR, February 2002

Gorlick, Brian. "Common burdens and standards: legal elements in assessing claims to refugee status" *Working Paper* #68 (October, 2002) Geneva: UNHCR.

Hovy, Bela. "Statistically Correct Asylum Data: Prospects and Limitations." *Working Paper* #37, Geneva: UNHCR, April, 2001.

Jacobsen, Karen. "Factors influencing the policy responses of host governments to mass refugee influxes" *International Migration Review* vol 30, # 3 (1996):655-678.

Jacobsen, Karen. "The forgotten solution: local integration for refugees in developing countries." *Working Paper* #45, Geneva: UNHCR, January, 2001

Jacobsen, Karen. "Can refugees benefit the state? Refugee resources and African state building." *Journal of Modern African Studies* vol. 40 #4 (2002): 577-596.

Kibreab, Gaim. "Local Settlements in Africa: A Misconceived Option?" *Journal of Refugee Studies*, vol. 2 #4 (1989): 468-489.

Mahiga, Augustine. "The United Nations Higher Commissioner for Refugees' Humanitarian Response to the Rwandan Emergency." Paper presented at the International Workshop on the Refugee Crisis in the Great Lakes Region, Arusha, Tanzania (August 16-19,1995).

Martin, Philip. "Comparative Migration Policies," *International Migration Review* vol. 28 #1 (Spring 1994): 164-170.

Perry, Duncan. "Macedonia's Quest for Security and Stability," *Current History* (March, 2000): 129-136.

Petrin, Sarah. "Refugee return and state reconstruction: a comparative analysis" *Working Paper* #66, Geneva: UNHCR, August, 2002

Sayigh, Rosemary. "Palestinian Refugees in Lebanon: Implantation, Transfer or Return?" *Middle East Policy* vol. VIII #1 (March, 2001): 94-105.

Stiles, Kendall. "Civil Society Empowerment and Multilateral Donors: The Centrality of International Institutions in the Transmission of New International Norms," *Global Governance,* vol. 4 #2 (May-July, 1998): 199-216.

Van Damme, Win. "How Liberian and Sierra Leonean Refugees Settled in the Forest Region of Guinea." *Journal of Refugee Studies,* vol. 12 #1 (1999): 36-53.

Whaites, Alan and Westwood, David. "Displacement and civil society in Peru." *World Vision* - Towards Peace and Justice: Discussion papers, No. 2, 1996.

Watson, C. "The Flight, Exile and Return of Chadian Refugees." Geneva: *UN Research Institute for Social Development,* 1996.

Rami Goldstein

CHAPTER THIRTEEN:

Forced Migration:
Legal Constrains and Future Possibilities

Introduction

T he two world wars, civil wars, territorial partitions, and the break up of a number of states along religious and ethnic lines, have caused the displacement of millions of people and large-scale influx situations all over the world. The UNHCR estimates that approximately 10.4 million were refugees in 2003[1] while additional 25 million have been Internally Displaced Persons. (IDPs).[2] Of the total IDPs only 5.3 million are IDPs of concern to UNHCR. Only about 1,146,232 are returned IDPs, and 1,014,300 asylum applications were pending worldwide. The total number of refugees and persons of concern worldwide was about 21 million.[3] The process of forced migration, which often involved eruptions of uncontrollable violence, created unexpected, complex legal problems that are hardly addressed.

The end of the cold war saw a new international emphasis on human rights. The protection of forced migrants[4] and refugees became an important dimension of the international human rights regime,[5] and a linkage was established between the international human rights regime and the international refugee regime.[6] The protection of refugees operates within a structure of individual rights and duties and state responsibilities, and human rights law is a prime source of existing refugee protection principles and structures; at the same time, it works to complement them.[7] The September 11 terrorist attack placed the issues of forced migration, international migration and national security at the top of the international agenda and has engendered a need by governments and other actors to reformulate the structure of the international refugee regime. Undoubtedly, since September 11 the international refugee regime, which intends to secure protection for refugees, is encountering new constraints and challenges. Other forced migrants including internally displaced persons (IDPs), stateless people and temporarily protected people, are also encountering continually new constraints. Clearly, the international regimes and regional instruments that regulate the complex problem of forced migration need reconstruction or reformulation.

It is our methodological assumption that tension between the international politics of forced migration and the internal politics of sovereign states are the cause for the legal constraints confronting the international refugee regime and the international human rights regime. Furthermore, sovereign states policies regarding forced migration, and especially policies pertaining to asylum seekers, constrain the mechanism that the international refugee regime is built upon and limit the legal possibilities to reform these regimes. This chapter focuses on the main legal constraints and possibilities that the phenomenon of forced migration is facing at the beginning of the third millennium.

Constraints That Derive from the 1951 Convention and the International Refugee Regime

The 1951 Convention Relating to the Status of Refugees (hereafter: 1951 Convention)[8] and the Protocol Relating to the Status of Refugees of January 31, 1967,[9] provide standards for the treatment of refugees that are almost universally accepted.[10] Notwithstanding all its deficiencies, the 1951 Convention definition of a refugee is one of the most widely accepted international norms. The 1951 Convention remains the sole legally binding international instrument that provides specific protection to refugees,[11] and it forms a central part of the international refugee regime. The 1951 Convention is a multilateral instrument of general and universal application, creating a special international legal regime for refugees in need of international protection.

However, some scholars argue that, in essence, the 1951 Convention, which was designed to address massive population movements of European refugees caused by World War II, betrays its dated origins as a humanitarian instrument and is indeed outdated and anachronistic.[12] In the past half century, the context of the international system and the politics of forced migration have completely changed, namely, international and national legal standards and practices have evolved significantly.[13] While the 1951 Convention provides a normative framework to address refugee problems and an accepted minimum standard of treatment, it does not address some important issues of refugee law. The 1951 refugee protection system could not predict and was not designed to address ethnic conflicts and civil wars resulting in massive influx situations. The long list of issues excluded and not addressed by the 1951 Conventions includes:

- Voluntary repatriation[14]
- Family reunification
- Special needs of women and children refugee
- Environmental Degradation
- Human trafficking

Some important operational aspects are also excluded. The 1951 Convention does not contain detailed provisions on responsibility sharing among all actors involved and the political and operational mechanics of international cooperation are left out.[15] In addition, there are diverging views on the interpretation of the refugee definition criterion itself,[16] the determination of refugee status; the *prima facie* mechanism, and the kind of procedures that should be employed for *prima facie* status determination.[17]

The 1951 Convention does not address the important question of under which circumstances a person seeking asylum as a refugee in a foreign state should be recognized as refugee and should be granted permanent or temporary asylum. It is the state of refuge that has the international legal right to grant asylum. This issue *inter alia* continues to be regulated solely by national laws, regulations and practices. The main constraint lies in the fact that many states are unwilling to subordinate their sovereignty to any international standard or obligation to receive refugees. Long before the September11 attack, different states were unwilling to accept and provide safe haven to refugees out of fear that they might be overwhelmed by an intolerable influx of refugees.[18] This policy has been motivated by a variety of concerns: dilution of national sovereignty (national interest), spread of international terrorism, rise of illegal immigration, and changes to the ethnic and religious composition of society.[19] Consequently, a clear tension has developed between the right of the state as a juristic entity, subject to certain duties and obligations under international law by which it is also entitled to certain rights,[20] and the state right to determine who will enter its borders. Moreover, international law stipulates that it is for each state to determine, by operation of internal law, who is a citizen.

Another constraint pertains to article 33 of the 1951 Convention, which established the principle of *non-refoulment*.[21] This principle, which is considered one of the main achievements of the 1951 Convention, means that states are obliged to refrain from forcibly returning a refugee to a state where he is likely to suffer persecution or danger to life or freedom. It is still controversial whether this principle has crystallized into a rule of customary international law and as such has the status of a binding rule of general international law.[22]

Despite the legal and moral strength of the principle of *non-refoulment* it has been difficult to secure its uniform observance. Often, states have refused the entrance of refugees. Entrance can turn into a nightmare when states use the practice of "warehousing" and in fact deny the refugees the right to integrate in the asylum state.[23] Several countries have resorted to forcible measures to discourage further inflows, namely, repulsion or exclusion and detention of claimants to refugee status in rigorous camps.[24] The principle of *non-refoulment*, which was intended to serve as a legal support tool for the asylum seekers, became a boomerang, resulting in severe anti-asylum measures. Thus, the principle of *non-refoulment* demonstrates the tension between the international politics of forced migration and the internal politics of states, or more specifically, the tension between the right of sovereign states to determine admission rules and the needs of people whose lives and freedoms are at risk and are in need of international protection.

Constraints Deriving From International Human Rights Regime

There is an obvious linkage between the international refugee regime and the international human rights regime. Refugees are, by definition, victims of human rights violations and "today's human rights abuses are tomorrow's refugee problems."[25] In the last decade human rights concerns have become an integral part of the UNHCR discourse and practice.[26] It is generally accepted that the interpretation of the 1951 Convention should be tied to human rights norms.[27] The complementary machinery of international human rights protection and the mechanism of the international refugee regime can together supply better instruments for dealing with forced migration problems. For this reason the UNHCR has incorporated a number of human rights principles and strategies in its policies and programs. Thus the UNHCR has been involved in recent years in activities such as protection activities in countries of origin; working with states in the area of legal rehabilitation, institution building, and law reform; enforcement of the rule of lawl and developing specific protection guidelines for refugee women and children.[28] The linkage that has developed between the system of international human rights protection and the international refugee regime, provides greater potential to ensure compliance with international refugee protection standards, whether in states which are parties to the 1951 Convention or otherwise.[29]

On the other hand, the international human rights regime puts essential constraints on the autonomous authority of the states, as Prof. James Hathaway notes:

"International human rights law is fundamentally a means of delimiting state sovereignty. Human rights including respect by states for a sphere of freedoms a commitment to meeting basic needs and the sharing of resources to effect these purposes-establish a benchmark for governments' right to claim sovereign authority over a people."[30]

Furthermore, the international refugee regime and the international human rights regime have often failed to provide effective protection for refugees or IDPs in dire circumstances.[31] There are serious doubts as to the effectiveness of the international human rights regime.[32] Despite these doubts, human rights principles have influenced and induced states to adopt fundamental changes in their domestic policies and laws. These changes clearly reflect the international principles.[33] Human rights organizations have also been involved, to a greater extent today than in the past, in intersecting with development agencies in rehabilitation, reconstruction, and repatriation activities, but "promoting respect for human rights values and creating conditions which make it possible for refugees to return home cannot be done by humanitarian agencies alone. Eliminating the causes of refugee flight requires continued commitment and timely political involvement by the international community…Humanitarian action can save lives, but it can never be a substitute for political action."[34]

Constraints Regarding the Complexity of Forced Migration, Especially in an Age of Terrorism

The increasingly complex nature of recent migrations movements is characterized by their composite flows that include asylum-seekers, refugees, migrant workers, victims of environmental degradation, or people in search of better life opportunities. All these groups are included in the UNHCR definition of "People of Concern" and they create new and complex problems for the international refugee regime, states, UNHCR, NGOs and other actors.[35] Also, the growing numbers of internally displaced persons and refugees who have returned to their countries of origin, too often under duress, in dire need of assistance or protection, and without opportunities for safe integration, have also come to the attention of the international community. Other categories include war-affected populations, torture victims, temporarily protected persons, and stateless people. While these categories are used to define the different forced migration situations, because of the dynamic elements of forced migration the categories are not mutually exclusive. Thus, forced migrants may belong simultaneously to more than one group, or in close sequence.[36]

The international refugee regime has to address complicated operational issues resulting from large-scale influx situations. These situations usually require comprehensive emergency responses often under difficult security and logistical conditions. The 2002 humanitarian operations in Afghanistan is a case in point. During 2001/2002, UNHCR had also to respond to other grave situations of new influxes of refugees elsewhere, especially in Africa and former Yugoslavia.[37]

The September 11 attack coerced the international refugee regime to confront unexpected difficulties. Security considerations have been given high priority and have permeated policy responses on a wide range of issues, especially the issue of asylum. However, dealing with the terrorist threat in the context of asylum does not necessarily call for a fundamental amendment of the international refugee regime or refugee definition, since under the 1951 Convention, provisions are explicitly put in for serious crimes to be excluded from refugee status.[38] The UNHCR and other international organizations had to admit that a review and tightening of procedural and security measures by individual states might be necessary. Consequently, most host countries incorporated exclusion clauses into national legislation for the first time.[39] Because of the complexity of exclusion cases and the possible infringement of human rights, this issue must be addressed carefully.

To date, the issue whether the exclusion cases should continue to be determined in the regular asylum procedure, or in admissibility stage, or in accelerated procedures, remains unresolved.[40] This issue constrains the international refugee regime and the international human rights regime, because national legislation on exclusion of those undeserving of international refugee protection, including those who are guilty of terrorist acts, not necessarily needs to incorporate the exclusion clauses of the 1951 Convention. The individual national legislation and different definitions of the exclusion practices lead to different policies and practice. Indispensability of national legislation leads to conflicting refugee laws and policies. This development inherently constrains the need to incorporate the international legal standards into national legislation and administrative procedures.

The growing threat of terrorism creates additional humanitarian needs and complicates efforts to alleviate it. Likewise, current anti-terrorist policies and programs, while ostensibly providing new space to enhance human security broadly understood, in themselves heighten the difficulty of humanitarian work and international protection.[41] Nonetheless, to avoid any unwarranted linkages between asylum-seekers, refugees, and terrorists, various regional organizations have adopted instruments and procedures to combat terrorism. The legal constraints are expressed by the definition of terrorist offences. If definitions are too broad and vague, as has been sometimes the case, there is a risk that the "terrorist" label might be abused for political ends, for example to criminalize legitimate activities of political opponents, in a manner amounting to persecution.[42]

Whether combating terrorism is seen primarily as an internal criminal law enforcement issue,[43] or whether the matter falls in the general framework of international criminal law,[44] the issues of the exclusion clauses of asylum seekers must be resolved in a manner which is not prejudicial to any, well founded claim to refugee status. In this context the mission of the international refugee regime is to prevent the abuse of the asylum channel. States must put in place measures, with appropriate legal safeguards, to ensure the effectiveness of the exclusion clauses of the 1951 Convention.[45]

Constraints Concerning Mandates and Responsibilities

The need to respond to the myriad and overlapping groups in need of protection and assistance force the international refugee regime to act within certain mandates and guidelines. On the other hand, drawing lines between categories and predetermined inflexible mandates and responsibilities may create obstacles in the ability of national, intergovernmental and non-governmental organizations (NGOs) to offer appropriate assistance and protection. Agencies may try to avoid responsibility by citing an inhibiting institutional mandate, or assistance agencies interested in intervening on behalf of a particular group may be prohibited from providing the service for lack of explicit mandate.[46]

Mandates and responsibilities have long been on the international agenda, particularly in the context of efforts to improve coordination.[47] Organizational mandates require understanding of three distinct phases of forced migration: prevention, responses, and solutions. Roles and responsibilities in the context of forced migration include (a) activities pertaining to early warning and prevention of forced migration, (b) emergency responses and longer-term assistance and protection for refugees and displaced persons, and (c) resolution of humanitarian emergencies via programs for repatriation, including post-conflict reconstruction, local integration and resettlement.[48]

Defining the mandates and responsibilities of all the actors involved in the current international refugee regime and the international human rights regime is not a simple mission, especially in an era of globalization, including global terrorism. States, NGOs intergovernmental organizations, and UN agencies have different approaches. For example, the UNHCR statute and mandate use two different approaches. While its statute is restrictive, the mandate is more dynamic. UNHCR operations do involve IDPs, although not all IDPs in all situations.[49] Because IDPs do not fit the refugee definition of the 1951 Convention,[50] they are at the mercy of domestic jurisdictions and are not eligible to any formal protection and assistance. This condition creates a major legal constraint. Establishing and strengthening links with both local and international NGOs and other civil society actors is essential in many of the operations of the international refugee regime. In southeastern Europe, for instance, since 1995, UNHCR has established an effective network of international and local NGOs assisting in the protection of refugees and returnees.[51] Clearly, NGOs efforts can complement official efforts to create a stable and effective legal regime.

Defining the governance of the international and regional regimes for responding to humanitarian emergencies requiring assistance is further complicated by the changing set of actors involved with forced migration. Formerly, the UNHCR was held the most responsible actor, mobilizing resources from sister agencies, within or outside the UN, and establishing partnerships with NGOs to provided services to refugees. In recent years there has been an increase in involvement by new sets of actors drawn from military, human rights, and developed communities. This involvement has exacerbated gaps in mandates and created difficulties in coordinating the transition from relief to development. The fact that numerous countries have engaged military forces in emergency relief operations to create secure environments[52] on behalf of forced migrants, namely, the provision of goods, food and shelter, and the construction of camps, such military interventions caused inconsistencies in mandates and responsibilities. The military involvement creates legal ambiguities and inconsistencies that might destabilize the international refugee regime and threaten the protection of the refugee.

The recent practice of protecting refugees in ad hoc "safe havens"[53] creates another legal mandate problem. Each safe haven has been created based on different international regimes, namely chapter VII of the UN charter (Rwanda and Bosnia), agreement and consent of the local state (Iraq and Seri Lanca) while others were created without the state consent.[54] In light of the abovementioned, the UNHCR has been seeking to improve the mechanism of partnerships with local civil societies, and local and international NGOs.

In 2002, the UNHCR executive committee concluded that the goals of the UNHCR Agenda for Protection should include:

♦ A demand that states examine how to accord NGOs improved legal status by creating a clear legal framework for their operations.

♦ UNHCR will continue to strengthen partnerships for protection and awareness raising, not only with host and donor governments (including national and regional legislatures), but also NGOs ,other actors or civil society, as well as refugee men, women and children.

♦ UNHCR and NGOs will intensify their cooperation to identify and address protection problems, especially where the latter have a field presence.

Constraints Regarding Enforceability

The goal of the international refugee regime, like that of public international law, is not enforceability in a strict sense, but rather to create a mechanism by which governments would consent to compromise their sovereign right to independent action in order to resolve the complex problem of forced migration.[55] This by itself must be considered as one of the critical constraints of the international refugee regime.

In this context Hathaway and Neve argue that:

"International refugee law was established precisely because it was seen to afford states a politically and socially acceptable way to maximize border control in the face of inevitable involuntary

migration. Refugee law has fallen out of favor because its mechanism no longer achieves its fundamental purpose of balancing the rights of involuntary migrants and those of the states to which refugees flee."[56]

The absence of an external central authority with the power to enforce the rules of international law in a regular and consistent manner raises the famous debate on the question of whether international law is "true" law. The issues of the binding force of international law and the extent to which sanctions (including sanctions by way of external force), are available under international law, are controversial.[57]

The main question in the context of forced migrants is enforceability, including the variances of scope and application in international treaties. The problem of enforcement is more difficult when it concerns the question of how to enforce the specific rights of the international human rights regime, since the international human rights regime focuses primarily on an extensive body of treaty law.[58] In the case of the principal UN human rights treaties, existing system of treaty bodies play a supervisory and enforcement role in ensuring compliance by state parties with the treaty provisions.[59] In the absence of effective international enforcement mechanisms, domestic courts have played an important role in the effort to enforce human rights norms.[60] It can be than, concluded, as some scholars argue, that the present set-up of ensuring compliance with international human rights standards is unsatisfactory and should be reformed.[61]

Many proposals to reform or reconstruct refugee law have been proposed. For example Prof. Peter Schuck proposed a system that would be based on an accepted norm of "proportional burden sharing" with each state agreeing to grant temporary protection or permanent settlement to refugees. According to this proposal, a new or existing international agency would have responsibility for assigning quotas of refugees to states. The states would be allowed to trade quotas by paying others to take on their obligations.[62] This proposal centers on a quota-based system and is intended to operate at the regional or sub-regional level in a constructive manner. However, it raises again the question of enforceability as, C.J. Harvey best illustrated: "Who is going to be able to ensure compliance by all states? The use of regional units as the basis for enforcement may well help but does raise other issues (notably moral objections)…"[63]

The probability of enhancing enforceability depends on the ability to reduce the political prerogatives of sovereign states since "The refugee protection system, however, has less to do with the legal niceties of the refugee Convention than with the political prerogatives of sovereign states. Each state judges for itself whether a particular migrant or group of migrants who reaches its territory or seeks resettlement there will receive that, or any, relief. Each state moreover, possesses powerful disincentives to provide relief, especially on its own territory."[64]

The issue of enforceability in the context of the political prerogatives of sovereign states has another impact. Since refugee issues, forced migration, and migration became matters of high internal politics, states may force emigration as a means to achieve different objectives. There are several different types of forced emigration. Governments may force emigration as a means of achieving cultural homogeneity or asserting the dominance of one ethnic community over another.[65] Secondly, governments use forced emigration as a means of eliminating political dissidents and class enemies.[66] Finally, forced emigration can be used as a strategy to achieve foreign policy objectives. Governments may, for example, force emigration as a way of putting tacit pressure on neighboring states (while publicly denying such intent), or forced emigration can be an instrument by which one state seeks deliberately to destabilize another.[67]

In summary, legal constraints regarding enforceability vis-à-vis the prerogatives of sovereign states are relevant on three levels: (a) protection of forced migrants and especially asylum seekers (internal-national level), (b) external international humanitarian intervention that requires operating within the boundaries of sovereign states, such as deployment of peace keeping forces, UNHCR field operations, and NGOs activities (international level), (c) the use of coercive intervention and enforcement of international law, norms and decisions, (global governance level).

Prospects for Emerging Responses to Forced Migration: Possible Legal Frameworks

The rise in ethnic and religious conflicts and the increase in the number of persons displaced or turned refugees require meaningful and effective international response. However, an adequate response can hardly be expected until new frameworks for possible action will emerge. Such frameworks must include legal, political, and social ground rules, and binding international conventions. Proposals to reform present refugee law and the current international regimes can hardly be pursued in a vacuum. Reconstruction or revision of the refugee law and the relevant regimes has to flow from a comprehensive diagnosis of three factors: (a) the causes and effects of the deficiencies of the present system,[68] (b) the politics conditioning the state of the existing international regimes, and (c) the lack of necessary and sufficient international cooperation among the numerous members of the legal and the political communities.[69] A progressive legal reform and a revision of the processes and policies concerning refugees and other forced migrants require extreme sensitivity to the national political-social context.[70] The following discussion addresses these issues.

A myriad of alternative models to reformulate or reconstruct the international refugee regime were presented in recent years in various forums. The all share common sets of objectives. First, most proposals suggest the replacement of the 1951 Convention obligations with a new set of obligations that will be accepted by both the local governments and the international community. Second, implementation will be made easy once all the parties involved will agree on the principles included in the benchmark proposals. However, the proposals that are based on the principle of a comprehensive reconstruction of the 1951 Convention ignore the fact that not all the support and protection operations follow the rules of the international conventions and they are hardly carried out in a very civil and principled manner.

Third, the creation of an international civilized, well-organized support and protection system requires the allocation of substantial resources that will greatly increase the cost of any support and protection operation. Fourth, in order to improve the quality of the protection from any type of physical harm that refugees often encounter in the first stages of their ordeal, it is necessary to direct resources especially to countries and regions of first asylum. Fifth, it is necessary to untie the refugee regime from migration, thus allowing states to insulate their refugee protection policies from economic migration, and to ease public concern over asylum-driven migration and people smuggling.[71]

Three main possible legal frameworks can address these issues resulting from and affecting the phenomenon of forced migration:

(I) Reconstruction of the international human rights and refugee regimes, namely, introducing a new regime for refugees and other forced migrants and changing *mutatis mutandis* of domestic laws. This legal framework will introduce new measures that would be adopted by the relevant regional bodies.

(II) Reformulating the current regimes, focusing on improving existing mechanisms of the current regimes in order to achieve cooperation and coordination of all the states and international organizations involved. Following this framework, the human rights regime will be maintained and strengthened, and it will include refugees and other forced migrants.

(III) Reformulating the international refugee law by incorporating new legal tools and increasing enforceability and deterrence. This revised regime will be based on new legal tools for an increased enforceability of the international refugee regime and human rights regime.

The following is a detailed analysis of the proposed frameworks.

I . Reconstruction of regimes and refugee law

The goal of all protection efforts is ultimately the reestablishment of a normal life for refugees and other forced migrants.[72] The UNHCR primary functions were defined as being twofold: first, to provide international protection for refugees and second, to seek permanent solutions to their problem.[73] The 1951 Convention and the 1967 Protocol are the foundation of the current international refugee regime that seeks to end the suffering of refugees. The fact that in the year 2004, 145 states are party to these principles and conventions can be seen as an indication of their importance.[74]

The consequence of establishing a new international refugee regime is that the existing instruments will lose their important role as multilateral instruments of general and universal application. It is questionable whether in the current situation of massive forced migration a complete overhaul and reconstruction of international regimes, regional instruments, and refugee law is desirable. Such a revision could undermine the existing protection systems—imperfect as they are—under international law.[75] Moreover, the third millennium poses considerable new challenges for states, big and small, as they try to reconcile their obligations under the 1951 Convention with problems raised by the mixed nature of forced migration movements.

Other major difficulties include misuse of the asylum system, increasing costs of protection operations, the threat of international terrorism, the growth in smuggling and trafficking of people,[76] and denial of access by states to UNHCR and other humanitarian agencies. These difficulties could be insurmountable, and in the foreseeable future, the establishment of new, effective refugee regimes will become impossible. Realistically, both the global and the regional conditions do not allow for fundamental, long lasting reconstruction frameworks in the international regime for the protection of refugees.

Two mitigating factors are helpful in the protection of forced migrants: First, the existing various human rights treaty monitoring bodies, and the jurisprudence developed by regional bodies, such as the European Court of Human Rights and the Inter-American court of Human Rights. They serve as influential and important actors as they complement the international refugee regime and apply it to all people, regardless of status.[77] Second, the frequent incorporation, over the years, of the principles contained in the 1951 Convention into regional instruments, national legislation and judicial decisions, constrain the ability to reconstruct the international refugee and human rights regimes and could reduce its effectiveness. As put by C.J. Harvey on this issue:

"It often appears that no matter how many grand schemes are developed to reform the legal regulation of forced migration, very little actually changes in practice. Suggested alterations can at times be so far removed from the practical realities of those engaged in systems of regulations that they have minimal impact."[78]

II. Reformulation of the Current Regimes by Extending Mechanisms

Reformulation and revitalizing the current regimes of international human rights and international refugee regime address international and regional instruments and bodies that are involved in the protection of forced migrants. This legal framework does not require the relinquishing of the current regimes. Rather, it suggests maintaining the basic mechanisms and principles that the existing regimes are build upon. In the last two decades this approach had received vast attention both in theory and practice.[79] *Inter alia,* this approach attempts to manifest international solidarity to resolve forced migrants situations. There is more than one way to implement this approach. For example, the framework will focus on the need to enhance international cooperation by sharing information, burdens and responsibilities. Another possibility is to focus on developing and adopting a more effective and objective mechanisms to achieve the fundamental purpose of balancing the rights of forced migrants with the rights of host sovereign states. This legal framework requires the construction of a mechanism, which will reduce the tension between the international politics of forced migration and the internal asylum politics of sovereign states.

Hathaway and Neve who offered a project to reformulate the international refugee regime correctly illustrated the problem:

> We therefore believe that the answer is to affirm the need for international law to bring both order and principle to bear on the way states address refugee flows, while recognizing that international law will be respected by governments only if it is to be seen to be attentive to their basic concerns.[80]

Other scholars focus on human values and argue that human rights are more likely to be advanced through efforts to alter the thinking of populations and government officials than by more traditional legal tools.[81]

The greater the consensus generated among all the actors involved, the more likely the regime is to gain legitimacy. Therefore, the suggested reformulation approaches and the responses to them are best viewed as attempts to navigate between realism and idealism in convincing ways.[82] In the scope of the current international refugee regime, the office of the UNHCR has no power to force countries to provide refugees with even minimal humanitarian treatment. Thus, the UNHCR major instrument still remains diplomatic pressure to urge states to abide by international refugee law.[83]

It remains to be seen whether the state of the international refugee regime and the international human rights regime can be improved despite the ineffectiveness of international refugee law and international human rights law, and the constraints that internal politics and domestic laws impose upon these regimes.

III. Reformulation of International Refugee Law by Incorporating New Legal Tools and Increasing Enforceability and Deterrence

Jacques Derrida rightly stated on the issue of enforceability: " There are, to be sure, laws that are not enforced, but there is no law without enforceability, and no applicability or enforceability of the law without force, whether this force be direct or indirect, physical or symbolic, exterior or interior, brutal or subtly discursive and hermeneutic, coercive or regulative, and so forth."[85]

Because the nature of the international refugee regime is territorial, and the regime actually reinforces respect for sovereignty, it limits the ability of an international organization to act within national borders.[86] This is a structural paradox hindering the ability to enforce humanitarian and human rights laws. Obviously, the international community is not doing much to enforce existing norms although in principle the issue of enforcement is regarded as a central tenet of the international human rights law.[87]

Given the current situation, the legal possibilities for implementing the doctrines of the international refugee regime, international human rights regime, and the UNHCR operations depend on: (a) the relevant country's socio-political-economic conditions, (b) the political commitment on the part of governments involved to comply with international law standards, and (c) the local government will to cooperate with the UNHCR and other actors who influence the international politics of forced migration.[88] Thus, any approach that wishes to enhance enforcement of international refugee law and international human rights law and norms by using mainly existing legal tools, within the context of the current regimes, must take all these factors into consideration. Without proper enforceability and deterrence any new approach will be impossible to implement.

The move from temporary to durable solutions is one of the principal goals of the international refugee regime and the agenda of the UNHCR. However, durable solutions require, whenever possible, a coherent approach that integrates voluntary repatriation, local integration and resettlement into a single comprehensive approach.[89] Lack of ability to implement the norms of the relevant international regimes[90] will result in a failure to carry out and perform those temporary or durable solutions. If an effective international law will not be developed and adjusted to the new challenges of the forced migration problem, the international community will continue to face increasingly serious problems for both the forced migrants and the countries of their refuge.

Past experience shows that in coping with forced migration crises, temporary emergency responses and humanitarian intervention can alleviate human suffering to a good extent. However, to be fully effective, these measures must be complemented by decisive efforts on the part of the humanitarian establishment to address the basic causes of the flight in order to try and prevent the deterioration and spread of the conflict. Because the current international regimes are not provided with the proper legal tools to cope with the political and strategic complexities created by massive forced migration, the refugees often continue to be victims of persecution and terrorism, by either states or non-state aggressors. Unfortunately, the multiple legal constraints prevent the execution of meaningful and effective support operations for forced migrants and especially IDPs.

Indeed, on the one hand, mass human rights abuses trigger large-scale influxes of refugees and internal displaced persons, which the international community fails to prevent or deter. On the other hand, states have responded adversely by closing their borders, shifting responsibility to the countries and the regions which refugees have fled from. Again, the international refugee regime has proven powerless and ineffective in coping with these situations. The recent conflicts in Bosnia, Kosovo, Afghanistan and Iraq show that the tools available to respond to severe human right crises, as well as the tools to enforce international humanitarian norms, including international refugee law standards, remain limited and weak.[91]

The words of Arthur C. Helton best illustrated this situation:

> The small idea is that there is no single answer, no single tool or even formula or combination of tools to deal with a particular situation. It is to a great extent a question of nuance and timing as well as effective and expert humanitarian management. But the big idea is that, by solving refugee problems and dealing with fears and insecurities that both give rise to refugees and animate refugee responses, policy managers may begin to deal better with insecurities that characterize the new century. This world requires the institutionalization of preventive approaches and effective forms of international cooperation.[92]

The establishment of the permanent International Criminal Court (ICC)[93] has the potential to offer new legal possibilities for response to forced migration situations. It is obvious that this instrument is not entitled with the authority to provide protection or humanitarian aid to forced migrants, but it can have a deterrent effect on human rights violations and crimes against forced migrants, thus impacting situations which engender refugee flows. The UNHCR supported the establishment of the ICC :

> UNHCR strongly supports the establishment of an international criminal court. Its own experiences in such places as the former Yugoslavia and the Great Lakes region, where refugees and displaced persons under its mandate have been victims or witnesses of serious international crimes, show that criminal justice has been an important part to play in reconciliation and peace-building. Where crimes of international concern have

been committed and national criminal justice systems are unable or unwilling to cope, an establishment system of international justice would ensure that such crimes are not committed with impunity. An international criminal court with jurisdiction over international crimes would have a deterrent effect on such crimes, thus impacting positively situations which give rise to refugee flows.[94]

A promising development was the creation of two ad hoc international criminal tribunals that established new and creative jurisprudence.[95] These could clearly be considered as milestones and important tools for the protection of refugees and IDPs.

Another possibility for an emerging effective response is, for example, to create a new agency for all populations affected by emergency situations.[96] The idea is to establish a new, supranational agency, (or a combination of the UNHCR and the other intergovernmental organizations), that if provided with the authority and capacity to enforce the rules of international law could serve as a deterrence.[97] The possibility of creating a new legal framework might increase the effectiveness of the existing relevant regimes and could help to build a true enforcement regime. Thus far, such proposals have failed to garner support. When the United States suggested that the emergency functions of existing UN agencies be consolidated into a single new agency in charge of international emergencies, the proposal had to be withdrawn.[98] As the current inter and intra state violence does not seem to subside, and because situations of force migration are only getting worse, this new agency can offer the opportunity to validate the political will and to find the economical resources necessary to support those options. It is absolutely essential that new possibilities to contest with the new challenges be found to promptly resolve the problem.

Conclusion

International protection of refugees and forced migrants is not an abstract concept. It is a dynamic and action-oriented principle that is based on a delicate balancing mechanism. It encompasses a range of concrete activities, covering both policy and operational concerns, and it is carried out in cooperation with states, NGOs, intergovernmental organizations and other actors.[99] The goal of the international refugee regime and the international human rights regime is *inter alia* to enhance respect for the human rights of refugees and other forced migrants and resolve their problems through resettlement or repatriation.

There can be no doubt that the international community has been encountering new challenges regarding the complex situations of forced migration. The millions of people displaced by violent political conflicts and religious and ethnic clashes pose major global political, economic, and health threats. Neither the international regimes nor the individual governments seem able to find proper and constructive responses. The growing number of forced migration and displacement of populations within their own borders effect and destabilize trade, economic and political cooperation of both developed and developing nations.

In the aftermath of September 11, the complex and rapidly changing environment had placed a heavy toll on the countries hosting refugees. The traumatic terrorist attack directly affected the willingness and capacity of states to open their borders to refugees.The discussion of the causes of the legal constraints shows that they are found in three different levels and it is difficult to distinguish between the legal, political and operational constraints. However, it is possible and even necessary, to distinguish between internal and external constraints, namely, the domestic politics and the international and foreign politics.

As these two levels often do not overlap, and because conceptual conflicts arise between domestic policy makers and foreign policy makers over the definition of "national interest," the tension between the international politics and the domestic politics of forced migration create major legal constraints. In fact, a positive correlation exists between the intensity of this tension and the existence of legal constraints. Many host countries have carried out legislative changes aimed at migration control, and have developed methods limiting safeguards for asylum-seekers. The security dimension gained importance and forced states to amend and revise national immigration legislation. The focus of these legislations is to increase immigration restrictions to refugees by sovereign states. As reviewed in this chapter, it is the tension between the international politics of forced migration and the domestic/internal politics of sovereign states that creates major constraints on the support and protection of IDPs and refugees.

These legal constraints along with other operational and political constraints influence the effectiveness of the existing regimes and their ability to protect forced migrants. Reconstructing the international human rights and refugee regimes must be achieved gradually, especially after September 11, as states face considerable challenges and try to reconcile their obligations under the 1951 Convention with problems raised by the complex and problematic nature of forced migration movements.

In conclusion, the paradoxes, dilemmas and conflicting interests that exist in the global, regional and national environments make it almost impossible to establish, in the foreseeable future, completely new regimes. In particular, the adoption of proper legal tools for enhancing international refugee and international human rights laws, within the context of the current regimes, is urgently required. The international community has to create the opportunity to support new options and possibilities by allocating the necessary economic resources to build effective enforcement regimes.

Notes

1. The UNHCR (United Nations High Commissioner for Refugees), established on December 14, 1950 by the United Nations General Assembly, is the main intergovernmental humanitarian refugee agency. The agency is mandated mainly to lead and co-ordinate international action to protect refugees and resolve their problems.

2. Internal displaced persons are "Persons or groups of persons who have been forced or obliged to flee or leave their homes or places of habitual residence, in particular as a result of or in order to avoid the effects of armed conflict, situations of generalized violence, violations of human rights or natural or human-made disasters, and who have not crossed an internationally recognized state border." ("*Guiding Principles on Internal Displacement,*" UN OCHA, December 2000). IDPs have been outside the official definition of the 1951 refugee Convention and are not entitled to the benefits of the Convention. The *Analytical Report of the Secretary General on Internally Displaced Persons* uses the term to mean: "Persons who have been forced to

flee their homes suddenly or unexpectedly in larger numbers, as a result of armed conflict, internal strife, systematic violations of human rights or natural or man-made disasters; and who are within the territory of their own country." (UN Doc. E/CN.4/1992/23, p.5) as quoted in Luke T. Lee, "Internally Displaced Persons and Refugees: Toward Legal Synthesis" *Journal of Refugee Studies* 9 (1996): 28.

3. 2002 UNHCR Population Statistics (Provisional), accessed 6 April 2004; available from http://www.unhcr.ch/.cgi-bin/texis/vtx/statistics. According to the UNHCR Statistics, Refugees by Numbers 2002 Edition the estimated number of persons of concern to UNHCR reached the total number of 19,783,000. The Palestinians, who are covered by the mandate of UNRWA, are not included in those figures. However, Palestinians outside the UNRWA area of operation such as those in Iraq or Libya are considered to be of concern to UNHCR. At the end of 2001 their number was estimated by UNHCR as 349,100. Numbers play an important part in refugee situations, but there is a cloud of uncertainty and unreliability surrounding refugee statistics.
See: Jeff Crisp, "Who has Counted the Refugees UNHCR and the Politics of Numbers" Working Paper No. 12 in *New Issues in Refugee Research*, (Geneva: UNHCR, June 1999), 1-17.

4. Forced migrants can be defined: "persons who flee or are obliged to leave their homes or place of habitual residence because of events threatening to their lives or safety." See: Martin Suzan, "Forced Migration and the Evolving Humanitarian Regime" Working Paper No. 20 in *New issues in refugee research*, (Geneva: UNHCR, July 2000), 4.

5. The various role-players, who deal with refugee issues in the "international refugee regime," include the governments of countries of origin, host states, donors, intergovernmental organizations (INGOs), NGOs and some elements of the general public. This regime is also called the "international regime for the protection of refugees."

6. The various role-players who deal with refugee issues in the "international refugee regime" include the governments of countries of origin, host states, donors, intergovernmental organizations (INGOs), NGOs and some elements of the general public. This regime is also called the "international regime for the protection of refugees."

7. UNHCR, *Note On International Protection*, UN Doc.EC/48/SC/CRP.27 (1998), 1.

8. 189 UNTS, 150.

9. The Protocol Relating to the Status of the Refugees signed at New York on 31 January 1967, 606 UNTS, 267.

10. At the beginning of the year 2004, 145 states were party to the 1951 convention or the 1967 protocol or both of these instruments.

11. Laura Barnett, "Global Governance and the Evolution of the International Refugee Regime" Working Paper No.54, in *New Issues in Refugee Research*,(Geneva: UNHCR, February 2002), 7-8, quoting: Daniel J. Steinbock, "The Refugee Definition as Law: Issues of Interpretation" in Frances Nicholson and Patric Twomey eds, *Refugee Rights and Realities; Evolving International Concepts and Regimes* (Cambridge: Cambridge University Press,1999), 13.

12. Adrienne Millbank, "The Problem with the 1951 Convention"(*Parliament of Australia, Research Paper No. 5,2000-01)*, 8.

13. Brian Gorlick, Common burdens and standards: Legal elements in assessing claims to refugee status Working Paper No.68 in *New Issues in Refugee Research*, (Geneva: UNHCR, October 2002), 1.

14. See: Lee T. Luke, "The Refugee Convention and Internally Displaced Persons" *International Journal of Refugee Law* 13 (2000): 363-366; Lee T. Luke "Internally Displaced Persons and Refugees: Toward Legal Synthesis,".27-42. Over the years the General Assembly has allowed UNHCR to extend its protection to IDPs. The group of IDPs that received their first official assistance from UNHCR were in Sudan in 1972.See: Laura Barnett, "Global Governance and the Evolution of the International Refugee Regime," 9; Volker Turk, "The Role of the UNHCR in the Development of International Refugee Law" in Frances Nicholson and Patric Twomey, eds *Refugee Rights and Realities; Evolving International Concepts and Regimes,155*. About the problem of internally displaced persons see: Roberta Cohen and Francis M. Deng, *Masses in Flight: The Global Crisis of Internal Displacement* (Washington D.C.: Brookings Institute, 1998). Erin D. Mooney, suggests to

constitute a comprehensive regime for the protection of IDP's based on three separate components of standarts' institutional mechanisms and strategies of protection. According to Mooney, the UNHCR Guiding Principles on Internal Displacement can be an important unifying thread. See: Erin D. Mooney, "Towards a Protection Regime for Internally Displaced Persons" in Edward Newman and Joanne van Selm, eds, *Refugees and Forced Displacement: International Security, Human Vulnerability, and the State* (New York: United Nations University Press, 2003),159-181.

15 . For discussion on the issue of voluntary repatriation see: Guy Goodwin-Gill, "Voluntary Repatriation Legal and Policy Issues" in Gil Locester and Laila Monahan eds, *Refugees and International Relations* (Oxford: Oxford University Press, 1989), 255-291.

16. UNHCR, *Note On International Protection*, UN Doc.A/AC.96/930 (2000), 12.

17. *Ibid.,*

18. For discussion on the determination of status on a *prima facie* basis see: Bonaventure Rutinwa, "Prima Facie Status and Refugee Protection," UNHCR Working Paper No. 69 in *New Issues in Refugee Reaserch,* (Geneva:, October 2002), 1-19. A group determination on a *prima facia* basis means in essence the recognition by a state of refugee status on the basis of the readily apparent, objective circumstances in the country of origin giving rise to exodus. See: *Ibid.,* 1.

19. Ivan A. Shearer, *Starke's International Law* 11ed.(London: Butterworths,1994), 325-326

20. J.M. Castro-Magluff, "The Inadequacies of International Regime for the Protection of Refugees" in Janjay k. Roy ed. *Refugees and Human Rights Social and Political Dynamics of Refugee Problem in Eastern and North Eastern India* (Jaipur: Rawat Publishers, 2001), 70.

21. Daniel Warner, Refugees Law and Human Rights: Warner and Hathaway in Debate, *Journal of Refugee Studies,* 5 (1992), 162-163.

22. The discretion of a state to refuse asylum to refugees is substantially limited, by the principle of *non-refolement*. For a discussion on the principle of *non-refolement*, see: Elihu Lauterpacht and Daniel Bethlehem, "The Scope and Content of the Principle of Non-refoulment: Opinion" in Feller, Turk and Nicholson (eds) *Refugee Protection in International Law, UNHCR Global Consulations on International Protection* (Cambridge: Cambridge University Press, 2003), 87-178.

23. About the opinion that the meaning and scope of *non-refoulment* in the 1951 Convention is part of general international law and that article 33 of the 1951 Convention reflected or crystallized a rule of customary international law see: Ian A Shearer, Starke's *International Law* 11ed, 325-326; Goodwin-Gill Guy, *The Refugee in International Law*, 2nd ed. (Oxford: Oxford University Press, 1996),.167. For an opposite opinion see: James Hathaway, The Law of Refugee Status (Canada: Butterworths,1991), 24-25.

24. James C. Hathaway and Alexander R Neve. "Making International Refugee law Relevant Again: A Proposal for Collectivized and Solution-Oriented Protection" *Harvard Human Rights Journal* 10, (1997), 130-131.

25. Ibid., 326.

26. Gil Loescher, "Protection and Humanitarian Action in the Post-Cold War Area" in Aristide R. Zolberg and Peter M. Benda, *Global Migrants, Global Refugees Problems and Solutions* (New York: Berghan Books,2001), 171,184-185.

27. Brian Gorlick, "Human Rights and Refugees: Enhancing Protection Through International Human Rights Law," Working Paper No. 30 in *New Issues in Refugee Research* (Geneva: UNHCR, October 2000), 10.

28. Colin J. Harvey, "Talking about Refugee Law" *Journal of Refugee Studies* 12 (1999), 101.

29. Brian Gorlick, Human Rights and Refugees, 9.

30. *Ibid.,* 8.

31. James C. Hathaway, "Preconceiving Refugee Law as Human Rights Protection" *Journal of Refugee Studies* 4 (1991), 113.

32. Gil Loescher, "Protection and Humanitarian Action in the Post-Cold War Area," 188.

33. A. Mark Weisburd, "Implications of International Relations Theory For International Law of Human Rights" 38 Columbia Journal of Transnational Law, 45,48.

34. *Ibid.,* 67.

35. UNHCR Press Releases, "Sadaco Ogata Stresses Link Between Human Rights and Refugee Protection,"10 December,1998. Available from http://www.unhcr.ch/cgi-bin/texis/vtx/home/+jww.

36. UNHCR, Note on International Protection, UN Doc. A/AC.96/965, (2002), 5.

37. Suzan Martin, "Forced Migration and the Evolving Humanitarian Regime," Working paper No. 20 in *New Issues in Refugee Research*, (Geneva: UNHCR, July 2000), 3; and see the study team project of "International and Regional Regimes for Responding to Forced Migration Emergencies." Available from http://www.rsc.ox.ac.uk/TextWeb/rucastlevanhear.html/.

38. In south eastern Europe some 90,000 refugees fled the former Yugoslav Republic of Macedonia in the first part of 2001, before a peace accord was reached in August 2001. In Africa, some 77,000 refugees had fled from Liberia in the first half of 2002. There was also an influx into Cameroon of some 20,000 Nigerians fleeing ethnic clashes in northern Nigeria in early 2002. See: Note on International Protection, EXCOM of the High Commissioner's program, 53ed session A/Ac.96/965,11 September 2002, 14.

39. See: Article 1(F) of the 1951 Convention. This exclusion clause note that the provisions of the 1951 Convention "shall not apply to any person with respect to whom there are serious reasons for considering that: a) he has committed a crime against peace, a war crime, or crime against humanity, as defined in the international instruments drawn up to make provision in respect

of such crimes; b) he has committed a serious non-political crime outside the country of refuge prior to his admission to that country as a refugee; c) he has\been guilty of acts contrary to the purposes and principles of the United Nations." For detailed discussion on the issue of the relevancy of this exclusion in the aftermath of September 11,2001, see: Monette Zard, "Exclusion, Terrorism and the Refugee Convention," *Forced Migration Review* 13 (2002),.32-34. Article 33(2) of the 1951 Convention authorizes a government to refuse to protect a refugee whose presence threatens its most basic interests. Hathaway and Harvey argue that Articles 1(F) and 33(2) of the 1951 Convention serve complementary, but distinct purposes. See: James C. Hathaway and Colin Harvey, "Framing Refugee Protection in the New World Disorder,' *Cornell International Law Journal*, (Spring 2001), 257.

40. The United States, Britain, Canada and Germany, have introduced new laws or tightened existing legislation against refugees, asylum seekers, and immigrants.

41. UNHCR Note on international protection 2002, 12.

42. Larry Minear, "Humanitarian Action in an Age of Terrorism" Working Paper No.63 in *New Issues in Refugee Research* (Geneva: UNHCR, August 2002), 1.

43. *Ibid.*

44. UNHCR, Agenda for Protection Addendum, UN Doc.A/AC.96/965/Add.1,26 June 2002, 7.

45. Mark Drumbl, Judging the 11 September Terrorist Attack, *Human Rights Quarterly* 24: 323

46. UNHCR, Agenda for Protection Addendum, 26 June 2002, 7.

47. See the study team project of "International and Regional Regimes for Responding to Forced Migration Emergencies"; available from http://www.rsc.ox.ac.uk/TextWeb/rucastlevanhear.html.

48. Martin Suzan, "Forced Migration and the Evolving Humanitarian Regime," 3.

49. *Ibid.,* 9.

50. Laura Barnett, "Global Governance and the Evolution of the International Refugee Regime," 12-13 based on an interview with Jeff Crisp.

51. *Ibid.*

52 . UNHCR protection note, 2002, 17. In the year 2002 the focus of the UNHCR has been on capacity building in fund-raising techniques and on ensuring common standards of performance to enable local NGO's to sustain themselves after the scaling-down of UNHCR operations.

53. See the study team project of "International and Regional Regimes for Responding to Forced Migration Emergencies."

54. Safe havens have developed primarily as a substitute for refugee protection see: Paul Fridman, "International Intervention to Combat the Explosion of Refugees and Internally Displaced Persons," *Georgetown Immigration Law Journal* 9 (1995), 565.

55. Ahilan T. Arulanantham, "Restructured Safe Havens: A Proposal for Reform of the Refugee Protection Systems" *Human Rights Quarterly* (2000), 24

56 . James C. Hathaway and Alexander R. Neve "Making International Refugee law Relevant Again: A Proposal for Collectivized and Solution-Oriented Protection" *Harvard Human Rights Journal* 10 (1997),115,116 .

57. *Ibid.*

58. Ivan A. Shearer, Starke's *International Law*, 24-27.

59. See: A.M. Weisburd "Implications of International Relations Theory For International Law of Human Rights" *Columbia Journal of Transnational Law* 38, 48. The relevant treaties may be divided into three categories. (a) The Charter of the United Nations. (b) Number of treaties negotiated under the auspices of United Nations and open to all states as the International Convent on Civil and Political Rights (CCPR). (c)Regional human rights treaties.

60. Gorlick, "Human Rights and Refugees: Enhancing Protection Through International Human Rights Law," 7.

61 . Beth Stephens, "Translating Filartiga: A Comparative and International Law Analysis of Domestic Remedies For International Human Rights Violations" *Yale j. Int'L. 27* (winter 2002): 1-59.

62. *Ibid.*

63. Peter Schuck "Refugee Burden-Sharing: A Modest Proposal," Yale Journal of International Law, 22 (1997), p.243, Colin J. Harvey "Talking about Refugee Law," *Journal of Refugee Studies*,12 (1999), 106-107.

64. Harvey, "Talking about Refugee Law," 107.

65 . Schuck, "Refugee Burden-Sharing: A Modest Proposal," 252.

66. Myron Weiner, "Introduction: Security, Stability and International Migration," in Myron Weiner ed. *International Migration and Security* (Boulder, Colo.: Westview Press,1993), 5.

67. *Ibid.,* 6.

68 . *Ibid.,* 7-8.

69 . Harvey, "Talking about Refugee Law," 105.

70. *Ibid.,* 126.

71 . *Ibid.,* 127.

72. Millbank, "The Problem with the 1951 Convention," 24.

73 . UNHCR note on protection 2001, 25. The mandate of the UNHCR was expanded to IDPs although not all IDPs in all situations.

74. *UNHCR , The State of the World's Refugees 2000*: Fifty Years of Humanitarian Action (New York: Oxford University Press, 2000), 22.

75. The total number of states parties to the 1951 Convention as of 1 February 2004 is 142. The total Number of states parties to one of both instruments is 145. See: States Parties to the 1951 Convention as of 1 February 2004. Accessed 10 April, 2004. Available from http:www.unhcr.ch.cgi-bin/texis/vtx/+zwwBmeim_9.

76. Anker, Fitzpatric and Shacknove "Crisis and Cure: A reply to Hathaway/Neve and Schuck," Harvard Human Rights Journal 11 (1998), 295-310. Regional instruments ranging from the binding 1969 Convention of the Organization of African Unity (OAU) to the non-binding 1966 Joint Position of the European Union (EU) make direct reference to the 1951 Convention definition, albeit in the former to extent its content, and in the latter to restrict its interpretation. See: Jean-Yves Carlier, "The Geneva refugee definition and the 'theory of the three scales'" in Frances Nicholson and Patric Twomey eds, *Refugee Rights and Realities; Evolving International Concepts and Regimes* (Cambridge: Cambridge University Press,1999), 37,38.

77. UNHCR note on protection 2001: 1.

78. *Ibid.*, 2.

79. Harvey, "Talking about Refugee Law," 102.

80. For recent examples of reformulation proposals see: Hathaway's reformulation project. (See discussion note 80). Garvey's project attempts to move the international refugee regime towards the humanitarian approach to international refugee law. See: Garvey J.I., "Towards a Reformulation of International Refugee Law," *Harvard International Law Journal* 26 (1985), 483-500. Peter H. Schuck offers a refugee burden-sharing scheme to reduce the the burdens that the sudden, massive refugee flows impose on states. A. Arulanantham suggests a new model for implementing and protecting safe havens whenever they are necessary. This will be the key to changing the entire structure. See: Ahilan T. Arulanantham, "Restructured Safe Havens: A Proposal for Reform of the Refugee Protection Systems" *Human Rights Quaarterly*, 22 (2000): 1-56.

81 . Hathaway and Neve, "Making International Refugee law Relevant Again," 136-137. Hathaway's reformulation project basic premise is that refugee protection is in principle distinct from immigration. Therefore it must be dealt with other tools. Refugee protection is ideally, a situation of specific human rights remedy. This project is trying to encourage states to respect their international commitments and it advanced a collectivized approach building upon the notion of "interest–convergence groups." Both Hathaway's and Schuck's proposals advocate burden-sharing principals, but there are important differences between the two proposals. One of the most important differences is that Hathaway suggests fixed principles that should be used to determine where refugees should be sent, while Schuck argues for tradable quotas in refugee obligations.

82 . A. Mark Weisburd "Implications of International Relations Theory For International Law of Human Rights," *Columbia Journal of Transnational Law,* 38 (1999-2000): 45.

83. Harvey, 102-103.

84 . Gil Loescher, "Protection and Humanitarian Action in the Post-Cold War Area," 184-185.

85. See: Louis E. Wolcher, "The Paradox of Remedies: The Case of International Human Rights Law," *Columbia Journal of Transnational Law* 38 (1999-2000),.518,546 quoting: Jacques Derrida, "Force of Law: The Mystical Foundation of Authority" *Cardozo Law Review* 11 (1990): 920,943.

86. Barnett, "Global Governance and the Evolution of the International Refugee Regime," 7.

87. Mathew C.R. Craven, *The International Covenant on Economic, Social, and Cultural Rights: A Perspective on its development* (Oxford: Clarendon Press, 1995), 367.

88. Gorlick, Human Rights and Refugees, 9.

89. UNHCR note on protection 2002: 18.

90. About the norms regarding the international refugee regime and the international human rights regime see: Weiner Myron, "The Clash of Norms: Dilemmas in Refugee Policies," *Journal of Refuge Studies* 11 (1998): 433-453.

91. Gil Loescher, "Protection and Humanitarian Action in the Post-Cold War Area," 184-185.

92. Arthur C. Helton, *The Price of Indifference, Refugees and Humanitarian Action in the New Century* (Oxford: Oxford University press, 2002), 16-17.

93. The International Criminal Court (ICC) entered into force 1 July 2002, investigates and prosecutes individuals for crimes against humanity. The Rome Statute (UN Doc. A/CONF.183/9) provisions are: genocide, crimes against humanity:, and war crimes. The court is intended to have jurisdiction over crimes of concern to the international community, and it is complementary to national criminal justice systems. The definitions of those crimes are broad and some of the definitions are applicable directly or implicitly to crimes against refugees and other forced migrants. The court jurisdiction does not apply to armed attacks against civilians, denial of humanitarian assistance, forced displacement and planting of anti-personnel mines as well as attacks on humanitarian workers.

94. "UNHCR and the establishment of an International Criminal Court: Some Comments on the Draft Statute," *UNHCR Division on International Protection*, June 1998, 1. Available from http:// www.un.org/icc/unhcr.htm. The drafting history of the 1951 Convention reveals that the definitions of "crime against peace," "war crime" and "crime against humanity" in the exclusion clauses are not limited to those found in "international instruments" existing at the time that the 1951 Convention came into force. Thus, in interpreting the exclusion provision of the 1951 Convention, UNHCR has resorted to guidance from such recent instruments as the Statute of the International Criminal Tribunal for the former Yugoslavia (ICTY) and the Statute of the International Criminal Tribunal for Rwanda (ICTR). In this regard the Statute of the Court constitute another authoritative international instrument, which will guide UNHCR as well as States in the interpretation of concepts employed in the exclusion provision. See; "UNHCR and the Establishment of an International Criminal Court: Some Comments on the Draft Statute," *UNHCR Division on International Protection*: 1.

95. The International Criminal Tribunal for the former Yugoslavia (ICTY) and the International Criminal Tribunal for Rwanda (ICTR). See Navanethem Pillay, "International Criminal Tribunals as a Deterrent to Displacement" in Anne Bayefsky and Joan Fitzpatrick eds. *Human Rights and Forced Displacement* (Hague: Martinus Nijhoff Publishers, 2000), 262-267.

96. .Roberta Cohen and Francis M. Deng, *Masses in Flight: The Global Crisis of Internal Displacement* (Washington D.C.: Brookings Institute, 1998), 169.

97. Gil Loescher, "Protection and Humanitarian Action in the Post-Cold War Area," 185.

98. Cohen and Deng, Masses in Flight: The Global Crisis of Internal Displacement, *169*.

99. UNHCR protection note 2000: 2.

About the contributors...

Roberta Cohen is a Senior Fellow at the Brookings Institution, specializing in humanitarian and human rights issues. She is Co-Director of the Brookings Institution-Johns Hopkins SAIS Project on Internal Displacement and serves as Senior Adviser to the Representative of the UN Secretary-General on Internally Displaced Persons. She co-authored (with F. Deng) the first major study on internal displacement: *Masses in Flight: The Global Crisis of Internal Displacement* (Brookings, 1998). She is former Deputy Assistant Secretary of State for Human Rights: a Senior Adviser to the US Delegation to the UN, and is the recipient of the 2002 DACOR (State Department Diplomatic and Consular Officers Retired) award and the Fiftieth Anniversary Award for Exemplary Writing on Foreign Affairs and Diplomacy.

Nitza Nachmias is professor of Political Science at Towson University (USA) and Haifa University (Israel). Her research focuses on humanitarian aid and post conflict human development. Previously served as Executive Director of the National Council of Women of the USA. Among her publications: *The International Politics of Humanitarian Assistance* and *"Prolonged humanitarian assistance Operations: the case of UNRWA."*

Alan James is professor of International Relations, London School of Economics and Keele University. His recent works include: *Peacekeeping in International Politics* (1990); *Britain and the Congo Crisis, 1960-63* (1996); *Keeping the Peace in the Cyprus Crisis of 1963-64* (2002); and (with G R Berridge), *A Dictionary of Diplomacy (second edition, 2003).*

Leon Gordenker is professor emeritus of Politics at Princeton University and faculty associate of the Princeton Institute of International and Regional Studies. In addition to teaching at Princeton University, he has been a member of the UN Secretariat and consultant to several UN organizations.

He has published numerous books and articles on the international handling of refugee affairs and other complex emergencies.

Abby Stoddard is a researcher and policy analyst at the Center on International Cooperation at New York University, specializing in humanitarian assistance. Her practical experience includes work for the organizations CARE and Doctors of the World USA.

Claudena Skran is associate professor of Government and the director of the Program in International Studies at Lawrence University. She is the author of *Refugees in Interwar Europe: the Emergence of a Regime*, and has researched refugees assistance operations in Europe, Central America, and Africa. She earned her M.Phil and D.Phil from Oxford University.

Arne Strand specializes in post-war recovery operations in Afghanistan at the Chr. Michelsen Institute (CMI), Bergen. Norway. He has done fieldwork in Afghanistan for about 20 years, and his research includes economic recovery, peace building, and coordination of humanitarian assistance.

Petter Bauck is co-founder of The Norwegian Afghanistan Committee (1980), and he has been working on the issue of Afghanistan for more than 15 years. Between 2000 and to 2003 he lived and worked in Palestine on development issues. He published and co-edited several books on humanitarian aid among them *Afghanistan – focus on a genocide* (1987), *Eritrea,* (1978), and *Along the Nile (1977).*

Beth Elise Whitaker is assistant professor of Political Science at the University of North Carolina at Charlotte. She conducted research projects for the Brookings Institution, the UN Foundation, Save the Children (UK), CARE, the U.S. Institute of Peace, and the USAID. Her research focuses on refugee issues and security in central and southern Africa.

Joseph R. Rudolph, Jr. is professor of Political Science at Towson University. He is the author of numerous works on the politics of nationalism and served on numerous UN missions to Yugoslavia. His most recent publication is an *Encyclopedia of Modern Ethnic Conflicts* (2003).

Rami Goldstein is an expert on the history of the Middle East and has a background in International Law and International Relations. He is a legal advisor to the Registrar of NGO's in Israel. He participated as a lawyer in different projects concerning the Palestinian Refugees.

Sari Hanafi is Director of Palestinian Refugee and Diaspora Center, Shaml. His work has focused on economic, sociology and network analysis of the Palestinian refugees; relationships between Diaspora and center; NGOs, donors and international NGOs on the post-war period. He published numerous books and articles in French, Arabic and English and his books are quoted as main resources for the study of the Palestinian refugees. The last book (in the collaboration With Linda Taber) is *Donors, International organizations and Local NGOs. The Emergence of Palestinian Globalized Elite.*

Kendall Stiles is associate professor of Political Science at Brigham Young University. His research areas include international organizations and global governance. Among his numerous publications, his most recent book, *Civil Society by Design*, that explores the effects of international funding on the Bangladeshi NGO community.

-INDEX-

Nakbah ("Disaster"). 31; 225; 314; 323.

NATO. 55; 101; 108-110; 112; 116-120; 125; 130; 191; 199; 201-202; 205; 207; 217-218.

NGOs (Non-Government Organizations). 16; 20; 25; 27; 68-69; 75; 78; 90-91; 93-94; 97; 101; 111-113; 118; 137; 141-142; 147; 153; 155; 158-160; 172; 181; 197; 210; 333; 338; 348-349; 355; 368-369; 387; 402; 404-406; 408; 416; 418-419.

Pakistan. 24-25 ; 47 ; 52 ; 74 ; 105 ; 136-160 ; 204 ; 214 ; 366 ; 376-377.

Palestinian. *Authority:* 16 ; 226 ; 266 ; 285 ; 288 ; 308
      Diaspora: 30; 313-316; 319-321; 323; 335-337; 339; 340.
      Refugees: 6;13-16; 24; 28-31; 35;223-224; 227-232; 236-237; 242; 246; 249-251; 254-255; 265-266; 269-270; 272-273; 275-276; 278-279; 282-283; 285; 287-291;322-323;325; 328-329; 331; 341; 366; 375; 377; 389.

Pashtuns. 24 ; 138 ; 139 ; 152.

Peacekeeping. 14 ; 27 ; 110 ; 111 ; 112 ; 199 ; 201 ; 213

PLO (Palestinian Liberation Organization). 29-30; 239; 242; 245-251; 262; 269-270; 277-278; 283; 297; 302-303; 314-318; 320; 322; 329; 336.

Refugees. *Afghan:* 135-137; 140; 142; 153-156; 158; 159; 161; 359; 366; 380.
      Camps: 14; 20; 24-25; 27-28; 33; 51; 57; 59; 67-74; 110; 117-119; 142; 146; 151-152; 155-156; 159-160; 170; 172-182; 191; 202; 230-234; 237; 239-240; 242; 244; 246-250; 253; 276; 314; 319-320; 322; 325; 330; 349; 366; 370-374; 376-377; 383-384; 386-387; 400; 405
      Convention: 29; 102; 120; 141; 228; 297; 359; 380; 381; 407; 418; 419; 423.
      Repatriation. 21; 22; 25; 27; 28; 30; 69; 72; 74; 90; 97; 103; 103; 119; 136; 145; 146; 152; 156; 157; 170; 172-182; 186; 200; 228; 229; 251; 270; 276-280; 285; 286; 291; 331; 356; 362; 372; 385; 389; 391; 399; 402; 404; 413; 416; 420.

Printed in the United Kingdom
by Lightning Source UK Ltd.
119499UK00001B/63